POST-BROADCAST DEMOCRACY

How Media Choice Increases Inequality in Political Involvement and Polarizes Elections

Seventy years ago, commercial television did not exist, and print media were the most widely available source for news. Thirty-five years ago, television was universally available, but people had the choice of only a few channels. Today, the average viewer can choose from hundreds of channels, including several twenty-four-hour news channels. News is on cell phones, on iPods, and online; it has become a ubiquitous presence in modern society. The purpose of this book is to examine systematically how these differences in access and form of media affect political behavior. Using experiments and new survey data, it shows how changes in the media environment reverberate through the political system, affecting news exposure, political learning, turnout, and voting behavior. Before television, news could be difficult to understand for people with low reading skills. Only television, by virtue of being both easy to follow and hard to resist, drew the less educated into the news audience. In the 1970s and 1980s, more people watched television news than at any other time, but only because they had little choice. Today, cable television and the Internet offer people much more control and choice. To news junkies, politics has become a candy store. Others avoid news altogether. Political involvement has become more unequal, and elections more polarized as a result.

Markus Prior is an assistant professor of politics and public affairs at the Woodrow Wilson School of Public and International Affairs, Princeton University. The dissertation on which this book is based won the E. E. Schattschneider Award, awarded by the American Political Science Association, for the best dissertation in American government.

CAMBRIDGE STUDIES IN PUBLIC OPINION AND POLITICAL PSYCHOLOGY

Series Editors

Dennis Chong, *Northwestern University*
James H. Kuklinksi, *University of Illinois, Urbana-Champaign*

Cambridge Studies in Public Opinion and Political Psychology publishes innovative research from a variety of theoretical and methodological perspectives on the mass public foundations of politics and society. Research in the series focuses on the origins and influence of mass opinion; the dynamics of information and deliberation; and the emotional, normative, and instrumental bases of political choice. In addition to examining psychological processes, the series explores the organization of groups, the association between individual and collective preferences, and the impact of institutions on beliefs and behavior.

Cambridge Studies in Public Opinion and Political Psychology is dedicated to furthering theoretical and empirical research on the relationship between the political system and the attitudes and actions of citizens.

Books in the series are listed on the page following the Index.

POST-BROADCAST DEMOCRACY

How Media Choice Increases Inequality in Political Involvement and Polarizes Elections

MARKUS PRIOR

Princeton University

CAMBRIDGE
UNIVERSITY PRESS

CAMBRIDGE UNIVERSITY PRESS
Cambridge, New York, Melbourne, Madrid, Cape Town, Singapore, São Paulo

Cambridge University Press
32 Avenue of the Americas, New York, NY 10013-2473, USA

www.cambridge.org
Information on this title: www.cambridge.org/9780521858724

First published 2007

Printed in the United States of America

A catalog record for this publication is available from the British Library.

Library of Congress Cataloging in Publication Data

Prior, Markus, 1974–
Post-broadcast democracy : how media choice increases inequality in political
involvement and polarizes elections / Markus Prior.
    p.   cm. – (Cambridge studies in public opinion and political psychology)
Includes bibliographical references and index.
ISBN 13: 978-0-521-85872-4 (hardback)
ISBN 13: 978-0-521-67533-8 (pbk.)
1. Mass media – Political aspects.   2. Mass media – Influence.
I. Title.   II. Series.
P95.8.P756   2007
302.23 – dc22   2006025608

ISBN   978-0-521-85872-4 hardback
ISBN   978-0-521-67533-8 paperback

Für Mama und Papa

Contents

Contents

List of Tables

List of Tables

List of Figures

List of Figures

Acknowledgments

This project began as a Ph.D. dissertation in the Communication Department at Stanford a long time ago. I had the very good fortune of a stellar dissertation committee. In four remarkably different ways, Shanto Iyengar, Paul Sniderman, David Brady, and Mo Fiorina have challenged me to defend my arguments more convincingly and state them more precisely – and sometimes, to abandon them altogether. I learned something unique from each of the four that I will try to heed when this book is long finished. Shanto Iyengar, my advisor, taught me that establishing causality is the most important and most difficult aspect of social science. There is not enough random assignment in this project for Shanto, and I thank him for letting me pursue it nonetheless and for always being available for advice. Paul Sniderman introduced me to the power of embedding experiments in opinion surveys. Working for him, I observed firsthand how to craft a survey and a story. David Brady's most important contribution to this project is the first wave of the News & Entertainment Project, which I could not have conducted without him. He worked hard to socialize me properly into the American academic system. "This is not Europe; we share here," was one of his earliest pieces of advice. Humor is impossible to teach, but Mo Fiorina has impressed on me that social science research can be as smart and witty as a good work of fiction.

In addition to the members of my dissertation committee, others at Stanford provided reactions and advice on various aspects of my projects. For that I would like to thank Don Roberts, the late Steve Chaffee, Christian Sandvig, Karin Wahl-Jorgensen, Keith Krehbiel, and Simon Jackman.

I am grateful to the Center for the Study of Democratic Politics at Princeton for providing me with a fellowship just as I was finishing my dissertation. The collegial working environment at Princeton gave me a fantastic opportunity to try out new ideas and polish old ones. I could not have wished for smarter, kinder, and more dedicated colleagues than the ones I have at Princeton.

Acknowledgments

Doug Arnold, Larry Bartels, Marty Gilens, and Tali Mendelberg read entire versions of this manuscript and were always available for a quick piece of advice or a long conversation. Their comments, questions, and suggestions have improved this book a great deal. Chris Achen, Chuck Cameron, Josh Clinton, Paul DiMaggio, Fred Greenstein, Dave Lewis, Nolan McCarty, Paul Starr, and Keith Whittington also shared their thoughts on this project. And I thank Helene Wood for her assistance.

I owe a big debt of gratitude to several other people who read the entire manuscript and provided me with many helpful comments and reactions: Jay Hamilton, Sunshine Hillygus, Gabriel Lenz, Skip Lupia, Diana Mutz, and Michael Schudson. Scott Althaus and Matt Baum, who were among the reviewers of my manuscript, deserve special thanks for each of their fifteen pages of single-spaced reactions, suggestions, and constructive criticism. Jim Kuklinski helped throughout the revisions and the editing. I would also like to thank Lew Bateman, Sara Black, Jessica Cepelak, and Ernie Haim at Cambridge University Press for turning a manuscript into a book, and Ben Niles for the cover design.

Over the years, many other colleagues have offered their comments and suggestions on early conference papers, article drafts, or parts of what I have been calling the "almost final" manuscript for several years now: Steve Ansolabehere, Ted Brader, John Bullock, David Campbell, Dennis Chong, Stefano DellaVigna, Bob Entman, Bob Erikson, John Evans, John Geer, Matt Gentzkow, Vince Hutchings, Gary Jacobson, Elihu Katz, Orit Kedar, Scott Keeter, Don Kinder, Ken Kohlman, Yanna Krupnikov, Russ Neuman, Keiko Ono, Sam Popkin, Vince Price, Bob Putnam, Wendy Rahn, Eric Schickler, Danielle Shani, David Strömberg, Michael Traugott, Yariv Tsfati, Joe Turow, Nick Valentino, Sid Verba, James Webster, Herb Weisberg, Chris Wlezien, and Danna Goldthwaite Young. I am grateful to all of them. A special thank you goes to Michael Delli Carpini who patiently listened to my vague and wooly ideas and encouraged me to pursue this project before it even was a project.

I benefited from the comments of seminar participants after presenting parts of this project at the Annenberg School of Communication at the University of Pennsylvania, Columbia University, Cornell University, Duke University, Harvard University, the University of Michigan, the Univeristé de Montréal, Princeton University, and Temple University.

My understanding of news audiences would be much hazier without the input of several people who deal with these audiences daily in their professional lives: Horst Stipp at NBC, Michael Steinberg at the Katz Media Group, Jack Wakshlag at Turner Broadcasting, Ted Kneisler and Rob Schlaepfer at CBS, Evan Thomas at *Newsweek*, and Jay Mattlin at Mediamark Research. Although they can never share everything they know, I am indebted to them for the time they took from their busy

Acknowledgments

schedules and the patience with which they helped an academic better understand the business of reaching viewers.

Kathy Dykeman, Danielle Murray, and Chris Pippin at Knowledge Networks provided invaluable work on the implementation of the News & Entertainment Survey. The second wave of that survey owes its existence to the Center of the Study of Democratic Politics at Princeton University and the generosity of Mike Dennis at Knowledge Networks. Princeton provided me with a well-timed leave of absence to finish this manuscript.

Over the course of this project, Purcell Carson learned the hard way that an academic's work is never done. I thank her for her patience with me and for her support of this project. I happily acknowledge her responsibility for any signs of eloquence, the pruning of academic jargon, and the occasional dramatic overstatement. Remaining jargon, clumsy prose, and other shortcomings are in the book despite her and everyone else's best efforts and cannot be blamed on anyone but me.

I

Introduction

In 1935, commercial television did not exist. Two-thirds of all American households (and 9 percent of all automobiles) had a radio. Almost 600 AM stations were broadcasting throughout the country. Print media continued to be the most widely available source for news. The combined circulation of the roughly two thousand daily newspapers was about 41 million, one for every three Americans.[1]

Thirty-five years later, in 1970, television was universally available. In the average household, the television set was on for six hours each day. In more than half of all households, those hours were still in black and white. People's freedom to choose the content they liked was minimal: only half a dozen channels were available in an average household, a number that included noncommercial stations such as PBS affiliates and UHF stations, which were often received at poor quality, if at all. The three broadcast networks and their affiliates dominated television, capturing 80 percent of all viewing (with most of the remainder going to independent stations). Cable television, which delivered the lineup to about 6 percent of all homes, was still only a means to connect remote areas out of reach of over-the-air broadcast signals.

There was little to choose from, and choosing was work. Before the remote control revolution, couch potatoes had to cross the room to change channels. Perhaps it was healthy to have so little choice, as competing viewing preferences might have spelled trouble for the two-thirds of households with only one television set. News was the norm in American homes in the early evening. Of those who had their televisions on, three-quarters watched one of the network news programs.

1 The sources for the data in this and the following paragraphs are Stanley and Niemi (2006), Sterling (1984), Media Dynamics (2001), Nielsen Media Research (2000), Project for Excellence in Journalism (2004), and the Television Bureau of Advertising (at *www.tvb.org*).

Another 35 years later, in 2005, the television is on for eight hours per day on 2.6 screens in the average household. Over 85 percent of all households subscribe to cable or satellite television. The average viewer has a choice of about 100 channels. Several of those channels offer 24-hour news coverage. The broadcast networks and their affiliates capture less than 40 percent of all viewing, even though there are several additional networks. More than half of all viewing now goes to cable channels.

The audience for network news has declined. Less than a fifth of all households watch one of the network newscasts on an average weeknight. Many viewers turn to cable television for their news. Not counting prime time news magazines, the average American watches about 4 hours of broadcast news and 5 hours of cable news each month, according to data for the first eight months of 2005 collected by Nielsen Media Research. But these averages conceal growing inequality in news viewing. Many people watch a lot less than those 9 hours and have largely deserted the news audience, while cable has allowed others to become devoted television news junkies.

In 2005, it is possible to follow the news on cell phones, on iPods, and online. More than two-thirds of all Americans have access to the Internet. About half of those two-thirds connect via high-speed broadband that can conveniently deliver video content. Even though per-capita newspaper circulation has continued to drop to about one paper for every five Americans, many people are reading newspapers' online editions. The *New York Times*, for example, had a daily circulation of about 1.1 million in early 2005, but its website was accessed by 1.7 million unique visitors on an average day (and about 12 million in a month). Over the course of a month, the Web sites of newspapers in the top 125 U.S. markets are visited by about 45 million people. The most successful Web sites run by cable news channels, CNN.com and MSNBC.com, reach about 20 million different people per month.[2]

The differences between the media environments in 1935, 1970, and 2005 are impossible to miss. Americans in 1935 had to wait for newspapers to be printed and delivered if they wanted more than short radio news summaries. Newscasters and politicians were right in the living room of many Americans in 1970 on a routine basis, but they left at seven o'clock. For Americans in 2005, they stand by at every hour of the day, ready to

---

2 Data on online newspaper audiences is based on tracking of Internet use by Nielsen/NetRatings available from the Newspaper Association of America's Newspaper Audience Database (*www.naa.org/nadbase*) and from Timothy Williams, "NYTimes.com to Offer Subscription Service," *New York Times*, May 17, 2005. For online audiences for cable news channels, see Geraldine Fabrikant, "CNN Will Add Free Video to its Web Site," *New York Times*, May 16, 2005.

drop a mountain of information at the click of a mouse or the push of a remote.

It is difficult to imagine that differences as stark as these have no effect on politics. But how do they affect whether and how people encounter politics? Do they influence how much people learn about politics? Or how they make political decisions? Political science has surprisingly few answers to these questions.

It is not that political scientists fail to recognize the magnitude of the changes. Looking back in the early days of television, Converse (1962, 591), for example, states that

[t]he dramatic changes in information propagation are too familiar to require much elaboration.... The cumulative change has been of awesome proportions.... [C]onditions of information propagation have shifted in ways that affect a vast majority of the population.

Kinder (2003, 357) begins his recent review of mass communication and politics with the observation that

[o]ver the last half of the twentieth century, mass communications have transformed the landscape of American politics, vastly increasing the information about public affairs that is available to ordinary citizens. Through multiple channels... the volume of information relevant to politics circulating through American society is massive and increasing.

Yet the acknowledgement of these "massive" changes "of awesome proportions" has not been accompanied by an understanding of their political repercussions. Differences in media environments are rarely considered in theories of American politics. Kinder (2003, 376) concludes that "change in our thinking about mass communications and politics over the last 40 years has had to do with alterations in social science more than [with alterations] in communications technology." Methodological and conceptual shifts in social science have certainly been tremendously valuable, perhaps most refreshingly so in overcoming the prevailing view that media had little effect on political behavior at all (see also Iyengar and Simon 2000). But new findings that look like the result of methodological progress can sometimes be the effect of technological change. If changes in communications technology are consequential, neglecting them in our theories of the political process is a consequential mistake. Political science tends to treat ordinary people's political behavior as if it can be explained without reference to the media environment in which they live. Accepted generalizations about political behavior – that the actions of politicians and the reporting of the news media affect what people consider to be important political issues, that people can reach meaningful voting decisions even in the absence of comprehensive political knowledge, that party identification is a major determinant of vote choice, to name only

3

three – become ingrained in the literature as invariant patterns. Yet as the environment changes, so might the behavior.

With this book, I aim to give the media environment a more central place in our theories of the political process. My goal is to offer a systematic treatment of how the media environment affects political behavior. Before I introduce the general framework that connects the media environment to the political process, I offer two examples to illustrate how the availability of particular media affects political behaviors that scholars often assume are invariant. The first example emphasizes that many people do not voluntarily consume a lot of news. But when the media environment offers them political information as they go about their daily business, they often absorb it. The second example points out that some people do not go to the polls because a thorough examination of both parties' positions leads them to well-reasoned voting preferences. Instead, they vote if the environment reminds them of the upcoming election and provides them with a few simple reasons to pick one side or the other. In both examples, the media environment works in the background, but its effects can be substantial.

THE DEPENDENCE OF POLITICAL BEHAVIORS ON THE MEDIA ENVIRONMENT

"By-product learning" and the "floating voter," two concepts that have come back into fashion lately, were introduced at least half a century ago. Both are catchy ideas that have helped us understand how people learn and make political decisions. They have developed and expanded over time, but they were both conceived at a time when broadcast television had barely outgrown its infancy. As both concepts rely on the availability and flow of political information, it seems worth analyzing whether they apply to Americans in 2005 in the same way as they did to Americans in 1970, or 1935.

By-product Learning

Whether people learn about politics (and if so, how much) depends on the efficiency with which they can find the media content they seek. Due to a lack of efficiency, people often learn politically relevant facts as a by-product of nonpolitical routines. In his theoretical treatment of information seeking, Anthony Downs (1957) presents two subtly different scenarios to illustrate this point. First, free political information is sometimes obtained from entertainment-seeking behavior, as when, in Downs's example, moviegoers sit through a newsreel even though they came to be entertained by the main feature. Second, people may acquire political information "in the course of making production or consumption decisions." People learn about price developments while grocery shopping, even when they are not willing to engage in costly searches for information on the inflation rate (Popkin 1991). In both cases, individuals obtain political information for free, even though that was not the objective of their behavior. Hence, "accidental data are by-products of the non-political activities of a citizen; they accrue to him without any special effort on his part to find them" (Downs 1957, 223). The idea that people acquire political information in the course of other activities featured prominently in several recent studies of political learning (e.g., Baum 2003b; Popkin 1991).

Downs's two paths differ in one important aspect. The second path does not entail any sacrifices or loss of utility. If, in the course of buying your groceries, you learn about price inflation – information that you can use later when you decide how to cast your vote – you do not bear any additional costs just because you notice the price of groceries. In fact, it would probably be more costly to avoid noticing large price changes. "Just as exposed portions of the skin get tanned by the sun when people walk around out of doors, so people become informed as they go about their daily business" (Fiorina 1990, 338). The first path, on the other hand, does entail costs. Watching an unwanted newsreel imposes opportunity costs in the form of lost entertainment value. For most moviegoers, these opportunity costs would probably exceed the utility from exposure to the newsreel. Hence, they would have preferred to skip the newsreel and start the movie earlier, but many movie theaters did not offer the feature without the newsreel. (And moviegoers who arrived late to skip the newsreel risked not getting a good seat.) As far as Downs's first path is concerned, people who do not intend to learn about politics still do so because they cannot find exactly the media content they prefer.

This book is about the first path: about obtaining political information as a by-product in inefficient media environments. If you go to see a movie to satisfy your desire for entertainment, the newsreel is an inefficiency. People's exposure to political information and their political learning depend on these inefficiencies. The efficiency of the media environment – and hence the likelihood of non-political activities yielding political information as by-products – varies over time, often in response to technological change. Moviegoers today are no longer accidentally exposed to political information.[3]

---

3 In the case of newsreels, Downs may have overestimated both the opportunity costs and the amount of by-product learning. Newsreels rarely focused on political or social issues. (I provide a brief summary of newsreel content in Chapter 3.) Even so, most moviegoers presumably came for the movie, not the newsreel. According to Fielding (1972, 220), "theater owners generally viewed the newsreel as nothing more than a convenient house-clearing device to be inserted between feature attractions."

Downs (1957, 223) offers the newsreel example to illustrate a more general point:

Anyone with time to spare can acquire endless amounts of sought-for data, but variations in the quantity of accidental data received can result from other factors as well. In fact, systematic variations in the amount of free information received and ability to assimilate may strongly influence the distribution of political power in a democracy.

My central claim throughout this book is that the media environment – the types of media to which people have access – explains many "systematic variations in the amount of free information received." The media content available to people, its quantity, and the ease with which it can be obtained varies over time. Different media environments provide the media content people want at different levels of efficiency. For example, the available broadcast channels in 1970 were less likely than today's television lineup to offer programs that closely matched a viewer's ideal content – and even if they did, they rarely did so at the viewer's ideal time. Choosing one's preferred content was much less efficient in 1970 than it is today. Different media environments therefore offer different opportunities to obtain free information as a by-product. As it becomes easier to find the ideal content at the ideal time, the chances that viewers encounter political information as an unintended consequence of watching a less-than-ideal program, perhaps even a news program, dwindle. Changes in the set of available media thus affect who follows the news, who learns about politics, and who votes – in short, they affect "the distribution of political power in a democracy."

The Floating Voter

The floating voter is another concept that has attracted the continued attention of political scientists and, especially, campaign strategists and journalists. It, too, depends more on the media environment than commonly recognized. Floating voters are voters whose decisions are not noticeably influenced by a stable liberal or conservative ideology or a strong adherence to one party. As a result, they seldom approach an election with a firm sense of whom to vote for and do not always vote for the same party. Describing these patterns of fluctuations in voting behavior or vote intention, scholars have used many different terms, including "swing voters" and "marginal voters." Key (1966, 9–28) used the term "stand-patters" to describe those who voted for the same party in successive elections. "Switchers," on the other hand, voted for two different parties in the last two presidential elections. A third category, "new voters," includes those who voted in the current, but not in the preceding election. Campbell (1960, 399) made a similar distinction between "core voters" and "peripheral voters."

Zaller's (2004) chapter entitled "Floating Voters in U.S. Presidential Elections, 1948–2000" and Mayer's (2005) *The Swing Voters in American Presidential Elections* illustrate that the electoral significance of relatively uncommitted voters continues to interest political scientists. These works show that the behavior of floating voters has a disproportionate impact on the election outcome, especially in close elections (see also Burden and Kimball 2002; Kelley 1983). Many voters who do not consistently vote for the same party are less educated, less interested, less knowledgeable, and "more passive in their orientation to politics than . . . voters generally" (Kelley 1983, 149).[4]

Many floaters, swingers, and switchers behave capriciously not only when choosing between two candidates but also when deciding whether or not to vote. Even though he does not pursue the distinction, Key (1966, 22) notes that only some "new voters" have never voted before. Others just did not vote in the last election. He calls these voters "in-and-out voters."[5] While some of them "were prevented from voting four years earlier by causes beyond their control . . . , [o]thers, doubtless far more numerous, are persons with a low interest in politics, the apolitical, the apathetic, the indifferent, and those who vote only under the pressure of powerful stimuli."

The intensity of a campaign and the amount of political information that (potential) floating voters encounter thus affect their tendency to vote at all. Campbell's (1960) notion of "surge and decline" rests firmly on this connection between the strength of the campaign stimulus and the level of turnout. He distinguished between "high-stimulus" and "low-stimulus" elections. High-stimulus elections prompt even less interested citizens to cast a vote, while only the most interested vote in low-stimulus elections. Unfamiliar with ideological debates, floating voters – if they vote – decide based on candidate images or the controversy of the day. Both Campbell (1960) and Converse (1962) suggested this association as a way to explain why people's voting behavior in off-year elections is more consistent with their partisan identification and their ideology. Because the "stimulus" is not strong enough to inform less interested citizens, many of them are not sufficiently motivated to vote because they perceive

---

4 Key finds switchers about as interested and opinionated as standpatters, while new voters rank lower on measures of engagement. See Converse (1962) and Mayer (2005) for data supporting Kelley's conclusion.
5 Campbell (1960, 409) also used this term.

few differences between the political alternatives (e.g., Palfrey and Poole 1987). The weaker the stimulus, the greater the likelihood of "abstention due to indifference" (Fiorina 1999). This argument implies that a strong stimulus encourages higher turnout of Key's "in-and-out voters" – and hence less partisan voting behavior: "The volume of information flow can be seen as an important governor upon the magnitude of oscillations in party fortunes" (Converse 1962, 591).

If the magnitude of vote swings depends on the flow of information, the fundamental changes in the media environment over the last half-century may alter the significance of floating voters. Converse (1962, 598) recognized this and argued that "there should be an increasing amplitude of these [vote] swings as the information flow has increased during the current century." But even though Converse grappled with the dependence of electoral volatility on the flow of information, neither he nor Campbell considered the possibility that even a strong stimulus might be ignored or diluted. The amount of news coverage available today, the length of campaigns, and the money spent on advertising all suggest that the signal produced by election campaigns has increased in strength. Yet the opportunities to watch movies, sports, sitcoms, and crime shows have also increased. Even a signal that is arguably stronger than ever does not necessarily get through the noise of everyday distractions. The noise has also grown louder and more distracting in recent decades.

Although the presidential campaign in 2004 was regarded as intensely contested and very close until the end, it did not reach as wide a share of the electorate as past "high-stimulus" elections did. The presidential debates between George W. Bush and John Kerry in 2004 broke a long decline in the size of debate audiences. On average, about one in three households watched the three debates. This audience was large by comparison to presidential debates in the 1990s, but it still pales next to the roughly 60 percent of households that tuned in to watch Nixon and Kennedy in 1960.[6] The signal was certainly not weaker in 2004 than it was in 1960, but the debates reached a much lower share of the population. In 1966, 84 percent of all households watched coverage of the congressional election returns, according to Nielsen Media Research (*Variety* 1969). Congressional elections may have been "low stimulus" compared to presidential contests, but an audience of this size is unheard of today for any kind of election. In short, both on- and off-year elections have become increasingly "low-stimulus" in recent decades in the

---

6 The estimates for 1960 are from Nielsen Media Research (2000). The 2004 estimates come from press releases available on the company's Web site (*www.nielsenmedia. com*). The average rating for 2004 was 33.9, which does not include viewers on PBS stations and C-SPAN. About 5 percent of all debate viewers watched on PBS.

sense that they reach a declining share of the electorate.[7] It is more difficult for the same signal to get through to people who take advantage of increased media choice to avoid exposure to political information. From the point of view of these entertainment fans, the flow of political information has become much weaker in recent years as media choice has increased.

Because in-and-out voters vote only when the political stimulus they receive is strong enough to overcome their indifference to politics, the political significance of floating voters should thus change over time. A media environment that routinely reaches many floating voters will generate more fickle, less partisan voting behavior. If media messages reach committed voters, but are easy for less interested would-be floating voters to miss, elections should become increasingly dominated by partisan considerations. Changes in the media environment may therefore change the proportion of highly partisan voters and the variability in election outcomes over time. The assumption that Americans in 1935, 1970, and 2005 were all equally likely to be floating voters seems tenuous in light of the difference in what they could see, read, and hear about politics.

THE MEDIA ENVIRONMENT, 1920–2005

By-product learning and floating voters are just two examples of political behaviors that, upon closer view, seem to depend on what kind of media are available and how much choice they offer. The purpose of this book is to examine more systematically how the media environment affects political behavior. I chose 1935, 1970, and 2005 to emphasize the dramatic changes in the media environment that play leading roles in the next six chapters. The advent of television midway through the twentieth century and the expansion of choice for television viewers and new media users in its last two decades are arguably the most fundamental changes. But they are of course not the only ones, nor are technological advances the only reason for variation. In this section, I explain my main independent variable, the media environment.

A media environment is defined by the media available to people at a particular place and time and by the properties of these media. For a new medium to be available, the technology for local access must exist. In the early days of cable television, for example, availability was constrained by the physical infrastructure of cable systems, which did not pass all households immediately. Today, almost all U.S. households are physically

---

7 An exception may be the amount of political advertising. Of all news and campaign communications, advertising is most likely to reach less-interested segments of the electorate. I discuss this point more fully in Chapter 7.

ready to receive cable or satellite television. The media environment is thus partly determined by the state of technology.

The media available to people at a particular place and time often correspond to the availability of content that is necessary for political learning to occur: news programs, news channels, newspapers, and Web sites with political information, for example. Broadcast news was unavailable to people until a television station began operating somewhere close to them. Cable news channels are available only in households with cable or satellite access.

Once a medium is technically available, people often have to decide whether to obtain access to the medium. After broadcast signals become available, people have to buy a television set to watch television in their homes. To enjoy cable channels, viewers still have to subscribe to a cable or satellite system. At this stage, people's preferences and their ability to afford access begin to influence individual media environments. Though some of these decisions may be driven by the desire for specific content, buying a television set or subscribing to cable increases availability of many different types of programming. Broadcast channels, basic cable, and the Internet all bundle a variety of content – including some content that appears to media users to have little value. The content available through the medium often changes even after people have made the decision to gain access. This distinguishes the decision to gain access from the availability of specific content even further.[8]

---

8 The distinction between the decision to gain access and the availability of content is less meaningful when the decision to gain access and the decision to use the medium are made at the same time or when the content is highly specialized. People who subscribe to a newspaper find it on their doorstep every morning, regardless of whether they intend to read it that morning. Nonsubscribers who buy a paper at the newsstand, on the other hand, will have a strong inclination to read the paper that particular day. In a strict sense, the paper could still be thought of as part of the media environment, but it is no longer justified to treat the environment as largely independent of the particular content people like. This argument suggests a further distinction between two kinds of environments, the immediate media environment and the standing media environment.

The standing media environment refers only to the media that are *routinely* available to a person. The standing media environment would thus include the cable channels that are available to a cable subscriber and the paper that lands on the subscriber's doorstep every morning. It would not include the newspaper that a nonsubscriber buys occasionally. That paper would only be included in the immediate media environment, of which the standing environment is a subset. Throughout this book, I try to stay away from immediate media environments because they are difficult or even impossible to measure and because they make causal interpretation extremely difficult. Most of my analyses involve comparisons of people with different standing media environments.

Introduction

Media environments change over time, but they also vary geographically or across people at any point in time. Studying the importance of media environments by comparing the same units over time as the media environment changes is a very attractive analytic strategy because we can assume that the people or geographic areas remain the same. In Chapters 5 and 7, I assess the effect of cable television by relating changes in cable penetration in media markets over time to changes in turnout and vote outcomes in those media markets over time. In practice, this design is often difficult to implement because of data limitations or because the geographical units are not stable. For example, it is difficult to use a time series approach to study the effects of broadcast television in congressional districts because redistricting changed the districts frequently. It can also be tricky to tease apart the effects of technology and content when both change together (as when television stations spread across the country at the same time that the newscasts on the broadcast networks grew in length and became more sophisticated).

A second research design compares people or areas with different media environments at the same point in time. Such cross-sectional analyses raise doubt about the underlying causal mechanisms when it is difficult to determine to what extent people with different media environments behaved differently even before they gained access to the medium in question. Data limitations force me to rely on cross-sectional comparisons in many parts of this book. Fortunately, it is here that the distinction between the availability of a medium and the actual use of specific content is most helpful. If access to a medium is determined either by technological advances or by individual-level characteristics that are unrelated to the political outcomes of interest, causal interpretations are still relatively unambiguous. A cross-sectional relationship in the 1960s between the availability of television in an area and the turnout in that area implies a causal effect of television, unless television stations were more likely to begin operation in areas that already had high turnout. This selection effect, though by no means trivial, is far more tractable than the selection effects that might underlie a cross-sectional relationship between television news exposure and turnout. Those more likely to go to the polls in the first place probably also watch more television news. Even aside from measurement problems, inferring causality becomes an impossibility when the independent variable is media use.

There are cross-sectional variations in the media environment that do not emerge because of over-time change, but instead reflect persistent structural differences that have political implications. For example, citizens in markets with more than one newspaper name more political problems and reasons for their voting decisions (Chaffee and Wilson, 1977; Clarke and Fredin, 1978) and perceive newspaper coverage as more similar to their own views (Mutz and Martin, 2001). Citizens who receive their news from out-of-state pick up political information about that state, and are less well informed about the political situation in their own state (Delli Carpini et al., 1994; Keeter and Wilson, 1986; Zukin and Snyder, 1984). Arnold (2004) has recently documented large differences in how newspapers cover the members of Congress from their circulation areas. He concludes that "some citizens read newspapers regularly; some do not. But it now seems that even regular, seven-day-a-week readers are exposed to vastly different amounts of information about local representatives depending on where they live" (Arnold 2004, 63). Another example of structural variation in media environments, which I will cover in Chapter 6, is the overlap between congressional districts and media markets.

Cross-sectional variation in media environments often occurs because the transition to a new technology proceeds at different speeds in different parts of the country. Eventually, every household in this country was ready to receive a broadcast signal and display it on a television set. Yet throughout the 1950s and 1960s, some people remained out of television's reach (or, later, were reached only by weak, unreliable signals). Eventually, everybody will have high-speed Internet access, but in the early twenty-first century about half the population was still without any access to the Internet. For analytic purposes, these slow transitions are a boon because they allow us to compare before and after at the same point in time.

This book covers only the most sweeping changes in the media environment over the last fifty or so years and focuses on only a few key properties of the newly available media. Figure 1.1 illustrates the spread of the three most important new media during the last half-century: broadcast television, cable television, and the Internet. The rise of broadcast television led to arguably the single most important twentieth-century transformation in how Americans spend most of the hours during which they do not sleep or work. The growth of broadcast television remains the fastest diffusion of any mass medium. About a quarter century later, cable television began to open a heavily regulated, rigidly structured medium to economic competition and consumer choice (between different programming, though not between different cable providers).

Another twenty-five years later, Internet access became available. While not as fast as broadcast television, Internet penetration grew quickly over the last decade. Both its content and its technological capabilities remain a moving target and make a detailed comparison with older media difficult. Many observers claim that the Internet and the digital convergence of formerly separate media will rival and even surpass television in its impact on people's lives. I concentrate on one particular aspect of the Internet: its ability to provide content more efficiently than its predecessors, and the implications of that efficiency for political learning. We have seen this

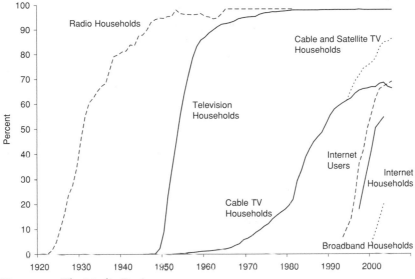

Figure 1.1. The Media Environment, 1920–2005.

Note: Radio households are from Sterling (1984). Television households are from *Broadcasting Yearbook* (different years). Cable television households and satellite television households are from *Broadcasting Yearbook* and the Television Bureau of Advertising (*www.tvb.org*). Internet households are assessed by the Current Population Survey.

Internet users are based on various Pew Surveys (June 2005, August 2004, June 2003, June 2002, June 2001, June 2000, June 1999, Early-August 1998, November 1997, July 1996, June 1995). The question wording was "Do you ever go online to access the Internet or World Wide Web or to send and receive email?", except in November 1993, when Pew asked "Do you or anyone in your household ever use the modem to connect to any computer bulletin boards, information services such as Compuserve or Prodigy, or other computers at other locations?" (Percentage reported here is for "respondent only" and "respondent and others.")

scenario play out once before with cable television. One of my main tasks is to examine what happened when cable television made it easier for viewers to choose the media content they liked. The Internet makes this choice easier still. Therefore the political implications of gaining Internet access – at least in this one regard – might resemble the implications of cable access.

Figure 1.1 also shows the growth of radio, which made up an important part of the media environment when broadcast television entered the scene in the 1940s. In terms of availability, newspapers and magazines are a constant for the time period shown in Figure 1.1 – at least in the simple sense that people could always buy or subscribe to daily and weekly print media. Chapter 3 describes the media environment in the 1940s in some detail, paying special attention to radio and newspapers before television. In recent years, the expansion of Internet access has made a greater number of print media widely available. Even though the number of daily newspapers and their circulation have declined since the mid-twentieth century, more newspapers are available to Internet users than were ever available to any individual before. Chapter 4 uses data on Internet usage in an attempt to quantify the magnitude of these shifts. In the core analyses, newspaper reading shows up as a control variable at best. The absence of fundamental change in availability and the dearth of suitable data justify this almost parenthetical treatment. (Opinion surveys rarely ask about newspaper subscriptions, and self-reports of newspaper reading are hopelessly inflated.) I also brush over many other, more nuanced features of the media environment. The VCR and talk radio, for example, come up only in passing.

Rather than treating the changes graphed in Figure 1.1 as isolated cases, I develop a theoretical framework that focuses on common patterns in how changes in the media environment affect exposure to political information and acquisition of political knowledge. Even though broadcast television and Internet technology represent dramatically different levels of advancement, it benefits our understanding to view the way in which they change political learning through the same lens. This lens is the mapping of individual-level factors – mostly preferences and abilities – into politically relevant outcomes. We know that these factors matter a great deal. Political interest and education, for example, are strong predictors of political knowledge and turnout (e.g., Delli Carpini and Keeter 1996; Verba, Schlozman, and Brady 1995). It has rarely been noticed, however, that some media environments leave a lot of room for people's interests and skills to guide their media use and political learning, while others impose strong constraints on everyone.

Over the last half-century, the media environment evolved from offering little political information and little choice to providing plenty of diverse media content, including, among many other options, copious and detailed political information. When we abandon the expectation that this evolution affects everyone in the same way, the significance of new media comes into clearer focus. Broadcast news offered little new information to well-educated Americans who read the newspaper on a daily basis. But to less educated citizens with weak reading skills, television shed light on the political world. Television offered politics in moving images and reported the news of the day in simple words. Politics now had faces.

The media environment of the broadcast era was characterized by homogeneity of content and limited opportunity to choose between genres. Cable television and the Internet remove constraints on content choice. This transition, too, means different things to different people. Some have seen the last newscast of their lives. To others, politics has become a candy store. Finally, it matters what people want. In short, changes in the media environment affect how individual-level factors work. I incorporate this dependence into a model of Conditional Political Learning. The model extends existing explanations of political learning by focusing on the way in which different prerequisites for learning jointly affect the acquisition of political knowledge. Conditional Political Learning addresses explicitly the way in which the effects of motivation and ability change when new media become available and old ones disappear or lose popularity.

The effects of such fundamental changes in the media environment have many important political implications. In the model, the availability of a new medium has its most immediate impact on news consumption. Changes in news consumption, in turn, influence how people learn about politics, whether or not they go to the polls, and to what extent partisan consideration drive election outcomes. Along this path from news consumption to election outcomes, changes in the media environment reverberate through the political system, leaving traces in many common indicators of public opinion and voting behavior.

The next chapter describes the Conditional Political Learning model and lays out the hypotheses it generates about the political implications of changing media environments. Chapters 3 to 7 then follow the repercussions over time to reveal their impact on political behavior. The result is a clearer picture of the media environment's contribution to stability and change in American politics. The next section provides a sketch of the journey.

STABILITY AND CHANGE

Despite being treated as if they were stable phenomena independent of context, some of our most widely used concepts and stylized facts are implicitly defined relative to the media environment. The floating voter may no longer vote at all in the high-choice environment. The idea of "low-information rationality," developed so effectively by Samuel Popkin (1991) from Downs's (1957) by-product argument, rests partly on the assumption that the media environment is inefficient enough to provide political cues even to citizens who are not motivated to actively seek any. But now that new media users can efficiently click from one entertainment program to the next, do they still encounter political cues by accident?

In the 1950s and 1960s, broadcast television tricked people who did not care very deeply about politics into watching the news. The popularity of television and the homogeneity of content on broadcast stations during the dinner hour led many Americans, even the less educated, less interested, and less partisan, to watch the news. Television was easy, it had pictures, and it was right there, in people's living rooms. And once they were "glued

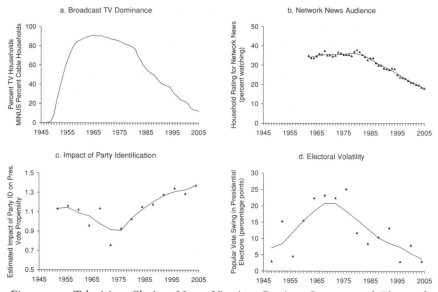

Figure 1.2. Television Choice, News Viewing, Partisan Impact, and Electoral Volatility.

Note: Television choice is based on Figure 1.1. Network news audience is the combined average yearly rating for the three evening newscasts on ABC, CBS, and NBC. The impact of party identification on presidential vote choice is estimated using Bartels's (2000) approach. Following Bartels (1998, 294–7), electoral volatility is the absolute difference between Republican vote margins in successive elections. Except for television choice, graphs plot raw data and moving averages generated by locally weighted regressions on time.

to the box" (Barwise, Ehrenberg, and Goodhardt 1982), they became captives of broadcast television. This marked a departure from pre-broadcast days when learning from the media, especially newspapers and magazines, required greater cognitive skills and motivation. It also contrasts markedly with the current media environment, in which most media users have a choice between many more television channels. A segment of dedicated news viewers continues to watch the news, even though they have greater choice than before. Others, however, used to watch the news only because nothing else was on. When cable began to offer them plentiful entertainment options at the same time that networks offered only news, these less intrinsically interested people reduced their news consumption.

In a heavily simplified way, graph (a) in Figure 1.2 shows this change in the degree of television content choice over the last six decades. It plots the extent to which the media environment was dominated by low-choice broadcast television, as measured by the percentage of households with access to broadcast television but not cable or satellite channels. It graphs, in other words, the share of the American public that would, for reasons that demand further examination, often watch whatever the three networks served them – including the news. Graph (b) in Figure 1.2 presents the percentage of American households that tuned to one of the three network newscasts (that is, the combined Nielsen ratings for *ABC Evening News*, *CBS Evening News*, and *NBC Nightly News*). At least in the period for which data are available, the size of the network news audience tracks the percentage of households with only broadcast channels very closely. The Pearson correlation between the two time series is .94 ($N = 44$).

The media environment of the broadcast era thus led people with little interest in public affairs to hear the political headlines of the day. Illustrating his idea of by-product learning, Downs (1957, 223) deduced that "entertainment sources sometimes yield political information as a surplus benefit from what is intended as an entertainment investment." He was writing at the beginning of the broadcast era and had the newsreel before the main movie feature in mind, but the same point can be made about a pleasant evening watching television with a little bit of political news as a "surplus benefit." People could skip the newsreel or turn off the television set, but many did not; instead they learned a thing or two about politics. Chapters 2 and 3 examine in detail why this happened and how the dominance of broadcast television affected political learning before the increase in media choice through cable television and the Internet.

With the advent of cable television, by-product learning became less common. As cable offered a choice between different program genres, content preferences began to guide people's viewing choices, and the habit of watching television in the evening did not by itself lead to political learning anymore. Chapters 4 and 5 analyze the transition from a world of three dominating networks to a media environment that provides much more plentiful and diverse media content. Media users now have many choices. The two chapters examine what happens to people who are sufficiently interested to watch news in the absence of alternatives, but not interested enough to stick with their choice when entertainment becomes an option. Downs's focus on obtaining information as a by-product should not distract us from the fact that some people are willing to expend considerable costs to learn about politics, simply because they enjoy it. And just as the opportunities for by-product learning depend on the available media, the amount of information available to those who enjoy politics is also a function of the media environment. Cable television and later the Internet offer news fans hours and hours of news updates, plenty of background analysis, and libraries full of political information. They should be able to learn a lot more about politics than in the past.

In the midst of profound political change caused by new media, there are areas of stability. If some people take advantage of greater media choice to become more knowledgeable, while others take advantage by avoiding politics altogether, average knowledge may not change. And indeed, mean levels of political knowledge in the population do not appear to have changed much over the last fifty years (Delli Carpini and Keeter 1996). Turnout too has been stable or barely declining after 1972 (Freeman 2004; McDonald and Popkin 2001). Yet if political knowledge and turnout have risen in some segments of the electorate, but declined in others, stability in means hides crucial changes.

Changes in the media environment will affect politics if they change the mix of people likely to go to the polls. If less educated citizens start to learn about politics from broadcast news and vote more, they may have had a moderating influence on election outcomes. Greater choice may remove the moderating influence exerted by some of these rather involuntarily drafted voters again. The effects of the media environments on the role of partisanship in voting behavior and the resulting changes in volatility and polarization of elections are the topic of Chapters 6 and 7. By allowing people to sort themselves more effectively into audiences for information or for entertainment, the expansion of media choice threatens to sepa-rate politically interested citizens who participate in the electoral process from those who favor entertainment and increasingly abstain from mak-ing political decisions. These two groups differ not only in their political interest but also in the strength of their partisan affiliations. If politically interested people who continue to follow the news despite the increasing allure of around-the-clock entertainment are also more partisan, the new media environment loses the moderating influence of people who are not particularly interested in politics but who used to vote because even their accidental exposure to broadcast news generated sufficient knowledge and motivation to get them to the polls. The result is more party-line vot-ing and increased polarization. Graph (c) in Figure 1.2 shows just such an increase in partisanship. It plots a measure of the impact of party identifi-cation on presidential vote decisions developed by Bartels (2000). (Party identification has a weaker but also rebounding impact in congressional elections.) Party identification regained its strong impact on vote choices at roughly the same time that broadcast dominance began to wane. The Pearson correlation between the two time series is $-.80$ ($N = 14$).

The changing composition of the voting public brings us back to the floating voters. Following the lead of Campbell (1960) and Converse (1962), I suggested earlier a connection between the media environment and the volatility of election outcomes. Even though the signal of elections has presumably grown in recent decades, it has to compete with new and noisy distractions from cable television and the Internet. As a result, it is less effective in reaching floating voters and motivating them to cast their fickle votes. With fewer floating voters, elections should become less volatile, a trend evident in graph (d) in Figure 1.2, which plots the vote swing from one presidential election to the next. The vote swing is the absolute difference in the Republican candidate's vote margin in consecutive elections (Bartels 1998). (For example, the vote swing in 2004 was 3 percentage points as George W. Bush won by 2.5 points in 2004 after receiving 0.5 fewer points than Al Gore in 2000.) Broadcast television dominance and electoral volatility move up and down together, generating a Pearson correlation of .76 ($N = 15$). Vote swings in House elections, too, increased in the 1960s and 1970s before declining again in recent decades (Jacobson 1990, 30–1; 2004, 16–18).

A higher percentage of Americans watched the news when choice on their television was low. When choice was low and audiences large, partisanship mattered less than either today or before television had reached most Americans. Television choice and electoral volatility also seem to go together. These correlations, while strong, could of course arise by coincidence or because some other factor influences all four trends. And I have only hinted at the causal mechanisms connecting the media environment with news exposure, partisanship, and electoral volatility. The remainder of this book is an attempt to provide theoretical justification and empirical evidence supporting these connections.

INDIVIDUAL-LEVEL VERSUS CONTEXTUAL EXPLANATIONS

When people stop watching the news, they must have lost interest in politics or become dissatisfied with the news. When voting patterns show increasing polarization along partisan lines, people must have become more partisan. These are common conjectures. They are also false. If changes in the media environment indeed contributed to the trends shown in Figure 1.2, then individual-level factors – people's political interest or attitudes toward government, for example – have less to do with these trends than is often assumed. It is tempting and easy to attribute trends in political behavior to individual-level change. It also misses a good part of the story.

In this book, I argue that news consumption, learning about politics, and electoral volatility have changed not so much because people are different today, but rather because the media environment is different. People have not necessarily changed; they have merely changed the channel. And they would have done it sooner, had they been given the chance.

There is no shortage of suggestions why fewer people watch network news than in the past. Typical explanations for the decline in the audience of network news include decreasing public interest in politics and the news, mounting cynicism and distrust toward government and media, and the vanishing of a generation of civic-minded people. These suggested

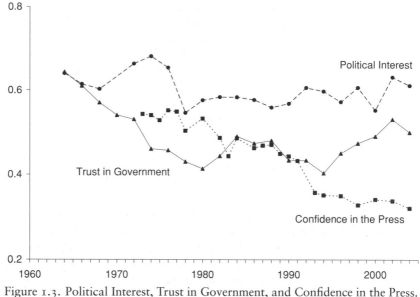

Figure 1.3. Political Interest, Trust in Government, and Confidence in the Press.

Note: All variables are means scaled to vary between 0 and 1. Data for political interest and trust in government are from the NES cumulative data set for 1948–2002 (variables 313 and 604) and the 2004 study. Confidence in the press is from the General Social Survey.

explanations all attribute lower news ratings to individuals' changing views of politics and the media. None of these variables, however, fit the trend in news audiences very well.

Interest in campaigns and attention to "government and public affairs" declined in the 1970s but remained at roughly the same level throughout the 1980s and 1990s. Figure 1.3 plots average levels of attention to public affairs over time using data from the National Election Studies (NES). (The trend is very similar for interest in campaigns.) Part of the decline in the 1970s, moreover, looks like an artifact of changes in the position of the relevant questions within the NES interview.[9] Regardless of whether

9 In 1978, unlike in earlier studies, the public affairs question was asked after several knowledge questions, which few respondents answered correctly. Bishop (1987) and Schwarz and Schuman (1997) have shown that survey respondents report "following what's going in government and public affairs" considerably less often when they are asked this question after several difficult political knowledge questions (compared to when they are asked the same interest question *before* the knowledge questions). In both studies, the percentage of respondents who say they follow public affairs "most" or "some of the time" dropped by almost 20 points when the knowledge questions preceded the interest item. Schwarz and Schuman (1997, 192) explain this

changes in the 1970s were real or not, the absence of a trend after 1978 seems to rule out political interest as a cause of declining news audiences. After all, network news audiences were still close to their peak in the early 1980s and have only declined in the past two decades.

Declining trust in government and cynicism toward elections and the political process do not seem to explain the decline in network news audiences either. After making adjustments for a change in question order, Bartels (2002) concludes that people's faith in elections – their belief that "having elections makes the government pay attention to what the people think" – has remained constant since the early 1970s. As Figure 1.3 shows, trust in government declined strongly throughout the 1960s and 1970s but has recovered somewhat since then. During the period of rather continuous audience decline, trust in government first increased, then decreased, and recently increased again. Other attitudes toward the political system declined before the 1980s, but have stabilized or even recovered since then (NES, Cumulative File, 1948–2002). None of these trends match the decline in news audiences. Network news continued to lose viewers during a period in which public attitudes toward the political system became, if anything, more positive. The usual suspects, according to so many casual observers, turn out to have nothing to do with declining network news audiences. Or, as in the case of faith in elections, they are related to it, but in the opposite direction than commonly suggested.

One other variable is often mentioned as an explanation for declining news audiences: rising distrust of the media (Cook, Gronke, and Rattliff 2000; Ladd 2006). A measure of this variable, confidence in the press, is only available (in the General Social Survey) going back to 1973, but its trend, graphed in Figure 1.3, fits the declining network news audience more closely than any other attitudinal change in the population. Confidence in the press has declined monotonically since it was first measured. Yet upon closer inspection, confidence in the press and network news audiences dropped in different ways. Whereas the network news audience fell linearly after about 1980, confidence in the press declined in two steps, one in the late 1970s, the other between 1991 and 1993. In

finding as follows: "Respondents have to assume that their lack of knowledge ... is due to their own behavior, namely that they don't follow public affairs."

Until 1976, the question about campaign interest was preceded by several items about the presidential campaign. Since then, it has been asked first in the pre-election interview. Bishop (2005, 86) suggests that "merely being made to think more about the presidential race in answering the question could be sufficient to get many respondents to think they were interested in the campaign."

between these two drops, confidence in the press remained pretty much constant.[10]

The disparity between most trends in attitudes toward politics and government and the size of the network news audience suggests that the decline in network news viewing may have more to do with a prominent change in the media environment, the spread of cable television. Although the trends shown in Figures 1.2 and 1.3 do not by any means constitute conclusive evidence, they raise sufficient doubt about individual-level change as a cause of declining network news audiences to encourage a more thorough examination of the link between the media environment and political behavior.

NO TECHNOLOGICAL DETERMINISM

Even if changes of the media environment cause political behavior to change, this does not imply that these effects were (pre)determined by the new technology alone. A new medium does not simply imprint its properties on people, and technology is not the only determinant of the media environment and the diffusion of media technologies graphed in Figure 1.1. Market mechanisms, policy regulation, and private initiative all affect both how fast and in what form a particular technology can grow, and what kind of content it offers (e.g., Hamilton 2004; Neuman 1991; 1996; Starr 2004; Turow 1997). The large audiences for network news before the spread of cable television, for example, were not an inevitable result of broadcast technology. They emerged because the networks and their affiliates decided to air news – a decision that was strongly encouraged by policy makers – and ended up, for economic reasons, airing it simultaneously in the early evening. These economic and political reasons, combined with the scarcity of the broadcast spectrum, created the

10 The trends in similar time series based on Harris polls and Pew data fit the decline in network news audiences even less well (Cook, Gronke, and Rattliff 2000). The difference in the respective declines is obviously not sufficient to rule out lower trust in the media as a cause of declining network news audiences. The differences in timing and the fact that cable news consumption actually increased as media trust declined (see Chapter 5) do demonstrate the limits of any simple correspondence between the trust in the media and television news viewing. The relationship is further complicated by the possibility that exposure to television news or the news media more generally depressed trust in the political system (Cappella and Jamieson 1997; Mutz and Reeves 2005; Patterson 1993; Robinson 1976), which could in turn affect trust in the media. Declining trust in the media could also be a post hoc rationalization by those who do not watch news anymore and now need a reason to justify that to themselves.

low-choice environment that made news hard to avoid. Furthermore, the political impact of broadcast television was so significant only because television was so popular – another feature that cannot be explained by technology alone. To be sure, the technological properties of the new medium, in particular its visual nature, which made it easier to understand than print media or radio, contributed to its political implications, but they were not deterministic.

Cable technology alone does not determine the number and political content of cable news channels. It does change the economic constraints for content providers. In a cable environment, it makes economic sense for the Fox News Channel to offer a more conservative political perspective than existing competitors. This strategy is unlikely to attract tens of millions of viewers, but no single news channel reaches such large audiences on a routine basis anymore. In the broadcast environment, the strategy pursued by Fox News would have been inferior to more middle-of-the-road political positions, which are acceptable to a larger audience than conservative views (Hamilton 2004, 3). As program choices increase, going after smaller audience segments becomes economically optimal (Owen and Wildman 1992). A proliferation of channels allows media outlets to specialize their content to attract smaller, but well-defined audience segments, which advertisers value because they can be efficiently targeted. Technology facilitates this content specialization, but the business strategies and profit motives of marketing firms accelerate it and influence its ultimate shape (Turow 1997).

How political actors use new media technologies also plays a role in determining the impact of a new medium (Bimber 2003).[11] At the heart of Chapter 6 is an excellent historical example of how the new medium of broadcast television provided some political actors – congressional incumbents – with the technological and economic means to dominate content and reap important electoral benefits. Incumbents were in a much better position than their challengers to appear on television, not because the technology inherently advantaged incumbents, but because they voted

---

11 Bimber (2003, 18) argues that "exogenous changes in the accessibility or structure of information cause changes in the structure of elite organizations that dominate political activity, and these in turn affect the broad character of democracy." According to Bimber, effects instigated by elite-level (organizational) changes are the key to understanding the political impact of the Internet. This book shows that altered mass behavior enabled by new media technologies deserves more consideration that Bimber gives it. My study is not equipped to evaluate the relative impact of changes among elites and in the general population. I discuss the role of elite mobilization on mass behavior in the concluding chapter.

themselves the privilege to produce content at subsidized rates and because regulation did not prevent them from blurring the lines between office-holders and journalists.

These examples illustrate Neuman's (1991, 19) more general point about the impact of new media technologies:

> The properties of the technology and the environment interact to produce an outcome: the social use of the technology. Thus, the outcome can be seen as a variable, rather than as being predetermined. At a different time or in a different context, the introduction of a new technology could have widely divergent effects.

In this book, I am concerned with new media as they developed in their economic and political environments. When I discuss the "effects of a medium," I thus refer to the effects of that medium in its particular form as determined by technology, economic considerations, regulatory constraints, and developing customs of use. For example, "implications of broadcast television for politics" is shorthand for "implications of changing from the pre-television media environment to a media environment that ended up being dominated by broadcast television for complex but observable reasons." This emphasis avoids the simplicity of technological determinism, but it can also make the analysis more complicated and the causal interpretation more difficult. If the new medium of broadcast television happened to be widely popular, was regulated in a particular way, and allowed incumbents to broadcast their own interview shows, can we still say that the change in the media environment caused subsequent changes in learning about politics and voting rates for incumbents? I will argue that we can because these political changes would not have occurred in the absence of broadcast television. But it is a conditional kind of technological effect – not a determinism.

The impact of changes in the media environment depends on how people use new media. Cautioning the digital optimists, Neuman (1991, 42) predicted that "[a]s evolving information technologies make new forms of education, exploration, and publication participation possible, deeply ingrained habits of passive, half-attentive media use constrain that potential." To understand changes in the media environment, we need to examine both the new opportunities and how people use these opportunities. The media environment is chiefly responsible for facilitating some behaviors while making others more difficult and less likely. Content preferences, for example, have different effects on news exposure, learning, and turnout in different media environments. Sometimes, a change caused by new media can suppress individual differences and makes everybody behave more alike. Broadcast television had this effect. Other changes in the media environment introduce more heterogeneity and inequality in media use and political behavior. When users have a lot of content to choose from, the diversity of individual preferences leads to increasing diversity in media exposure. Regardless of whether the outcome is higher or lower heterogeneity in political behaviors, the changes occur because the new media environment modifies how people's motivations and abilities work.

THE RELEVANCE OF MEDIA CONTENT
PREFERENCES FOR POLITICS

Some of the changes in political behavior I seek to explain happened half a century ago. Some of the concepts I draw on have been explicated and measured and employed in research for many decades. But one of the key elements of my analysis is completely new. Media content preferences – what type of media content people prefer – have not been used in the study of politics. They turn out to be very powerful predictors of political behavior in our current high-choice media environment. As Chapter 4 demonstrates, the effect of content preferences on knowledge and turnout already exceeds the impact of education and other resource variables, even though most Americans still have only analog cable access and dial-up internet connections.

The strength of one's preferences for different media content is not directly political. Whether or not I would die for a prime time comedy or another episode of my favorite soap opera is not generally seen as a pressing question for political scientists. But in a high-choice media environment where options abound and information and entertainment compete constantly, content preferences assume a political relevance they did not have before cable and Internet. The more I like comedy shows or soap operas, the less time I have for the news. Preferences for entertainment content affect political behavior.

Political science is not well prepared for the new importance of media content preferences. Most survey research relies on little more than a rather blunt measure of political interest – something like, "How interested are you in politics; a lot, a little, or not at all?" – that generates little variance, does not distinguish between an interest in politics and an interest in the news more generally, and fails to compare people's taste for the news to their desire for other media content. As the media environment gives people more room to seek out the media content that interests them, finer measures of interests and preferences are needed. By offering empirical measures of content preference, I hope to contribute to our understanding of politics in a high-choice media environment even after all Americans have gained access to digital cable and high-speed Internet.

The effect of preference in the current media environment contrasts pointedly with their unimportance under conditions of low choice.

Broadcast television leveled the playing field. For the politically interested and cognitively sophisticated segments of the population, broadcast
television changed relatively little. For those less motivated and able to
follow the news, however, the introduction of television had two important effects. It provided more easily comprehensible political information,
and it imposed this information on a captive audience. In contrast, the
most consequential change caused by cable television and the Internet is
to provide additional media content of every type and genre at a variety
of difficulty levels. In a media environment that is no longer constrained
by a sophistication requirement or the lack of choice, people's individual choices become more important. Political information in the current
media environment comes mostly to those who want it. In the starkest
terms, broadcast television reduced the importance of individual content
preferences, while cable and Internet raise them to a level of importance
not seen before.

   To appreciate the promises and dangers of new media, we need to first
understand the old ones. That is why this story begins in 1935. The role of
content preferences in the current media environment is only one of several
instances in which the arrival of a new medium profoundly changed the
impact of an individual-level factor. But these changes are easy to miss if
we happen to study a period in which the media environment is stable.
The theoretical framework that I introduce in the next chapter explicitly
recognizes the conditional nature of individual-level effects on political
behavior. Politics does not happen in empty space; it happens in a media
environment.

2

Conditional Political Learning

Political information and exposure to news motivate people to go to the polls. In the media environment dominated by broadcast television, many Americans watched the news. Some viewers turned on the news out of a strong interest in politics and public affairs. Others happened to be watching television and took the path of least resistance to the next entertainment opportunity: Do not leave the couch, do not turn the dial. For many of these less politically interested viewers, exposure to a few newscasts each week made just the difference between voting and not voting. As the media environment changed, they could find content more to their liking than news. As a result, they stayed home on Election Day.

This chapter begins to investigate the media environment's power to change whether and how people encounter politics and what they learn about it. Choice between different media content is the key variable for understanding the impact of changing media environments. In a low-choice environment, people's preferences have little power to influence media exposure. When choices abound, people do what they like best, so preferences drive exposure. The chapter introduces the theoretical framework and illustrates empirically its core mechanism, the impact of media choice on political involvement. I draw on past research and my own experimental demonstration of these mechanisms to explain the Conditional Political Learning model. From this model, I derive a set of hypotheses concerning the political implications of moving from the pre-television to the broadcast television environment and then to the cable and Internet environment.

In subsequent chapters, I describe changes in the media environment in greater detail and add depth to the empirical tests of my hypotheses. The virtue of this chapter is its simplicity. Though simple, the chapter covers considerable ground, reaching all the way from the media environment to the polarization of contemporary elections. By necessity, this chapter glances over nuances and raises new questions about the connections between the media environment, news exposure, political learning, turnout, and polarization. In Chapters 3 to 7, I hope to anticipate and answer most of those questions.

DEVELOPING A MODEL OF CONDITIONAL POLITICAL LEARNING

Political knowledge has different elements, including factual knowledge, a sense of the connections between different political ideas, and an ability to derive informed opinions. Theoretically, all these elements can be affected by the media environment. Throughout this book, I use the term "political knowledge" to describe knowledge of specific political facts and concepts as well as knowledge of recent noteworthy political events.[1] Political learning refers to the acquisition of these types of information. Political knowledge can decline over time, either because people forget what they used to know or because a particular fact is no longer true (as when a new person is appointed to a political office, but someone continues to believe that the predecessor is still in office). Political scientists know more about learning than about forgetting or failing to update. I simply assume that an individual's political knowledge can decline when he or she is no longer exposed to political information.

Political Knowledge and the OMA Framework

The most influential studies of political learning are based on the notion that factors in three broad areas guide the acquisition of political knowledge: opportunity, motivation, and ability (Delli Carpini and Keeter 1996; Luskin 1990). Opportunity refers to the availability of political information; ability, to people's skills in absorbing and comprehending the available information; and motivation, to whether people are actually interested in doing so.

Delli Carpini and Keeter (1996) define opportunity as a product of "the state of knowledge about the topic in question..., the frequency with which information is made available..., [and] the communications technology available." Opportunity encompasses many different factors, but the media environment is an important one. In Chapter 1, I introduced my definition of the media environment: A media environment is defined by the different media sources routinely available to people at any point

---

1 The concentration on factual knowledge is largely dictated by data limitations. For over-time comparisons, I need to draw on survey data collected in the past. As factual knowledge is the most common measure of knowledge in these data sets, I rely on it for my analyses.

in time. The properties of the media to which people have access and of the media markets and circulation areas in which they live have direct and indirect effects on their political knowledge and behavior. The classical studies in this tradition examined the effects of television in the 1950s by comparing areas already covered by the new medium to areas not yet covered (Parker 1963; Simon and Stern 1955). A variation of this approach studies the (temporary) absence of a medium in a certain area. Mondak (1995), for example, took advantage of a local newspaper strike in Pittsburgh to study what happens when a medium is unavailable for a period of time. Studies that follow this tradition show that people are more knowledgeable about state politics in areas served by the newspapers of the state's capital city (Delli Carpini, Keeter, and Kennamer 1994). Those who receive their news from out-of-state pick up less political information about that state, and are less well informed about the political situation in their own state (Delli Carpini, Keeter, and Kennamer 1994; Keeter and Wilson 1986; Zukin and Snyder 1984). These studies illustrate one of the components of the opportunity-motivation-ability (OMA) framework: Different media environments provide different opportunities to learn about politics.

The other two factors that explain political learning according to the OMA framework are individual characteristics: ability and motivation. Ability affects how much people learn from their exposure to politics, given particular levels of motivation and opportunity. It "covers a fairly wide range of skills, talents, and attributes, from the physical (the ability to see and hear, for example) to the cognitive (the ability to process and retain information) to the social (the ability to read and write)" (Delli Carpini and Keeter 1996). Both innate and learnable skills fall in this category. Luskin (1990), for example, demonstrates the effect of intelligence on political sophistication.[2] Nie, Junn, and Stehlik-Barry (1996) show that verbal proficiency, which is itself determined by education, increases political knowledge.

In Delli Carpini and Keeter's (1996, 114) account, the third factor, motivation, encompasses self-interest, noninstrumental curiosity about politics, as well as a sense of efficacy and civic duty:

> The motivation to follow politics, and thus to learn about it, comes from several places. It results from interest – both a general interest in national and international affairs, and a more focused interest based on personal needs or concerns. It results from a sense of efficacy, the belief that one's involvement in politics is a good

2 Political sophistication (or political expertise) is not the same as political knowledge because it also includes a notion of integration of knowledge akin to Converse's (1964) "constraints" of belief systems. Political knowledge is the best single predictor of political sophistication, however (Luskin 1987).

investment of one's time, that it will produce either psychic, solidary, or substantive rewards. And it results from a sense of civic duty, the belief that one should be involved in politics regardless of one's personal interest or the likelihood of an identifiable payoff.

While Delli Carpini and Keeter focus more on motivation as a set of factors that influence whether an individual chooses to seek out political information, research on message processing (e.g., Chaiken 1980; Petty and Cacioppo 1986) demonstrates that motivation also influences learning directly as higher motivation leads to different, more thorough, processing of a message. Numerous studies have shown that political interest, a sense of civic duty, and efficacy affect how much people know about politics.

Many Americans are not overly interested in politics. They do not consider political involvement a "good investment of their time" and gain greater "psychic, solidary, and substantive rewards" from working, socializing, or using entertainment media. The OMA framework suggests why these modestly interested people still pick up some political information along the way: The environment offers it to them. If people have the ability required to understand this information, they learn even when their interest is low.

Different Types of Learning: Motivated and Accidental

Another theoretical perspective also features this kind of environment-driven learning. Downs (1957) and later Fiorina (1990) and Popkin (1991) discuss the notion of obtaining information as a by-product. Even when it is not their goal to learn about politics, people acquire new information if the environment offers it to them as they are engaged in their everyday activities. Unlike the OMA framework, Downs's by-product model of learning explains *why* the environment can increase knowledge in the absence of a motivation to learn.

Downs's goal was to explain why rational citizens learn about politics at all, even though they receive few if any tangible benefits from acquiring political knowledge. It would be "rational" to remain ignorant, yet few people do. As a solution to this puzzle, Downs argues that people 'pay' only for the pleasure and enjoyment of entertainment, but sometimes pick up free political information on the side. The benefits from entertainment are tangible, so it is rational to pay for them (by actually paying money for the experience or by accepting the opportunity costs of not being able to enjoy something else).

Some people derive tangible benefits from following the news. Yet, these benefits derive not from the value of the information people acquire, but from enjoying the experience. They watch news because of its consumption value. So, as Fiorina (1990, 337) points out, some people – "informed citizens as fans" – learn simply because they like following politics. This is very similar to Delli Carpini and Keeter's (1996, 114) argument that for some people political knowledge provides "psychic" rewards or satisfies "personal needs."

But not everybody derives consumption value from following the news. Downs's major contribution is to explain why people who do *not* enjoy politics or the news may still pick up political information. Even people who do not derive consumption value from news exposure learn about politics when political information is presented as part of an activity that offers payoffs from *entertainment*. As discussed in Chapter 1, Downs presented the newsreel before the main movie feature as an example. If watching the movie maximizes the consumption or entertainment value for a politically uninterested person, she will decide to tolerate the news-reel even though she does not derive any value from the experience or from the information she might obtain. A similar argument has been made about news as an interruption of entertainment programming on the broadcast networks before cable:

Television news reaches both those who generally monitor politics *and* those who would have virtually *no* news were it not for television. . . . Television touches those millions who will sit through the news because of what follows or what comes before, but who would rarely expend the energy to read through print information. Consequently, TV produces two audiences – the advertent (those who watch for the news) and the inadvertent audience (those who fall into the news). (Robinson 1976, 426, emphasis in the original)

Two different paths – accidental exposure and enjoyment of politics – both lead to political learning. Some people learn about politics because they are motivated to do so; others learn because they cannot help it and it is free.

The Media Environment as a Condition for Learning

In the early twenty-first century, Robinson's description of television sounds outdated. Today, few people "sit through the news because of what follows or what comes before." But if the description of television viewing is outdated, then so are the consequences that Robinson outlines. The "inadvertent audience" is becoming an anachronism. And if that is true, then the very argument at the core of Downsian by-product learning is aging fast.

By-product learning is a variable that depends on the efficiency with which we can get what we want from the media. At a particular level of inefficiency in the media environment – just a few broadcast channels all of which offer the same program type at the same time, or movie features preceded by newsreels – we observe the same behavior, news exposure, in the "advertent" and the "inadvertent audience." Yet for the former, the behavior is driven by intrinsic motivations, whereas structural factors explain the behavior for the latter audience segment. If we ignore that accidental exposure to political information is not a constant but depends on the media environment, we misunderstand the role that learning as a by-product is likely to play in the future. The by-product view does *not* specify two different and independently sufficient conditions for political learning, enjoyment of news and politics (which leads to direct learning effects), and entertainment-seeking media exposure (which leads to learning through accidental exposure). The latter condition is not in itself sufficient. In an efficient media environment, people who use media only to gratify their entertainment needs do not acquire even basic political information through accidental exposure. When the structure, and hence the efficiency, of the media environment changes, behavior too should change, especially for the inadvertent news viewers who only watch because of the environmental inefficiency.[3]

The realization that accidental exposure to political information is not an unalterable fact of life calls for a more nuanced view of political learning. Opportunity – a characteristic of the environment – interacts with motivation and ability – characteristics of the individual – to produce political knowledge. When newsreels preceded movies, people were exposed to and maybe learned about politics even if they were not motivated to seek out political information. Once theaters abandoned the newsreel, those unmotivated to seek out political information became less likely to encounter politics. Put differently, the relationship between motivation and political knowledge becomes stronger as the environment becomes a more efficient provider of the media content people want. Opportunity not only influences political learning directly; it also conditions the impact of individual-level factors.

These interactive effects of environment and individual characteristics are not developed in the existing OMA framework proposed by Luskin (1990) and Delli Carpini and Keeter (1996). Instead, these authors mostly

---

3 I use the term "efficiency" to refer to the ease with which media content can be accessed in a media environment. Efficiency in this sense is similar to "audience autonomy" (Napoli 2003, 145). Economists sometimes use the term "efficiency" more broadly to describe social welfare implications. I do not mean to suggest that a high-choice media environment necessarily increases the efficiency of the democratic system or society as a whole.

consider the direct effects of the three factors on political knowledge and treat them as independent of each other.[4]

The OMA framework and Downs's by-product model both give a role to the media environment in explaining political learning, but it is a relatively underwritten and static role in both theories. The media environment has a greater impact than both OMA and Downs grant it. A change in the media environment is enough to change how the other two factors, motivation and ability, work. To equip the OMA framework to deal with changing media environments, I extend it to incorporate explicitly the interactions between opportunity on the one hand, and motivation and ability on the other. The effect of individual characteristics on political learning is thus conditional on the media environment. My model is a model of Conditional Political Learning.

In the Conditional Political Learning model, *the effect of motivation on political learning depends on the media environment.* Specifically, the impact of program preferences and political interest on political knowledge varies with the media environment. A model of political learning from media thus requires two components: one individual-level component that captures what media content people like, and one aggregate component that takes account of the availability of political information. Together, the two components can not only predict overall learning but also distinguish the likelihood of learning as a by-product from learning as a result of deliberate news-seeking. As a media environment becomes more efficient, people who obtain greatest gratification from entertainment content pick up less information because they encounter fewer opportunities for learning as a by-product. For those who obtain gratification from news exposure, on the other hand, higher efficiency of a media system may mean more opportunities to watch news and learn about politics. The effect of motivation depends on the opportunities that exist in a particular media environment to satisfy these preferences.

The effect of the second individual-level factor that comes out of the OMA framework is conditional, too: *The effect of ability on political learning depends on the media environment.* The role of people's skills in political learning depends in part on the kinds of skills that the available media require. Delli Carpini and Keeter (1996) and Luskin (1990) describe opportunity largely in terms of the information that is available

---

4 Delli Carpini and Keeter (1996) acknowledge the importance of interactions between opportunity and individual-level factors explicitly (p. 8), but their empirical analysis does not incorporate this idea. In their model of political knowledge (p. 181), "behavioral" and "structural" factors are correlated, but their effects on political knowledge are independent.

to people as they go about their lives. But this information is not equally useful to all people to whom it is available. People need a certain level of expertise to take advantage of the information. For some information opportunities, such as television news, many people have this expertise. Other opportunities – government documents written in a foreign language and stored in the Library of Congress – require qualifications that few people have. Hence, just as some media environments leave more room for motivation, the effect of the second individual-level factor in the OMA framework, ability, depends on the media environment as well. Processing and comprehending a message requires greater ability for some media than for others.

With the addition of interactions between individual factors and the media environment, the theoretical foundation for the analyses in the following chapters is in place. Before I flesh out the Conditional Political Learning model to link changes in the media environment to election outcomes, I offer an empirical test of the core principle of the model. A simple experiment provides a first glimpse at the conditioning power of media environments. It also serves as a focal point for the integration of different literatures: not only the OMA framework and studies of political learning conducted mostly in political science but also research on audience behavior and program choice more common in communication and economics.

THE LOW-CHOICE/HIGH-CHOICE EXPERIMENT

Choice is the primary feature of cable television that increased the efficiency of the media environment over what it was in the broadcast era. With cable access, viewers have a wider choice of genres and programs, both overall and at any point in time. Isolating the impact of media choice is one of the major goals of this book. For a stylized comparison of media choice during the broadcast era and media choice in a cable environment, I designed the Low-Choice/High-Choice Experiment. The experiment was embedded in the News & Entertainment Survey, on which I will rely in several chapters of the book. For now, it is only necessary to know that 2,358 randomly selected U.S. residents were interviewed for this survey in 2002. At the very beginning of the interview, respondents were asked the following question: "If you had free time at 6 o'clock at night and the following programs were available, which one would you watch, or would you not watch television then?"

Respondents were randomly assigned to one of two conditions. The two conditions were designed to resemble the choices people have in a broadcast and a cable environment, respectively. Approximating the broadcast environment, the low-choice condition gave respondents only

34

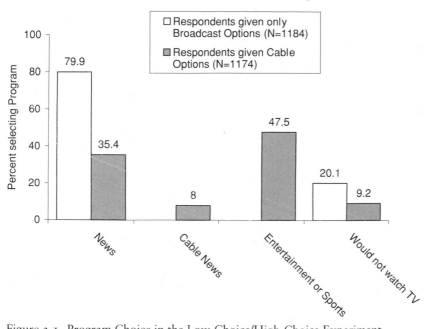

Figure 2.1. Program Choice in the Low-Choice/High-Choice Experiment.

Note: The bars in this figure show the frequency of responses in the two conditions of the Low-Choice/High-Choice Experiment.

Source: News & Entertainment Survey.

five response options: ABC Nightly News, NBC Nightly News, CBS Nightly News, the *Newshour with Jim Lehrer,* and finally the option to turn off the television. In the high-choice condition, respondents were presented with the same five options plus several additional programs that are available only on cable. Their choices included additional news channels (Fox News, "CNN or MSNBC") and several entertainment options ("a comedy or sitcom program like *Friends* or *The Simpsons,*" "a drama program like *ER* or *Law and Order,*" "a science fiction program like *X-Files* or *Star Trek Voyager,*" "a Reality TV like *Survivor* or *Cops,*" and "a Sports program"). Just as real cable subscribers, respondents in the high-choice condition could select from a greater number of viewing options – eleven compared to four in the low-choice condition – and greater variety of genres.[5] The results, shown in Figure 2.1, are stunningly

---

5 Response options were presented on screen in two columns and randomized within news and entertainment categories. In the high-choice condition, the first option in the left column was always an entertainment program; the first option in the right column was always a news option.

clear. In the low-choice condition, 80 percent of the respondents selected one of the four news programs, while the remaining 20 percent reported that they would not watch television given those choices. In the high-choice condition, the news audience is virtually cut in half. Only 35 percent of the respondents in the high-choice condition said they would watch one of the four broadcast newscasts. An additional 8 percent picked cable news. Half of the hypothetical cable audience, however, selected an entertainment program or sports. Given more alternatives, fewer people cannot find anything they like, reducing by half the percentage of respondents who responded that they would turn off the set.[6]

The point of the Low-Choice/High-Choice Experiment was to strip the comparison of broadcast and cable of all extraneous noise. Doing so risks getting rid of all realism. And yet, the experimental results are surprisingly similar to real-world trends in the size of the network news audience over the last four decades. Between 1963, when CBS and NBC expanded their evening newscasts to thirty minutes, and the early 1980s, the average audience rating for the three network newscasts combined was pretty stable at about 36. An average 36 percent of all American homes watched the network news each weekday in those years. The highest-ever combined yearly average was a 38 rating in 1980. In 2003, the combined rating fell below 20, and a year later it was less than half of its maximum value. During this period, the percentage of households with cable (or satellite) access more than quadrupled from 20 percent to over 80 percent.

At the same time that cable television increased entertainment options, the networks repeatedly moved their newscasts to earlier time slots. Observers have mentioned this scheduling change as a mundane

---

6 At first glance, the distributions appear to be consistent with respondents' selecting answers randomly. Because four of the five options in the low-choice condition are news programs, random responding would generate an 80–20 split. In the high-choice condition, with six news options and five entertainment options, the distribution generated by random responding would be 50 percent news, 42 percent entertainment, and 8 percent "would not watch TV." Yet even though both random distributions are close to the empirically obtained distributions *in the aggregate*, responses were clearly not random. For example, in the low-choice condition, 33 percent of the respondents selected NBC News, while only 15 percent picked ABC News, and only 6 percent the *Lehrer Newshour*. In the high-choice condition, where random responding would lead to 8 percent for each response option, 22 percent selected the "comedy or sitcom," while less than 5 percent chose reality TV, sports, the *Lehrer Newshour*, FOX News, or "CNN or MSNBC News." Social desirability bias does not offer a straightforward explanation either why so many respondents selected news in the low-choice condition. If they did so only to impress the researcher, they should be less willing to select entertainment options in the high-choice condition. Moreover, they completed the survey on a computer screen without any impressionable interviewer around.

explanation for the ratings decline because it keeps people from watching who are still at work. Yet, little of the ratings decline seems to be explained by the increasingly earlier airing of network news. A different audience measure, the market share, holds constant the available audience by dividing the number of households watching a program by the number of households watching television at the time. Until the early 1980s, the combined market share for the three network newscasts was about 75. Three out of four households watching television at the time had their set tuned to the network news. In 2004, the combined share fell below 40 for the first time. Just as in the Low-Choice/High-Choice Experiment, the news audience in the current high-choice environment is half of what it was during the low-choice days of broadcast television.

The experimental results also correspond to audience research that shows local news audiences to be smaller when other channels offer entertainment programs in the same time slot (Webster 1984; Webster and Newton 1988; Webster and Wakshlag 1983). A systematic comparison of local news across different media markets in 1982 found the market share for news programs to be about 20 percent lower among cable viewers under 50 than among viewers in the same age group who could watch only broadcast channels (Webster 1982).[7] Offering people more choice – be it in a hypothetical survey question about television or on their actual television sets – has remarkable effects on their news consumption. Why does choice make such a big difference? Why do so many people select news in the low-choice condition? To understand the impact of choice, we need to know how people choose.

Models of Program Choice

The literature on program choice developed by economists and communication scholars helps explain the pattern of responses in the Low-Choice/High-Choice Experiment and the behavior of television viewers as they decide whether or not to watch the news. The most parsimonious models of program choice are proposed by economists (for an overview, see Owen and Wildman 1992). Viewers maximize utility by selecting the program that is closest to their "ideal program." The fit between the programs offered at any particular time and viewers' ideal programs is evaluated either in terms of underlying program characteristics (Bowman 1975; Lehmann 1971) or program types (Hawkins et al. 2001; Youn 1994). Content preferences clearly outperform demographic

---

7 These are my calculations based on Webster's data. Differences were somewhat smaller for viewers above the age of 50, who are generally more interested in the news.

variables as predictors of program choice (e.g., Lehmann 1971). The uses-and-gratifications approach prominent in the communication literature (e.g., Gantz 1978; Katz, Blumler, and Gurevitch 1973; Katz, Gurevitch, and Haas 1973) argues that content preferences capture only one aspect of program choice. According to uses-and-gratifications, media use is driven by people's motivation to gratify their needs, which also include social and emotional needs. Subsequent theoretical extensions have added an expected-utility component. People have expectations regarding the level of gratification they are likely to obtain from different media content and select the content that maximizes their expected gratifications (Becker and Schoenbach 1989). Mirroring the Downsian by-product view, this model emphasizes the difference between the primary effect of satisfying needs through media use and secondary effects such as knowledge gains.

Even though economic models focus more on well-defined preferences, whereas uses-and-gratifications emphasizes a broader and more diffuse set of needs, these models have in common that viewers are treated as maximizing expected satisfaction given a set of programming options. More recently, Matt Baum (2002; Baum and Kernell 1999) has employed a similar model of television watching. People's expectation about the utility of information they can gain from different programs determines their program choice. People weigh the benefits from obtaining information against the time, effort, and money it takes to acquire the information (transaction costs) and the costs associated with not being able to do something else, like watching an entertainment show (opportunity costs). The models by Baum and Becker and Schönbach as well as a major strand of the uses-and-gratifications literature (e.g., Rubin 1984) juxtapose information and entertainment seeking as the two main motivations for media use. When viewers have a choice between news and entertainment programming, many do not watch news programs because the opportunity costs involved in forfeiting payoffs from entertainment are too high.

With greater choice through cable access, the impact of program type preferences on program choice increases, so "indiscriminate viewing" is less likely among cable subscribers (Youn 1994). Viewing shares for broadcast networks decrease at the expense of cable channels. Even though any particular specialty cable channel is not viewed by large shares of the total audience, many specialty channels attract small numbers of dedicated heavy users (Webster 1986). Hence, while the channel repertoire for cable subscribers (the number of frequently viewed channels) is not dramatically higher than for nonsubscribers (Heeter 1985), their repertoire reflects a set of channels that are more closely related to their genre preferences. Cable television and greater choice in general produce "a degree of audience polarization unprecedented in our experience with traditional forms of television" (Webster 1986, 89).

The responses in the high-choice condition of the Low-Choice/High-Choice Experiment are thus not surprising. People select content they like. Yet the impact of choice in the experiment and the decline in network news audiences in the cable era are only so large because the reference point is so high. Why do 80 percent of the survey respondents say that they would watch the news in the low-choice condition? Why did almost 40 percent of all households turn on the network news on an average weekday in 1980? The explanation has to do with the fact that viewers are reluctant to turn off their sets even when the programs offered at the time do not meet their preferences well. Rather than purposefully turning on the set to watch a particular program, people's decision to watch television and their subsequent selection of a program are largely independent. One study conducted in the early seventies showed that 40 percent of the respondents reported watching programs because they appeared on the channel they were already watching or because someone else wanted to see them (LoSciuto 1972). Habit plays a role in deciding when to watch television. Even though weekday and weekend programming differs significantly, people tend to watch at similar times of the day on weekdays and weekends (Rosenstein and Grant 1997).

To account for such results, audience research has proposed a two-stage model according to which people first decide to watch television and then pick the available program they like best. Klein (1972, 77) called this model of television viewing the "Theory of Least Objectionable Program." The two-stage model explains a variety of empirical patterns summarized as "viewer inertia." Audience research shows that the size of program audiences benefits from lead-in (or inheritance) effects (Rosenstein and Grant 1997; Tiedge and Ksobiech 1986; Webster and Phalen 1997). Because part of the audience simply keeps watching the next program on the channel that is already on, program ratings depend partly on the popularity of the preceding program. Lead-in effects occur even when the genre of the two adjacent programs is not the same (Walker 1988). Empirical evidence for the two-step model also comes from analysis of audience data showing relatively low repeat-viewing rates. Repeat viewing measures what percentage of an audience watches the same show or a program in the same genre a day or a week later. Although different studies have produced a range of different estimates, repeat viewing is seldom higher than 50 percent and can be much lower (Barwise, Ehrenberg, and Goodhardt 1982; Headen, Klompmaker, and Rust 1979; Webster and Wang 1992). At most half the viewers of a particular program watch the same program on the following day or in the following week. Repeat viewing of genres rather than programs is not noticeably higher (Barwise and Ehrenberg 1988). If viewers selectively turned on the set for particular programs or genres, repeat-viewing rates should be higher.

Compared to other media, broadcast television left relatively little room for motivation in general, and content preferences in particular, to make a difference. In the broadcast era, programming strategies, most notably the monopoly for local and network news in the early evening hours, reduced people's television viewing to a choice between watching news or turning off their television sets. In their study of presidential television appearances, Baum and Kernell (1999, 101) show that audiences were larger when cable penetration was still low and when all broadcast networks carried the appearance. "[T]he combination of limited channels, an unwillingness to turn off the set, and the networks' joint suspension of commercial programming during a presidential appearance" produced a captive audience. The same logic extends to news in general. Independent of their content preference, viewers set to watch television at the dinner hour or after prime time constituted a captive audience for news. A major share of television viewing in the broadcast era did not follow a deliberate choice of a program. Instead, convenience, availability of spare time, and the decision to spend that time watching television determined viewing behavior (see also Comstock and Scharrer 1999; Neuman 1991, 94). Hence, even though many people watched television primarily to be entertained, not to obtain political information, many of them were routinely exposed to news in the broadcast era. Based on self-reports, Patterson and McClure (1976, 165, note 5) report that "regular viewers of television entertainment programs have, compared with the total population, almost identical . . . news exposure levels." Epstein (1973, 90) observed that

[t]hose viewers who can be counted on to watch a news program are not at all drawn to their set from their various pursuits by the appeal of the program; for the main part they are already watching television at that hour, or disposed to watch it then, according to the audience-research studies that networks have conducted over the years.

Combining utility-maximizing program selection and the two-stage model of viewing can explain why politically uninterested citizens are routinely exposed to political information as long as choice is limited. Viewers turn on their television sets because watching television promises to be more gratifying than anything else they could do at the same time. They then select the most preferred program available, even if that happens to be a news program and their absolute liking of news is low. As Barwise and Ehrenberg (1988, 57) conclude, simultaneous scheduling of news programs on all networks in the broadcast era "goes with lower audience appreciation among those viewing at these times (i.e. *they did not all necessarily want to watch news then*)" (emphasis added).

Conditional Political Learning

A lot, then, depends on whether news is the only program genre available at the time. Before cable television, it often was. Today, most Americans can choose from dozens or hundreds of alternative programs. As a result, former news viewers switch to entertainment, and Robinson's "inadvertent" news audience disappears. People no longer "fall into the news."

Perhaps the most remarkable aspect of the Low-Choice/High-Choice Experiment is not the magnitude of the shift but the fact that it is entirely due to the manipulation of people's choices. Because of the random assignment to one of the two conditions, respondents did not differ systematically on any other dimension than the viewing choices they were given. In other words, the transition from a low-choice to a high-choice environment cut the news audience in half, even though respondents in both conditions were equally interested in politics, equally likely to get their news from other media, equally bound to follow the news by a sense of civic duty, and equally likely to believe that learning about politics is worthwhile. Hence, the decline of the news audience we have observed over the past decades is not necessarily an indication of reduced political interest or changes in other attitudes. The experiment demonstrates that it could possibly be caused by changes in the media environment alone. People's media use may change in a modified media environment, even if their preferences have remained constant.

The Switchers

Comparing responses in the low-choice and the high-choice conditions of my experiment, or audience ratings early and late in the diffusion of cable television, yields conclusions about aggregate changes in the news audience. Individual-level data are needed to identify which individuals are most affected by the expansion of viewing choices. I extended the Low-Choice/High-Choice Experiment to yield such data. The last question of the interview, asked half an hour after the first for the median respondent, repeated the text of the first question. Respondents were again asked to select the program they would most likely watch at 6 o'clock at night. The response options given in the low-choice and high-choice conditions remained just as in the first question. Respondents assigned to the low-choice condition in the first question were now asked to select from the long list of options. The reverse was true for respondents initially in the high-choice condition. Over the course of the interview, every respondent thus answered the question twice, once in the low-choice condition and once in the high-choice condition. This makes it possible to determine for each respondent how she modifies her viewing behavior when faced

Table 2.1. *News Exposure in Low-Choice and High-Choice Media Environments*

Group		Frequency	Political Interest	
			"Very interested"	"Very" or "Somewhat interested"
Always news	Watch news in both environments	43.2%	37%	80%
Cable news only	Move from not watching to (cable) news when offered the choice	2.2%	39%	81%
Switchers	Move from news to entertainment when offered the choice	34.1%	18%	66%
Entertainment only	Move from not watching to entertainment when offered the choice	10.3%	11%	51%
Non-viewers	Do not watch anything in either scenario	7.1%	16%	59%
Overwhelmed	Move from news to not watching television when offered more choice	3.0%	28%	73%

Note: This table offers a typology of news exposure in low-choice and high-choice media environments. The table provides estimates of the frequency of each exposure pattern based on the (repeated) Low-Choice/High-Choice Experiment. The two rightmost columns show average political interest within each group of viewers.
Source: News & Entertainment Survey ($N = 2,310$).

with an expansion of choice.[8] Table 2.1 shows the frequency of different modifications.

The largest group of respondents, 43 percent, selected a news program regardless of whether they were given the short or the long list of viewing

8 In the high-choice condition, the marginals for the last question differed significantly from the responses in the first question. When asked in the last question, 41.6% of the respondents selected entertainment, 40.6% broadcast news, 6.7% cable news, and 11.1% said they would not watch television. Hence, of the respondents who answered the high-choice question at the end of the interview, 47% selected a news program, compared to 43% of the respondents who were asked the high-choice question at the start. The χ^2 statistic for the difference between this distribution and the distribution obtained in the first question is 12.3, $p < .01$. Since it is unclear which distribution is the "correct" one, the following analysis uses the entire sample. In the low-choice condition, 80.3% selected news and 19.7% selected not watching television when asked in the last question. This distribution is not different from the one obtained in the first question ($\chi^2 = .07$).

options. I call this group the Always News group. Another 2 percent selected a news program – cable news in most cases – in the high-choice condition but would not watch if offered only the short list of options. I label this group the Cable News Only group. The second largest group with 34 percent, the Switchers, picked a news program in the low-choice condition but switched to entertainment in the high-choice condition. Few respondents, only 10 percent of the sample, would rather turn off the television set than watch news, if that is their choice. This small group is the Entertainment Only group. Finally, the Non-Viewers (7 percent) report that they would not watch television in either condition, and a small group of respondents (3 percent) violates logic by selecting news in the low-choice condition, yet not watching when offered additional choices.[9]

Consistent with theories of program choice, those most affected by the expansion of choice, the Switchers, are not particularly interested in politics. Only 18 percent of them say they are "very interested" in politics, which is significantly lower than in the Always News and the Cable News Only groups. These two groups are the most politically interested with 37 and 39 percent being very interested (see last two columns in Table 2.1).[10] Switchers are, on the other hand, *more* interested than

9 This behavior does not appear to be caused by exposure to political content during the interview because the percentage of people who move from news to not watching does not depend on whether the high-choice condition occurred in the first or last question. Most likely, it reflects simple measurement error.

Studying consumer choice more generally, Iyengar and Lepper (2000) have shown that although people enjoy choice, having too many options can keep people from making a choice. In one field experiment, they offered participants either 6 or 24 different kinds of jam. Participants in the "limited-choice" condition were much more likely to buy jam. This argument does not seem to apply to greater media choice. Television viewing has continued to increase as media choice expanded (and so has Internet usage). People do not turn off their television sets in response to "choice overload" on television. Even if they do not evaluate all choices systematically (by consulting a TV guide or zapping through the entire lineup), the behavior of television viewers appears to resemble satisficing (Simon 1957). Viewers do not always select the optimal program, but search until they find a program they like enough. Iyengar and Lepper also find that people with many options display lower satisfaction with their eventual choice. Drawing on a more cultural approach, Springsteen (1992) suggests that this problem may apply to television choice as well.

10 Political interest was measured by the following question: "In general, how interested are you in politics and public affairs?" Response options were "very interested," "somewhat interested," "slightly interested," and "not at all interested." Table 2.1 also provides the share of respondents of each viewer type that are either "very" or "somewhat" interested. Results show the same pattern when the entire scale is used.

those in the Entertainment Only group, in which 11 percent voice strong political interest. While the most politically interested people select news regardless of other choices and the least interested cannot be bothered to watch news even if the alternative is not watching television at all (at least hypothetically), people at mid-levels of political interest switch. They are sufficiently interested to watch news in the absence of alternatives, but not interested enough to stick with their choice when entertainment becomes an option. And they appear to make up a substantial portion of viewers. The Low-Choice/High-Choice Experiment identifies one-third of the population as Switchers.

Did Switchers Learn?

The significance of Switchers' leaving the news audience as media choice increases depends on what they got out of their time in the inadvertent audience. If Switchers used to learn about politics in the broadcast environment, their reduced news consumption in favor of entertainment programming is of direct political relevance. Providing Switchers with more choices would then pose a problem for a democratic system that is based on voluntary participation because fewer of the benefits of political knowledge would accrue to them or the electorate as a whole. If Switchers learn less about politics in the high-choice environment, their political participation will drop, their political decisions may match their underlying predispositions less well, and collective decisions may be increasingly distorted (see, e.g., Althaus 1998; Bartels 1996; Delli Carpini and Keeter 1996).

But do Switchers actually learn anything in the captive news audience? We have already seen that they are not as interested as the rest of the audience. And attention to the news helps comprehension and retention of political information (Chaffee and Schleuder 1986; Chang and Krosnick 2002). Yet, even though a captive news audience does not exhibit the same political interest as a self-selected, intrinsically motivated news audience and may therefore not learn as much about politics, the research on passive learning (Krugman and Hartley 1970) suggests that even unmotivated exposure can produce learning (Keeter and Wilson 1986; Zukin and Snyder 1984). Graber (1988) has found that "people who are exposed to large amounts of news will remember many stories despite lack of interest because mere exposure produces learning." Zukin and Snyder (1984) show that even many politically uninterested New Jersey citizens who received their broadcast news from New York City stations recalled the names of New York's mayoral candidates, even though they could not vote for any of the candidates. Viewers learn from exposure to thirty-second political commercials (Ansolabehere and Iyengar 1995), even though their attention and motivation are presumably low during commercial breaks (see also Krugman 1965). Hence, broadcast viewers are likely to learn about politics even in the absence of strong intrinsic political interest. Even those who would prefer to watch entertainment programs acquire at least basic political knowledge in passing if they happen to turn on their television at a time when only news is on.

The Low-Choice/High-Choice Experiment offers an opportunity to examine Switchers' political knowledge in different media environments. So far, the experiment has identified people who switch from news to entertainment if given a chance. Whether or not Switchers already have that chance – and whether or not they still learn about politics passively – depends on their real-life media environment. The Switchers with access to cable television should already be watching entertainment in real life, and their political knowledge should have suffered. The Switchers who are still waiting for cable, on the other hand, should continue to watch newscasts for lack of better alternatives and learn from them. Switchers' political knowledge should thus depend on whether they have cable access or not. In contrast, political knowledge levels of the other prominent groups, the Always News and the Entertainment Only groups, should not differ by cable access. Respondents in the Always News group have indicated that they would follow the news regardless of the alternatives, while those in the Entertainment Only group are unlikely to watch news even if their options are limited.[11]

Figure 2.2 shows political knowledge scores for these three groups separately for cable subscribers and nonsubscribers. The proportion of cable subscribers in each group is almost identical. In the weighted sample, the percentage of cable subscribers is 81 percent overall and between 81 and 82 percent in each of the three groups. The graph shows the predicted values from an ordinary least squares (OLS) regression of an eight-item index of current events knowledge[12] on cable access and its interactions with viewer type. Cable access is correlated with demographic variables like income and education. Because I am interested in the difference cable access makes for political knowledge, not in the knowledge differences that happen to exist in the first place between the kind of people with and without cable access, the model adjusts for the impact of demographic variables. (The set of control variables is listed in the note to Figure 2.2.)

---

11 People in the Always News group might want to watch more news than is offered on over-the-air channels and therefore learn more about politics with cable access. This effect will become evident in subsequent chapters with more precise measures. Subsequent chapters also examine the effect of Internet access, which should be similar.

12 The items that make up the knowledge index were included in the first wave of the News & Entertainment Survey and are described in the appendix to Chapter 4.

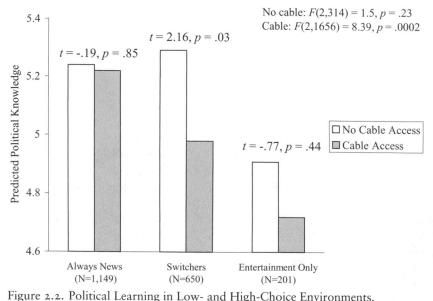

Figure 2.2. Political Learning in Low- and High-Choice Environments.

Note: The graph shows predicted values from an OLS regression of Wave 1 current events knowledge on cable access and its interactions with viewer type. The model also included control variables for income, education, age, gender, race, native English speaker, Internet access, newspaper reading, media market size, and the order in which the Low-Choice/High-Choice Experiment was administered. The F tests in the upper-right corner evaluate whether the addition of viewer types to the model with control variables improves the model fit (separately for cable and no cable).

Source: News & Entertainment Survey.

As expected, political knowledge is high in the Always News group whether or not respondents have cable access. The Entertainment Only group is the least knowledgeable segment. Cable access appears to lower political knowledge for this group, but the difference is not statistically significant. Only for the knowledge levels of Switchers does cable access make a significant difference. Switchers who do not yet have access to cable television resemble the Always News group and are significantly more knowledgeable than Switchers with cable access ($t = 2.16, p = .03$), whose knowledge levels are not distinguishable from the Entertainment Only group. These results confirm that television news exposure informs even less motivated viewers (Neuman, Just, and Crigler 1992). Switchers without cable access – people who would abandon the news as soon as they are offered a few alternatives – are as knowledgeable as the news junkies who stick with the news as choice increases.

The experiment illustrates that content preferences – revealed in this case by respondents' repeated answers to the hypothetical exposure questions – only begin to affect political knowledge when people have a choice.

Adding information about viewer types to the standard knowledge model does not improve the model fit for respondents without cable access ($F[2, 314] = 1.49$, $p = .23$). Among cable subscribers, however, viewer type adds significantly to the explanation of political knowledge ($F[2, 1656] = 8.39$, $p < .001$). In short, the (repeated) Low-Choice/High-Choice Experiment reveals respondents' preferences for news and entertainment content, and these preferences interact with their media environment – cable access, in this case – to influence their political knowledge levels. The first, and rather simplified, test of Conditional Political Learning thus provides empirical support.

If it is in fact the difference in the media environment, not interest or education, that explains this knowledge difference within the Switcher group, then political interest and education among Switchers should not be lower for cable subscribers. And, indeed, Switchers with and without cable access are equally interested in politics ($t = .75$, $p = .46$) and equally well educated ($t = .79$, $p = .47$). The transition from a low-choice to a high-choice media environment rather than individual-level factors explains differences in political knowledge for this segment of the population. In a nutshell, Switchers without cable access represent learning in the old broadcast environment; Switchers with cable access embody learning (or the lack thereof) in the current high-choice environment.

SEVEN HYPOTHESES

Cable television is primarily a conduit for media entertainment. But it would be a serious mistake to dismiss its effects as politically irrelevant for that reason. Entertainment media affect politics literally every minute of the day because they compete for the news viewer's attention. Media choice has begun to reveal its power to affect news exposure and political learning in the Low-Choice/High-Choice Experiment. It may not stop there. If the proliferation of media choices can transport people from a world in which people learn even if they do not care much about politics to a world where only those who care remain informed, it can change politics more widely. Knowledge affects turnout. Turnout affects elections. The repercussions of a major change in the media environment have the potential to reverberate through the political system.

Only the contrast with the high-choice media environment, both in the experiment and in the real world, truly drives home the reach of broadcast news when choice was still low. Reaching two-fifths of all households for thirty minutes on an average weeknight is something that even the most popular entertainment shows can only dream of. (*I Love Lucy* had average season ratings that were higher, but the show aired only once a week and at a time when fewer Americans had television sets. The rating for the last episode of *Seinfeld*, 41.3, barely exceeded the *average* weekday rating that the three network newscasts received year in and year out in the low-choice environment.)

In Figure 2.1, a second important change in the media environment is hidden in plain sight: the transition from the pre-television environment to the low-choice world of broadcast television. Did television in fact create the circumstances that allowed news to reach so widely? Or were so many Americans exposed to news on a routine basis even earlier, just not through television? Especially if the former is true, the advent of broadcast television, too, may have had far-reaching effects on politics. To fully appreciate the political impact of modern media environments, we therefore have to go back to the time before television.

Television as a medium has often been denigrated as "dumb." The words of an entire television newscast, after all, fit easily on one page of a newspaper. And yet, according to my *first hypothesis*, broadcast television increased political knowledge among less cognitively skilled or educated people. This effect may not have been large and certainly did not erase knowledge difference between more and less educated individuals. But it was large enough to narrow this knowledge gap, especially since broadcast television hardly allowed skilled people to learn more about politics than they did before the rise of television. Because learning from print media is more difficult than learning from television, the relationship between the ingredients of ability mentioned by Delli Carpini and Keeter – literacy, information processing skills, and retention, in particular – and political knowledge should be strong in a media environment dominated by print media. The rise of television lowered the importance of ability in acquiring political information. Compared to existing sources for information, television posed decidedly lower demands on people's cognitive skills. Research in psychology and communication indicates that picking up information from television news requires less attention and less cognitive effort than learning from print media (Neuman, Just, and Crigler 1992; Singer 1980). Television news decreases the gap between well- and poorly informed news viewers by presenting political information in a form that can be easily processed even by less educated or less interested people (Eveland and Scheufele 2000; Kwak 1999; Scheufele and Shah 2000). By offering visual information, television provides people with an alternative to verbal processing as a way to learn about politics (Graber 1988; 1990). Broadcast television thus should have made it easier for people with low ability to learn about politics. Moreover, television was very popular, and, for reasons I detail in Chapter 3, many people watched the nightly news.

The days of large network news audiences came to an end as cable television expanded, according to my *second hypothesis*. More efficient choice reduced the audience for regular evening news which had benefited most from the "roadblock" strategy of simultaneously scheduling news on all (or most) broadcast channels. This hypothesis follows from the two-step model of television viewing, and the Low-Choice/High-Choice Experiment presented in this chapter has already provided the first empirical support.

Average political knowledge levels have changed much over the fifty years (e.g., Delli Carpini and Keeter 1996). But that does not mean that all Americans are as knowledgeable as in the past. My *third hypothesis* states that the advent of cable increased the knowledge gap between people with a preference for news and people with a preference for other media content. The low-choice inefficiency of broadcast television was conducive to (passive) learning even among those with little interest in politics and the news. The growth of cable television reduced occurrences of passive learning about politics by making choice more efficient, as illustrated by the Low-Choice/High-Choice Experiment. Yet access to cable television also enables people who like news to watch more of it and increase their political knowledge. As choice increases, individual content preferences should thus become better predictors of exposure to political information and political learning. Even though the Low-Choice/High-Choice Experiment demonstrated the effect of choice in lowering audiences for "roadblocked" news programs, it did not incorporate the crucial element of the high-choice environment from the viewpoint of people who like news – the chance to watch a lot more news than before by taking advantage of twenty-four-hour cable news channels. A segment of the Always News group identified in the experiment is bound to become more knowledgeable in the high-choice environment. In addition to cable news, political information available on the Internet provides a feast for news junkies. The third hypothesis, then, covers the effects of both cable television and the Internet. I test it in Chapter 4, drawing on more refined measure of people's preference for news versus entertainment than the simply binary choice in the Low-Choice/High-Choice Experiment.[13]

The political implications of changes in the media environment go far beyond news exposure and learning. According to my *fourth hypothesis*, broadcast television also narrowed the turnout gap between more

---

13 Just as broadcast television changed little for individuals with a strong political interest, the shift from low-choice broadcast television to the current high-choice media environment probably leaves the conditional effect of ability unchanged. It is not inconceivable that greater choice changes the impact of ability in subtle ways. Cable television and, more likely, political Web sites might fit the learning styles of interested citizens better than print media did. I examine this question briefly in Chapter 4.

and less educated Americans. Shifts in news exposure affect turnout levels. For several reasons, exposure to political information increases the likelihood that an individual will cast a vote on Election Day. Exposure increases political knowledge, which in turn increases turnout (e.g., Delli Carpini and Keeter 1996; Verba, Schlozman, and Brady 1995) because people know when, how, and for whom to vote. Furthermore, knowledgeable people are more likely to perceive differences between candidates and thus less likely to abstain due to indifference (Brady and Ansolabehere 1989; Palfrey and Poole 1987). As Popkin and Dimock (1999, 122) state forcefully, "nonvoting results from a lack of knowledge about what government is doing and where parties and candidates stand, not from a knowledgeable rejection of government or parties." Independent of learning effects, exposure to political information is likely to increase people's political interest (e.g., Bartels and Rahn 2000). Interest, in turn, affects turnout even when one controls for political knowledge (Verba, Schlozman, and Brady 1995). When the peculiar nature of the low-choice broadcast environment increased exposure and political knowledge among less educated Americans, it thus should have affected turnout rates as well. If the availability of broadcast television increased basic political knowledge of less educated citizens, it should thereby have increased their likelihood of voting. I discuss in Chapter 3 that the overall effect on turnout is difficult to predict because we do not know the extent to which television news replaced newspapers as a news source for more educated people. This replacement effect may have been sufficiently large to offset the knowledge gains among less educated people. More importantly, however, it does follow that relative to their more educated counterparts, Americans of lower education should have begun to turn out at higher rates as broadcast television spread across the country. (This does not necessarily imply that absolute turnout rates in either segment increased because other factors may have depressed turnout.)

My *fifth hypothesis* predicts a widening turnout gap in the current environment, as people who prefer news vote at higher rates and those with other preferences increasingly stay home from the polls. Entertainment fans with a cable box or Internet connection increasingly miss both the interest- and the information-based effect of broadcast news on turnout. People who like news, on the other hand, should become more likely to go to the polls because they watch, read, and hear an even higher dose of informative, motivating news.

Relative changes in the turnout rates of different population segments can affect election outcomes. According to my *sixth hypothesis*, broadcast television reduced the impact of partisanship on vote decisions, at least in nonpresidential elections where party labels are not as strongly emphasized. Politically interested and knowledgeable people are more likely to vote in part because they perceive clearer differences between parties and candidates. Knowledge, political interest, and strong partisanship go together, both theoretically and empirically (Neuman 1986; Palfrey and Poole 1987). If broadcast television did indeed increase the proportion of less educated voters, and if these less educated voters were disproportionately politically moderate or indifferent, television should have indirectly increased the proportion of less partisan voters. Broadcast television may thus have decreased the influence of partisan considerations in the average voter's electoral decision making. It may have motivated less educated citizens to go to the polls, but, being less partisan, they cast their votes based not on partisanship but on nonpartisan criteria such as incumbency. These implications of broadcast television for aggregate voting behavior are the subject of Chapter 6.

My *seventh hypothesis* predicts that partisan polarization among voters resurges in the transition to today's high-choice environment. The more interested citizens who take advantage of abundant political information and vote at higher rates are also more partisan. Those who do not care for news and political information – or do not care as much as they care for entertainment – are also more moderate or indifferent. As their turnout rates drop as a result of increased media choice, greater polarization *among voters* should follow, even in the absence of polarization *in the electorate*. I cover this final hypothesis in Chapter 7.

CONCLUSION

At the heart of this chapter was an old puzzle: Why do people acquire political information, even though the benefits from doing so are infinitesimally small? Some people follow politics for the mere fun of it and become knowledgeable that way. But the question remains why some citizens with little interest in politics or sense of civic duty are (or were?) fairly knowledgeable about politics. As a solution to this puzzle, Downs (1957) suggested that some people obtain costless political information as a by-product of their everyday activities. What has been largely neglected is Downs's qualification, made only in passing, that acquiring political information as a by-product depends partly[14] on the structure of the environment. The "inadvertent" members of the news audience in the low-choice broadcast environment – those news viewers who watched

---

14 As mentioned at the beginning of this chapter, Downs, and later Fiorina (1990), distinguish different ways of by-product learning. The media environment is not relevant for by-product learning that occurs "in the course of making production or consumption decisions" (Downs 1957, 223). Popkin's (1991) model of low-information rationality rests mostly on this path of costless political learning.

Table 2.2. *Seven Hypotheses*

Hypothesis	Chapter
News Exposure and Political Knowledge	
1. Broadcast television increased political knowledge among less educated people, narrowing the knowledge gap between more and less educated people.	3
2. Cable television reduced the audience for regular evening news.	4, 5
3. Cable television and the Internet increased the knowledge gap between people with a preference for news and people with a preference for other media content.	4
Turnout	
4. Broadcast television narrowed the turnout gap between more and less educated Americans.	3
5. Cable television and the Internet increased the turnout gap between people with a preference for news and people with a preference for other media content.	4, 5
Aggregate Voting Behavior	
6. Broadcast television increased the proportion of less partisan voters and reduced the impact of partisanship on vote decisions.	6
7. Cable television and the Internet increased political polarization among voters, but not in the electorate as a whole.	7

only because nothing more entertaining was on – were the prototypical by-product learners. As media choice increases, they switch to their true destiny, entertainment, and reduce occurrences of by-product learning. I incorporate this qualification into a more general theory of political learning that takes into account the role of the media environment. Building on the OMA framework of political learning (Delli Carpini and Keeter 1996; Luskin 1990), I propose that the effects of motivation and ability both depend on the media environment.

In the remainder of this book, I use the Conditional Political Learning framework to explain how the rise of broadcast television, the addition of cable channels, and the growth of the Internet have affected politics in the United States. Table 2.2 summarizes the hypotheses I have derived from this theoretical framework. The next five chapters are devoted to testing them. According to these hypotheses, broadcast television narrowed knowledge and turnout gaps in the electorate, while cable and the Internet widened these gaps again. Broadcast television produced political moderation, while cable and the Internet led to resurging partisan polarization among voters. If these hypotheses are supported, the media environment does indeed exert a considerable impact on, in Downs's (1957, 223) words, "the distribution of political power in a democracy."

Part I

The Participatory Effects of Media Choice

3

Broadcast Television, Political Knowledge, and Turnout

The growth of broadcast television is a text book example of a fundamental change in the media environment. Whether measured by the percentage of Americans watching television regularly, by the amount of time spent watching every day, or by the dominance of broadcast television over other media, broadcast television at its prime was the paradigm of a mass medium. More people than ever before and ever again followed the same homogenous programming as a daily routine. In this chapter, I show that this change in the media environment affected how Americans learned about politics, and whether or not they would go to the polls. Broadcast television brought Americans closer together in their political knowledge and their involvement in the electoral process. It did so by striking a bargain with many of those Americans who had previously ignored politics because it seemed too difficult to keep up with: "We will bring moving pictures right into your living room that you will find impossible to resist for many hours each day – but for an hour or two, the irresistible moving pictures will show you news and politics."

To set the stage, this chapter begins with a brief description of the media environment before television. Next, I sketch the growth of television and the maturing of television news. The popularity of the medium and the conventions surrounding the scheduling of news generated large news audiences in this oddly irresistible low-choice environment. This change was of particular importance for the political behavior of less educated Americans. I then present a series of statistical analyses to demonstrate that television increased political knowledge and turnout rates among the less educated. Because the more educated were not noticeably affected, the rise of television reduced inequality in political knowledge and turnout. For a few decades, low choice was a profound political equalizer.

BROADCAST TELEVISION AND THE NEWS

Before Television

Even though newspapers and radio news were widely available, it was reserved to television to bring the news into many new living rooms on a routine basis, especially the living rooms of less educated Americans. Before television, no other medium enjoyed the dominance that broadcast television would come to enjoy in the 1970s. Even though almost 90 percent of American households owned a radio, when surveys first asked about radio ownership in the 1930s, "a rough equality between the mass media remained" (Baughman 1997, 9). Americans read newspapers and magazines, listened to radio news, and watched newsreels when they went to the movies.[1] Between the mid 1930s and the late 1950s, about 80 percent of the adult population read a daily newspaper "regularly," according to a variety of different surveys. Radio gained the advantage after Pearl Harbor and continued to be the primary news source for the remainder of the war (Cantril 1951, 523–4). In response to Gallup polls in 1939, about 60 percent of the respondents said that they listened "regularly" to radio news. This number increased slightly in the following years, up to 74 percent in 1944 (Cantril 1951, 706–7). It is impossible to know what "regularly" meant to respondents, and those numbers – as all self-reports of news exposure – probably exaggerate news consumption considerably.[2]

---

1 Newsreels covered politics on occasion, but shied away from controversy, were "often shallow, trivial, and even fraudulent," and "included so much frivolous material that the audience found it difficult to take [them] very seriously" (Fielding 1972, 4, 230). Entertaining and visually arresting footage was more important than newsworthiness. In the first half of the 1940s, coverage of World War II dominated newsreels. According to one analysis, less than 10 percent of the content of newsreels was news about government or politics (Handel 1950). According to Castleman and Podrazik (1982, 17), newsreels "barely qualified as news. The newsreels were light, upbeat, and oriented toward highly visual events such as far-off natural disasters, the christening of a new ship, or the finals of a beauty pageant. There was ... no in-depth reporting." Fielding (1972, 233) concludes that "at best, the journalistic contribution of the conventional newsreel had always been second rate, both in intent and in performance." The documentary-style *The March of Time* series was an exception in its more serious tone, but it did not cover daily news. Jamieson (1996, 29–34) describes several newsreels about candidates who were widely seen during campaigns, including reels about Truman and Dewey in 1948. Although moviegoers were occasionally exposed to news about politics and public affairs, newsreels probably contained less political information than even the early television newscasts.

2 By comparison, over 80 percent said in Pew polls conducted throughout the late 1980s and 1990s that they watched television news "regularly" – at a time when the network news audience was already in decline.

But they demonstrate that no single medium dominated the media environment as far as news was concerned.

When people were asked directly to name their primary news source, roughly equal numbers selected newspapers and radio before television became widely available (Mayer 1993, 599–600). After a thorough review of public opinion data, Mayer (1993, 594) concludes that "radio never established itself in the public mind as the nation's principal source of news" except for a brief period during World War II. As early as 1958, "TV absorb[ed] considerably more time and attention than radio did in its heyday" (Bogart 1972, 114).

Radio became a mass medium in the 1930s, though not yet a regular and substantial source of news. Judging by the spread of radio stations, 1922 was the year that radio grew up. Within twelve months, the number of radio stations on air increased from 30 to 556. Yet only about 60,000 radio sets were in use at the time – one for every 500 homes. It took until 1927 for a quarter of all households to have radio sets, and until 1937 for three quarters to be reached. Radio penetration in the South lagged considerably behind the rest of the country (Craig 2000, 9–13; Television Digest 1960, 22). In the 1930s, news offerings on radio were relatively scarce, "with most reports consisting of a few headlines supplied by the major newspaper wire services, or leisurely observations by commentators" (Castleman and Podrazik 1982, 17). Less than 10 percent of the networks' prime-time radio programming was news. Daytime news was not common (Lichty and Topping 1975, 429–31). During World War II, radio broadcast a lot more news, typified by Edward R. Murrow's reports from London during the Nazi bombings. In the late 1930s, the radio networks broadcast a total of less than 1,000 hours of news per year. That number increased to 2,400 in 1940 and over 5,000 in 1943 and 1944 (Lichty and Topping 1975, 434).

Local stations did not always rely on network programming for their news. They could either produce their own local news or not program as much news as the networks offered. Beyond evidence for a few individual stations, it is difficult to know exactly how much news was broadcast on radio. An early content analysis of New York's nineteen radio stations in 1927 found only 3 percent of the airtime devoted to "news" – and that category included weather reports and "police alarms." The vast majority of airtime went to music (Lundberg 1975). Early radio news was brief and offered only once a day. One reason for the slow start was radio stations' reliance on wire service for their news, which was fought by newspapers because they depended on the same material and could not offer it as fast as radio (Danna 1975; Lichty and Bohn 1975, 325–6). According to an account of broadcast news in the 1960s, "television networks and stations are considerably more active than their radio counterparts in providing news and other information" (Summers and Summers 1966, 329).

In addition to news programs, radio gave airtime to politicians and government officials directly. During the 1928 presidential campaign, radio stations aired speeches by the candidates and party leaders on a weekly and, in the last weeks before the election, even daily basis. As president, Hoover addressed the radio audience in almost eighty broadcasts. Broadcasting of candidate speeches continued in 1932, which also saw the first five-minute ads. Cabinet members and congressional leaders were also given airtime on occasion. Under Roosevelt, presidential radio addresses continued at a similar frequency. Most presidential speeches and other governmental broadcasts lasted no more than fifteen minutes, and the organizers generally avoided interrupting or preempting popular entertainment programming. In the twelve years of his presidency, FDR also held thirty-one of his now-famous "fireside chats."

Modern mythology occasionally depicts the fireside chats as FDR speaking to the entire nation on a regular basis. For the years before the United States entered the war, that notion is clearly exaggerated. In a 1939 survey, 24 percent of those interviewed said they "usually" listened to these fireside chats, but another 37 percent "never" did (Craig 2000, 147–59, 195). According to ratings collected by C. E. Hooper, an early audience research firm, less than a quarter of the population listened to radio broadcasts by the president during his first two terms in office (Lichty and Topping 1975, 520). These results match findings by Lazarsfeld and Berelson (1968, 120–5) that radio's reach was not particularly broad. Audiences for news and candidate speeches even in the last days of the campaign in 1940 were concentrated among the educated. Even according to typically quite inflated self-reports, about half of all Americans did not listen to any of the major speeches just before Election Day. Campaign exposure through different media was strongly related, indicating that radio and print often duplicated audiences. Citizens with low reading skills apparently did not turn to the radio as an easier alternative to print media in large numbers.

Audience interest in news and presidential speeches increased temporarily during World War II. Hooper ratings for several fireside chats in 1941 and 1942 indicated that more than three-quarters of the population tuned in. As mentioned earlier, more Americans listened to radio news during the war than before. In times of crisis, people tend to turn to the news medium that informs them most quickly about the latest events. Just as television news – and especially twenty-four-hour news channels – saw their audiences increase after the events of 9/11 and during the military confrontation with Iraq in 1991 (Althaus 2002; Prior 2002), large majorities listened to radio news in 1943–5. But these spurts of mass news consumption do not typify the routine in more normal times. With the exception of the last war years, radio was primarily an entertainment medium and its newscasts short and easily avoided. (Radio offered many more channels than television because there were more stations – more than 2,500 in 1947, about a quarter of which were FM stations – and because the radio signal has a wider reach.) Television, too, was an entertainment medium, but television news turned out to be unusually persistent.

Although radio did not dominate to the same extent as television would, it did affect political behavior. Analyzing county-level census data, Strömberg (2004) documents that radio penetration increased turnout in gubernatorial elections between 1920 and 1940. Radio had a bigger impact in close elections. Strömberg offers two possible explanations for the turnout increase, both related to the distribution of information. Either radio covered close elections more intensely and thereby motivated more people to vote, or radio simply broadcast information about the closeness of the election, which gave people a better sense of whether their vote was important.

From Radio to Television: Fast and Slow

Measured by the growth of U.S. households with television sets, television emerged in a single decade, the 1950s. In 1949, only 2.3 percent of all households in America had a television set. [3] By 1955, that percentage had risen to 55. At the end of the decade, 87 percent of all households had sets (Broadcasting Publications 1969). This growth rate makes television the fastest mass medium to be adopted in U.S. history. Even the Internet, though diffusing very quickly in the 1990s, did not spread as fast as broadcast television (see Figure 1.1).

The popularity of television was immense. Bower (1973, 66) concludes from survey data collected in 1960 and 1970 that "there is not much going on at home for most people that can vie with the attractions of the TV set all evening long." Starting in 1959, Roper asked respondents which medium they would like to keep if they could keep only one. As the time series in Figure 3.1 shows, people were more attached to their television than to any other medium in 1959, and the gap widened at the expense of radio and in particular newspapers. Even though the number of people who would keep television if they had to pick one medium continued to grow, the 1950s were special. Asked for their reasons for watching television in 1960, 55 percent of Americans agreed that it was

---

3 This section and the next rely on a variety of historical accounts of early television, including general histories by Sterling and Kittross (1990), Walker and Ferguson (1998), and Castleman and Podrazik (1982).

"Suppose that you could continue to have only one of the following–radio, television, newspapers or magazines–which one of the four would you most want to keep?"

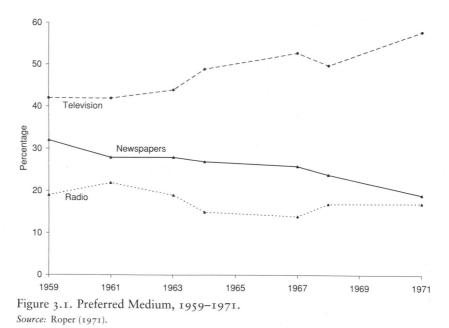

Figure 3.1. Preferred Medium, 1959–1971.
Source: Roper (1971).

"usually . . . a pleasant way to spend an evening" (my emphasis). Ten years later, that number was down to 41 percent, and by 1980 only 35 percent agreed (Bower 1985, 85). The 1950s, it seems, had all the marks of a honeymoon in which the new medium could do no wrong. A few decades later, Americans still did not want to cash it in for something else, but their enthusiasm had cooled.

The record-breaking pace at which Americans bought television sets and embraced the content in the 1950s masks a slower and more gradual transition to the new medium, however (Sterling and Kittross 1990; Walker and Ferguson 1998). The first commercial stations had emerged a decade earlier. As early as 1928, a few radio stations were experimenting with video. That year, a Schenectady station broadcast the first television drama. The number of experimental television stations had grown to 18 by 1937. When Franklin D. Roosevelt opened the World's Fair in New York in 1939, he was the first president to be seen on television – on about 200 sets, the number in use in New York at the time. (The cheapest model was available for $200 – about $2,800 in today's dollars.) The party conventions in 1940 were also televised. In 1941, the Federal Communication Commission (FCC) authorized the start of commercial television.

Stations that had previously operated on an experimental basis turned into commercial television stations. By early 1942, ten commercial stations were on air in New York, Philadelphia, Chicago, Schenectady, and Los Angeles. That did not mean, however, that most people even in those cities were watching television every night. Not only were the stations on air for only fifteen hours a week, following FCC regulation, but few people had television sets. Few sets were for sale – as few as ninety sets were sold per month in New York, the hottest market in the country by far, early in 1942 – and prices remained very high. In 1945, less than 1 percent of all U.S. families owned a television set. Only 22 percent of the population claimed that they had ever seen one in operation, and 11 percent did not even know what television was, according to a Gallup survey (Mayer 1993, 600–1).

Two events slowed the growth of television further. During World War II, several stations shut down, and no new stations were allowed to be built. Each network broadcast only one evening per week during the last war years. Because electronic parts were needed for military use, no new television sets were produced. After the war, production resumed slowly. In 1946, only 6,500 sets were manufactured. In 1948, only 102,000 television sets were in use – two-thirds of which were in New York (Bogart 1972, 8–9). In 1949, when only 2.3 percent of all households had a TV set, 52 percent said they had seen "a program of any kind on a television set," but only 10 percent had seen it in their own home (Mayer 1993, 600–1).

The second holdup was the TV freeze of 1948 which stopped the licensing of new stations until 1952. During the early period of television, the UHF (ultra high frequency) spectrum was not yet used for television (except for experimental television), and there was no national plan governing the assignment of frequencies. In 1948, the FCC, concluding that nationwide television was impossible on this basis, stopped licensing new television stations in order to draft a comprehensive policy of television growth first. When the freeze was announced in September 1948, 37 television stations in 22 cities were broadcasting to a total of about one million TV sets. Anticipated to last six months, the freeze remained in effect until April 1952. The FCC decided to use the UHF spectrum in addition to the VHF (very high frequency) spectrum for commercial television. The nationwide expansion of television was coordinated by a plan of initially more than 2,000 frequency assignments. (These were commercial and noncommercial stations, not all of which eventually started operation.)

The freeze did not halt the growth of television completely. Several dozen stations, whose applications had been approved before 1948, began operation after the freeze had started. That is why the number of operating stations increased from 50 in January 1948 to 107 in January 1951. Americans also continued to buy TV sets. Between the beginning and the end of the freeze, the number of sets in use increased from fewer than 1 million in 1949 to 20 million in early 1953.

Hence, even though the history of television starts long before the 1950s, most Americans discovered the new medium in that decade. But the evolution of television did not slow down at the end of the 1950s, after most Americans had acquired their first TV set. In the 1960s, almost every American household had a television, but what people could see when they turned it on continued to change. For a start, some people could not see very much at all. The new UHF stations were inferior to the established VHF stations because receivers were not optimally equipped for UHF and the signals did not cover areas as large as VHF signals did (Owen and Wildman 1992). VHF stations reliably covered sixty-five to seventy miles, whereas UHF had a reach of only thirty to forty miles. These inequalities persisted even when the FCC allowed UHF stations to use more powerful antennas. The higher frequency UHF is also more vulnerable to interference. Moreover, all TV sets produced before 1952 and more than 80 percent of those manufactured between 1952 and 1963 could not receive UHF channels. In 1960, only 8 percent of all households had sets that were equipped for UHF reception. After the FCC mandated UHF capabilities for sets made after 1964, that percentage rose to 52 percent in 1970 (Bower 1973, 4).

Television News

What people could see on their sets changed considerably as well in the 1960s. Of greatest political relevance, the newshole expanded and the quality of news programming improved, creating a noticeably different product than the early "radio with pictures." Most stations offered local and network news during the dinner hour as well as after prime time (at 10 or 11 o'clock at night) in the 1950s and 1960s.

Regularly scheduled, daily fifteen-minute network newscasts premiered on NBC and CBS in the first network season in 1948.[4] Before that time, news on television consisted of rebroadcast of newsreels purchased from the theatrical newsreel companies or the wire services. CBS's *Douglas Edwards with the News* premiered on May 3, 1948. It aired at 7:30 P.M. until September 1955, when it moved to 6:45 P.M. NBC's *Camel News Caravan* started in February 1949, but it had been in existence for a year as

---

4 For information about specific programs, see McNeil (1984); for scheduling, see Castleman and Podrazik (1984).

The Camel Newsreel Theatre, a ten-minute collection of newsreels. NBC's time slot for network news was 7:45 P.M. until the fall of 1957, when it moved to 6:45 P.M. ABC, the youngest and weakest of the three networks, took longer to find a stable news format. A fifteen-minute *News and Views* aired in 1948–9, but because ABC had fewer affiliates than NBC and CBS and few of its existing affiliates decided to carry the program, it disappeared after one season. Its eventual successor, *John Daly and the News*, began in 1953 as a fifteen-minute newscast at 7:15 P.M. In the following years, the program was repeatedly moved to earlier time slots – 6.45 P.M. in 1959, 6 P.M. a year later, and 5:30 P.M. in 1965.

In 1963, the network evening news on CBS and NBC expanded to thirty minutes. A special interview with President Kennedy was broadcast on the first half-hour long *CBS Evening News* on September 2, 1963. NBC's *Huntley-Brinkley Report* grew to half an hour the following week, also with a JFK exclusive on its first airing. Barely ten weeks later, the president was dead, but television news was more alive than ever. Opening domestic bureaus outside New York, Los Angeles, and Chicago and taking advantage of technological advances, "network news had done more than double in length; its quality had improved tremendously in the process" (Castleman and Podrazik 1982, 164). For the next two decades, both programs were broadcast by the networks at 6:30 P.M. *ABC Evening News* expanded to thirty minutes only in 1967 and aired at 6 P.M.

The networks offered national news and political coverage at other times than the early evening. NBC's *Today Show* premiered in 1952, offering a two-hour mix of news and interviews from 7 to 9 in the morning. The other networks struggled initially to come up with an equally attractive alternative, but in 1969 CBS increased its *Morning News* to a full hour (and later to two hours), and in 1975 ABC started *Good Morning America*. In 1982, all networks began offering news in the 6 A.M. slot. Network television's oldest continuing program, NBC's *Meet the Press*, aired first on television in 1947 and had a regular Sunday evening slot for several decades. *Face the Nation*, its CBS counterpart, premiered in 1954. In the 1960s, networks also offered five-minute news summaries during the day. Each network scheduled up to four of the summaries between the end of the morning news shows and the early evening news. These five-minute news formats became less common in the 1970s and the last one aired on CBS in May 1980. Documentary and magazine shows such as the early *See it Now*, *60 Minutes*, and, starting in 1980, ABC's *Nightline* offered hard news on network television. During election campaigns, specials and program time bought by the candidates added substantial airtime for politics. In each of the three presidential campaigns in the 1960s, special news programming and candidate-initiated communication added up to about fifty to sixty hours of network programming in the two months preceding the election (Lichty, Ripley, and Summers 1965; Topping and Lichty 1971).

The first time that CBS and NBC offered their evening newscasts in the same time slot was in 1957. ABC's evening news joined them only briefly in 1959, before moving to an earlier time. Nonetheless, the early evening was effectively "roadblocked" with news for most viewers. Before the mid-1950s, many markets had only one or two network affiliates, and most independents broadcast on UHF frequencies, which few viewers could receive. The ABC network did not have affiliates in many markets yet, and its affiliates broadcast on UHF in others.

Local affiliates were not required to carry the network broadcast live. In fact, they were not required to carry it at all. The reach of ABC's *Evening News* lagged behind the other two networks. In 1965, CBS's and NBC's newscasts were carried on 192 and 187 affiliates, respectively, but ABC *Evening News* only on 106 (Nielsen 1975, 422). It took ABC until 1972 to convince all its affiliates to carry the *Evening News*. The ABC affiliates in Flint, Michigan, and Birmingham, Alabama, were the last to be converted. After recording technology became available in the late 1950s, many network affiliates decided not to broadcast the evening newscast live, especially in the Western time zones. The first network newscast to be rebroadcast there was CBS's *Douglas Edwards with the News* in 1956.

Local authority over scheduling makes it difficult to estimate how many Americans were regularly presented with the exciting choice between *ABC Evening News*, *CBS Evening News*, and *NBC Nightly News*. In the 1971–2 season, for example, CBS and NBC affiliates aired their national newscasts at the same time in three-quarters of the hundred biggest media markets (Nielsen Media Research 1972). All three national newscasts aired simultaneously in far fewer markets, partly because some ABC affiliates did not carry the newscasts at all. More importantly, however, even if network newscasts were not scheduled simultaneously, most local stations offered either national or local news at least between 6 and 7 P.M., and even earlier in many markets. In the 1960s, when ABC increased its number of affiliates and UHF stations began to be received by more television sets, it was uncommon to counterprogram national newscasts with entertainment (Sharbutt 1987).

Despite the increasing importance of the networks, local newscasts too expanded in the 1950s and 1960s (Mickelson 1989, 160; Sterling and Kittross 1990). The locals had increased their time on air from the meager fifteen hours a week in the 1940s to mornings and afternoons in addition to the earlier evening programs, so the demand for content grew parallel to the networks' technological capabilities. Before the first network season in 1948, most of the local stations were affiliated with one of the networks but produced their programs locally. To carry network news, a station had to be connected to the network, which reached the West Coast only in 1952. Until then, only 45 percent of all television homes had been hooked up to the network. The rest could not yet watch live network television. Once linked to the network, local stations usually carried at least a thirty-minute local newscast prior to the network news and a recap after the network slot at 11 P.M. When network news expanded to thirty minutes in 1963, local news coverage also grew to up to two hours in the early evening plus noon and late evening news programs.

The overall amount of news varied from market to market. Dallas Smythe conducted studies in several markets in the early 1950s, assessing the overall airtime devoted to different genres over the course of a week (Kingson 1952; Smythe 1953a; 1953b; Smythe and Campbell 1951). In January 1951, 1952, and 1953, the New York market offered between 30 and 35 hours of news per week on its seven stations, which represented about 6 percent of all broadcast hours in that period. (Political features, coverage of public events, and discussion of public issues added another 2 to 3 percent.) In one week in May 1951, the eight stations in the Los Angeles market (including one from San Diego) aired a total of 17 hours of news plus another 13 hours of public affairs discussion and feature programming. New Haven's only station, WNHC, broadcast almost 5 hours of news in a week in May 1952, slightly less than the average station in New York. It devoted another ninety minutes to political discussion and features.

Smythe's team counted commercials as well. In the early days of television, advertising took up less airtime than today. Almost 90 percent of the news hours were devoted to programming, compared to less than two-thirds today (Project for Excellence in Journalism 2004). In a (small) random sample of markets with independent stations, network affiliates broadcast about two hours of local news per day in 1971. Independent VHF stations still offered almost an hour and a half, whereas independent UHF stations only provided half an hour of local news (Nestvold 1973). According to Nestvold, it was the "industry consensus" at the time that only network affiliates and independent VHF stations offered a considerable amount of news. The now-defunct Television Information Office conducted annual surveys of network affiliates to tabulate the amount of local news offered. In the mid-1980s, the average network affiliate offered forty-five minutes of local news in the early evening. About 40 percent of all affiliates had early evening local newscasts of one hour or longer. More than half of these long local newscasts were split to both precede and follow the network news (PR Newswire 1987a; 1987b).

One reason for the relative prominence of television news was that the networks saw it as their responsibility to inform the public and as a matter of prestige to do so better than their competitors. Another reason was a set of FCC licensing rules and conventions. The Prime Time Access Rule required local stations to broadcast nonnetwork programs during one hour between 7 and 11 P.M. Local stations could broadcast local news and documentaries (but also network news or children's programming) to fulfill the local programming requirement. Even though the FCC did not issue precise guidelines for the required programming share devoted to news and public affairs, its 1946 "Blue Book" (Federal Communications Commission 1946) stated that "the Commission, in determining whether a station has served the public interest, will take into consideration the amount of time which has been or will be devoted to the discussion of public issues" (cited in Simmons 1978, 40). In subsequent rulings, the FCC continued to emphasize this part of the Fairness Doctrine, but failed to provide precise definitions of the amount of public affairs programming that would be considered appropriate (Neuman 1991, 133). Informally, broadcasters could anticipate a "5-5-10 rule," according to which "5 percent of programming should be for local affairs, 5 percent for news and public affairs, and 10 percent for nonentertainment programs" (Graber 1980, 42). Despite violations of these (informal) rules, no broadcast license was revoked or not renewed in this period for failure to broadcast enough public affairs content. Based on an interview with an FCC attorney, Baum (2003b, 300) reports that broadcasters were checked more carefully at license renewal if they had not met the minimum requirement for news and public affairs.

Although FCC regulations were imprecise and confusing, FCC content data shows that many stations devoted more than the required airtime to local news and public affairs. In a survey of local stations published by the FCC in 1973, the median of the fifty VHF stations with the highest revenues devoted 15.5 percent to news and public affairs. (The median for the next fifty VHF stations was 13.9 percent.) Annual Programming Reports filed with the FCC in the mid-seventies revealed similar numbers (Simmons 1978, 247, fn. 207). Summarizing the impact of technology, regulation, and common practice, Allen (2001, 14) concludes that "every city graced with a new TV station also had a new source of local news." Two conditions for learning from television were thus met by the 1960s, if not earlier: Television offered several hours of news programming every day, and almost all Americans could watch television in their homes. But did they watch *the news*?

Television's Dominance and the Limits of Choice

Television changed people's lives dramatically. Even in the early days of the medium, Nielsen estimated that the television was on for four or five hours in the average television household. How did people make time for an extra four or five hours of their new favorite pastime? Newspapers, magazines, radio, and newsreels continued to be available. Nothing barred people from going to the movies or listening to the radio. And to some extent, people simply added television use to their existing media routine. Studies conducted in the early 1950s found increased overall media use in homes with television access (Bogart 1972, 66).

More importantly, however, television replaced a considerable amount of radio listening and movie going. Radio use declined in the 1950s. According to Nielsen estimates, the duration of daily radio use dropped from about four hours in the 1930s and 1940s to barely over two hours by the mid-1950s. The average evening radio program reached about 4.8 million homes in 1948, but only 2 million seven years later. In the early 1950s, radios were on for about two hours more per day in homes without television sets than in television homes (Bogart 1972, 115, 117). This gap remained almost constant as television penetration increased from around one-quarter to more than 70 percent, clearly pointing to a sizable replacement of radio by television use. Radio did not disappear completely. During the day, people continued to listen to the radio. Radio suffered most in prime time, both because television viewing was the quintessential after-work activity and because television's most popular shows were on in prime time (Bogart 1972, 77; Gould 1951a).

Movie attendance fell dramatically just as television penetration grew. Between 1946 and 1960, the average weekly audience for motion pictures dropped in half from 82 million to 41 million. By 1970, it had fallen to 19 million (Bogart 1972, 163, 412; see also Gould 1951b). Audiences declined even in areas without television, so only part of the decline can be attributed to simple time displacement by the new medium.

Replacement of newspaper reading by television kicked in more slowly. Eventually, newspaper circulation and self-reported use declined, but the evidence for an early replacement effect is not clear. Comparisons of households with and without television revealed little change in self-reported newspaper reading in the early 1950s, but these data are difficult to interpret because the first households to own television sets were also the most likely to read newspapers (Bogart 1972, 152–6). Although newspaper circulation fell between 1946 and 1952 in large cities, all of which had television stations, circulation grew by about the same percentage in smaller cities with and without stations (Bogart 1972, 161). Bogart (1972, 156) described television as "an important supplement to newspaper accounts" for more educated Americans in the mid-1950s, "visualizing and dramatizing the events and personalities of the day." In 1970, Bower (1973, 68) surveyed a sample of Minneapolis-St. Paul residents who were keeping a viewing diary for the American Research Bureau (a television ratings service at the time). How much television respondents watched was unrelated to whether or not they reported reading a newspaper every day. Gentzkow (2006), on the other hand, has shown that in the 1940s and 1950s newspaper circulation declined more in states that already had television access, suggesting replacement. Whether caused by television or not, the decline in newspaper reading, evident in circulation data, is picked up by a question asked repeatedly by the General Social Survey (and, in 1967, NORC). The first time it was asked, in 1967, 74 percent of the respondents said they read the newspaper "every day" (Mayer 1993, 605). The percentage of daily readers dropped below 60 in 1978, below 50 in 1993, and below 40 in 2000.

The dominance of television and the availability of several hours of news programming alone do not imply any necessary changes for news exposure. But add to that the low number of broadcast channels in any given television household and the simultaneous scheduling of news programs on most or even all of those channels, and you have a captive audience for news. Ironically, the most popular mass medium ever offered the lowest degree of content choice of any mass medium. The average number of stations per market in the top 100 media markets was 3 in 1965 and 3.5 in 1975 (Parkman 1982). More people lived in larger markets, which had more stations earlier. Since viewers, especially in small markets, received signals from neighboring markets, the average viewer could choose between more than three stations even in the mid-1950s, when about 70 percent of television homes received four or more stations. In 1971, Nielsen estimated that proportion to be 90 percent. The average household received 6.8 stations (Bogart 1972, 12, 356).

But 6.8 stations did not equal 6.8 different programming options at a time. Stations with the same network affiliation mostly duplicated programming options (except, importantly, for local news). Reception of channels from other markets was weaker. Some of those 6.8 stations per market were UHF stations, yet they represented an actual viewing alternative to few people because of their reduced reach and greater interference problems. According to Nielsen estimates for 1971, 43 percent of the stations in the twenty largest media markets were UHF stations, but they achieved only a 6 percent audience share in prime time (Bogart 1972, 477). In 1970, Minneapolis-St. Paul had two UHF stations. According to one survey, only 25 percent of local residents could receive one of those stations, and only half of those would get a "good picture." Even worse, "no one in the sample could receive the second UHF station" (Bower 1973, 130).

Scheduling practices reduced choice between different genres even further, leading to virtual absence of choice for several hours each day. Certain time slots were devoted to only one type of programming on all channels, either because the slots were reserved for public affairs or children's programming by FCC regulation or because all networks maximized prime-time audiences by offering entertainment programs. Horizontal diversity – the number of program types available at a given time – was generally low on the networks (e.g., Signorielli 1986; Steiner 1952): "If all television programmers are compelled to cater to the same mass audience, it is impossible, or at least imprudent, for one channel to offer content of a type that is systematically different from the channels with which it competes. In the U.S. context, this has meant that there is no significant difference in what a viewer can see on ABC, CBS, or NBC" (Webster 1986, 79). Entertainment competition for news in the early evening was similarly limited. Even for independents with tough network competition, offering cheaply produced newscasts had financial advantages because stations saved the fees for showing syndicated content and did not have to share advertising revenues. Some of the independent stations were educational stations, which did not offer entertainment programming.

Low choice had little effect on the overall amount of viewing. To overstate the point only slightly, moving images in the living rooms were so exciting that any program was worth watching. Watching television was "essentially a pastime activity indulged in for its own sake rather than for its content" (Bogart 1972, xvii). The Hooper ratings service used the "coincidental method," calling large samples of Americans to ask what program, if any, they were watching when the phone rang. The results illustrate the irrelevance of choice in television viewing. Regardless of how many channels were available in respondents' communities, the same percentage of them had their television on when Hooper called. An American Research Bureau (ARB) study conducted in 1955 and Nielsen data in 1968 document the same lack of a relationship between choice and the amount of viewing (Bogart 1972, 85–6, 379). On an average evening in 1968, the television was on in 60 percent of all television homes – regardless of the number of channels received. People were not picky with regard to content; receiving only one or two channels did not keep them from watching as much television as those with three or more channels. The 1955 ARB study found that Americans in areas with only one or two channels were no more likely than those with more channels to listen to the radio instead of watching the program that their channel served them. Most people liked watching television too much to turn it off, but they had too little choice to always or even often select programming they really liked.

The Captive News Audience

In the absence of choice, there was little room for content preferences to have any impact on media exposure. When news blanketed their television screens in the early evening or after prime time, Americans were reluctant to stop watching. Even if another channel might offer more entertaining fare, people did not get up right away to change the channel. Writing in the mid-1950s, Bogart (1972, 82) explains the reluctance to switch channels: "A substantial part of the TV audience stays with the same station, partly out of deliberate choice..., partly because it may be the clearest image that they are watching, but also partly because it represents the path of least resistance and effort." Without a remote control, switching channels took effort. As a result, people watched news, even when the news covered serious politics:

The very passivity of most people's viewing may help to make television an important source of political information. When the local and national newscasts mix some political stories in with the others, as they usually do, the passive and not-very-political viewers in the inadvertent audience do not bother to switch channels. It is less effort to leave the set alone, knowing that in a minute or two the political stuff will be followed by other, more interesting stories. So the viewers absorb some political information even when they do not seek it. (Ranney 1983, 12–13)

Global medium preference (preferring watching television to not watching) trumped particular content preference (preferring entertainment to news). In a survey conducted in 1950, only 11.5 percent of respondents who owned a television set reported that they did not watch news (Mayer 1993, 602). It is not surprising, then, that television became the primary news source for more and more people. Figure 3.2 shows the percentage of people who "usually get most of [their] news about what's going on in the world today" from newspapers and television. It takes until 1963 for the two lines to cross, indicating that television became the average American's primary news source in the mid-sixties. Respondents could offer multiple answers to the question. Figure 3.2 also plots the percentage of respondents who mentioned television as their only source of news. It is another sign of television's growing dominance that this percentage roughly doubled between the early 1960s and the mid-1970s.

In 1960, most Americans (59 percent) still believed that newspapers gave them "the most complete news coverage," and few (only 19 percent) thought that television fit that description. Ten years later, about 40 percent mentioned each medium in response to the same question. By 1980, the balance had further shifted to television. Half of all Americans now deemed news coverage on television "most complete," compared to only 33 percent for newspaper coverage (Bower 1985, 17; see also

Broadcast TV, Political Knowledge, and Turnout

"I'd like to ask you where you usually get most of your news about what's going on in the world--from the newspapers or radio or television or magazines or talking to people or where?" (multiple responses allowed)

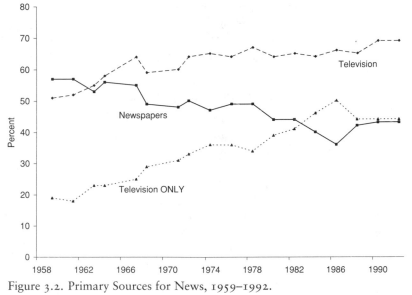

Figure 3.2. Primary Sources for News, 1959–1992.
Source: Mayer (1993, 603–4).

Converse 1962, 592). These are clearly not accurate descriptions of the news coverage provided by both media. They reflect people's attitudes about their options and illustrate vividly how Americans came around to relying on television for their news.

The positive attitudes toward news on television were matched by the size of the news audience. Many of those who said that television offered the most complete news coverage and that they got most of their news from that medium were probably not in fact very keen on following the news regularly. But be it for lack of alternatives or genuine interest, many Americans watched the news in the broadcast era. The average audience for the three network newscasts put together was fairly stable throughout the 1960s and 1970s. About 35 to 38 percent of all households with televisions were watching the news on an average weekday evening in those years. The market share for network news was around 75 percent in this period, indicating that three out of four households with their sets on at the time were watching the network news.

Local news was at least as widely watched as network news. The average rating for early evening local newscasts in the top 100 Nielsen markets was 40 in 1965 and 43 in 1975. In the late evening – at 11 o'clock in most markets in the Eastern and Pacific time zones, and at 10 o'clock in other markets – between 39 (1965) and 35 (1975) percent of all households watched the news (calculated from Parkman 1982). By comparison, the combined ratings for the three evening network newscasts were 35 in 1965 and 36 in 1975. Ratings data reported by Epstein (1973, 87) for 1969, Adams (1977, 83) for 1976, and Hess (1991, 37) for 1986–7 also show larger audiences for local than network news.

Who Benefits from Television News?

Television as a – perhaps inadvertent – new source of news was particularly important for less educated segments of the population. Even before television, the educated found plenty of news in newspapers and magazines. Radio audiences for political events, too, had an upper-class bias (though probably less so during the last war years, when most Americans listened to the news). Lazarsfeld (1940, 25–8), for example, found that listeners of high socioeconomic status were considerably more likely to tune into several radio addresses in 1937 and 1938 by President Roosevelt and Supreme Court nominee Hugo Black. Television differed very clearly from previous media in that it attracted an audience that was, if anything, less educated than the population as a whole. Even though many of the less educated may have been mostly interested in the entertainment content, this educational homogeneity extended to television news. Survey data paints less educated viewers as even less discriminating in their program choices than the more educated. To the extent that it happened at all, the educated were more likely to watch selectively (Bower 1973, 56–9). Even though less educated people tend to be decidedly less interested in politics, they were at least as likely to watch television news as the more educated. While Nielsen data for 1966 showed no difference by education in the proportion of viewers watching informational programs (Bogart 1972, 383), several other studies found that less educated viewers watched more news programs than more educated viewers (Adams 1977; Bower 1973, 132; Robinson 1976; Steiner 1963).

For people who had difficulties reading newspapers or magazines in particular, news on television represented a new opportunity to learn about politics that required less attention and cognitive effort than print media (Eveland and Scheufele 2000; Kwak 1999; Neuman, Just, and Crigler 1992; Singer 1980) and, unlike radio, offered visuals which can improve learning (Graber 1988; 1990). There is no doubt that newspapers offered more political information of almost any kind than television news, be it local or national. People can learn a lot more about politics from newspapers than from television news – *but only if they read the articles*. Those who do not buy or borrow a paper do not learn. The functionally illiterate, who "eschew any serious reading that is not imperative" and whose share "is often estimated to be as high as 60 per cent" (Converse 1962, 592), learn little. Subscribers or occasional readers who skip directly to the sports pages or the cartoons and never look back to the front section of the newspaper do not learn anything about politics. For many people, television news was a more easily understandable and therefore perhaps more attractive source of news. As members of the captive audience, the sports fans, the functionally illiterate, and the committed nonreaders would now learn about politics. Not a lot perhaps, but more than before.[5]

In a national survey conducted in 1960 (Steiner 1963), almost 50 percent of the respondents who only attended grade school picked television as the medium that gives them "the clearest understanding of the candidates and issues in national elections," while less than 15 percent of the college-educated did so. Thirty-five percent of the least educated respondents said that television was the medium that "presents things most intelligently," while less than 5 percent of the most educated said so. Twenty years later, when another representative sample of Americans was asked the same questions, everyone had even more favorable attitudes about television, compared to other media, but the least educated remained the most enthusiastic. The share that selected television was 81 percent for the "clearest understanding" and 71 for intelligent presentation among those with no more than a grade school education (only around 10 percent at this point). Among the college-educated, 46 percent agreed with the first statement, 31 percent with the second statement (Bower 1985, 53). These findings suggest that television led to a wider dissemination of basic political information especially among citizens not sufficiently interested or able to read about politics in newspapers or magazines.

The effect of television on political knowledge among more educated people is difficult to predict. Evidence reviewed earlier in the chapter pointed to a replacement of radio and newspaper use by the rising amount of television viewing. As radio and, in particular, print users were disproportionately educated, the availability of television may have led to the substitution of newspaper and radio use in that demographic. Although

---

5 Some have argued that network news, although easier than print news, was still too hard to follow for many Americans (Barber 1979; Graber 2001, 112). Knowledge levels in the inadvertent news audience could have been even higher, if network news had used more accessible language and tried harder to make audio and video correspond, an element of news stories that increases comprehension (e.g., Brosius 1989; Grimes 1991; Lang 1995).

television news was easier to understand, it did not provide the same depth and detail as newspaper coverage of politics, so the replacement may have lowered knowledge levels among more educated people who used to read the paper to get their news. Whether or not knowledge declined among the more educated as a result, the predicted effect of television on the overall distribution of knowledge is unambiguous. Many less educated began to encounter news on a routine basis, and the more educated, if anything, learned less. Hence, education should have made less of a difference for learning about politics as television spread across the country.

THE IMPACT OF TELEVISION ACCESS ON LEARNING ABOUT POLITICS

To test directly if television's peculiar combination of high popularity, easy news, and low content choice reduced the gap in political knowledge between more and less educated segments of the electorate, I draw on data from the National Election Studies. Beginning in 1952, the NES has asked random samples of voting-age Americans about their political opinions and voting behavior before and after each presidential election (as well as after all midterm congressional elections except for 1954). In most years, the survey included several factual knowledge questions about politics. I use these questions to create a measure of the respondent's political knowledge. Each year contains a different set of questions, and the selection of these questions is by necessity quite arbitrary. I include the studies conducted between 1952 and 1968. Respondents in 1956 were asked only one knowledge question, and the 1962 survey did not contain any knowledge questions, but in other years in the period, I can draw on at least five (in 1952) and often more than twice as many questions. The appendix to this chapter provides detailed information on all items. For each year, I sum up the number of correct answers and transform the resulting index to the 0–100 interval. This index is very similar to Zaller's (1992) measure of awareness, although I do not use the interviewer ratings of political knowledge that the NES introduced in 1966.

To examine whether television affected people's political knowledge, I create a measure of television access by combining NES data with data from the *Television Factbook* on the television stations in operation and their coverage areas at the time of the survey. The NES data sets contain information on each respondent's county (or city) of residence, and *Factbooks* after 1960 list the stations operating in each county. This coverage information is based on periodic studies conducted by the American Research Bureau (which later became Arbitron) that asked residents across the country which television stations they were watching. For each NES respondent, I use the *Factbooks* to determine how many and what type of television stations operated in his or her county of residence. I only count stations that reach at least 50 percent of the county, according to the ARB coverage studies.[6]

Following the theoretical expectation that the impact of local television should be larger among less educated people, I initially divide the sample into respondents who did not finish high school and those who did. For the period between 1952 and 1968, this splits the sample almost exactly in half. Knowledge gains for less educated citizens should differ depending on which types of stations deliver their broadcast signals. Even though I included only counties with at least 50 percent coverage, VHF stations should still provide a clearer picture. Network affiliation was the best way to guarantee professional programming and, important for my purposes, regular national newscasts. The following estimates therefore distinguish network affiliates broadcasting on VHF frequencies, independent VHF stations, and UHF network affiliates. (The data set did not include any independent stations on UHF frequencies that reached more than 50 percent of a county in which NES respondents resided.)

I begin by examining how the local television stations affected political knowledge without making any assumptions about the cumulative effect in markets with more than one station. On the one hand, the first television station in a particular area may have a particularly strong effect on learning about politics because it brings the new source of news and entertainment into people's living rooms. Most people may wish that entertainment programming were available around the clock, but they tolerate a newscast once or twice during the day. If the second station in the area shows the same amount of news at the same time, it should not have any additional effect on people's political knowledge. Viewers can now select

---

6 The ARB distinguished three types of counties: counties where a station reached more than 50 percent of all households, counties in which 25 to 50 percent of the households received the station, and counties in which 5 to 24 percent of households did so. In my analysis, I consider only the effect of TV stations that cover more than 50 percent of a county based on the assumption that stations with lower coverage are less likely to affect a respondent. I verified the validity of this assumption by running the analysis with stations of all coverage levels, but found no significant effects for stations that did not reach 50 percent of a county.

Prior to the 1960 ARB coverage study, the *Factbooks* did not contain coverage information. For stations in operation in 1952, 1956, and 1958, I therefore have to rely on 1960 coverage data. Only a handful of stations changed the height of their antenna or the power of their signal between 1952 and 1960 (which would make the 1960 coverage data for marginal counties inapplicable to earlier years), so this extrapolation poses few problems. In the few cases where a station's reach changed and a county with NES respondents was likely to be affected by this change, I adjusted the coverage data based on the difference in antenna height.

between two different newscasts, but they can still not select entertainment programming during the news hour. In the initially unlikely case that the second station offered appealing entertainment content in the same time slot that the first station reserved for news, the marginal effect of the second station on news exposure and political knowledge could even be negative. For network affiliates with their coordinated focus on news in several day parts this was unusual, but it might describe the scheduling practice of some independent stations.

There are reasons, on the other hand, why adding the second or third station in a market might still increase learning. The stations in a market did not all have the same reach. The most obvious distinction is between UHF and higher-reach VHF stations, but even for stations that use the same band, reach still depends on the geographical location, the strength of the signal, and the height of their antenna. Hence, the marginal effect of the second station should be positive because for some viewers in the media market the second station is in fact the first station they can receive (or receive with little noise).

The analysis in Table 3.1 does not impose any functional form on the effect of television stations but simply estimates the effect of the first, second, and third station separately. Statistically, this is not the most efficient approach, but it offers a clear view of the cumulative effects of television stations. The dependent variable in the OLS regression models in Table 3.1 is the knowledge index. The models include a number of control variables to ensure that I do not incorrectly attribute knowledge differences to television, when they in fact arise as a result of another factor that is correlated with the number of local stations in the respondent's county. Political knowledge may have increased disproportionately in cities because they have more media outlets and campaigns can most effectively target areas of high population density. Previous studies have shown that minorities tend to be less knowledgeable about politics. If they are also more likely to live in areas with many television stations, this could confound the estimation. Other control variables include gender, age, and whether or not the respondent lived in the South, which did not have the same level of political competition in the period studied here. All models also include year effects (which are not shown in the tables) to adjust for differences between presidential election years and off-years and, most importantly, to remove the year-to-year differences that emerge simply because each year uses a different set of knowledge questions.

The results in the first column of Table 3.1 reveal a positive effect of television on political knowledge among less educated respondents. With one exception, the television variables are positive and, despite the inefficient dummy estimation, many approach statistical significance. But the main purpose of this analysis is to compare the effects of different types

Broadcast TV, Political Knowledge, and Turnout

Table 3.1. *Television and Political Knowledge, by Education*

	Low Education (No High School Diploma)		High Education (High School Diploma)	
VHF Network Affiliates				
1 (11%)	2.81 (2.07)		2.94 (2.30)	
2 (17%)	2.93 (2.07)		3.45 (2.21)	
3 (56%)	8.00** (2.00)		4.23* (2.09)	
4 + (8%)	2.51 (2.53)		3.90 (2.44)	
VHF Independents				
1 (14%)	4.15** (1.44)		−0.44 (1.20)	
2 + (13%)	−1.33 (1.58)		−3.14** (1.31)	
UHF Network Affiliates				
1 (4%)	2.04 (2.33)		0.69 (2.00)	
2 (2%)	5.78 (3.51)		−1.84 (3.16)	
3 + (2%)	7.79* (3.51)		2.93 (3.37)	
Number of VHF Stations (logged)		3.00** (.73)		0.10 (.73)
Number of UHF Stations (logged)		2.72* (1.19)		−0.33 (1.09)
Gender	−14.8** (.9)	−14.9** (.9)	−7.6** (.8)	−7.6** (.8)
Race	−13.8** (1.3)	−13.7** (1.3)	−10.8** (1.8)	−10.9** (1.8)
Age	0.034 (.027)	0.034 (.027)	0.17** (.03)	0.17** (.03)
Suburban area	−4.3** (1.2)	−4.8** (1.2)	1.1 (1.0)	1.2 (1.0)
Rural area	−5.3** (1.2)	−5.7** (1.2)	−0.3 (1.1)	0.1 (1.1)
South	−1.5 (1.1)	−1.4 (1.1)	0.7 (1.1)	0.8 (1.0)
R^2	0.16	0.16	0.17	0.17
N	5,032	5,032	5,182	5,182

* $p < .05$, ** $p < .01$ (one-tailed).

Note: The dependent variable in all models is a political knowledge index scored 0–100 (see appendix to this chapter for questions). The models are estimates by OLS regression. Cell entries are unstandardized regression coefficients with standard errors in parentheses. Year dummies are included. The log transformation is TV = ln (TV) + 1, if TV ≠ 0; TV = 0 else.

Source: NES 1952–60, 64–8, merged with Television Access Data Set.

and numbers of stations. The results reveal that the effect of television increases as the number of VHF network affiliates increases, but only up to the third station. More than three stations of this type reduce the effect of television again. Most likely, this effect emerges because counties with more than three network affiliates are squeezed awkwardly between two television markets (like Somerset County in New Jersey, which receives VHF signals from network affiliates in both New York and Philadelphia). Whatever the reason, the effect of VHF network affiliates is not linear. The same is true for UHF affiliates, but the results do not suggest negative marginal effects. One independent station in the county also increased political knowledge, by slightly more than the first VHF network affiliate. The impact of independent stations disappears when there is more than one. This might be a result of different programming strategies by independents, especially when they compete with other independents.

Based on these results, I decided to combine all VHF stations into one variable and model their impact on knowledge with decreasing, but not negative, marginal effects by using a logarithmic transformation of the number of stations.[7] I keep a separate measure of UHF stations, not because Table 3.1 suggests large differences but because the few UHF stations in the sample would otherwise be overwhelmed by the ubiquitous VHF stations.

The second column in Table 3.1 uses the logged number of VHF and UHF stations, respectively, instead of dummy variables. Both have clearly significant positive effects on political knowledge of less educated respondents. The results confirm that knowledge was lower in suburban and rural areas than in cities for other reasons as well, but after controlling for this effect, the presence of television still had a sizable independent effect. Columns 3 and 4 of Table 3.1 show the same analysis for the more educated half of the sample. Overall, they reveal few effects of television on political knowledge.

The causal interpretation of the television effect is relatively unambiguous because the allocation of new local stations was an exogenous process and it is implausible that less educated but knowledgeable individuals would selectively and disproportionately move to areas with television stations. The spread of television across the country lowered the knowledge gap between more and less educated segments of the population by increasing knowledge among the less educated while leaving it unchanged among the more educated.

The models in Table 3.1 do not adjust for the impact of people's motivation to learn about politics. Perhaps people's interest in politics increased disproportionately in cities during the same period in which television grew, but for unrelated reasons. Or the increased reach of political information into the lives of less educated citizens, made possible by television, had a directly related effect on political interest, increasing the curiosity of the captive news audience. The models in Table 3.2 test these hypotheses.

---

7 The reduced effect of television in counties with more than three VHF network affiliates and more than one independent station might justify a quadratic term to model negative marginal effects. However, both cases are relatively rare. Statistically, logarithmic and quadratic effects fit about equally well. I therefore decided to use the same functional form for both VHF and UHF stations. (UHF stations clearly do not suggest negative marginal effects.) The exact transformation is $TV = \ln(TV) + 1$, if $TV \neq 0$; $TV = 0$ else.

Table 3.2. *Television, Political Knowledge, and Political Interest*

	"Total" Effect (DV: Knowledge)	Direct Effect (DV: Knowledge)	Indirect Effect (DV: Political Interest)
Number of VHF Stations (logged)	3.40** (.86)	2.18** (.84)	.054** (.01)
Number of VHF Stations (logged) × Education	−0.74** (.25)	−0.50* (.25)	−0.014** (.003)
Number of UHF Stations (logged)	2.58* (1.51)	1.36 (1.46)	0.053** (.017)
Number of UHF Stations (logged) × Education	−0.53 (.46)	−0.24 (.44)	−0.016** (.005)
Education	7.08** (.55)	5.10** (.54)	0.092** (.006)
Female	−10.2** (.6)	−8.9** (.56)	−0.061** (.007)
African American	−12.1** (1.0)	−11.6** (.99)	−0.02 (.012)
Age	0.10** (.02)	0.08** (.02)	0.002** (.0002)
Suburban area	−1.8* (.8)	−1.5* (.76)	−0.011 (.009)
Rural area	−2.2** (.8)	−2.1** (.75)	−0.015* (.009)
South	−1.4* (.7)	−1.6* (.70)	−0.004 (.008)
Political Interest (by year)	not included	included	–
R^2	0.22	0.29	0.18
N	10,214	10,151	11,493

* $p < .05$, ** $p < .01$ (one-tailed).
Note: The dependent variable in the first two models is a political knowledge index scored 0–100 (see appendix to this chapter for questions). The dependent variable in the third model is political interest. All models are estimates by OLS regression. Cell entries are unstandardized regression coefficients with standard errors in parentheses. Year dummies are included. The log transformation is TV = ln (TV) + 1, if TV ≠ 0; TV = 0 else.
Source: NES 1952–60, 64–8, merged with Television Access Data Set.

The model in the first column estimates the impact of television for the whole sample – instead of dividing the sample, as in Table 3.1 – by including an interaction between education and the number of television stations (separately for VHF and UHF stations). Education is measured on a six-point scale that ranges from less than nine grades of schooling to the highest level of at least a Bachelor's degree. For VHF stations, this interaction term is negative and highly significant. For UHF stations, it only approaches significance. The main effect of VHF stations, too, is larger than the main effect for UHF stations, although both are statistically significant. These results support my hypothesis, but suggest that the limited reach of UHF stations attenuated their effect.

The second column adds controls for political interest to the model. The NES did not ask the same political interest question in all years. To account for possible measurement differences and to allow the effect of political interest to vary for on- and off-year elections, the interest measure is interacted with the year dummies. Controlling for campaign interest reduces the television effect by between a third (for VHF stations) and half (for UHF stations). To the extent that television increased political interest, however, the model in column 2 underestimates the total effect of television. Column 3, in which political interest is the dependent variable, shows that television did indeed encourage political interest among less educated Americans. Both VHF and UHF stations increased political interest significantly, and this effect – just as the effect on political knowledge – declines among more educated respondents. Television thus increased political knowledge among Americans of low education directly and indirectly – directly by exposing them to more political information than before, and indirectly by motivating them to seek out more political information.[8]

The magnitudes of these effects are illustrated in Figures 3.3 and 3.4, which plot the results for all three models shown in Table 3.2. The first panel in Figure 3.3, labeled "direct effect," is derived from the second model. It depicts the direct effect of the number of VHF stations on political knowledge at different levels of education, while holding constant respondents' political interest.[9] At the 75th percentile of education (some nonacademic training after high school, shown by the dotted line) and even at the mean level of education, which corresponds to finishing high school in this period (and is shown by the dashed line), television had only a small and statistically insignificant effect on political knowledge. Among respondents who finished no more than eight grades of school (the 25th education percentile, shown by the solid line), however, television had a significant positive effect. The difference between no VHF stations and three VHF stations – the median number in the late 1960s – amounts to a 7 percent increase in political knowledge. But this is an underestimate of the true effect because it ignores the indirect effect through political interest. The second panel in Figure 3.3 plots the effect based on the first model in Table 3.2 – without controls for political interest. The television effect here is larger. The equivalent difference between zero and

---

8 Including a control variable for self-reported frequency of newspaper reading does not change the results much. It decreases the TV effect slightly in column 1 of Table 3.2, and increases it slightly in column 2. I do not include the variable in the reported results because it is only available in four NES surveys, so its inclusion would cut the number of cases considerably.

9 Other independent variables are held constant at their sample means. All models include different intercepts for each year (year dummies). When plotting predicted values, I set the value of each dummy to the proportion of cases for the particular year (that is, to its sample mean).

Broadcast TV, Political Knowledge, and Turnout

a) Direct Effect

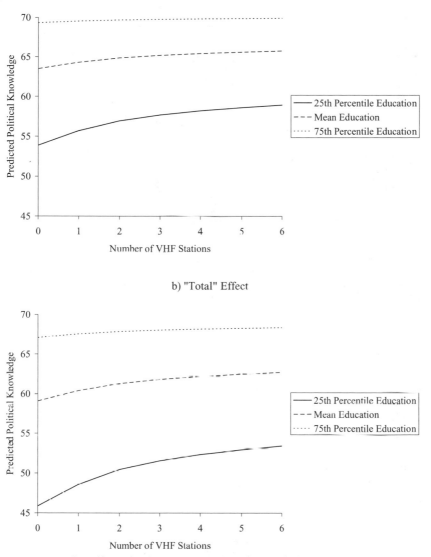

b) "Total" Effect

Figure 3.3. The Effect of Television on Political Knowledge.

Note: The graphs plot people's predicted political knowledge as a function of the number of VHF stations in their county for three levels of education based on the first two models in Table 3.2.

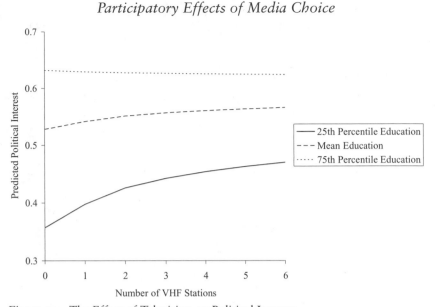

Figure 3.4. The Effect of Television on Political Interest.

Note: The graph plots people's predicted political interest as a function of the number of VHF stations in their county for three levels of education based on the third model in Table 3.2.

three stations at the 25th education percentile is a 12 percent increase in political knowledge.

The effects based on the model without political interest, on the other hand, are a slight overestimate because not the entire impact of political interest is caused by television. Respondents in areas with television are somewhat more interested even when the interest-generating effect of television is adjusted for. When unrelated differences in political interest are subtracted, the total effect of the first three VHF stations is an 11 percent increase in political knowledge among less educated Americans.[10] Among the more educated, television left knowledge levels largely unchanged, thus narrowing the knowledge gap between more and

10 Figure 3.4, which plots the effect of television on political interest derived from column 3 in Table 3.2, indicates that the first three VHF stations increased political interest from .36 to .44 (on a 0–1 scale) at the 25th percentile of education. The average coefficient for campaign interest on knowledge across years is 22.6, which suggests an indirect effect of about 2 points on the knowledge scale. This is almost as much as the difference between the TV effect with and without political interest in the model. In other words, almost the entire effect in the second panel in Figure 3.3 is caused by television. (That is why the second panel is labeled "total" effect, even though it only approximates the total effect, that is, the sum of direct and indirect effect.)

less educated citizens. This effect of television was relatively stable across the two decades I examine, and it was evident even in 1952 when a substantial number of Americans still had no television access whatsoever.[11]

The Conditional Political Learning model emphasizes the changing impact of education as a variable in learning about politics. Television made it easier to learn about politics for less educated Americans. The model does not suggest changes in the effect of interest in news and politics. Broadcast television should have lowered the impact of education on political learning without increasing the importance of political interest. Most people were exposed to the limited amount of news coverage on television, which did not require much education to understand, but did not provide more interested people with the option of choosing in-depth coverage either. Yet an alternative hypothesis is not implausible either, according to which political interest became more important once educational barriers to following politics were removed. After all, with television, highly interested individuals had an additional source of political information. I tested these opposite claims by including an interaction of campaign interest and the number of television stations. Whether or not the interaction of education and number of stations remains in the model, the political interest interaction with television does not have a significant effect on political knowledge. The main effect of political interest on political knowledge is strong, but television did not increase the importance of motivation in determining who learned about politics and who did not. Consistent with the Conditional Political Learning model, the impact of broadcast television was to produce learning effects even among less educated people, while providing fewer opportunities for more interested (or educated) individuals to learn more than they did without access to television.

---

11 Running the first model in Table 3.2 separately for 1952–8 and 1960–8 generates very similar and statistically significant estimates for both VHF and UHF stations. Television stations reached more and more Americans over time, but the effect of a given number of stations did not change. The results also remain significant at $p < .01$ and of similar magnitude as the pooled results when the model is estimated for 1952 only. This is important because most variation after 1952 is between respondents with access to just one or two stations and respondents with access to up to half a dozen stations. Across the entire data set, only 8 percent of the respondents lived in areas without any VHF network affiliates, and some of them had access to UHF stations (see Table 3.1). Only in 1952 did a significant number of NES respondents have no access to TV at all. In that year, 29 percent of them lived in counties in which not a single TV station reached the 50 percent coverage mark. To the extent that NES data allow it, this analysis thus establishes that any access to the new medium – rather than just later differences between a few and a few more channels – contributed to a narrowing of the knowledge gap.

It is clear from Table 3.2 that television did not eliminate all knowledge inequalities. As in almost all other studies, women, African Americans, and the less educated stand out because of their low political knowledge. The important point is that broadcast television reduced these inequalities. I focus on knowledge differences between more and less educated Americans, but similar results emerge for gender and race differences. The positive effect of television on political knowledge was somewhat stronger among women and African Americans. The decreasing marginal effects of television among the more educated were weaker among women. Television had a particularly strong main effect on knowledge levels of African Americans. It thus relieved knowledge inequalities of several different kinds.

THE IMPACT OF TELEVISION ACCESS ON TURNOUT

To the extent that exposure to news and increased political knowledge motivate former nonvoters to go to the polls, the growth of television should have increased the proportion of less educated voters. Television made less educated Americans more politically knowledgeable and should therefore also have made them more likely to turn out. Because knowledge levels among the more educated changed little, their turnout rates should not have changed as much. Taken together, these findings suggest that television increased the number of less educated voters as a percentage of all voters.

To test the turnout hypothesis, I estimated the same model as before with self-reported turnout[12] as the dependent variable. The key independent variables are again the logged number of television stations and the interaction between education and the number of stations. The first column in Table 3.3 shows the results. The main and interaction effects of VHF stations are in the predicted directions and statistically precise, indicating that turnout rose among less educated respondents as the number of VHF stations that reached their county increased. The impact of UHF stations, on the other hand, is statistically and substantively negligible. Figure 3.5 illustrates the effect of VHF stations on turnout. While people with mean or higher levels of education were largely unaffected by television, the new medium increased the likelihood that less educated citizens would go to the polls. The predicted probability of voting at the 25th percentile rises from .53 without television to .60 with three VHF stations – a 12 percent increase. Television narrowed the turnout gap between more and less educated segments of the electorate.

12 I use variable 702 from the NES 1948–2002 Cumulative Data File.

Table 3.3. *The Effect of Television on Turnout*

	"Total" Effect	Direct Effect Controlling for Political Knowledge	Direct Effect Controlling for Political Interest
Number of VHF Stations (logged)	0.186** (.070)	0.117 (.075)	0.086 (.073)
Number of VHF Stations (logged) × Education	−0.055** (.023)	−0.036 (.025)	−0.037 (.024)
Number of UHF Stations (logged)	−0.041 (.115)	−0.14 (.13)	−0.17 (.12)
Number of UHF Stations (logged) × Education	−0.004 (.039)	0.011 (.042)	0.025 (.041)
Education	0.48** (.05)	0.36** (.05)	0.33** (.05)
Political knowledge	–	0.018** (.001)	–
Female	−0.44** (.05)	−0.28** (.05)	−0.34** (.05)
African American	−0.63** (.07)	−0.42** (.08)	0.65** (.08)
Age	0.028** (.002)	0.026** (.002)	0.027** (.002)
Suburban area	0.047 (.063)	0.080 (.070)	0.072 (.066)
Rural area	0.030 (.062)	0.086 (.069)	0.049 (.065)
South	−0.93** (.05)	−0.97** (.06)	−1.03** (.06)
Political Interest (by year)	Not included	Not included	Included
Log likelihood	−5914.4	−4887.0	−5425.0
R^2	0.13	0.17	0.20
N	11,209	9,873	11,145

* $p < .05$, ** $p < .01$ (one-tailed).

Note: The dependent variable in these models is self-reported turnout. Cell entries are logit coefficients with standard errors in parentheses. Year dummies are included. The log transformation is TV = ln (TV) + 1, if TV ≠ 0; TV = 0 else.

Source: NES 1952–68, merged with Television Access Data Set.

What part of this turnout increase is explained by television's positive impact on political knowledge among the less educated? About a third, according to the second column in Table 3.3, which adds the political knowledge measure as a control variable. This estimate can only be a rough approximation (since knowledge is measured by only a few items in some years), but it suggests that the direct motivational effect from watching news on television accounts for a substantial part of the turnout effect. This conclusion is also supported by the role of political interest. The model in the third column controls for political interest (again allowing its impact to vary each year). The effect of VHF stations is roughly cut in half. But because television increased political interest among the less educated, which in turn increased their likelihood of going to the polls, column 3 misses the indirect effect of television on turnout. The direct effect at the 25th education percentile is now only a probability

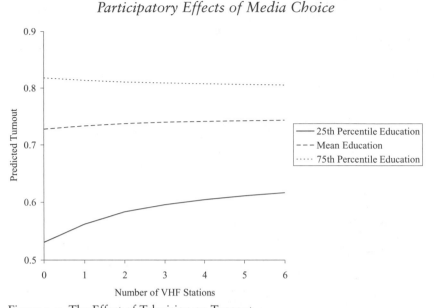

Figure 3.5. The Effect of Television on Turnout.

Note: The graph plots people's predicted likelihood of turning out as a function of the number of VHF stations in their county for three levels of education based on the first model in Table 3.3.

difference of .03, but the effect of three television stations on political interest at that level of education adds at least another .03, bringing the total effect close to the probability difference in Figure 3.5 of .07. As in the case of political knowledge, the reduction in the television effect when political interest is added to the model is almost entirely due to the indirect effect of television that works through political interest. Television thus narrowed the turnout gap by motivating and informing less educated Americans.

Two papers have recently examined the impact of television on turnout at the aggregate level – with somewhat different conclusions. Both Strömberg (2001) and Gentzkow (2006) examine county-level turnout, but they use different measures of television penetration. Strömberg finds that turnout increased more between 1950 and 1960 in counties with a higher proportion of television households. Examining national elections between 1946 and 1970, Gentzkow shows that turnout declined in years after the first television station began operating in a county. Turnout declined first in areas that received television stations early, and this decline cannot be explained by other differences between these areas and those that got television later (such as higher levels of education or greater population density in cities). The magnitude of the television effect is substantial, according to Gentzkow's analysis. He concludes that television accounts for a quarter of the overall turnout decline in presidential elections and half of the decline in off-years.[13]

My analysis does not indicate a strong effect of television on average turnout. The Conditional Political Learning model does not offer a firm prediction because of ambiguities related to the replacement of newspaper reading by television viewing. If newspaper readers complement their news diet with television newscasts, they should not become less likely to vote. Yet, if they replace some of their newspaper reading with television news, turnout in this (most educated) segment may have declined as television spread. Distinguishing between these two possibilities is difficult for several reasons. First, the degree of replacement changed over time, as is evident in the overall circulation of newspapers and television audience estimates. Second, asking people about their media use and whether or not they voted yields notoriously unreliable results (Prior 2005b; Vavreck 2005). Modeling the rate of replacement and its turnout effects is impossible with the self-report data available for this period.

The more important result to emerge from this chapter concerns the relative levels of turnout. Even though the Conditional Political Learning model does not yield predictions for absolute turnout levels, it clearly predicts declining inequality between Americans of different educational attainment. And here the empirical evidence, both in this chapter and in other work, is much less ambiguous. Even though Gentzkow and Strömberg reach different conclusions about the impact of television on absolute turnout levels, their results agree with my conclusions regarding the relative trends in turnout at different levels of education. Gentzkow finds that television depresses turnout more strongly in the third of counties with the highest percentage of high school graduates.[14] Strömberg finds the largest turnout increases between 1950 and 1960 in counties with the lowest education levels. Both of these studies are thus consistent with the present results, providing robust support for the proposition that television increased turnout among the less educated relative to the more educated. Regardless of its absolute effect, television changed the composition of the voting public by increasing the proportion of less educated voters.[15]

---

13 The contradictory findings by Gentzkow and Strömberg might be explained by a changing impact of television over time or the difference in the measurement of television penetration.

14 It is not entirely clear what to make of this result, however, because the interaction of television with average education in the county flips signs when several other county demographics are included in the model.

15 Empirically, the stratification of turnout by education has not diminished (Freeman 2004). For two reasons, it is difficult to gauge the overall impact of broadcast television on the educational composition of the voting public. First, we only observe

CONCLUSION

Many years ago, when broadcast television was still growing, Converse (1962, 592) suggested that television might have a positive aggregate effect on knowledge levels. He pointed to "functional illiteracy" rates of up to 60 percent to argue that television was likely to reach many people who hardly ever picked up a newspaper or magazine. The substitution effect among the most interested individuals, on the other had, was going to be curbed by the lack of political information in newspapers. Converse had knowledge about congressional candidates in mind and, not having found much information about them in the papers, believed that knowledge levels among the "literate" and motivated could therefore not decline much even if they sacrificed some of their newspaper reading to watch television. The empirical evidence I have offered in this chapter clearly supports the first part of Converse's intuition. Less educated Americans, who found newspapers or magazines too difficult or unappealing to read, became more knowledgeable once television was available to them.

The second part of Converse's argument does not fully apply to general political knowledge. Even if newspapers really contained as little information about congressional candidates as Converse came to believe, they surely offered plenty of information about the kind of national and international topics covered by the knowledge questions I used in this chapter. If the more educated did increasingly turn their attention from newspapers to television, they should keep up less well with the latest political developments, certainly with the kind of details that newspapers offer in the fourth or fifth paragraph of a story at a time when the equivalent report on television has long ended. Yet my empirical results are not as far

---

the voting public in a television environment. The most interesting question, however, is what would have happened in the absence of television. The proportion of the less educated among voters has declined after 1964 (Freeman 2004; Leighley and Nagler 1992). My analyses show that this decline was lower in areas covered by television. If my hypothesis is correct, the effect of television was to prevent an even further drop, not to reduce or eliminate turnout inequality. My precise claim is that – holding everything else constant – television decreased the difference in turnout rates of more and less educated Americans. Everything else was not constant. In time, a host of other factors may have contributed to absolute increase in turnout inequality by education. And of course, overall education levels increased. This raises the second difficulty. The proportion of Americans without a high school diploma was larger at the beginning of my period of analysis, in 1952, than at the end of it, in 1970. Despite this overall increase in education, the least educated still benefited from television at the end of this period. When I restrict my analysis to the second half of the 1960s, television continues to have a positive effect on political knowledge among the less educated.

from Converse's prediction as this line of reasoning suggests. The increasing reach of television did not lower political knowledge among the more educated, according to my analysis. Why not? First and foremost, the knowledge questions asked by the National Election Studies were rarely about the kind of detail that people would find in newspapers, but not on television. Perhaps the educated did indeed substitute television for newspapers and become less knowledgeable about details, but this analysis is too coarse to pick up this effect. There is some evidence for a slight (and not statistically reliable) decline at the highest levels of education.[16] But perhaps educated Americans did not in fact abandon newspapers. The evidence for replacement of newspaper reading by television is not as unambiguous as for the replacement of radio listening. The clearest political change brought about by television concerned the less educated: They gained a new source of political information more suitable to their tastes and capabilities. For educated, politically interested Americans, television did not change the amount of available political information.[17]

Some of the properties of television that produced learning effects among the less educated were present in radio. Nonetheless, Converse emphasized the effect of television on the illiterate, not the effect of radio, even though radio did not require reading skills either. Radio did carry news summaries, so it is conceivable that greater political involvement of the less educated began before television. Strömberg's (2004) finding that radio penetration increased turnout in gubernatorial elections between 1920 and 1940 might be evidence for such an effect. Most of the research reviewed in this chapter, however, agrees with Converse's proposition that the impact of television was of major importance for those unable to follow the news in print. It appears that news and political speeches on the radio did not have the same large audiences among less educated listeners that television would attract. The most likely reason for this difference in audience composition is that radio even early on offered greater choice than television. Radio signals traveled farther than broadcast signals, and there were more radio stations to begin with. The radio audience was not a captive audience, at least compared to television viewers in the broadcast

---

16 The main effect for the number of television stations, entered without the education interaction, is not significant in any of the models. This result is consistent with Delli Carpini and Keeter's (1996) finding that average knowledge levels have remained constant over the last fifty years.

17 Television did change the level of distraction and the amount of entertainment vying for the attention of educated people. Chapter 4 examines the distraction potential of entertainment television. Broadcast television also changed politics because Americans could now *see* their candidates on a nightly basis. My study is not intended to evaluate the implications of this change.

era. Greater movie attendance before television also supports this conclusion. Radio thus did not encourage accidental news exposure to the
same extent as television. And when people listened to the news, they may
not have learned as much as television news viewers. Research has clearly
demonstrated the benefits of visuals for people's ability to learn information presented to them in the news, especially among the less educated
(Graber 1988; 1990; Neuman, Just, and Crigler 1992). In short, even if
television was not an entirely clean break in the media environment –
and even if television accelerated a process that had already started with
radio – the combination of visuals, great popularity, and low choice made
television a major innovation for people's learning about politics.

From the very beginning of television, the medium was seen as a form
of entertainment. Its informative function was generally mentioned as an
afterthought. Yet for a sizable segment of the population the first exposure to politics came through broadcast news. Why does a medium that
is primarily seen as a source for entertainment increase knowledge, political interest, and turnout in a segment of the population that is notoriously hard to reach? According to Conditional Political Learning, the
low degree of choice on broadcast television and its unprecedented popularity are the key factors. Most people watched television for several
hours every night and often regardless of what programs were on. People
watched news because they did not want to turn off the television. Hence,
news programs enjoyed their largest audiences in the decades of broadcast
dominance despite the primary function of television as an entertainment
medium. When one considers the circumstances under which network
and local news attracted their sky-high ratings in the 1960s and 1970s,
the "popularity" of news looks somewhat less impressive. In the absence
of competition from entertainment programming, many Americans did
watch the news on a more or less daily basis. To read that as evidence
for genuine, widespread interest would be a mistake, however. Yet, interested or not, Americans watched their Cronkite and the local news that
followed or preceded him. It was not necessary for television *news* to be
popular – television as a medium just had to be more attractive than the
alternatives, and the two or three channels people could watch had to
offer their newscasts at the same time.

Regardless of whether the less educated were tricked into watching
by the lack of choice or developed a genuine interest in the news once
it was presented in a more comprehensible form, television expanded
the audience for political information. Yet, it is easy to carry this argument too far – the amount of political information presented in the news
was limited, and even if less educated people could be recruited into the
news audience, their capacity to learn remained low (Grabe et al. 2000).
But even cursory and unmotivated exposure to newscasts may have been

enough to teach these new audience members some simple facts about the important political issues of the day and motivate them to go to the polls (Krugman and Hartley 1970; Zukin and Snyder 1984).

The findings in this chapter seem to match well with the notion of television as a "knowledge leveler" (Neuman 1976, 122) that reduces differences in political knowledge by presenting information in less cognitively demanding ways (Eveland and Scheufele 2000; Kwak 1999). Yet the "leveling" was done not by television per se, but by *television news*. The broadcast environment with low choice and high popularity ensured that access to television and exposure to television news were synonymous for a surprisingly large portion of the population. These conditions – and with them the declining gaps in knowledge and turnout – were only temporary, however. In the 1970s and 1980s, political learning and turnout began to be affected by the next fundamental change in the media environment: cable television.

Appendix to Chapter 3: Measuring Political Knowledge, NES 1952–1968

The following items were used to create the measure of political knowledge:

NES 1952: Has heard of Taft-Hartley Act; knows that Democrats are more likely to spend money on education, housing, and unemployment; knows that working class and labor unionists are more likely to vote for Democratic Party (2 items); does not answer "Don't Know" regarding parties' involvement in world affairs

NES 1956: Knows that working class is more likely to vote for Democratic Party

NES 1958: Knowledge of House majority party before and after the election; correct recall of House incumbent; knows which of the two House candidates is the incumbent (or says correctly that there was no incumbent); remembers something incumbent has done for district; claims to know incumbent's religion

NES 1960: Knows that Republicans are more conservative than Democrats; knowledge of House majority party before and after the election; knows home state, religion, and age of each presidential candidate

NES 1964: Knows that Republicans are more conservative than Democrats; knows that Cuba is communist; knows that most of China is communist and not member of United Nations (2 points); knowledge of House majority party before and after the election; correct recall of House incumbent; knows which of the two House candidates is the incumbent (or says correctly that there was no incumbent); knows home state, religion, and position on civil rights bill of each presidential candidate

NES 1966: Knowledge of House majority party before and after the election; correct recall of House incumbent; knows which party ran candidates in the district; knows which of the two House candidates is the incumbent (or says correctly that there was no incumbent); number of Supreme Court justices correctly named (up to three)

NES 1968: Knows that Republicans are more conservative than Democrats; knows that Cuba is communist; knows that most of China is communist and not member of United Nations (2 points); knowledge of House majority party before and after the election; correct recall of House incumbent; knows which party ran candidates in the district; knows which of the two House candidates is the incumbent (or says correctly that there was no incumbent); places Humphrey to the left of Wallace on urban unrest scale. Respondents were asked to name the percentage of the federal budget devoted to defense, social welfare, and foreign aid. For the first two items, all responses within 10 points of the correct value were coded as correct. For foreign aid, any percentage below 5 was considered correct.

4

From Low Choice to High Choice: The Impact of Cable Television and Internet on News Exposure, Political Knowledge, and Turnout

Choosing every night between a scant three or four channels, television viewers in the broadcast period inspired the term "captive" audience. When the networks scheduled news, people watched news. Starting in the 1970s, the captives' chains were loosened, albeit slowly. Early cable television only served to bring broadcast signals to rural or mountainous areas. The percentage of homes with cable television was less than 2 percent before 1965 and only 7.6 percent in 1970. Before it became more commercial in the seventies, cable television was just another transmission device, not yet a source of original programming. This began to change in the 1970s when cable channels such as Home Box Office (HBO), Ted Turner's WTBS, and Sports Programming Network (now ESPN) began operating. Slowly, more and more Americans became subscribers. Cable reached a third of all households by 1983 and more than half of them by 1989. In the mid-1990s, satellite technology offered another way to leave the broadcast days. Cable or satellite television was in 70 percent of all homes by 1997 and passed the 85 percent mark in 2004.[1]

When alternatives increase, people have more choice, and their own motivations for watching become more important in predicting their viewing behavior. With the advent of cable, the supply of programming in many television genres expanded (e.g., Becker and Schoenbach 1989; Weimann 1996). Cable subscribers are offered more movies than captive audiences with only an antenna. They are offered more sports programs, more news, more cooking shows, more weather reports, and so on and

---

[1] Cable and satellite penetration is only one measure of access. The number of channels available through cable access has increased considerably (Comstock and Scharrer 1999). Digital cable offers more channels than analog; premium or pay-per-view cable offers more than basic service. The basic premise holds regardless: Cable (or satellite) television increases subscribers' choices dramatically compared to broadcast television.

so on. Cable subscribers will not watch more of everything, but they will watch more of some genres – the genres they like the most. For most new cable subscribers, the number of frequently viewed channels, often called the "channel repertoire," increases only modestly (Heeter 1985). Even cable subscribers with several hundred channels at their disposal tend to watch fewer than twenty of them (Webster 2005). Yet the new repertoire of channels reflects cable subscribers' genre preferences more closely than the broadcast repertoire did. Parts of the audience, hungry for around-the-clock entertainment, have seen the last newscast of their lives and take the opportunity to watch entertainment programming during the hours formerly dominated by news. Others happily greet the day when they do not have to accept soap operas and celebrity talk in the afternoon, but can watch a twenty-four-hour cable news channel. The most important point I seek to demonstrate in this chapter is that more choice leads to better sorting of the television audience by taste. Viewers still cannot watch what they want all the time, but compared to the broadcast era they no longer merely watch what is on.

To know who gets more news and who escapes news more efficiently than before, we need to know people's preferences for television programming. This chapter picks up where the Low-Choice/High-Choice Experiment left off in examining the consequences of greater choice for news exposure, political knowledge, and turnout. It extends the analysis by considering the role of the Internet in expanding media choice and the effect of greater choice on turnout. Most importantly, this chapter introduces a direct measure of people's media content preferences. In the Low-Choice/High-Choice Experiment, the Switchers did not have an opportunity to express just how grateful they are that news programs no longer "roadblock" their early evenings. The experiment covered just one hypothetical choice, so it could not establish if some in the Always News group might take advantage of greater choice at other times to watch more news than in the low-choice environment. Finally, the Low-Choice/High-Choice Experiment is not actually about viewing preferences. Those in the Always News group might stick with the news not because they like the news more than the Switchers, but because they felt a greater obligation to keep up with politics and public affairs. In this chapter, I use a direct measure of content preference to show that people who like news learn more about politics in a high-choice media environment than they used to, while political knowledge drops for those who prefer entertainment. The transition from a low-choice to a high-choice media environment thus increased the knowledge gap that had previously been narrowed by broadcast television. In the high-choice media environment, television ceases to be the "knowledge leveler" (Neuman 1976) that it was in its early days.

A change in the media environment that arises for technological reasons has profound but unintended implications for politics because it affects how evenly political knowledge is distributed in the population. Political scientists have devoted far more effort to studying the average levels of political knowledge and their consequences. There is plenty of evidence that an informed citizenry benefits a political system. Among other things, more knowledgeable people are more tolerant, more likely to vote, and more likely to hold consistent opinions. And although knowledge levels are low, they have not changed much over time. Delli Carpini and Keeter (1996) documented relatively stable knowledge levels since the advent of survey research (see also Smith 1989). More recent studies have confirmed their findings (Gilens, Vavreck, and Cohen 2005) or even indicated the possibility of a slight increase (Althaus 2003). At least, most would argue, the problem is not getting worse. This conclusion ignores an increasingly unequal distribution of political knowledge.

Knowledge inequality is difficult to track. Issues and candidates change, forcing scholars to revise their measures of political knowledge. Changes in the variance of knowledge scales over time can emerge for purely methodological reasons, either because questions have changed or because the same questions have become more or less difficult to answer. To examine inequality by analyzing differences between different groups over time (for example, the difference in political knowledge of Americans with and without a college degree), it is necessary to identify (and measure) the distinguishing variable. Before this study, the concept of Relative Entertainment Preference had not been used. As a result, the widening knowledge and turnout gaps between news and entertainment fans that become evident in this chapter have gone unnoticed.[2]

Even when average knowledge levels remain stable, rising inequality may cause concern. According to Delli Carpini and Keeter (1996, 1):

The more equitably information is distributed among citizens, the more likely it is that the actions of government will reflect the public interest and, thus, that the public will be supportive of those actions. In short, a broadly and equitably

---

2 These conceptual and methodological problems with measuring political knowledge over time make it particularly difficult to examine the dynamics of gaps in general knowledge (as opposed to issue- or event-specific knowledge) over time. I tried in vain to use survey data to analyze temporal variance in knowledge. In addition to the difficulties described in the paragraph, the small number of factual knowledge questions in the National Election Studies frustrated my efforts. Although not a measure of factual knowledge, the items in the NES Survey which ask respondents what they like and dislike about the two political parties and the presidential candidates offer two time series going back to 1952. For both series, the variance in the total number of likes and dislikes has increased considerably since the 1970s.

informed citizenry helps assure a democracy that is both responsive and responsible.

Rising inequality in political involvement can reinforce economic inequality both because lack of knowledge leads citizens to support policies that hurt their economic interests (e.g., Bartels 2005) and because politicians pay more attention to the demands of the politically involved. Even if roughly equal segments of the population have become more and less knowledgeable, respectively, the more knowledgeable cannot correct the mistakes of those who tune out. In the 1990s, political science found some comfort in the notion that aggregation of preferences and the use of heuristics make up for information shortfalls. Aggregation of preferences that appear ill-informed at the individual level could lead to collective preferences that closely approximate rational (enlightened) positions because the allegedly random errors in individual opinions cancel out (Page and Shapiro 1992). Yet, as Althaus (2003) has shown, random errors cancel out only under unrealistic assumptions, and, more importantly, less knowledgeable individuals tend to make the same kind of "errors" because they rely on the same prominent cues emphasized in the media or by the survey context. The errors are not random, in other words, and therefore do not cancel out. Inequality in political knowledge has a direct negative effect on the quality of public opinion.

According to the heuristics argument, people do not obtain encyclopedic information about politics because the benefits from being highly informed are low, but they pick up politically relevant cues by accident. In their decision making, people employ heuristics such as party identification, ideology, liking for the candidates, and demographic similarities with the candidates (Lupia 1994; Popkin 1991; Sniderman, Brody, and Tetlock 1991). Even though only Popkin (1991) made the claim explicitly, this literature has come to embody the view that decisions based on heuristics approximate decisions that people would make if armed with complete information.[3] This view has been criticized because the votes of less knowledgeable people do in fact differ systematically from "fully informed" voters (Althaus 1998; 2001; Bartels 1996; Lau and Redlawsk 2001). People do not always have the necessary information to employ heuristics "intelligently," in part because the news media fail to cover certain cues (Delli Carpini 2000b; Kinder 1998, 786; Kuklinski and Quirk

---

3 One of the earliest applications to political science (Brady and Sniderman 1985) showed the affect-based likeability heuristic to be *more* consequential among well-informed citizens. It is incorrect that only poorly informed people use heuristics. Rather, for the poorly informed, heuristics are relatively more crucial than factual information.

2000). A further drop in knowledge among the least-informed, who would seem to need cues the most, only exacerbates such concerns. People most dependent on cues are also most likely to abandon news for entertainment and may thus no longer pick up enough information to apply heuristics in ways that further either their own or the electorate's collective interest.

The case for equality is even more straightforward in the case of turnout. Citizens who do not exercise their right to vote risk that their views will not be represented (e.g., Griffin and Newman 2005; Rosenstone and Hansen 1993). This might be less of a problem for people who abstain after careful deliberation. Yet, the growing differences in turnout rates documented in this chapter arise because of a lack of interest and knowledge. Rising inequality in political knowledge feeds inequality in turnout.[4] Even if the level of political involvement in the population does not appear to drop, the growing inequality of this involvement, which is the direct consequence of greater media choice, poses serious problems for post-broadcast democracies.

CABLE TELEVISION AND THE NETWORK NEWS AUDIENCE

The widening knowledge gap in the high-choice environment follows from a widening exposure gap. The exposure gap occurs because greater media choice reduces the homogenizing impact of the media environment and increases the impact of individual users' motivations. Because different users have widely different preferences, the result is audience fragmentation. Some people will use their newfound media freedom to watch, read, and hear more about politics than they used to. The flipside of greater choice is that some viewers abandon television news. This decline can only occur because of the particular circumstances that brought the viewers to television news in the first place. I discussed these circumstances – the general popularity of television paired with low choice and the "road-blocking" strategy employed by the networks and their affiliates – in the previous chapter.

Removing constraints on choice will thus most strongly depress audiences for news programs that benefited to the greatest extent from the structure of the broadcast environment. These programs are network and

---

4 By "rising inequality in turnout" and "widening turnout gaps" I mean an increase in the variance of people's probabilities of voting (which are not directly observed but can be inferred). A more intuitive way to think about turnout inequality is in terms of average turnout rates across groups of people (e.g., turnout rates among entertainment fans compared to turnout rates among news junkies) or across time (i.e., increasing variance in the number of votes cast by individuals over a period of time). (See also Freeman 2004, 716–23.)

local newscasts in the early evening and the late-night local news after prime time. Presidential debates and other presidential appearances that were televised by all networks are also prime candidates for audience decline (Baum and Kernell 1999). Although the end of effective road-blocking is a dominant reason for the declining reach of news, the general rise in competition also contributes. Like other programs, news programs and presidential appearances suffer from reduced lead-in effects, which decrease as the number of alternative programs increases (Tiedge and Ksobiech 1986; Walker 1988). News audiences depend partly on the lead-in they receive from preceding programming (Webster and Newton 1988), so reduced overall viewing of network channels by cable subscribers also lowers the audience for news. Network news programs may have lost additional viewers to cable news channels or the Internet as news junkies now have more choices among news formats. (This creates a difficult situation for the networks' news divisions because they need to appeal to viewers who want – and can now get – more entertainment and to viewers who are looking for more hard news. It is generally assumed that the former group is much larger, although exact measurement is very difficult.)

The expected effect on network news audiences is clear. According to my second hypothesis (see Table 2.2), they decline as cable and Internet penetration rises. To investigate the impact of cable penetration on network news audiences, I turn to audience data collected by Nielsen Media Research. Nielsen data are not affected by methodological concerns with self-reports that plague survey measures of media use (about which more follows) because they are recorded automatically.[5] Nielsen presents its national audience estimates separately for households with and without

---

5 Nielsen uses "people meters" for its national sample of viewers and for tracking the largest media markets. Viewing data for smaller markets is still collected using time diaries. I use only data from their national people meter sample in this chapter. Person-level measurement requires Nielsen panel members to push a button on the people meter when they start watching. Failing to do so creates measurement error. Household data do not have this limitation because all television activity is automatically recorded. Of course, without relying on person data, the number of viewers per household cannot be tracked.

The biggest advantage of Nielsen's people meter data is that they are not confounded by recall and social desirability biases that plague self-reports of media use (Prior 2005b). Although I consider people meter data more accurate than self-reports, it should be clear that any audience measurement is an estimation process with both random and systematic error (see, e.g., Napoli 2003, 71–95). The accuracy of household estimates based on people meters still depends on the quality of the viewer sample. Nielsen estimates do not track viewers' attention (or, in fact, their presence).

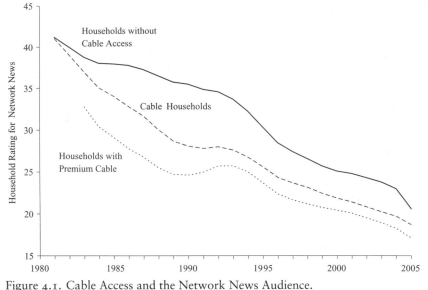

Figure 4.1. Cable Access and the Network News Audience.

Note: Ratings are combined Nielsen ratings for three network newscasts (Monday through Friday) in March of each year. The graph plots moving averages generated by locally weighted regressions with a bandwidth of .33.

cable access. Figure 4.1 plots the combined weekday ratings for the three national network newscasts over the last twenty-five years for three types of households: households that receive only broadcast channels, households with any kind of cable access (and, in recent years, satellite access), and households that subscribe to premium cable channels such as HBO or Showtime. The measures are average for one month per year (March). To eliminate some of the measurement error, the graph shows moving averages generated by locally weighted regressions.

Network news ratings for cable and broadcast households were at the same level in the early 1980s. In the 1960s and 1970s, cable technology delivered television to remote areas, but no original programming, so we should not expect large differences in news consumption between cable and broadcast households. By 1981, the beginning of the time series in Figure 4.1, cable systems did offer various entertainment options. At this point, however, only about 20 percent of all households had cable access, and people in these households were better educated and wealthier than the national average – and therefore quite likely to watch the news. The trend for premium cable households, which begins in 1983, suggests that some cable households did immediately reduce their network news viewing. Premium cable presumably attracted movie and sports buffs, a particularly entertainment-focused audience segment. It fits the Conditional

Political Learning model that their news viewing is the lowest of all segments.[6]

The strongest evidence in support of a cable effect on network news audiences appears for the period between the early 1980s and the mid-1990s. In this period, the decline in news viewing was much steeper in cable households. The network news ratings in homes without cable access were still around 35 as late as 1994, almost 10 rating points higher than in cable households. Whereas cable households looked like broadcast households in the early 1980s, their network news consumption approached the low levels of premium cable households by the mid-1990s. In this period, when network news ratings in cable households dropped by more than a third, cable penetration increased from 20 to 60 percent.[7]

Even though the early half of Figure 4.1 appears to support the hypothesis that cable did it, we cannot draw causal inferences from the figure. The trends for the last ten years illustrate the problem. Since the mid-1990s, network news audiences have declined considerably even in households without cable access. After 1995, the three trend lines are almost parallel. This may be partly due to the addition of several smaller broadcast networks (Fox, UPN, and WP) which increased entertainment options even for households without cable. The number of independent UHF stations also increased steeply in the 1980s and 1990s (Nielsen Media Research 2005; Owen and Wildman 1992, 21,22).[8]

Especially in recent years, declining news viewing in broadcast-only homes could also reflect a selection effect. By 2005, the share of

6 The percentage of households with premium cable increased from under 10 percent in 1981 to 25 percent in 1985. It then fluctuated between a quarter and a third for most years. Nielsen's reclassification of former premium channels as regular cable channels explains some of the fluctuation. The average between 2001 and 2005 is 35 percent.

7 Zaller (1999; forthcoming) has argued that before cable began to compete for viewers, network newscasts offered news of a higher "quality" than the public wanted. Journalists took pride in offering high-quality news. Many viewers would have preferred softer news, but had nowhere else to go. If this reasoning is correct, the audience decline in Figure 4.1 understates the extent to which less interested segments put up with content they did not much care for. Americans in the broadcast era not only watched more news, they watched news that was more detailed, longer, and, in their eyes, more boring than the network news today. Perhaps the captive audience would have learned even more from their unintended news exposure if television news had been simpler (Barber 1979; Graber 2001, 112).

8 As Baldwin, Barrett, and Bates (1992) point out, analyzing the same trends between 1982 and 1989, increasing attractiveness of independent stations in the 1980s may explain the modest decline of network news ratings in broadcast-only households.

households without cable (or satellite) access was down to under 15 percent. This segment is becoming increasingly less representative of the population as a whole. Some people do not watch much television at all and therefore have little reason to acquire access to more channels. If more and more of the remaining noncable viewers fall in this category, average news viewing in noncable households should decline, but not because broadcast-only viewers watch less news than they did in the past. They never watched news, but they make up a larger and larger share of noncable viewers. The data in Figure 4.1 cannot tell us if the people who are without cable in 2005 ever watched more news.[9]

Another trend that confounds any causal interpretation of Figure 4.1 is the rise in Internet access after 1995. Former network news viewers in broadcast-only households may increasingly get their news online. Although the CNN channel did not attract enough viewers in the 1980s and 1990s to account for all those former network news viewers that have gone missing, the Internet may explain some of the drop beginning in the late 1990s. Though the early decline of network news audiences almost certainly means that people watched less news overall, the recent decline might have more to do with replacement of one kind of news with another. In all, Figure 4.1 reveals suggestive trends early on indicating that cable television lowered network news audiences. But these data cannot distinguish between individual-level change and selection effects. For that, we must turn to survey data.

MEASURING PREFERENCE FOR ENTERTAINMENT

To measure people's preferences for different media content and assess their impact on political involvement, I designed the News & Entertainment Survey (N&E Survey), a panel survey of 2,358 randomly selected U.S. residents. It was conducted by Knowledge Networks in two waves in 2002 and 2003. Knowledge Networks (KN) interviews national probability samples over the Internet by providing a large panel, selected through

---

9 The network news programs air earlier today than in the past (Cancian, Bills, and Bergstrom 1995; Sharbutt 1987). This is sometimes mentioned as one of the causes for the decline in viewership as more people are still at work and cannot watch the news. Yet this implies a decline in ratings, but not market share. (Market share denotes the size of the audience as a percentage of all households watching television at the time.) Earlier time slots for news should not affect the share because the percentage of households with their TV on would also be lower if more people are still at work. Empirically, however, ratings and shares for network news have declined by roughly the same degree.

Random Digit Dialing (RDD), with WebTV units and free Internet connections in exchange for taking surveys. The participants for this study constitute a randomly selected subset of the KN panel and are thus close to a random sample of the U.S. adult population.[10] The first survey wave was conducted in February and March 2002; the second wave occurred in April 2003. Of the 2,358 first-wave respondents, the 1957 who were still part of the Knowledge Networks panel in April 2003[11] were contacted again. Of these, 1,650 panelists were reinterviewed, generating a reinterview rate of 84 percent.

At any given time, television viewers must commit to one particular program. They can watch either entertainment or news, but not both. This notion implies that viewers evaluate the different programming options relative to each other. I designed two measures of Relative Entertainment Preference (REP). The first REP measure is based on ranking of news relative to other programming genres. Respondents were shown a list of ten genres and asked to select the one they liked best:

Science fiction shows like *X-Files* or *Star Trek Voyager*
Comedies/sitcoms like *Friends* or *The Simpsons*
Drama shows like *ER* or *Law and Order*
Soap operas like *General Hospital* or *One Life to Live*
Reality TV shows like *Survivor* or *Cops*
Sports
Game shows like *Jeopardy* or *Who wants to be a millionaire?*
News
Documentary programs on channels like History Channel or Discovery Channel
Music videos

The meaning of "news" was not elaborated because just before ranking the genres, respondents had been asked to evaluate various different types

---

10 The household cooperation rate for the initial panel recruitment during the period of the two surveys was 53 percent. The survey completion rate for the first wave was 85 percent. For details on the sampling mechanism used by Knowledge Networks, see Krotki and Dennis (2001). In a comparison of KN data to an RDD telephone survey, Krosnick and Chang (2001) found the KN sample to be representative of the U.S. population in terms of demographics and political attitudes.

11 Almost all of the remaining 400 respondents had voluntarily withdrawn from the KN panel by the time of the second survey wave. Because few of the surveys KN panelists complete cover politics, this panel attrition should not be of great concern for my analysis. Empirically, respondents who withdrew did not differ significantly on most key variables from respondents who remained active (see discussion that follows).

of news (see Prior 2003), a task that encouraged them to think of their favorite type of news. After respondents marked their favorite genre, the next screen showed the remaining nine genres and again asked for the most liked genre. This procedure was repeated twice more, yielding a ranking of respondents' four most preferred television genres. Then, respondents were given a chance to mark all the remaining genres that they "really dislike." For the purpose of this study, I am interested only in the ranking of news vis-à-vis all other genres. The appeal of news is greatest for respondents who select news as their favorite genre. At the opposite end are respondents who specifically mark news as one genre they dislike. The measure of people's relative preferences for entertainment over news is thus coded 5 if the respondent dislikes news, 4 if the respondent neither dislikes it nor selects it as one of his top four genres, and 3, 2, 1, and 0 if the respondent selects news as his fourth-, third-, second- or most liked genre, respectively. Three percent dislike news explicitly. Exactly half of the respondents are indifferent to news, neither ranking it nor marking it as "disliked." The remaining respondents rank it fourth (17 percent), third (14 percent), second (11 percent), or first (5 percent).

The second measure of Relative Entertainment Preference uses the concept of "probabilistic polling," a measurement approach developed by Charles Manski (1999; 2002), which allows respondents to express the uncertainty of their survey responses. Respondents were asked which of four cable premium channels they would order, assuming that they would not have to pay a monthly charge. The four alternatives were a music channel, a news channel, a "movie and entertainment channel," and a sports channel. Instead of making respondents pick one channel, Manski's approach allows them to assign a "percent chance" to each of the four channels. Respondents can thus express their preference structure more precisely. At the same time, the item measures relative preferences because the sum of the four percent chances must total one hundred percent.[12] The question was phrased as follows:

Suppose you could pick one cable premium channel for no monthly charge. For each of the four channels below, please indicate the percent chance that you would choose that channel.

You have 100 percentage points to allocate among all four choices. For example, if you are absolutely certain that you would pick one particular channel, you might

[12] Respondents whose percent chance allocation did not add to 100 were reminded of that fact and asked to modify their answers. After changing their allocation, respondents were then allowed to move to the next question (even if the percent chances still did not sum to 100). Of the 4.3 percent of respondents who did not provide a correct allocation, most did not enter any numbers.

assign a 95 to 100 percent chance to that channel and a minimal percent chance to all others. Or, if you cannot decide between two channels, you might assign each of them a 40 to 50 percent chance and minimal chances to the other two. These are only examples.

Please indicate the percent chances that you would pick each channel now.[13]

The movie channel was most popular with an average percent chance of 50 (and a standard deviation of 28). The news channel was next with 23 (s.d. = 22), followed by sport (14, s.d. = 19) and music (13, s.d. = 17). My second measure of REP is the total of points that respondents assigned to the three nonnews channels (or, put differently, 100 minus the percent chance assigned to the news channel).

Even though the two measures of REP employ different measurement approaches (ranking versus rating), they are closely related. Respondents who disliked the news according to the ranking measure allocated almost all of their percentage points (89.6) to the three entertainment options. Those indifferent to news on the ranking measure were also quite fond of entertainment, assigning 83.8 points to entertainment. Respondents who ranked news among their four most liked genres allocated a higher percentage chance to the twenty-four-hour news channel. But the differences between ranking news fourth or third and ranking news as the most liked genre are large. The points assigned to entertainment declined from 74.6 among those who ranked news fourth to 67.3 (ranked third), 61.8 (ranked second), and only 51.4 among those who ranked news first. The Pearson correlation between the two REP measures is .44.

Because both REP measures are strongly related, the most efficient way to present the following results is to combine the two measures. (To demonstrate that they have highly similar effects, I present separate results in the next analysis, before adopting the combined measures.[14]) I combined the two variables by taking the mean of their z-scores and transforming it to the 0–1 interval. For 101 respondents, the combined REP is missing because they did not complete the Manski questions. For the remaining 2,257 respondents, the combined REP has a mean of .66 and a standard deviation of .19. Figure 4.2 shows a histogram of this key independent variable. Though REP is not normally distributed, respondents spread over the entire range of the measure, creating a clear distinction between strong news and entertainment fans. (The sharp drop-off at high

---

13 The wording of the response options was "24-hour music channel," "24-hour news channel," "24-hour movie and entertainment channel," and "24-hour sports channel."

14 In a previous paper (Prior 2005a), I used only the ranking component of REP to examine effects on knowledge and turnout. Results are essentially the same.

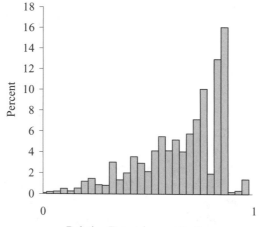

Figure 4.2. Relative Entertainment Preference (Combined Measure).

Note: This figure shows the frequency distribution of the combined REP measure in the N&E Survey.

levels of REP occurs because very few respondents marked news as "disliked" on the ranking measure.)

The preference distribution on the ranking measure of REP among second-wave respondents differs minimally (by no more than 1 percentage point per category) from the whole sample, indicating that respondents with a preference for entertainment were no more or less likely to complete the second survey. Respondents who completed the second wave scored 4 points (or .18 of one standard deviation) lower on the Manski REP measure, a substantively small but significant difference that suggests a somewhat higher level of news interest among continuing panelists. On the other hand, the difference in political knowledge between first- and second-wave respondents is insignificant. Even though the threat from panel attrition for the representativeness of the Wave 2 sample is modest at best, the remainder of this chapter also offers results that rely only on the Wave 1 sample for comparison.

Relative Entertainment Preference is different from political interest. Most obviously, the former refers to news, the latter to politics. More importantly, however, REP is a relative evaluation of different media content, whereas political interest is an absolute concept. Political interest does not take into account people's competing interests. Curious or enthusiastic people may profess strong interest in almost everything we ask them about. Yet they will not have the time to act upon all those interests. A relative evaluation of news avoids this problem by asking respondents to figure in how much they like other media content. The many demands on their time and the countless competing leisure attractions constantly require people to weigh different alternatives. Theoretically, a relative evaluation of news (or politics) compared to those alternatives seems more appropriate in explaining their behavior.

A relative measure of people's interests may also reduce social desirability pressures on respondents. Empirically, very few respondents confess that they are not particularly interested in politics. The standard political interest question makes it harder to admit low political interest than the REP measures, which allow respondents to select genres they like *even better* than the news. Framing the question in terms of "liking" may encourage the intended subjective assessment, rather than responses that are tinted by normative considerations (for example, that one should be interested in politics on normative grounds).

RELATIVE ENTERTAINMENT PREFERENCE AND SELF-REPORTED EXPOSURE TO NEWS

Viewers' content preferences become more powerful predictors of their news exposure when they have a choice between different media content, according to Conditional Political Learning. Among cable subscribers, only those who really like news should watch news programs. Those without cable, on the other hand, are not as discriminating and watch news for lack of better options even if they do not have a strong preference for news. To complement the aggregate analysis of audience data for network news, I examine the joint effect of content preference and cable access on television news exposure as reported by respondents in the N&E Survey. The dependent variable in Table 4.1 is measured by asking respondents, "How many days in the past week did you watch at least one news program on TV?" I regress it on cable access, Relative Entertainment Preference, and the interactions with cable access.[15] The models also include several control variables that may affect news exposure and correlate with REP or cable access.

Table 4.1 shows three models using three different measures of Relative Entertainment Preference: the ranking measure, the Manski measure,

[15] News exposure has a mean of 4.5 days and a standard deviation of 2.5. Cable access is coded as a dummy variable based on the question "Do you have either cable or satellite television?" Eighty-one percent of the respondents said they did. The 2002 Pew Media Consumption asked separately about cable and satellite television. According to that survey, conducted in April/May 2002, 66 percent of all Americans had cable access; another 14 percent had access to satellite TV. Questions in previous Pew surveys referred jointly to cable and satellite access. The empirical analyses in this chapter treat the two as equivalent. For comparison, Nielsen Media Research estimated that 70 percent of all U.S. households had cable access in May 2002 and 15 percent had satellite access.

Table 4.1. *The Effect of Relative Entertainment Preference on News Exposure*
(N&E Survey)

	"How many days in the past week did you watch at least one news program on television?"		
Cable access	0.57* (.31)	1.11** (.41)	1.00** (.42)
REP: Ranking (0–5)	−0.32** (.085)	–	–
REP: Manski (0–100)	–	−0.019** (.005)	–
REP: Mean (0–1)	–	–	−2.84** (.56)
REP × Cable access	−0.17* (.094)	−0.013** (.005)	−1.34* (.62)
Education	−0.020 (.042)	−0.019 (.041)	−0.034 (.041)
Income	−0.018 (.014)	−0.009 (.014)	−0.020 (.014)
R's primary language is English	0.34 (.30)	0.16 (.30)	0.31 (.30)
Gender	0.076 (.096)	−0.051 (.095)	0.034 (.094)
Age	0.05** (.003)	0.05** (.003)	0.05** (.003)
TV Households, Nielsen 2002–3 (in 1,000,000)	0.038 (.03)	0.032 (.029)	0.033 (.029)
R has premium cable	0.29** (.11)	0.32** (.10)	0.33** (.10)
R owns VCR	0.24* (.11)	0.22* (.11)	0.23* (.11)
R owns home computer	0.13 (.12)	0.16 (.11)	0.14 (.11)
Internet access	−0.011 (.11)	−0.081 (.11)	−0.047 (.11)
Constant	2.55** (.48)	3.07** (.53)	3.70** (.55)
R^2	0.21	0.22	0.24
N	2,161	2,161	2,161

$** p < .01, * p < .05$ (one-tailed).
Note: The dependent variable in these three OLS regressions is news exposure. Cell entries are unstandardized regression coefficients with standard errors in parentheses.

and the combined measure. Figuring in the differences in scaling, all three measures yield very similar estimates. Respondents' Relative Entertainment Preference has a negative main effect on news exposure, indicating that people who like entertainment are less likely to report news exposure even if they do not have cable access. The interaction of REP with cable access is also negative and shows that the relationship between preferences and exposure is about 50 percent stronger among cable subscribers. Both coefficients are clearly statistically significant in all three models. Cable access also has a significant, but positive effect. At low levels of REP, news exposure is driven mostly by this main effect of cable. Even if they are equally well educated, of equal age, and of the same gender and race, news fans with cable report higher news exposure than news fans without cable.

Figure 4.3 graphs the relationship estimated by the third model in Table 4.1, holding other independent variables at their means. The line for respondents with cable access is steeper, indicating a stronger relationship for cable subscribers. This pattern – greater elasticity between preferences

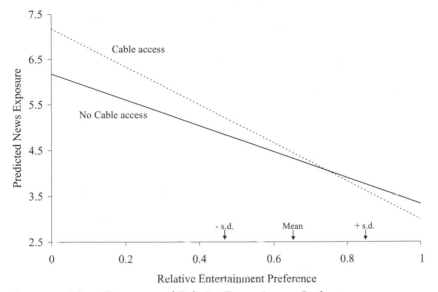

Figure 4.3. News Exposure and Relative Entertainment Preference.

Note: The graph plots predicted news exposure for the range of REP and different media environments based on the third model in Table 4.1.
Source: N&E Survey.

and political behavior among people in high-choice media environments – will emerge many times in this chapter. It illustrates one key insight of the Conditional Political Learning model: Increase people's media options, and preferences will more noticeably guide their choices and behaviors.

I present the analysis of news exposure only reluctantly because it is well known that survey measures of media use suffer from a number of serious problems. They are highly unreliable because people are not very good at remembering the time they spend using media, and because following the news closely and often is socially desirable, leading people to overreport their exposure (Ansolabehere and Iyengar 1998; Price and Zaller 1993; Prior 2005b). In the context of this study, it is of even greater concern that some people's self-reports are more biased than others'. For example, politically interested people who go to the polls regularly are more likely to incorrectly recall seeing political commercials on television (Ansolabehere, Iyengar, and Simon 1999). If media environments or content preferences were systematically related to bias in self-reported media exposure, then including exposure in the model could lead to incorrect estimates. It is not implausible that cable subscribers, who spend more time watching television than nonsubscribers (Becker et al. 1989), over-estimate their news exposure to a greater extent. Someone who watches five hours of television a day might be more likely to assume that he saw some news, whereas this might be less true for someone whose television is on for only an hour or two. There is evidence of self-report problems in Table 4.1. People who subscribe to premium cable channels reported significantly higher news exposure than basic cable subscribers, even though there is virtually no news programming on premium channels. The effect of premium channels remains significant despite controls for media content preferences, education, income, and several other demographic variables. The most plausible explanation for this finding is that access to premium channels increases the bias in self-reported news exposure.

The preceding analysis thus needs to be viewed with appropriate caution. The trends in Nielsen ratings shown in Figure 4.1 become a much-needed, though indirect, piece of confirmatory evidence, for they are not threatened by self-report bias in the same way. The Nielsen data showed a decline in network news audiences, which, according to Chapter 3, were inflated by a lack of choice in the broadcast environment and were watched even by some entertainment fans. As cable penetration increased, network news audiences dropped. Until the mid-1990s, this drop was more pronounced in cable households. Using cross-sectional data, the survey analysis has shown lower news audiences among entertainment fans with cable access than among those without.

Despite all its flaws, the analysis so far confirms the expectation that cable access increases news exposure for some people – those with a high appreciation of news – but lowers it for those who watch television primarily to be entertained.[16] Previous research on learning from television suggests that larger exposure differences should result in larger differences in political knowledge. The causal mechanism by which media choice affects learning thus involves changes in exposure to news and political information. A cable user who enjoys news will watch more news than before, especially at times when broadcast channels do not offer any. A subscriber more keen on entertainment will lower his exposure to political information. These changes in news exposure affect people's political knowledge. At first glance, a path model might be able to capture the successive effects of people's preferences on exposure and knowledge. Because of their methodological problems, however, I will not use any exposure measures in the following analysis of political knowledge, neither as control variables nor as intervening variables in a path model. This omission is less crucial than in might initially seem. Conditional Political Learning does not assume that the relationship between news exposure

---

16 Secondary data used for replication later in this chapter offered additional tests. They consistently generated the same pattern of results as the analysis of the N&E Survey.

and political knowledge is constant across levels of news and entertainment preference. In fact, it is quite likely that people who watched news for lack of more entertaining alternatives may not learn as much as people who watch news out of an intrinsic interest. Conditional Political Learning only stipulates, in keeping with the literature on passive learning, that those who prefer entertainment learn *at least something* from their accidental exposure to the news. The mediating impact of content preferences on learning from exposure to the news is an interesting topic for future research, but it requires experimental rather than survey research. Because it is not a central point in my theoretical framework, I instead focus on the direct link between content preferences and political knowledge. If people with a preference for entertainment did in fact watch without learning anything at all, then the following analysis should not reveal any differences between entertainment-seekers with and without cable access.

THE INTERNET AND MEDIA CHOICE

Cable television is only one technological advance that increases people's media choices. This chapter adds the Internet to the analysis. Cable was an important first step because it loosened the severe limits on choice in the most popular mass medium in history to date. But in terms of control and degree of choice, it is, or certainly will soon be, dwarfed by the Internet. The Internet resembles cable television insofar as both media multiply the amount and variety of content available. Hence, understanding the impact that cable television had on democratic politics may help us anticipate the impact of the Internet.

To the extent that content choice on the Internet follows similar patterns, Internet access should supply news-seekers with political information and offer plentiful distraction to those who want to avoid the news, thereby contributing to an increasing knowledge gap. While the two media are undoubtedly very different in many respects, access to the Internet, just like cable access, makes media choice more efficient. Internet users can, after all, spend their time online on entertainment or news Web sites. For example, according to a recent survey (Pew Internet and American Life Project 2003), similar numbers of Internet users report looking for political information, sports coverage, and "information about movies, books, or other leisure activities" on a typical day. Playing games and "looking for information from a government website" are equally likely uses. The variety of content people access online appears to be at least as large as the diversity of cable programming.[17]

17 Including an interaction of Internet access and REP in the exposure analysis (Table 4.1) should produce a smaller coefficient than the interaction of cable access and

Even though both cable television and the Internet increase media users' content choice, they are not perfect substitutes for each other. Compared at least to dial-up Internet service, cable offers greater immediacy and more visuals. The Web offers more detailed information and can be customized to a greater extent. Both media, in other words, have unique features, and access to both of them offers users the greatest flexibility. People with access to both media can watch a campaign speech on cable before later comparing online how different newspapers cover the event. Depending on their needs or the issue that interests them, they can actively search a wealth of political information online or passively consume cable politics. There is every reason to believe, then, that the effects of cable television and Internet access are additive and that the knowledge gap is largest for people with access to both new media.

According to the first wave of the N&E Survey, 39 percent had access to the Internet in early 2002. This percentage refers to respondents who connect to the Internet using their home computers. Because Knowledge Networks conducts interviews through WebTV, all respondents in the N&E Survey have basic Internet access on their television. Access through WebTV is much less convenient than through an Internet browser. For example, screen resolution is lower, and users do not have a mouse to navigate Web sites. It is still possible that respondents with WebTV can match content and preference more efficiently than people who do not have any Internet access whatsoever. Analytically, this is not a major concern because, if anything, it would produce conservative estimates of the true effect. If respondents with WebTV as their only means of using the Internet did indeed behave just as Internet users with dial-up or broadband connections, then the effect of content preference should be the same for all respondents in the N&E Survey. It would be harder to find significant differences between respondents defined as having no Internet access and those with dial-up or broadband access. For further reassurance, I later draw on data collected by the National Election Studies and the Pew Center for the People and the Press to replicate the results from the N&E Survey. Both NES and Pew samples include many respondents who do not have any Internet access.

REP because news fans with Internet (but not cable) access cannot watch more TV news. They can visit more Web sites, but the dependent variable does not measure online news exposure (which was not assessed in the N&E Survey). Internet users without cable access but a strong preference for entertainment should watch less TV news. Empirical analysis suggests this effect, but it does not offer enough cases for a proper test. (Only 120 respondents have an Internet connection other than WebTV, but no cable or satellite access.)

RELATIVE ENTERTAINMENT PREFERENCE AND
POLITICAL KNOWLEDGE

When television viewers have a choice between different media content, their preferences should predict what programs they will select and, by extension, how much they will learn about politics. Relative Entertainment Preference should thus affect political knowledge significantly more among cable subscribers than among nonsubscribers. Similarly, REP should have a stronger effect for Internet users. To test these hypotheses, I regress political knowledge on cable and Internet access, REP, and the interaction between REP and media access. This yields different estimates of the relationship between preferences and knowledge for those with and without access to each of the two media. I use the summary measure of REP by combining the genre ranking and the Manski measure. The dependent variable in the first model shown in Table 4.2 is knowledge of current events as measured in the second wave of the N&E Survey by a total of twelve knowledge questions (listed in the appendix to this chapter). The independent variables are from the first wave and were measured a year before the dependent variable. The model thus estimates the joint effect of preference and media access as of spring 2002 on political knowledge a year later.

One of the control variables is political knowledge in the first wave. Substantively, including respondents' political knowledge from fourteen months earlier makes the model a model of knowledge change, that is, political learning. It examines which respondents know more or less about politics than expected based on what they knew a year earlier. Technically, controlling for the lagged value of the dependent variable reduces problems of selection bias or reverse causation because the change in knowledge between the two waves cannot affect first-wave content preferences. I include other control variables to account for alternative explanations of political learning. Because cable is not affordable for all Americans, access is correlated with demographic variables, notably income and education. Also included are measures of the respondent's media environment that might affect political knowledge directly (e.g., the size of the respondent's media market and whether the respondent owns a VCR).[18]

The panel analysis provides clear support for the predicted effect of increased media choice. The two interactions of cable and Internet access

---

18 I excluded five respondents who answered all or all but one current events question correctly in Wave 1, but only one or none at all in Wave 2. These dramatic differences probably arise because respondents lacked the motivation to complete the knowledge items in the second wave.

Table 4.2. *The Effect of Relative Entertainment Preference on Changes in Political Knowledge (N&E Survey)*

	Panel Data	Cross-Sectional Data	
		Wave 2 Respondents Only	All Respondents
Cable access	1.12* (.55)	0.44 (.30)	0.59* (.27)
Internet access	0.99* (.49)	0.74** (.26)	0.20 (.23)
Relative Entertainment Preference, Mean (REP)	−0.49 (.78)	−0.19 (.43)	−0.51 (.37)
REP × Cable	**−1.75*** (.82)	**−0.75*** (.45)	**−0.83*** (.40)
REP × Internet	**−1.23*** (.70)	**−1.14*** (.37)	−0.36 (.32)
Wave 1 political knowledge	0.70** (.03)	–	–
Wave 1 civics knowledge	–	0.69** (.037)	0.61** (.03)
Education	0.093 (.059)	0.11** (.03)	0.17** (.027)
Income	0.057** (.019)	0.018* (.011)	0.017* (.009)
Gender	−0.28* (.13)	−0.24** (.07)	−0.32** (.06)
Age	0.022** (.004)	0.001 (.002)	0.001 (.002)
R's primary language is English	1.15** (.44)	0.33 (.27)	−0.020 (.19)
Racial minority	0.20 (.18)	−0.078 (.10)	−0.17* (.082)
Democrat	0.15 (.16)	−0.085 (.083)	−0.031 (.071)
Republican	0.22 (.17)	−0.022 (.092)	0.014 (.077)
R reports being registered to vote	0.36* (.19)	0.19* (.11)	0.11 (.083)
TV households, Nielsen 2002–3 (in 1,000,000)	0.039 (.038)	0.047* (.022)	0.022 (.019)
R owns home computer	−0.037 (.17)	−0.061 (.097)	0.070 (.082)
R owns VCR	−0.20 (.14)	−0.003 (.077)	−0.053 (.065)
Constant	−2.58** (.77)	2.03** (.44)	2.64** (.36)
Joint *F*-test for REP × Cable and REP × Internet	4.0, $p = .02$	6.5, $p = .002$	3.1, $p = .05$
R^2	0.41	0.32	0.30
N	1,545	1,550	2,201

** $p < .01$, * $p < .05$ (one-tailed).

Note: The dependent variable in the first model is current events knowledge in the second panel wave. The dependent variable in models two and three is current events knowledge in the first wave. All models are estimated by OLS. Cell entries are unstandardized regression coefficients with standard errors in parentheses.

with Relative Entertainment Preference are statistically significant in the predicted direction. The two main effects of media access are sizable and positive, indicating that greater choice significantly increased political knowledge between the two panel waves for respondents with a weak entertainment preference. To illustrate the interactions, Figure 4.4 plots

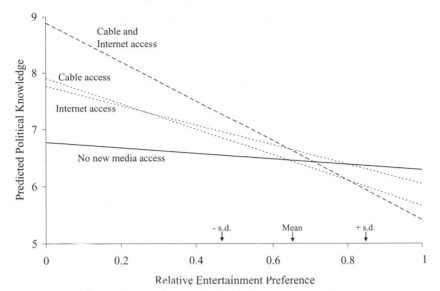

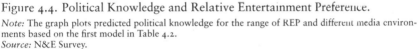

Figure 4.4. Political Knowledge and Relative Entertainment Preference.

Note: The graph plots predicted political knowledge for the range of REP and different media environments based on the first model in Table 4.2.

Source: N&E Survey.

the predicted values for different levels of media choice. REP has little effect on political knowledge for respondents with neither cable nor Internet access. In a media environment where people cannot choose between entertainment and news, it does not matter very much if they prefer one or the other. Among those with access to both new media, on the other hand, the impact of entertainment preference is substantial. The difference between someone with a strong preference for entertainment over news (one standard deviation above the mean of REP) and someone with a weak relative preference for entertainment (one standard deviation below) amounts to a knowledge gain of about 23 percent.[19]

19 Other control variables may have different effects for cable subscribers and non-subscribers. If these controls are correlated with their content preferences, the coefficients for the REP × Cable and REP × Internet interactions might be inflated. One way to check this is to enter interactions between cable (and Internet) access and all other variables. Despite considerable multicollinearity, this does not change the results very much at all. The REP × Cable interaction is −1.60 (instead of −1.75 in Table 4.2) with a standard error of .93, and the REP × Internet interaction −1.71 (instead of −1.23) with a standard error of .76, so both coefficients remain clearly statistically significant. Including the self-reported frequency of listening to radio news and reading a newspaper does not change the coefficients much either.

The strong impact of content preferences is perhaps most clearly revealed by a comparison with the effect of education, typically one of the strongest predictors of political knowledge (Delli Carpini and Keeter 1996). The effect of education does not even reach statistical significance when REP and its interactions with the media environment are included in the model. Without them, the coefficient for education is significant and 25 percent larger than in the first column of Table 4.2, suggesting that part of the learning effect we normally attribute to education is in fact better explained by differences in media content preferences. (And as I show later, content preferences are practically unrelated to education.) The change in knowledge associated with the difference between the most and the least educated respondents is little more than half an item on the twelve-item knowledge scale, clearly less than the effect of Relative Entertainment Preference among new media users.[20] According to Nie, Junn, and Stehlik-Barry (1996), "formal education is almost without exception the strongest factor in explaining what citizens do in politics and how they think about politics." In a high-choice environment, this does not appear to be true anymore. People's media content preference becomes a better predictor of political learning than even their level of education.

At first glance, the shape of the interactions in Figure 4.4 suggests that the increase in knowledge among news fans (those with low REP values) clearly exceeds the decrease in knowledge among entertainment fans (at the right end of the REP scale). This interpretation ignores the actual distribution of Relative Entertainment Preference, however. The majority of respondents are located on the right side of the REP scale. The mean REP score and its standard deviation, marked by arrows in Figure 4.4, show where respondents concentrate. Within the range between one standard deviation below and above the mean, the interaction effect looks a lot more symmetric and suggests that knowledge gains and losses may roughly balance out. Counteracting the symmetry around the mean is the long left tail of the distribution (recall Figure 4.2). The 10th percentile of REP is .37, which indicates that a small segment of the population has very strong preferences for news and is becoming noticeably more knowledgeable in the high-choice media environment. Ultimately, the comparison of gains and losses is tricky. I will return to it in the next chapter.

---

20 When the effect of education, too, is allowed to differ depending on the media environment, the interaction of education and Internet access approaches statistical significance ($p < .09$, one-tailed test), indicating that the impact of education on political learning is somewhat greater among Internet users. Even among them, it remains smaller than the effect of REP, however. Furthermore, the interactions between REP and media access remain statistically significant. The effect of education is the same for respondents with and without cable access.

The panel design provides a very rigorous test of my hypotheses because it assesses the change in political knowledge compared to a baseline set by performance in the first panel wave.[21] Without such a baseline, the estimation could be compromised by selection effects. According to the Conditional Political Learning model, preferences remain stable, but their effect on political learning changes when the media environment changes. A modification of the media environment, then, is the causal factor that over time produces knowledge increases (in the case of a preference for news) or decreases (if entertainment programming is preferred). Alternatively, however, more knowledgeable respondents with a preference for news may be more likely than less knowledgeable, but equally interested, respondents to have new media access in the first place. If the reverse happened for respondents who prefer entertainment, an interaction effect of content preferences and new media access would emerge, but the knowledge gap would not in fact have widened as a result of new media. The differences in the dependent variable would emerge not because individuals' political knowledge changed after they gained access to cable or the Internet but because of how individuals selected new media. The panel survey is the best method to rule out this alternative.

The panel analysis constitutes direct evidence for my hypothesis that knowledge gaps widen over time. Entertainment fans without cable and Internet access learned more over the course of fourteen months than entertainment fans with access to new media. This is not consistent with the counterhypothesis that sorting rather than changes in political knowledge explain the interactions of preferences and media environment. According to the sorting hypothesis, entertainment fans never knew more about politics than today because, although they may have been exposed to more news, they did not learn. The counterhypothesis is also inconsistent with the empirical evidence for passive learning (e.g., Graber 1988; Keeter and Wilson 1986; Krugman 1965; Krugman and Hartley 1970; Zukin and Snyder 1984).[22]

---

21 The results remain essentially the same when the panel model is specified using a differenced dependent variable (the difference in knowledge in the two panel waves), instead of including its lagged value as an independent variable.

22 A second aspect of the assumed dynamics of the widening knowledge gap cannot be tested with the available data. According to the theory, political knowledge changes are most likely when people have gained access to new media and adjusted their media use to their new media environment. I cannot test this proposition because the two panel waves of the N&E Survey were conducted only fourteen months apart, so few respondents actually gained new media access. The role of forgetting would complicate this analysis. Even a strong entertainment fan who gains access to the Internet, never watches TV news again, and never visits a political Web site does not immediately forget everything he knew about politics from his days in the

Despite the clear advantages of panel data, I now proceed to estimate the effects with a cross-sectional design using only Wave 1 data for one reason: If a cross-sectional design can detect the conditional effects of changes in the media environment too, then I can use other data sets that do not include a panel component to replicate the results. The N&E Survey is the only panel data set that includes the measures necessary to test my hypothesis. For corroboration, I have to rely on cross-sectional data.

A cross-sectional design still makes it possible to show static gaps in knowledge (rather than learning over time) among people with greater media access. In the cross-sectional case, however, the "baseline" cannot be knowledge assessed at an earlier point in time. Instead, I use knowledge that respondents presumably acquired earlier. Knowledge about governmental processes and institutions probably fits that description both because it is emphasized in civics education and because the correct answers do not change as frequently as the correct answers to questions about current events. If a respondent knows today that the Republican Party is more conservative than the Democratic Party or that a president can serve only two four-year terms, there is a reasonable probability that the respondent also knew these things last year or five years ago. Answers to questions about current events, on the other hand, are by definition not knowable in advance. Hence, I can use civics knowledge as a quasi-lagged dependent variable in the cross-sectional data set. The dependent variable in columns 2 and 3 of Table 4.2 is thus Wave 1 knowledge of current events, while civics knowledge, also measured in Wave 1, serves as a control variable.[23] Column 2 includes only respondents who were

captive audience. It might thus take some time before the knowledge gap starts to widen between news and entertainment fans after they have gained access to a new medium.

For the same reason, the panel specification may understate the true effect of content preferences because first wave political knowledge itself is partly determined by preferences among respondents who have enjoyed cable or Internet access for some time. For them, the effects of transitioning from low choice to high choice may have occurred already by the time of the first wave. The cross-sectional models that follow avoid this problem but raise their own methodological concerns.

23 The civics knowledge index is the number of correct responses to the questions about judicial review, presidential veto, maximum number of presidential terms, and the more conservative party (see appendix for this chapter).

This approach is inconsistent with a strong interpretation of political knowledge as a "general," unidimensional construct (Delli Carpini and Keeter 1996; Zaller 1986), but convincing evidence exists in favor of different, domain-specific types of political knowledge (Hutchings 2001; Iyengar 1990). If civics knowledge is indeed acquired earlier and is more stable, running the models in Table 4.2 with civics knowledge as the dependent variable should not yield the same strong interaction effects. And in fact it does not.

also interviewed in Wave 2, while column 3 shows the same model for all Wave 1 respondents.

The results for the cross-sectional analysis are slightly weaker than for the panel setup, but they reveal the same pattern of interaction effects between preferences and media access. In the model in column 3, only the interaction of REP and cable access is significant. In both models, however, the joint addition of the two interaction terms increases the model fit significantly (see bottom of Table 4.2). Including civics knowledge in the model as an independent variable controls for "initial" differences in knowledge between respondents and makes it more difficult to argue that a selection effect drives the results. If people with a preference for news had been more knowledgeable to begin with – and access to new media did not affect their knowledge at all – then civics knowledge should have left little variance to explain for REP and its interaction with new media access. The results throughout this chapter indicate that this is not the case. A panel design with two measures of knowledge at different points in time is even better because it does not need to rely on the assumption that baseline knowledge was in fact acquired before the change in the media environment occurred.[24] But it is useful to know that even cross-sectional data analysis can demonstrate the presence of wider knowledge gaps between news and entertainment fans in a high-choice media environment because it allows me to use several cross-sectional data sets to replicate the results later in this chapter.[25]

24 Using the first wave current knowledge index is not completely straightforward either because the two sets of items used to measure current knowledge in the two panel waves are not specific enough to test knowledge of issues that were in the news exactly during the time of the interview. For example, a respondent who in the second wave answers correctly that Donald Rumsfeld is the secretary of defense may have learned this even before the first panel wave as the correct answer remained the same since then. Even if this respondent had cable access and a strong preference for entertainment, and therefore became less likely to learn about new political issues, he or she may still remember several answers in the second panel wave. This argument suggests that the panel setup might underestimate the effect of cable and the Internet. It also emphasizes the conceptual distinction between different kinds of knowledge questions.

25 The Pearson correlation between the current events knowledge in Wave 1 and Wave 2 is .57. The correlation between civics knowledge and current knowledge is .51 in Wave 1 and .49 in Wave 2. Empirically, the panel and cross-sectional relationships are of similar strength, but conceptually the former speaks primarily to the persistence of knowledge over time, whereas the latter tell us about domain-specificity – how likely people with knowledge of one "domain" of politics are to also know the answer to a question about another domain (Iyengar 1990; Zaller 1986).

Participatory Effects of Media Choice

The analysis of news exposure presented earlier in the chapter is important to properly interpret the growing knowledge gap between entertainment fans and news-seekers. Without the exposure evidence, an alternative explanation for the knowledge gap would have been conceivable. Learning among entertainment fans with cable access might decline even though they continued to watch network news if the substitution of hard news with softer features makes the news less informative. According to this alternative hypothesis, changes in the content of news, not media choice, would be the cause of their lower knowledge. Or entertainment fans with cable could have shifted their news consumption to cable news formats that are not as enlightening as the network news. Again, media choice would be part of the explanation, but in a different way than I have argued.

The exposure analysis is inconsistent with these alternative explanations of the widening knowledge gap. It strongly suggests that entertainment fans with cable access watch less television news than their otherwise similar counterparts without cable. Likewise, news fans with cable watch more news than news fans without cable. These diverging patterns of exposure lead to a widening knowledge gap among cable subscribers. If the alternative hypothesis were correct, modifying the content of news to make it more informative could lower knowledge gaps again. The notion of Conditional Political Learning and the empirical evidence presented in this chapter offer no such easy way out. Entertainment fans with new media access are less knowledgeable because they have abandoned the news audience altogether, not because they have switched to less informative news.

RELATIVE ENTERTAINMENT PREFERENCE AND TURNOUT

Exposure to political information increases the likelihood that an individual will go to the polls on Election Day. As discussed in greater detail in Chapter 3, exposure motivates people and increases their political knowledge, which in turn makes it more likely that they will notice a difference between candidates or see a reason to care about an election. Knowledge of facts like these increases people's probability of turning out. Among those who use new media to access more political information, turnout should therefore increase. Entertainment fans with a cable box or Internet connection, on the other hand, will miss both the interest- and the information-based effect of broadcast news on turnout. Hence, increasing penetration of new media technologies should widen the turnout gap. People who prefer news vote at higher rates, and those with other preferences increasingly stay home from the polls, so turnout difference between the two groups should increase. This is my fifth hypothesis (see Table 2.2).

Table 4.3. *The Effect of Relative Entertainment Preference on Turnout*
(N&E Survey)

	Wave 2	Wave 1	
		Wave 2 Respondents Only	All Respondents
Cable access	0.46 (.59)	1.59** (.67)	1.26* (.57)
Internet access	0.96* (.57)	1.02 (.67)	0.29 (.53)
Relative Entertainment Preference, Mean (REP)	0.17 (.82)	0.47 (.89)	0.22 (.75)
REP× Cable	−0.68 (.88)	−1.75* (.98)	−1.37* (.82)
REP× Internet	−1.40* (.79)	−1.89* (.93)	−0.86 (.73)
Wave 1 political knowledge	0.17** (.03)	0.15** (.033)	0.13** (.028)
Education	0.23** (.06)	0.031 (.069)	0.16** (.056)
Gender	0.22 (.14)	0.54** (.16)	0.42** (.12)
Age	0.038** (.005)	0.029** (.005)	0.032** (.004)
Income	0.069** (.02)	0.059** (.023)	0.041* (.018)
R's primary language is English	1.07 (.65)	−0.27 (.77)	−1.17* (.52)
Racial minority	0.10 (.18)	0.091 (.21)	0.034 (.16)
Democrat	1.13** (.17)	0.014 (.18)	0.22 (.14)
Republican	1.00** (.16)	0.21 (.20)	0.48** (.16)
R reports being registered to vote	3.20** (.33)	3.15** (.22)	3.01** (.17)
TV households, Nielsen 2002–3 (in 1,000,000)	−0.057 (.039)	−0.057 (.048)	−0.080* (.038)
R owns home computer	0.18 (.18)	0.22 (.21)	0.22 (.17)
R owns VCR	0.32* (.15)	0.31* (.17)	0.36** (.13)
Constant	−9.41** (1.07)	−5.65** (1.13)	−4.88** (.81)
Joint LR test for REP × Cable and REP × Internet	3.9, $p = .14$	7.6, $p = .02$	4.5, $p = .10$
Pseudo R^2	0.30	0.31	0.32
Log likelihood	720.1	−587.4	−889.2
N	1,507	1,515	2,158

** $p < .01$, * $p < .05$ (one-tailed).

Note: The dependent variable in the first model is self-reported turnout in 2002, measured in the second panel wave. The dependent variable in models two and three is self-reported turnout in the 2000 congressional elections, measured in the first wave. Cell entries are logit coefficients with standard errors in parentheses.

The models in Table 4.3 test the hypothesis by regressing turnout on Relative Entertainment Preference, access to cable and Internet, and their interactions (plus demographic controls). The model in the first column uses Wave 2 data. The dependent variable is self-reported turnout in the

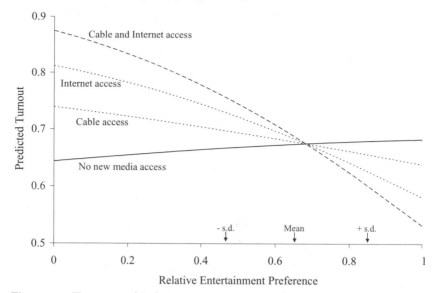

Figure 4.5. Turnout and Relative Entertainment Preference.

Note: The graph plots the predicted probability of turnout for the range of REP and different media environments from the model in column 1 of Table 4.3.

Source: N&E Survey.

2002 House election. The models in the second and third column use Wave 1 data and self-reported turnout in the 2000 House election as the dependent variable. Unlike column 3, which uses all respondents, column 2 includes only respondents who were later reinterviewed. The difference between columns 2 and 3 gives some indication as to the importance of panel attrition. Comparing the coefficients for the six interactions in Table 4.3, all are in the predicted direction, but two of them fail to reach statistical significance – one with cable ($p = .22$ in column 1) and one with Internet access ($p = .12$ in column 3). The joint likelihood ratio tests indicate that the addition of the two interaction terms improves the model fit significantly in two of the three models. For the third model, the improvement is only marginally significant. Yet while a few of the estimates lack statistical precision, the substantive size of the main and interaction effects provides strong support for the hypothesis, as shown by the predicted values in Figure 4.5 (derived from the first model in Table 4.3).

After people obtain access to new media, their content preferences become a powerful predictor of turnout. Among respondents without either cable or Internet access, the relationship between content preference and turnout is not statistically different from zero. For cable subscribers and Internet users, in contrast, the effects of REP are sizable. With access to both media, the predicted turnout probability for a person who prefers entertainment to news quite strongly (one standard deviation above the mean of REP) is .61. Holding everything else equal, but moving to one standard deviation below the mean of REP, a weak relative preference for entertainment, generates a predicted probability of .76, a 26 percent increase in the probability of voting. As in the case of political knowledge, the effect of preferences in the high-choice environment appears roughly symmetric once the distribution of REP is considered.

Including political knowledge in the models reduces the magnitude of the effects by less than a third (and only for the cable effect). This result could arise for two reasons: Either my measure of political knowledge does not capture the type of knowledge most relevant to encouraging turnout or exposure to political information motivates people to vote even when it does not affect their political knowledge. Regardless of which reason is more important, greater media choice makes content preferences a major influence on turnout. Again, just as in the case of political knowledge, the effect of preference exceeds the effect of education, typically one of the strongest predictors.[26]

REPLICATING RESULTS FOR DIFFERENT CONTEXTS: NES AND PEW

The N&E Survey handily supports the hypothesis that greater media choice increased inequality in the distributions of political knowledge and turnout. Yet it can only do so for a time when most Americans had enjoyed access to cable television for many years, and the Internet had reached about half of all households. The main purpose of replicating the analysis using additional (secondary) data – in addition to providing a general robustness check – is to determine if the results hold in different contexts and for different points in the diffusion process of cable television and the Internet. Survey data for the replications come from the National Election Studies and the Media Consumption Surveys (MCS) conducted biannually by the Pew Center for the People and the Press. The NES conducts both face-to-face and telephone interviews; Pew uses phone interviews. Unfortunately, the main drawback of secondary data is a big one. Neither the NES nor Pew's MCS include direct measures

---

26 Including the lagged dependent variable (self-reported turnout in the 2000 House election, as measured in the first panel wave) in the model of 2002 turnout leaves the result largely unchanged. The coefficient for the cable interaction increases (in absolute value) to −0.74 (.91), while the coefficient for the Internet interaction decreases to −1.02 (.81). Conducting the same analysis using only the ranking measures of REP produces slightly stronger results that reach statistical significance (Prior 2005a).

of the key concept, entertainment preference. Instead, only a few questions about exposure to entertainment shows are available. Hence, no measure derived from these data comes even close in construct validity to the measure in the N&E Survey. The two NES data sets that ask about cable and Internet access – the NES 1996 and 2000 – include a variety of knowledge items. For each data set, a knowledge measure is created by summing the number of correct responses to fourteen knowledge questions (listed in the appendix to this chapter). Turnout in the NES 1996 is assessed by respondent's self-reported vote in the 1996 House election. Vote measures in the Pew surveys are based on questions about voting in the last presidential (and, in the MCS 1996, House) election.[27]

Although secondary data sources provide no direct preference measures, it is possible to infer respondents' relative preferences approximately from the type of content they report watching. High entertainment exposure per se does not necessarily indicate a greater preference for entertainment. Respondents with high entertainment exposure may watch a lot of television in general, without necessarily preferring entertainment strongly to other genres. Hence, the mix of exposure to different genres, rather than absolute exposure to entertainment alone, should be a (very rough) indicator of underlying relative preference. Respondents who watch entertainment programs but little or no news probably do so out of a preference for entertainment. High news exposure and low entertainment exposure would reflect a preference for news. The ratio of entertainment viewing to overall viewing thus yields the best possible measure of Relative Entertainment Preference in NES and Pew data. This ratio is defined as follows:

$$\text{Relative Entertainment Preference (REP)} = \frac{\text{Entertainment Viewing}}{\text{Entertainment Viewing} + \text{News Viewing}}$$

News Viewing is the average number of days per week the respondent watched national and local news. The particular operationalization

27 Any specific candidate named is coded as 1; "did not vote," "don't know," and not remembering which candidate the vote was cast for are coded as 0. The resulting measures show less overreporting than common in the NES: 50 percent turnout in the MCS 2000, 55 percent in the MCS 1998, and 46 percent (1994 House election) and 62 percent (1992 presidential election) in the MCS 1996. By comparison, turnout in the 1996 presidential election was 76 percent according to the NES 1996 post-election interview. To avoid the most severe bias due to overreporting, I use the NES turnout measure of voting in the 1996 House election instead (71 percent). Respondents who did not know whether they voted or who refused to answer (1996, 3.8 percent; 1998, 6.1 percent; 2000, 7.3 percent) could be excluded from the analysis. Respondents who reported voting, but did not remember whom they voted for (1996, 5.1 percent; 1998, 6.7 percent; 2000, 8.8 percent), could be coded as not having voted. The results change little for these alternative specifications.

of Entertainment Viewing depends on the items in the surveys. For the NES 2000, Entertainment viewing is average exposure to *Jeopardy, Wheel of Fortune,* and "television talk shows such as *Oprah Winfrey, Rosie O'Donnell,* or *Jerry Springer.*" The NES 1996 measures entertainment viewing as the average daily viewing of "*Jeopardy* or *Wheel of Fortune*" and *Dr Quinn, Medicine Woman.* In the Pew data, Entertainment Viewing is operationalized as watching *Entertainment Tonight, Jerry Springer,* and *Oprah* (MCS 2000), watching *Entertainment Tonight* and MTV and reading *People Magazine* (MCS 1998), and watching *Hardcopy, Jerry Springer,* and MTV (MCS 1996). All items used four-point response formats ("regularly," "sometimes," "hardly ever," "never"). REP cannot be computed for respondents who reported no information and entertainment viewing at all. These respondents are excluded from the analysis (2.4 percent in the MCS 1996, 2 percent in the MCS 1998, 4.5 percent in the MCS 2000, 5.8 percent in the NES 1996, and 9.9 percent in the NES 2000).

The resulting REP measures range from 0 to 1 and have means of between .21 (NES 1996) and .28 (MCS 2000) with standard deviations between .19 and .28. Evidently, the ratio measures are skewed toward news preference. This is not surprising because the surveys asked about very few entertainment programs and – with the exception of the NES 2000 talk show item – only about specific programs rather than genres. Many respondents surely reported low entertainment exposure not because they do not like entertainment, but because they were not asked about their favorite shows. Yet even though the REP measures built from NES and Pew data underestimate people's preference for entertainment, they still identify a set of respondents to whom entertainment programming is relatively more attractive. To verify that measures of REP are roughly comparable for the different data sets, I examined the relationship between demographics and REP for each data source. Demographics have very similar effects on the more precise REP measure in the N&E Survey and on the somewhat noisier ones in NES and Pew surveys.

To test the knowledge and turnout hypotheses, political knowledge (Table 4.4) and turnout (Table 4.5) are again regressed on access to cable television and the Internet, Relative Entertainment Preference, and the respective interactions. Overall, the replications clearly support the hypothesis that greater media choice makes content preferences better predictors of people's political knowledge and turnout. All interaction terms of cable access and REP are in the predicted direction and six of the seven are statistically significant. The conditioning effect of Internet access is evident for turnout only. To summarize the joint effect of preferences and media access in these replications, I use the average of the coefficients across the two knowledge models and the five turnout models, respectively, to graph predicted values for the range of REP in Figure 4.6.

Table 4.4. *The Effect of Relative Entertainment Preference on Political Knowledge (NES Surveys)*

	NES 1996	NES 2000
Cable access	0.26 (.22)	0.04 (.23)
Internet access	0.15 (.22)	0.39* (.21)
Relative Entertainment Preference (REP)	−0.17 (.60)	0.06 (.59)
REP × Cable	−1.33* (.68)	−1.38* (.64)
REP × Internet	0.80 (.68)	0.09 (.52)
Education	0.44** (.05)	0.58** (.05)
Gender	−0.64** (.15)	−0.88** (.14)
Age	0.03** (.01)	0.04** (.005)
Income (MV imputed)	0.07** (.02)	0.08** (.02)
Income was imputed	−0.22 (.26)	−0.14 (.19)
African American	−1.35** (.25)	−0.78** (.24)
Hispanic or Latino	−	−0.41 (.31)
Other minority	−0.15 (.45)	−0.07 (.30)
R works 20+ hours per week	0.01 (.18)	−0.38* (.17)
R lives in the South	−0.31* (.16)	−0.74** (.15)
Party ID	0.02 (.03)	−0.02 (.04)
Strength of party ID	0.37** (.08)	0.43** (.07)
Frequency of political discussion with friends or family	1.60** (.24)	1.29** (.17)
Constant	3.52** (.46)	−0.25 (.44)
R^2	0.29	0.40
N	1,284	1,334

** $p < .01$, * $p < .05$ (one-tailed).

Note: The dependent variables in both models are summary knowledge scales. Cell entries are unstandardized OLS coefficients and standard errors in parentheses.

Political knowledge of respondents without access to cable or Internet is unrelated to their content preference. For those with access to cable television, on the other hand, moving from low to high entertainment preference corresponds to a 20 percent drop in political knowledge. The effect of REP among Internet users is insignificant and not even in the predicted direction. This result is the only replication failure. The results for Internet users suggest the possibility that early adopters differed somewhat from those who obtained access later and that the control variables cannot adjust for these differences. Three of the four interactions between REP and Internet access in the earliest data sets (from 1996) are not significant (although the fourth is large and significant in the predicted direction). In 1996, the Internet was still relatively new. Less than 18 percent of all U.S.

Table 4.5. *The Effect of Relative Entertainment Preference on Turnout (NES and Pew Surveys)*

	NES 1996	Pew 2000	Pew 1998	Pew 1996	
	1996 House	1996 Pres.	1996 Pres.	1992 Pres.	1994 House
Cable	0.49** (.21)	0.25** (.11)	0.18* (.10)	0.59** (.15)	0.36* (.14)
Internet	0.21 (.21)	0.62** (.11)	0.54** (.12)	0.58** (.18)	0.34* (.17)
REP	0.44 (.54)	0.08 (.27)	0.05 (.24)	-0.84* (.38)	-0.64 (.40)
REP× Cable	**-1.28* (.61)**	**-0.57* (.29)**	**-0.26 (.28)**	**-0.99* (.44)**	**-1.15* (.46)**
REP× Internet	**0.39 (.66)**	**-0.67** (.28)**	**-0.79** (.30)**	**-1.11* (.52)**	**-0.10 (.53)**
Education	0.31** (.05)	0.22** (.02)	0.26** (.02)	0.23** (.03)	0.22** (.03)
Income (Imputations for MV)	0.07** (.01)	0.10** (.02)	0.11** (.02)	0.08** (.02)	0.15** (.02)
Income missing	0.21 (.27)	-0.91** (.09)	-0.79** (.08)	-0.60* (.14)	0.07 (.14)
Gender	0.19 (.14)	-0.10 (.06)	0.13* (.06)	-0.21** (.08)	-0.13* (.08)
Age	0.04** (.005)	0.04** (.002)	0.04** (.002)	0.04** (.003)	0.05** (.003)
Employment status	0.09 (.17)	0.19** (.07)	0.17** (.07)	0.26** (.08)	-0.19* (.08)
Size of town	–	-0.07* (.03)	-0.02 (.03)	-0.02 (.04)	0.05 (.04)
Party ID	0.11** (.04)	–	–	–	–
Strength of party ID	0.61** (.08)	–	–	–	–
Constant	-4.87** (.46)	-3.25** (.21)	-3.19** (.18)	-2.45** (.26)	-3.70** (.27)
Log likelihood	-677.5	-3109.9	-3560.9	-2090.2	-2089.7
N	1,410	2,910	2,856	1,674	1,620

$** p < .01, * p < .05$ (one-tailed).

Note: The dependent variable in these models is self-reported turnout. Cell entries are logit coefficients and standard errors in parentheses.

Participatory Effects of Media Choice

a) Political Knowledge

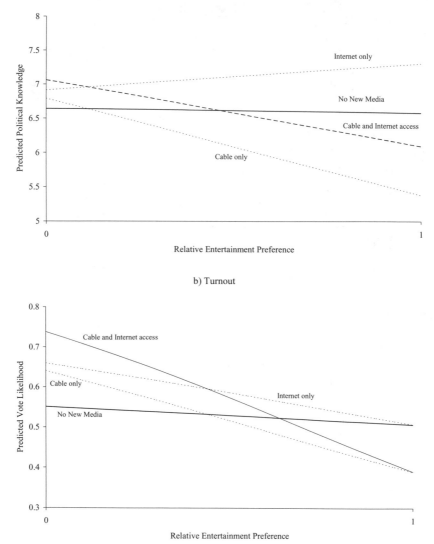

b) Turnout

Figure 4.6. Pew and NES Replications, Average Effects on Political Knowledge and Turnout.

Note: The graphs plot predicted values based on the average of the coefficients in Tables 4.3 and 4.4.

households could connect to the Internet in 1997 according to the Current Population Survey. Some people without a connection at home used the Internet at work, but presumably their online activity was largely limited to work-related use, thus constraining the effect of content preferences. In surveys conducted after 1996 (including the N&E Survey), the interaction of REP and Internet access is negative and statistically significant in four of the five tests.

The turnout effects in the replications mirror the N&E analysis quite precisely. The likelihood of turnout among people without access to cable or the Internet is just above chance regardless of their entertainment preference. For those with cable and the Internet, the likelihood of casting a vote drops from over .7 among people with the least interest in entertainment to .4 among those with the strongest preference for entertainment.

To rule out that the technological savvy of new media users or their "lifestyle" accounts for the observed results, I used a number of variables in the MCS 2000 that asked respondents whether they owned a cell phone, a pager, a DVD player, and a palm pilot. I ran the same model of vote likelihood as in Table 4.5 with these variables instead of cable and Internet access. Whereas the coefficients for the interactions with cable and Internet access were large and statistically significant, none of the interactions of the REP index with the other technological devices produced results that even approached significance. Consequently, increased media choice, not some other aspect related to new media technology or its users, is the likely cause of the observed effects.

Beyond replicating the N&E results, the analysis of NES and Pew data adds an important element by demonstrating that access to new media conditioned the effect of preferences as early as 1996 (the first year for which we have data to test the hypothesis). According to a competing hypothesis, respondents with strong content preferences may have had access to these media earlier. In that case, the fact that political knowledge and turnout are higher among news-seekers and lower among entertainment-seekers with greater media would not imply any changes in knowledge and turnout levels, only that these two segments were the most and least knowledgeable in the first place. The results of the N&E Survey panel analysis make this claim hard to sustain. The fact that Relative Entertainment Preference was a better predictor among cable viewers and Internet users repeatedly between 1996 and 2003 adds further evidence against the alternative hypothesis (although the very early Internet users may be an exception). During this period, the percentage of cable subscribers rose from 69 percent in 1996 (MCS 1996) to 81 percent in 2003 (N&E Survey), and the percentage of Americans with Internet access increased from a mere 21 percent in April of 1996 (MCS 1996) to

62 percent in 2000 (NES 2000). Demographic similarities between Internet users and the public as a whole increased (Bimber 2003, 213). At some point in this diffusion process, even people with moderate content preferences would have obtained access to new media.

Yet this analysis has shown significant effects both in 1996 (even for Internet users in one instance), when only 15 percent of the population had access to both cable and the Internet, and in 2000, when 53 percent did. It thus becomes implausible to argue that over the period of this analysis, respondents with strong content preferences were *always* more likely to have greater media choice. The effect of increased choice appears to be quite stable over the past decade, even though more and more people gained access to cable television and the Internet.

With only a few exceptions, the impact of cable television and the Internet – both their main and interactive effects – were statistically and substantively similar in this chapter's analyses. Even though the various survey questions designed to assess Relative Entertainment Preference all made reference to television, the resulting measures proved equally capable of predicting turnout changes for Internet users. These results suggest that preferences become better predictors of media use as content choice increases, regardless of the medium. People who like news use both the Internet and their additional cable channels as sources of news and political information.

Successful replication minimizes concerns about one other methodological issue noted earlier: Knowledge Networks, the company that conducted the N&E Survey, provides its respondents with WebTV to conduct periodic interviews. Strictly speaking, the N&E Survey therefore does not permit inferences about the effect of Internet access. That dial-up (and broadband) Internet access does significantly boost the impact of content preference compared to a WebTV connection suggests that accessing the Internet on a television set is not quite the same thing as even a dial-up connection. Still, replicating results on data sets that include respondents with no Internet connection at all bolsters the robustness of my findings. Substantively, the more important point is that differences in the efficiency of media access probably matter as much as the difference between no access and presently typical dial-up connections. As Internet connections become faster, the impact of content preferences is likely to increase further.

In all, replication using a number of different data sets was successful. The hypothesized conditioning effect of media choice has been shown for very different points in the diffusion process of cable television and the Internet (1996 to 2003), for different interview modes (phone, face-to-face, and Web-based) and political contexts (during election campaigns and mid-term), as well as for different measures of Relative Entertainment Preference.

THE DEMOGRAPHIC PROFILES OF NEWS JUNKIES
AND ENTERTAINMENT FANS

In the high-choice media environment, content preferences become powerful determinants of news exposure, political knowledge, and turnout. So who are the people who like news better than entertainment? Who prefers entertainment? These are important questions for two reasons. First, the significance of Relative Entertainment Preference as a predictor of political involvement would be somewhat limited if it was just a proxy for demographic characteristics. If, on the other hand, demographics were only weakly related to REP, its effects would represent an independent and previously little noticed influence on several important dimensions of political involvement.

Second, analysis of the relationship between REP and demographic variables begins to address the implications of greater media choice for political representation. If the demographics of news and entertainment fans were similar, news fans might be able to represent the interests of entertainment fans whose electoral participation declines. Demographic similarity between news and entertainment fans is not a sufficient condition for effective representation, of course. It does not imply shared political values or issue preferences. But an absence of demographic similarity would all but rule out effective representation.

To present the demographic profiles of news junkies and entertainment fans, I regressed the combined measure of Relative Entertainment Preference in the N&E Survey on a variety of demographic variables and several indicators of the respondent's media environment. Figure 4.7 presents the results graphically, as deviations from the Relative Entertainment Preference of a demographic profile that corresponds almost exactly to the mean REP value in the sample of .659 (on the 0–1 scale).[28] A white married employed male with average education, age, and income whose first language is English and who lives in a household in a medium-sized media market with basic cable access and a VCR, but no Internet access or personal computer, has a predicted Relative Entertainment Preference of .659. The vertical line in Figure 4.7 marks the predicted REP value for this profile. The bars in the figure show deviations from this reference group for other demographics. For example, the predicted REP for a respondent

---

28 The regression also controls for English as first language, but those results are not shown because only sixty respondents did not speak English as a first language.

Figure 4.7. The Demographic Predictors of Relative Entertainment Preference.

Note: This figure shows Relative Entertainment Preference for different demographic groups. These values are based on an OLS regression of the combined REP measure on the listed variables (as well as English as first language). The vertical line is the predicted REP value for a white married employed male with average education, age, and income whose first language is English and who lives in a household in a medium-sized media market with basic cable access and a VCR, but no Internet access or personal computer. The bars in the figure represent deviations from this reference profile. The horizontal axis at the top characterizes the distribution of REP by its mean, standard deviation, as well as 10th, 25th, 75th, and 90th percentiles.

Source: N&E Survey.

with an otherwise identical demographic profile but a college degree is .037 lower (i.e., .622). A woman with otherwise identical demographics has a predicted REP of .667, .008 higher than the reference profile. The horizontal axis at the bottom of the graph indicates these deviations in units of REP.

The magnitude of demographic differences becomes clear when it is compared to the horizontal axis at the top, which summarizes the overall variation in Relative Entertainment Preference. It characterizes the distribution of REP by its mean and its standard deviation, as well as its 10th, 25th, 75th, and 90th percentiles. (See Figure 4.2 for a plot of the distribution.) The difference in REP between someone at the mean level of education and a college educated respondent, for example, is equivalent to one-fifth of one standard deviation of REP. The difference between a man and woman is one-twentieth of one standard deviation.

The size of the bars in Figure 4.7 provides an intuitive illustration of the fact that demographic variables do not explain REP well. A preference for entertainment is not a stand-in for education or socioeconomic status. Although college-educated people, men, and the wealthy and the unemployed are significantly fonder of news (as indicated by lower REP values), these differences are substantively very small (less than a fifth of one standard deviation of REP). Respondents who own a VCR or subscribe to premium cable channels like entertainment a little better, but these differences too are small by substantive standards. The only sizable predictor of Relative Entertainment Preference is age. Young people enjoy entertainment a lot more than news and political information, while people over 64 prefer news quite strongly. Without age in the model, the demographic variables in Figure 4.7 explain only 7 percent of the variance in Relative Entertainment Preference. Even with the four age categories, the R^2 is only .13. When it comes to Relative Entertainment Preference, there is little accounting for taste.

The failure of socioeconomic status to explain REP points to an important attribute of content preferences that only increases the importance of their effects. Content preferences cut across gender, race, income, and levels of education. The chances that a wealthy, well-educated American and a poor American without a high-school diploma prefer entertainment to news are essentially the same. As a result, the chances are essentially the same that either one of them will abandon the news in the high-choice media environment. This analysis thus does not close the door to descriptive representation (Pitkin 1967) of entertainment fans by news junkies. As far as demographics are concerned, news junkies look like potential stand-ins for the political dropouts of the high-choice media environment. Neither do news junkies have a fundamentally different view of politics. Respondents' party identification and ideology are not related to Relative Entertainment Preference either. News junkies are not systematically more liberal, more conservative, more Republican, or more Democratic than entertainment fans. They do differ in one important aspect that will become important in Chapter 7: Entertainment fans are decidedly less partisan than news fans.[29] Final judgment on the promise of news junkies as representatives of entertainment fans has to wait.

CONCLUSION

Even though political information is abundant and more readily available than ever before, political knowledge has decreased for a substantial portion of the electorate: entertainment fans with access to new media. Ironically, the share of politically uninformed people has risen since we entered the so-called "information age." Television as a medium has often been denigrated as "dumb," but, helped by the features of the broadcast environment, it was more successful in reaching less educated and less interested segments of the population than the "encyclopedic" Internet. It is true that the words of an entire television newscast fit easily on one page of a newspaper. It is true that the Internet offers more politically relevant information than many libraries. But it would be a mistake to base our expectation about the impact of a medium on its content alone.

Many early assessments of the political impact of the Internet had the distinct flavor of blessing or disaster. The Internet would either lift everyone up into the strata of good and effective citizens or spread universal chaos by balkanizing and privatizing politics. While these predictions differed dramatically in their directions, they agreed that everyone would be affected to more or less the same extent. In the old tradition of McLuhian determinism, forecasters expected the Internet to imprint its properties on people, and the controversy was only about what these properties were.

---

29 Relative Entertainment Preference correlates with political interest. This is to be expected since both variables measure an intrinsic motivation to follow public life. The correlation is not as strong as one might expect, however. When a standard four-point scale of political interest is added to the demographic model discussed in this section, the R^2 increases to .17 and the difference between the highest and lowest category of political interest amounts to .13 on the REP scale – about two-thirds of a standard deviation. Without any other variables in the model, this difference increases to .19, but that is still only one standard deviation of REP. One reason for the relatively weak relationship is that the two variables refer to different domains (news or politics). Another likely reason is the limited theoretical range of the political interest measure. By making respondents choose between only four levels of interest (where the lowest is so socially undesirable that very few respondents selected it), standard political interest measures squander a lot of meaningful variance.

The Impact of Cable TV and Internet

This study developed and confirmed fundamentally different expectations regarding the impact of the Internet on political behavior. Cable television and the Internet clearly do not affect everyone in the same way. Both media offer their audience the opportunity to learn more about politics and find additional motivation to go to the polls, but only people who enjoy the news take advantage of this opportunity. For those who prefer entertainment, the temptations of new media lead elsewhere. Content preferences have little effect on turnout in the absence of media choice. Only in a high-choice environment does turnout depend on people's relative preferences for news and entertainment. With access to cable television and the Internet, however, content preferences become an important predictor of turnout, rivaling even education in its impact. Even though predicted turnout levels do not differ by content preferences for respondents with neither cable nor Internet access, an avid news-seeker becomes almost twice as likely to go to the polls as a devoted entertainment fan when both have access to these two new media.

The Conditional Political Learning model emphasizes that changes in the availability of media content can affect news consumption, learning, and turnout, *even in the absence of preference changes*. People's media use may change in a modified media environment, even if their preferences have not. By this logic, the increasing share of people who avoid news completely is *not* an indication of reduced political interest. Interest in politics may never have been as high as audience shares for evening news led us to believe. There was simply nothing else to watch. With the growth of cable television, the conditions for passive learning about politics came to an end. Analyses of three different sets of surveys all show that individual preferences become better predictors of political knowledge and turnout in a media environment that offers more content diversity and choice. They reveal that those who prefer entertainment and have access to new media display the lowest levels of political knowledge and turnout.

The analysis in the past two chapters has examined how changes in the media environment affect the distribution of political knowledge in the population. The surprising finding about entertainment fans is not that their knowledge and turnout rates are quite low, but that there were times when their knowledge and turnout were significantly higher than today. In Chapter 3, I argued that the media environment of the time can explain their unexpected political involvement. In this chapter, the surprising result about people who like the news is that there appears to be room for knowledge and turnout increases in the high-choice media environment. According to our typical picture of these highly interested people, they always knew a lot and were pretty much certain to vote. They did, after all, always have newspapers, magazines, and books with which to educate themselves about politics. The results in this chapter demonstrate that cable news, political Web sites, emailed news summaries, newsgroups, and blogs make a difference, even compared to a supposedly pretty high baseline. My data do not allow me to determine if people with a preference for news know more about politics today because more political information is available or because information-rich media sources in the low-choice environment were more clumsy to handle, but contained just as much information. Without a doubt, cable news channels and the Internet make political information available faster and more easily than print media used to do. Political information online is also cheaper than it used to be when people had to buy the paper every day or subscribe. In sum, it is probably a lot more rewarding (and time-consuming) to be a news junkie today than it was three decades ago.

Following the formulation of the knowledge gap hypothesis by Tichenor, Donohue, and Olien (1970), numerous studies have examined the diffusion of information in the population and the differences that emerge between more and less informed individuals (for reviews see Gaziano 1997; Viswanath and Finnegan 1996). Surprisingly, research in the knowledge gap tradition has almost completely ignored the role of media environments in general and of content choice in particular. Even though Tichenor, Donohue, and Olien's (1970) original publication focused on differences by level of education, subsequent research has shown knowledge gaps between more and less interested or motivated people as well, often presenting interest-based explanations as competing with the original education-based formulation (e.g., Genova and Greenberg 1979). The past two chapters have shown, however, that the impact of education and interest depends on characteristics of the available media at a particular point in time. Education was an important conditioning variable for political learning in the pre-broadcast media environment. The advent of broadcast television diminished the importance of education as a necessary condition for exposure and learning. Interest (or content preference) has gained considerable significance in the high-choice cable and Internet environment.

Tichenor, Donohue, and Olien (1970) applied the knowledge gap hypothesis to print media and cautioned that television might play a rather different role in the diffusion of information. Later studies confirmed that television may indeed function as a "knowledge leveler" (Neuman 1976, 122) because it presents information in less cognitively demanding ways. These studies provided one of the theoretical foundations for my analysis of broadcast television in the last chapter. Television reduced knowledge differences between more and less educated segments of the electorate by presenting political information in less cognitively demanding ways than print media and radio. It is important to note, however, that a necessary condition for this effect was the severely limited choice on broadcast television. The leveling effect occurred only because less educated television viewers had no choice but to watch the news from time to time. As opportunities for selective exposure multiplied with the increase in the number of channels and passive learning about politics became less likely, the leveling effect of television ended and even reversed into the opposite. Neuman (1976), Kwak (1999), and Eveland and Scheufele (2000) can only conclude that television news narrows the knowledge gap because they treat exposure as a given. Television news may narrow the gap *among viewers*. As the transition to a high-choice environment generates more and more people who are never exposed to news, television as a "knowledge leveler" loses its punch. Unlike previous studies, this one predicts and finds an increasing knowledge gap as cable television and the Internet reach more people.

The gap between news and entertainment fans that opens in the high-choice environment could not be more different from the much-lamented digital divide. The digital divide is and was between people who can afford access to new media (and afford to learn how to use them) and those who do not have the means to do so. The digital divide emerged because socioeconomic inequalities generated inequalities in access to new media. Without belittling the costs involved in gaining access and acquiring the necessary skills, this study casts doubt on the view that the socioeconomic dimension of the digital divide is the greatest obstacle to an informed and participating electorate.

Many casual observers emphasize the great promise new technologies hold for democracy. Optimists predicted increasing political knowledge and participation among currently disadvantaged people once these inequalities have been overcome (e.g., National Telecommunications and Information Administration 2002; Negroponte 1995). Yet this ignores the inequalities that continue to affect new media use after inequalities in new media access have been reduced. Greater media choice leads to greater *voluntary* segmentation of the electorate. The present study suggests that gaps based on socioeconomic status will be eclipsed by preference-based gaps once access to new media becomes cheaper and more widely available. Gaps created by unequal distribution of resources and skills often emerged due to circumstances outside of people's control. The preference-based gaps documented in this book are self-imposed as many people abandon the news for entertainment simply because they like it better. Inequality in political knowledge and turnout increases as a result of voluntary, not circumstantial, consumption decisions.

Appendix to Chapter 4:
Description of Knowledge Measures

Note: correct answers to multiple-choice questions are bolded.

Political Knowledge, Wave 1 (Twelve-Item Index)

Current Events Knowledge

"Which of the following countries shares a border with Afghanistan?" (Russia / **Pakistan** / Iraq / Kazakhstan)

"In the war in Afghanistan, which of the following groups fought on the side of the coalition led by the United States and Britain?" (The Islamic Jihad / The Taliban / **The Northern Alliance** / Al-Qaeda)

"Which of the following agencies was founded in the wake of the terrorist attacks on September 11?" (**Office for Homeland Security** / Delta Force / National Security Agency / Department of Civilian Defense)

"Would you say there is more, less, or about the same amount of crime in the United States today as compared to 10 years ago?" (more / **less** / same)

"Please give me your best guess for this next question. For every dollar spent by the federal government in Washington, how much of each dollar do you think goes for foreign aid to help other countries?" (following Gilens (2001), 5 percent or less is coded as correct)

"Do you happen to know which party currently has the most members in the House of Representatives in Washington?" (Democrats / **Republicans**)

"On this page, you see four photographs. Do you happen to know which of the photographs shows John McCain?"

"On this page, you see four photographs. Do you happen to know which of the photographs shows Vladimir Putin?"

Description of Knowledge Measures

Civics Knowledge

"Whose responsibility is it to determine if a law is constitutional or not?" (President / Congress / **Supreme Court**)

"How much of a majority is required for the U.S. Senate and House to override a presidential veto?" (one-half plus one vote / three-fifths / **two-thirds** / three-quarters)

"How many four-year terms can the president of the United States serve?" (1 / **2** / 3 / unlimited number of terms)

"In general, thinking about the political parties in Washington, would you say that Democrats are more conservative than Republicans, or Republicans are more conservative than Democrats?" (Democrats more conservative / **Republicans more conservative**)

Political Knowledge, Wave 2 (Fifteen-Item Index)

Current Events Knowledge

"Who is the current secretary of defense?" (**Donald Rumsfeld** / John Ashcroft / George Tenet / Colin Powell)

"Who is the current Senate majority leader?" (**Bill Frist** / Trent Lott / Dick Gephardt / John Kerry)

"Who is the Chief Justice on the U.S. Supreme Court?" (**William Rehnquist** / Clarence Thomas / Antonin Scalia / Anthony Kennedy)

"What office is currently held by Condoleezza ("Condi") Rice?" (U.S. Attorney General / **National Security Advisor** / Secretary of Defense / White House Chief of Staff)

"What position is currently held by Ari Fleischer?" (White House Chief of Staff / **White House Press Secretary** / Education Secretary / Senior Presidential Campaign Advisor)

"What position is currently held by Alan Greenspan?" (Director of the Central Intelligence Agency / Treasury Secretary / **Chairman of the Federal Reserve** / Commerce Secretary)

"For each of the following politicians, please indicate to which party they belong: Tom Daschle, Christine Todd Whitman, Howard Dean, Ralph Nader." (Democrat, Republican, Green Party, Reform Party)

"Do you happen to know which party currently has the most members in the House of Representatives in Washington?" (Democrats / **Republicans**)

"Do you happen to know which party currently has the most members in the Senate?" (Democrats / **Republicans**)

Civics Knowledge

"Whose responsibility is it to determine if a law is constitutional or not?" (President / Congress / **Supreme Court**)

"How much of a majority is required for the U.S. Senate and House to override a presidential veto?" (one-half plus one vote / three-fifths / **two-thirds** / three-quarters)

"In general, thinking about the political parties in Washington, would you say that Democrats are more conservative than Republicans, or Republicans are more conservative than Democrats?" (Democrats more conservative / **Republicans more conservative**)

Note: One half of the respondents were randomly assigned to a visual condition in which photographs of the politicians instead of their names were shown on screen. For the purpose of this study, I simply average across this (random) variation.

NES 2000

Political Knowledge (Fourteen-Item Index)

Knows which party had majority in the House before election

Knows which party had majority in the Senate before election

Correctly responds that Trent Lott's current job is Senate majority leader (open-ended)

Correctly responds that William Rehnquist's current job is chief justice of the Supreme Court (open-ended)

Correctly responds that Tony Blair's current job is prime minister of England / Great Britain (open-ended)

Correctly responds that Janet Reno's current job is attorney general (open-ended)

Correctly recalls incumbent / challenger

Recognizes incumbent / challenger (rated on feeling thermometer)

Correctly identifies incumbent in the district

Remembers something about incumbent in district

Gives response other than "Don't Know" to "Do you happen to know about how many years [incumbent] has been in the House of Representatives?"

Gives response other than "Don't Know" to "How good a job would you say U.S. Representative [NAME] does of keeping in touch with the people in your district?"

Description of Knowledge Measures

NES 1996

Political Knowledge (Fourteen-Item Index)

Knows which party had majority in the House before election

Knows which party had majority in the Senate before election

Correctly responds that Al Gore's current job is vice-president (open-ended)

Correctly responds that William Rehnquist's current job is chief justice of the Supreme Court (open-ended)

Correctly responds that Boris Yeltsin's current job is president (leader) of Russia (open-ended)

Correctly responds that Newt Gingrich's current job is Speaker of the House (open-ended)

Correctly recalls incumbent / challenger

Recognizes incumbent / challenger (rated on feeling thermometer)

Correctly identifies incumbent in the district

Gives response other than "Don't Know" to "Did Representative [NAME] vote for or against the welfare reform bill?"

Gives response other than "Don't Know" to "How often has Representative [NAME] supported President Clinton's legislative proposals?"

Gives response other than "Don't Know" to "How good a job would you say U.S. Representative [NAME] does of keeping in touch with the people in your district?"

5

From Low Choice to High Choice: Does Greater Media Choice Affect Total News Consumption and Average Turnout?

Greater media choice increases inequality in political involvement. The last chapter demonstrated that the growing reach of cable television and the Internet has widened gaps in news exposure, political knowledge, and turnout between those who like news and those who prefer entertainment. But the Conditional Political Learning model and the empirical analysis had little to say about *average* political involvement. Increases in news exposure, knowledge, and turnout among news-seekers offset declines among entertainment fans. My theory does not predict whether or not one change exceeds the other to produce changes in average political involvement. Yet, even in the absence of firm theoretical expectations, the effects of new media on the size of the news audience and the level of electoral participation are important and have recently been subject to wide speculation.

In this chapter, I examine the effects of greater media choice on average news exposure and turnout. As far as turnout is concerned, assessing the relevant average is straightforward – it is simply the turnout rate. The following analysis examines if increasing cable penetration in the 1970s and 1980s affected average turnout in presidential and congressional elections. It relates changes in cable penetration in different media markets to changes in turnout rates in those markets. This time series research design provides rigorous estimates of cable television's causal effect on average turnout. It also allows an additional test of the Conditional Political Learning model because cable offered very little news before CNN began operation. During an expansion of choice that adds entertainment options, but not news, my theory predicts a turnout decline.

With respect to news exposure, it is far more challenging to determine the average. We have pretty good measures of news exposure through individual media outlets. Newspaper circulation can be tracked over time. A history of audience estimates for different television news programs is available from Nielsen Media Research. Combining news exposure through different media into one estimate of total news consumption is far more difficult. In fact, estimates at the subnational level would be so unreliable as to cast doubt on any causal inference based on them. An analysis of cable television's impact on average news consumption that parallels the turnout analysis is therefore not feasible. Instead, I provide some rough estimates of the trend in total news consumption since the early 1980s, a period in which cable and Internet penetration rose dramatically. This approach does not allow causal inferences, but it describes a quantity – the total amount of news consumed in the United States – that has so far escaped measurement. Considering the incessant talk of declining news audiences, the analysis offers a surprising conclusion.

DID CABLE TELEVISION AFFECT AVERAGE TURNOUT LEVELS?

The analysis of survey data in the previous chapter has revealed increasing differences in the turnout rates of news and entertainment fans as they gain access to new media. Survey data suggest a rough balance of effects among news- and entertainment-seekers.[1] For a more precise assessment that does not depend on self-reports of turnout, I turn to an analysis of actual vote returns. As Figure 1.1 indicated, cable penetration grew most strongly between the mid-1970s and the mid-1980s. Survey data sets that measure both cable access and the relevant political variables are not available for that period, but aggregate data are. Using the media market as the unit of analysis, I estimate the effect of rising cable penetration on turnout between 1972 and 1990.

For the first half of this period, the Conditional Political Learning model does in fact provide theoretical expectations about the effect of increasing cable penetration. Before the first all-news cable channel, CNN, reached a sufficient number of cable households, cable provided more entertainment options, but no additional news options. In those early years of cable television, the Conditional Political Learning model therefore predicts a decline in turnout as a result of increasing cable penetration because entertainment fans with cable access watched less news, learned less, and voted less, while news fans could not yet take advantage

---

1 In the News & Entertainment Survey, the main effects of cable and Internet access on turnout are not statistically distinguishable from zero when their interactions with Relative Entertainment Preference are excluded (and regardless of whether or not past turnout is included as a control variable in the panel analysis). In the replication analyses, several main effects for cable and Internet are positive and statistically significant.

of greater news offerings. Other things being equal, turnout among news fans should have remained constant until they could receive CNN, thus not yet offsetting turnout declines among entertainment fans. Turner Broadcasting launched CNN in 1980. By the mid-1980s, almost all cable households received CNN and/or CNN Headline News. (Satellite NewsChannels, created by ABC and Westinghouse in 1982, also offered cable news for fifteen months before it was bought and shut down by Turner.) The aggregate analysis thus provides another test of the Conditional Political Learning framework. According to the model, cable television should have depressed turnout in the 1970s and early 1980s, but not necessarily thereafter.

The data set I created to test this hypothesis and assess the overall effect of cable on turnout includes information on cable penetration and turnout (as well as several demographic indicators) in media markets for presidential and midterm elections between 1972 and 1990. I use the data set again in Chapter 7 to study the effect of cable penetration on partisan polarization. The unit of analysis is the media market (using Nielsen's Designated Market Area or DMA). Data on cable penetration is available at the media market level. Election returns and population data are not. But with only a handful of exceptions, Nielsen assigns each county to exactly one DMA. County-level election and population data can therefore be aggregated to the DMA.[2] Turnout is calculated by dividing the total number of votes cast in presidential or House elections in the county by the voting-age population. For noncensus years, this denominator is derived by linear interpolation, as are all other variables based on census data. The dependent variable is the change in turnout in the DMA compared to the last election of the same type (presidential or midterm) four years earlier.

Cable penetration and change in cable penetration are both only weakly related to the size of the media market (see also Waldfogel 2002). In the pooled data set, the Pearson correlation between cable penetration and DMA size is −.21. The correlation between change in cable penetration and DMA size is .05. Estimates of the political effects of cable television are therefore not likely to be confounded by the higher number of news outlets in larger markets.

Even though nationwide only 9 percent of television households had access to cable in 1972, cable penetration across DMAs ranged from 0 to 61 percent. In 1990, average cable penetration was 58 percent with a range from 41 to 85 percent. In short, there was considerable variation in cable penetration both over time and across DMAs. Because most

---

2 Election data come from the Interuniversity Consortium for Political and Social Research (ICPSR) data set 13. Population data come from various county data books issued by the Census Bureau.

DMAs included the same geographic area (counties) for all or most of the study period,[3] I can use a time series approach to estimate the effect of cable penetration. Comparing the effect of changes in cable penetration since the last election on changes in turnout within a media market is a more powerful design than correlating cable penetration and turnout in the same year across markets.

Table 5.1 presents the results of the aggregate analysis. I conducted the analysis separately for turnout in presidential elections and for turnout in midterm elections to the House of Representatives. The dependent variable is the change in turnout of the voting-age population in a media market compared to four years earlier.[4] It is regressed on the change in cable penetration over the previous four years. A negative coefficient would thus indicate that increasing cable penetration lowered turnout. The regression models control for the effects of several demographic variables and are weighted by the size of the voting-age population in the DMA (to prevent smaller markets from having disproportionate influence).

The growth of cable television did not significantly affect turnout in the average presidential election between 1976 and 1988, according to the results in the first column of Table 5.1. The model in the second column tests specifically whether cable had a stronger effect in elections before CNN became widely available (that is, in the elections of 1976 and 1980, compared to those of 1984 and 1988). The results indicate that an increase in cable penetration did in fact lower turnout in 1976 and 1980 by a significant amount. After 1980, cable had no discernable effect. This pattern supports the Conditional Political Learning model, according to which cable television reduced turnout as long as it offered only (or mostly) entertainment programming.

3 Most DMAs contain the same counties in consecutive election years. But during the period of study, Nielsen reassigned some counties to other DMAs and created a few new DMAs. To approximate a time series data set that preserves the same geographical units over time, I treated small new DMAs that split off from larger ones (often only for a few years) as part of the original DMA. Nonetheless, some DMAs changed over time. For each DMA, I calculated the share of the population that left the DMA and the share of the population in newly added counties. In the analyses reported in this chapter and in Chapter 7, I excluded DMAs for which the sum of the two shares exceeded 15 percent. This cutoff reduced the number of cases by 47 for presidential elections (columns 1 and 2 in Table 5.1) and by 38 for midterm elections (columns 3 and 4 in Table 5.1). The results change hardly at all when other cutoffs are used (or when all DMAs are included regardless of how much they changed).

4 An analysis of House turnout in presidential election years produces essentially the same results. I use a four-year difference because turnout fluctuations between presidential and midterm elections make two-year differences more difficult to interpret.

Table 5.1. *The Effect of Increasing Cable Penetration on Turnout (DMA Data Set)*

	Change in Turnout to Four Years Earlier			
	Presidential Elections		Midterm Elections	
Change in cable penetration	−0.016 (.016)	−0.087** (.028)	−0.093** (.033)	−0.19** (.08)
Change in cable penetration × After 1980		0.105** (.035)		0.12 (.09)
TV households (in millions)	−0.014 (.11)	−0.006 (.11)	−0.55** (.22)	−0.56** (.22)
Population density	−0.94* (.44)	−0.96* (.44)	−0.85 (.94)	−0.81 (.94)
% white	−0.060** (.01)	−0.059** (.01)	−0.045* (.021)	−0.045* (.02)
Change in % white	0.63** (.08)	0.64** (.08)	−0.09 (.18)	−0.10 (.18)
% with College degree	−0.031 (.042)	−0.023 (.041)	−0.19* (.08)	−0.19* (.08)
Change in % with college degree	−0.28 (.24)	−0.31 (.24)	0.79 (.53)	0.80 (.53)
Median age	−0.20** (.05)	−0.19** (.05)	−0.07 (.13)	−0.06 (.13)
Change in median age	−0.14 (.11)	−0.14 (.11)	−0.30 (.25)	−0.31 (.25)
Unemployment rate	−0.21** (.06)	−0.19** (.06)	−0.39** (.13)	−0.38** (.13)
Change in unemployment rate	0.44** (.13)	0.42** (.13)	0.35 (.33)	0.34 (.33)
Median income (in $1,000)	−0.07 (.06)	−0.10 (.06)	0.04 (.11)	0.03 (.11)
Change in median income	0.51** (.15)	0.54** (.15)	0.32 (.32)	0.31 (.32)
1980	0.39 (.34)	0.53 (.34)		
1982			6.6** (.8)	5.8** (1.0)
1984	3.7** (.6)	2.8** (.6)		
1986			−1.1 (1.1)	−1.8* (1.2)
1988	−0.8 (.7)	−1.3* (.7)		
1990			2.4 (1.6)	1.9 (1.6)
Constant	11.8** (1.7)	12.2** (1.7)	7.6* (4.1)	8.0* (4.1)
R^2	0.46	0.47	0.33	0.33
N	741	741	681	681

** $p < .01$, * $p < .05$ (one-tailed).

Note: The dependent variable in these models is the change in turnout of the voting-age population in a media market compared to four years earlier. Models are estimated by OLS regressions. The data are weighted by the voting-age population in the DMA. Cell entries are unstandardized regression coefficients with standard error in parentheses.

Cable television also depressed turnout in midterm elections before 1980, according the fourth column of Table 5.1. The negative effect was larger than in presidential elections, persisting at a reduced magnitude even after CNN began to inform and motivate news junkies. As a result, the average effect of cable penetration in midterm elections between 1978 and 1990 is negative and statistically significant (column 3).

To illustrate the impact of cable television implied by the results in Table 5.1, I plot predicted values for each election in Figure 5.1. In two panels (for presidential and midterm election years), the figure compares the actual turnout trend to the estimated turnout if cable penetration had not increased beyond its level at the beginning of the analysis.[5] Both panels show that in every election of the period, more people would have voted if cable penetration had remained low (shown by the dashed lines). The differences are small in presidential elections, amounting to about one per-centage point. Cable made only a slightly larger difference in the midterm elections of 1978 and 1982 (about 1.5 points). Hence, even though cable access had the predicted negative effect on turnout early on when CNN was not yet available, this effect was muted by the still low levels of cable penetration. Cable made the biggest difference in the midterm election of 1986. Had penetration remained at its 1982 level, turnout in 1986 would have been higher by an estimated 2.5 percentage points. Even though most cable subscribers could receive CNN by this point, the growth of cable penetration was at its peak, and many new entertainment fans gained access in those years.

In the late 1980s, the solid and the dashed lines in Figure 5.1 move closer together again. Eventually, cable penetration began to slow down the decline in turnout. Between 1986 and 1990, an additional 9 per-cent of households gained cable access, but midterm turnout declined only marginally, by 0.2 points. Without the increase in cable penetra-tion, turnout would have declined by more than two points in those four years, according to my estimates. Aggregate data make it impossible to determine conclusively if this relative turnout recovery is in fact a result of more cable news viewing, but Conditional Political Learning and the earlier individual-level analysis support this conclusion.

5 To generate predicted values for individual elections, interactions of change in cable penetration and year dummies are added to the models in column 1 and 3 of Table 5.1. For presidential turnout, the effects of change in cable penetration are -0.10 (.04) in 1976, -0.08 (.04) in 1980, -0.02 (.02) in 1984, and 0.09 (.03) in 1988. For midterm elections, yearly effects are -0.20 (.08) in 1978, -0.03 (.06) in 1982, -0.16 (.05) in 1986, and 0.20 (.10) in 1990. Demographic variables are set to their yearly averages. The average increase in cable penetration was 4.9% for 1972–6, 5.6% for 1974–8, 6.2% for 1976–80, 16.2% for 1978–82, 21.5% for 1980–4, 15.6% for 1982–6, 9.9% for 1984–8, and 9.5% for 1986–90.

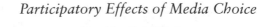

a. Presidential Elections

Without post-1972 increase in cable

With actual increase in cable penetration

b. Midterm Elections

Without post-1972 increase in cable

With actual increase in cable penetration

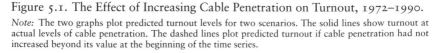

Figure 5.1. The Effect of Increasing Cable Penetration on Turnout, 1972–1990.

Note: The two graphs plot predicted turnout levels for two scenarios. The solid lines show turnout at actual levels of cable penetration. The dashed lines plot predicted turnout if cable penetration had not increased beyond its value at the beginning of the time series.

In sum, the aggregate analysis of voter turnout establishes a small negative effect of cable penetration on average turnout levels. Cable television's potential to depress turnout was largest in the 1970s and early 1980s because it did not yet offer news programming to those who wanted it. Turnout did not drop even further in this period because still relatively few Americans subscribed to cable. This analysis confirms that the primary impact of cable television was not to change average levels of turnout. Much more consequential was its opposite impact on turnout rates of news and entertainment fans. Cable penetration decreased the share of Americans who went to the polls by little more than a whisker, but it increased the turnout gap between news and entertainment fans by a lot.

These results are consistent with the absence of a strong trend in turnout at the national level since 1972 (Freeman 2004; McDonald and Popkin 2001). In principle, a similar analysis could be conducted to test the effect of cable television on average political knowledge. In practice, this is impossible because we do not know how knowledge changed over time at the level of the media market (or at any other subnational geographical level). Even the conclusion that average political knowledge has been very stable over the last half-century (Delli Carpini and Keeter 1996; Smith 1989) rests on more assumptions than the same conclusion with respect to turnout. In the case of political knowledge, survey analysis presented in the last chapter is the clearest evidence for stable means, but growing inequality.[6]

For my third measure of political involvement, news exposure, the measurement problems are even more complex. Unlike for political knowledge and turnout, we do not even have estimates of trends in the total amount of news that Americans consume. Average (or total) levels of news consumption are generally assessed only for news on specific media. Whether news consumption on all media combined is higher or lower than in the past is an important question that analysts have neglected almost completely. In the next section, I offer a rough estimate of the trend in Total News Consumption.

GREATER MEDIA CHOICE AND TOTAL NEWS CONSUMPTION

For a specific television news program, Nielsen's audience estimates provide us with a time trend. The audience for the news flagships of the broadcast era, the evening network news, has declined by half from its peak in the early 1980s (see Figures 1.2 and 4.2). I have already presented

---

6 When the interaction effects between Relative Entertainment Preference and the media environment are removed from the N&E Survey panel model in Chapter 4, the main effects of cable and Internet access on political learning are indistinguishable from zero. This is also true in most cross-sectional models.

the evidence for growing cable penetration as a cause for this decline. But over roughly the same period of the network news decline, cable news channels have increased their audience. News fans watch more news than in the past; entertainment fans watch less. As in the case of knowledge and turnout, the Conditional Political Leaning model does not offer a global prediction for the effect of greater media choice on overall television news exposure. This section provides an empirical assessment of the trends in overall television news exposure.

Cable news is not the only news outlet that has enjoyed audience gains in recent years. Many Americans get their news from Web sites devoted to politics and public affairs. Considering only overall television news exposure thus misses a major source of news in the high-choice media environment. Likewise, any assessment of total news consumption would be incomplete if it ignored the decline in newspaper circulation. Comparing trends in audiences for news on different media raises a thorny issue: How do we compare watching a news program on television to visiting a Web site or buying a newspaper? The purpose of this section is to provide at least a rough estimate of whether Americans consume more or less news than in the past.

The diversification of news options has made measurement more challenging. Signs of audience fragmentation are taken prematurely as indication of declining news consumption. Traditional indicators of news media use – network news ratings and daily newspaper circulation – are indeed down. But news options that were not available in the past or have expanded in scope have gained audiences. Cable television, all-news radio, news Web sites, and the online editions of newspapers all add to the overall news audience. Individually, these new audiences may seem rather small, but together they make up a large share of news media use.[7]

Even though many people consume less news than in the past, the total amount of news consumed has not necessarily declined. In fact, new media generate so much more news media use that the American public probably consumes more news than in the past. Conceptually, Total News Consumption is straightforward to define. It is the total amount of

---

7 Two analyses in Chapter 4 illustrate this point. Figure 4.1 showed audience estimates for one particular type of news – the evening network newscasts – and demonstrated a clear decline as cable penetration increased. The survey analysis in Table 4.1 examined exposure to any kind of television news. At least as far as self-reports are concerned, there is little evidence that aggregate news exposure was lower among cable users. The reason for this difference is obvious: By making available twenty-four-hour news channels, cable increased news exposure for people with a high appreciation of news, but this effect is only picked up when overall news exposure is analyzed. As far as network news viewing in particular is concerned, there is little room for news-seekers with cable access to watch more than they did without cable.

news consumed in a given interval by a group of people, in this case the American public. It is measured in time units. That is where the problems start. People are bad at estimating the amount of time they spend doing things, so survey measurement of Total News Consumption would yield flawed results. Audience research firms monitor television viewing to provide consumption estimates that do not depend on self-assessment. A similar measurement approach may be conceivable for online news consumption, but consumption of (offline) print media is generally assessed by the number of copies in circulation. It is not obvious how newspaper circulation can be compared to time spent viewing television news. (Neither is it obvious what kind of programs or articles or Web sites should count as "news.") In light of these measurement problems, the following is no more than a back-of-the-envelope estimate. To provide at least a very rough sense of trends in Total News Consumption, I simplify the task and consider television and newspapers separately.

As a result of greater media choice, fewer Americans watch the news and learn about politics than in the past. That is one main conclusion from the Conditional Political Learning model supported by the empirical analysis in the previous chapter. It is widely believed that Americans as a whole also watch less news than in the past. This belief is based on a flawed interpretation of the available data. Central to the misinterpretation is the impression that a 38 rating for the three evening network news programs – the highest-ever combined yearly average – is more news than an average 1.4 rating for the three major cable networks (CNN, Fox News Channel, and MSNBC) – their combined average in 2004. It is not. The 38 rating means that on a typical weekday in 1980, 38 percent of all U.S. households watched one of the three evening network newscasts – thirty minutes of news (including commercial breaks). For the average household, this amounts to 11.4 minutes (30 minutes × .38) of news per weekday. A 1.4 rating for the three cable networks means that 1.4 percent of all U.S. households watched one of the three cable networks *during the average minute of the day*. For the average household, this amounts to 20.2 minutes (60 minutes × 24 hours × .014) of news per day.[8]

As far as television news is concerned, the most interesting question is whether the rise of cable news viewing can make up for the decline

---

8 In this example, the 1.4 rating is the rating for all U.S. households. Media reports often give the rating within the coverage area of each cable channel. The 38 rating for network news refers to newscasts during the week. If weekend newscasts, which are generally not as widely viewed, are included, the comparison would be even more skewed in favor of cable. Net of advertising, the number of news minutes per day would of course be lower. The comparison assumes that the ratio of news to advertising is similar for network news and cable news channels.

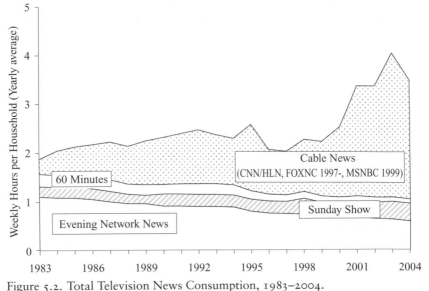

Figure 5.2. Total Television News Consumption, 1983–2004.

Note: Nightly network news ratings were only available for weekdays. Audiences are smaller on the weekend. I assumed that weekend audiences are two-thirds of the weekday averages, a ratio that roughly applied in 2000. Ratings for news magazines and Sunday interview shows are averages compiled from Lexis-Nexis.

in broadcast news audiences (network and local). To compare the two, I draw on Nielsen ratings to calculate the average weekly household news consumption of broadcast and cable news. To derive yearly household television news consumption from ratings data, I multiplied ratings, which measure the size of the audience for the average minute of a program or cable channel, by the length of the program. As in the preceding examples, this yields the number of news minutes viewed in a particular time period. In Figure 5.2, I report the results in hours per week for years since 1983. In 1983, for example, the average household watched just over an hour of nightly network news each week. By 2004, this number was down to little more than half an hour.

Prime-time news magazines and Sunday morning talk shows on the networks also contribute to overall news consumption. To capture the contribution of prime-time news magazines, the figure includes the average viewing time of the most popular news magazine, *60 Minutes*. The other networks aired similar shows for most of this period, but their audiences were smaller and declined at a similar rate as *60 Minutes*. Adding them to the graph would increase news consumption slightly more in the early years. The networks also schedule news on Sunday mornings, each offering an interview program (*This Week, Face the Nation, Meet the*

Press, and, since 1996, *Fox News Sunday* on the Fox Broadcast Network). Figure 5.2 illustrates that these weekly programs add relatively little to overall news consumption, largely because they draw small audiences. The extension of *Meet the Press* to one hour in 1992 and the addition of *Fox News Sunday* in 1996 actually increased average news consumption of the Sunday morning shows slightly. The graph does not include the audience for weekday morning news on ABC, CBS, and NBC, which has been very stable over the last two decades, so its exclusion will not affect conclusions about the overall trends in news viewing.

Systematic data for local news consumption are not available to me. Periodic reports would suggest a declining trend similar to that of the nightly network news and at a slightly higher level, as local newscasts tend to draw somewhat larger audiences (see Chapter 3). In recent years, local newscasts received an average audience rating of about 8 percent, both in the early evening and after prime time (Project for Excellence in Journalism 2005). Thirty years earlier, the average rating for a local newscasts in the top 100 markets was 12 in the early evening and 10 in the late evening (Parkman 1982). Estimation of local news consumption is complicated by two factors. First, the number and length of news programs varies by media market and has changed over time. Second, Nielsen bases its market-level audience estimates on much smaller samples. In most markets, audience measurement is still not automatic (using diaries instead of people meters).

For cable news, I include any viewing of the domestic CNN feed, CNN Headline News, the Fox News Channel (since 1997), and MSNBC (since 1999). Instead of using program ratings, the calculation for cable channels requires multiplication of the average daily household audiences by their twenty-four-hour airing period. A Nielsen analysis cited by Wilbert (2004) confirms the validity of my method. According to that analysis, the average weekly household consumption of cable news was 3:06 hours in 2003 and 2:25 hours in 2002. My method yields 2:55 hours for 2003 and 2:16 hours for 2002. The small difference might be due to the fact that I cannot exclude sports (on MSNBC) or paid programming. I also do not include CNBC and other financial news channels such as Bloomberg. These have very small audiences.

Adding up the time that the American public spends watching cable and broadcast news shows remarkably stable television news consumption between the early 1980s, when CNN appeared on the scene, and the end of the 1990s, when broadcast news had lost a considerable share of its audience and cable access had reached two-thirds of all American households. If local news and network news magazines other than *60 Minutes* were included in Figure 5.2, the slight suggestion of an increase in the first half of the time period would disappear.

Driven by increased cable news viewing, Total Television News Consumption increased by about 50 percent in 2001 in the aftermath of 9/11 and has stayed at this higher level since (sustained, at least in part, by the war in Iraq and perhaps by the addition of the successful Fox News Channel). By this rough approximation, there is no indication that Americans watch less news today than twenty years ago. In fact, in recent years they have watched more.[9]

A similar argument applies to newspaper reading. Between 1995 and 2004, daily newspaper circulation has declined from 58.2 million to 54.6 million, according to *Editor & Publisher*. (Circulation of weekly newspapers increased slightly in this period (Waldfogel 2002).) These circulation numbers do not take into account online newspaper reading. Drawing on Web usage data, a recent study by the Newspaper Association of America found that in 2005 about 46 million people visited a newspaper Web site in a given month (from within the United States). On average, each of these 46 million people accessed newspaper Web sites seven times each month and spent a total of thirty-eight minutes per month on those sites.[10] Although it is difficult to compare these data to daily circulation numbers, they suggest that the declining print circulation is offset by increased online reading. Forty-six million visitors who spend an average of 38 minutes per month on the websites generate 971,111 hours of daily online

---

9 All of this, of course, ignores the fact that the average minute of a news program on cable is quite different than the average network news minute. It also makes no adjustment for changes in the content of network or cable news programs. To the extent that the average minute of news contains less news now than in the past, a more detailed measurement approach would have to discount recent news minutes by a larger factor.

10 These numbers imply a great number of very short visits (a little over a minute per day, on average). It is prudent to assume that only a small fraction of the over 46 million unique monthly visitors actually read articles on a more or less daily basis. Even those serious readers may be enough to compensate for the decline in print circulation. The number of daily visitors to the *New York Times* Web site, for example, exceeds the number of copies it sells (Timothy Williams, "NYTimes.com to Offer Subscription Service," *New York Times*, May 17, 2005).

A more general problem with assessments of print news consumption is the ambiguous meaning of newspaper circulation or newspaper reading. First, circulation does not reflect that newspapers contain more news than in the past (Stepp 1999). It might take fewer newspapers today to get the same amount of news. Second, survey questions about newspaper consumption usually do distinguish different newspaper content. The percentage of Americans who say they read a daily newspaper does not tell us the share of Americans who read more than just the sports pages and the cartoons. Circulation numbers present the same problem. The decline in circulation and self-reported newspaper reading could simply indicate that fewer Americans need newspapers to get their daily dose of cartoons.

newspaper consumption (46 million × 38 minutes/30/60). By comparison, the circulation decline of 3.6 million since 1995 corresponds to a loss of 900,000 hours of daily news consumption if each newspaper would have been read for 15 minutes (3.6 million × 15 minutes/60). Total Newspaper Consumption may in fact be on the rise.

In sum, there is little evidence that the overall amount of television news viewing or newspaper reading has declined. Radio news consumption, too, appears to be relatively stable. National Public Radio has recently increased its audience (Keaggy 2004; Project for Excellence in Journalism 2006). The audience for political talk radio has at least been stable in the last decade (Project for Excellence in Journalism 2004, 2006; Sanders 2005). And by definition, online sources of news other than newspaper Web sites have added to news consumption. Even though I cannot offer an exact estimate of trends in Total News Consumption, there is no evidence for a decline since the advent of cable news and the Internet. Most likely, Total News Consumption is up.

A QUESTION OF CONCENTRATION: HOW MANY NEWS JUNKIES ARE THERE?

Just as many observers take comfort in relatively stable levels of knowledge and turnout, they may be encouraged by the absence of a decline in Total News Consumption. If we judge the health of a political system by the total amount of news watched, read, and heard, there is no more reason for concern today than in past decades. This finding runs counter to many alarmist portrayals of alleged declines in news media use in the United States.

But as in the cases of knowledge and turnout, a stable average tells only half of the story. The potential problem for the functioning of the democratic system is that news consumption is more heavily concentrated. In the past, many people consumed a little news; today a few people consume a lot of news. Just how few of these news junkies there are is not easy to estimate. In this section, I attempt to roughly quantify the share of news junkies in the population, drawing on both cumulative audience data and the News & Entertainment Survey.

Even though Americans may consume more news, more Americans also tune out the news altogether. Total consumption calculations do not address the question of concentration: If in the past one person read the *Los Angeles Times*, and another the *Boston Globe*, how likely is it that today the first person reads the print version of the *Times* and checks the *Globe*'s Web site, while the other person reads no newspaper at all? How much do the remaining network news viewers contribute to the increased cable news audiences? The Conditional Political Learning model suggests that this kind of concentration is increasingly common.

Analyses in previous chapters have shown that a considerable number of Switchers flee the news. News junkies move in the opposite direction, consuming more news than ever. There are probably fewer news junkies than there are Switchers. The High-Choice/Low-Choice Experiment presented in Chapter 2 identified about a third of the population as Switchers. The ratings for network news have decreased by about 20 percentage points as cable penetration increased from 20 to 85 percent. By comparison, fewer people voice a strong relative preference for news. Five percent of the N&E Survey respondents ranked news ahead of all other genres. Another 11 percent ranked it second. The distribution of the combined REP measure in Figure 4.2 reveals a small number of very dedicated news fans. Among them, the gains in knowledge and turnout are substantial.

Most observers agree that Switchers outnumber news junkies. Patterson (2000b, 247), for example, believes that "although cable has fostered a core of 'news junkies' who immerse themselves in CNN and C-SPAN, its more significant effect has been to contribute to a steep decline in the overall size of the news audience." One advantage of identifying news junkies based on questions about their preferences – rather than their actual behavior – is that between-media comparisons are easier. The downside is that preferences do not always translate into behavior. Some people who greatly prefer news to other media content might still not have the time to follow it closely. Determining the share of news junkies by their behavior – for example, by how much time people spent watching television news or visiting news Web sites – is not straightforward because it is not clear how much news is enough to make someone a news junkie. What, to use Patterson's term, counts as "immersion"? To compare the rough estimates based on preference measures – perhaps 10–15 percent news junkies and at least twice as many Switchers – to behavioral data, I briefly review some audience research data.

Patterns of cable news viewing are more helpful than network news viewing in analyzing the concentration of news exposure because the amount of network news is very limited. Ideally, any type of news viewing should be considered, but the appropriate data are not publicly available. According to Nielsen data in Webster (2005), 27 percent of the voting-age population watched the Fox News Channel (FNC) during an average week in February 2003. More people, 35 percent, tuned in to CNN for at least a minute during the same period. (This measure is known as the cumulative audience or "cume.")[11] Yet while FNC has fewer viewers, its

---

11 The minimum amount of viewing necessary for a viewer to be included in the cumulative audience varies. The most common minimum is six minutes on the

viewers watch for longer periods. Viewers of the Fox News Channel spent an average 193 minutes per week watching the channel, compared to only 118 for CNN viewers (see also Farhi 2003).[12] Three other cable news channels attracted smaller audiences. MSNBC had a weekly cumulative audience of 23 percent, and those 23 percent watched for an average of 76 minutes per week. The cumulative audience for CNBC was 14 percent at an average viewing time of 51 minutes. CNN Headline News, which was measured separately from the CNN news channel, was seen by 25 percent of all viewers for an average 51 minutes. Due to the impending U.S. military intervention in Iraq, news audiences were unusually large in February 2003. Weekly cumulative audiences in 2005 were closer to 20 percent for both CNN and FNC and under 15 percent for MSNBC and CNN Headline News. Data for the first eight months of 2005 have Fox News viewers watching for 144 minutes per week, CNN viewers for 63 minutes, MSNBC viewers for 43 minutes, CNN Headline News viewers for 42 minutes, and CNBC viewers for 29 minutes.

These numbers provide another important corrective to the common view that cable news audiences must be very small because their average audiences are small. But they do not yet offer a clear picture of the news junkie. How many different viewers account for the bulk of all this cable news viewing? Do Fox News viewers also watch CNN? This is an important question not only because it addresses the concentration of cable news viewing, but also because it begins to shed light on audience polarization in a fragmented news environment. If heavy Fox News viewers also watch a lot of CNN and MSNBC, they remain exposed to a host of different viewpoints, even when any one channel exhibits a bias. Such a pattern would reduce concerns by theorists like Sunstein (2001b) and Turow (1997) about audience fragmentation into small, self-contained segments consisting of like-minded users exposed only to content that is consistent with their existing attitudes.

Webster (2005) provides some additional insights into the concentration of news viewing.[13] Those who watched at least some Fox News spent 7.5 percent of their overall viewing time with the Fox News Channel, but another 6 percent with the other four cable networks (CNN, CNN Headline News, CNBC, MSNBC). Viewers who never watched Fox News also

same day, but Webster's data also include viewers who only watched between one and five minutes of the particular channel.

12 Use of the two cable channels' Web sites reveals a similar pattern: CNN.com attracts more unique visitors, but visitors to FoxNews.com spend more time on the Web site (Project for Excellence in Journalism 2004).

13 I am grateful to James Webster for sharing with me the data that did not make it into his article.

spent less time, under 3 percent of their total television consumption, watching other cable news channels. Likewise, CNN viewers, who spent 4.7 percent of their viewing time watching CNN, devoted another 6.8 percent of their viewing to the other four cable channels, including 3.7 percent to Fox News. The 65 percent of viewers who never watched CNN also rarely watched other cable channels (for less than 3 percent of their total viewing time). MSNBC viewers – 23 percent of the adult population who spent 3 percent of their viewing time with MSNBC – watched other news channels for an additional 9 percent of their total television use. For viewers who avoided MSNBC, that share is only 4.2 percent. Even though these averages may hide more polarized viewing patterns among small subsets of cable news viewers, they offer little support for claims that the fragmentation of the cable news environment fosters political polarization by encouraging selective exposure to only one side of an issue.[14]

These data point to considerable concentration of cable news viewing. Fox News viewers – about a quarter of the population – spent 13.5 percent of their overall time watching cable news, compared to less than 3 percent for the other three-quarters of viewers. CNN viewers were a somewhat larger group at 35 percent. They devoted 11.5 percent of their viewing total to cable news, compared to less than 3 percent for non-CNN viewers. MSNBC viewers, the smallest group with 23 percent of all adults, also spent 11.5 percent on cable news, compared to 4.2 percent who did not watch MSNBC.

Webster's data do not allow us to determine the exact overlap between these three groups or the distribution of viewing time among news viewers. A Nielsen measure that addresses this issue is the "exclusive cume," which records the number of unique viewers for a network (or program) that do not watch a specified set of other networks (or programs). In December 2004, for example, the cumulative audience for CNN was 55 million (i.e., 55 million different people watched CNN for at least six minutes on at least one day of the month). In reference to the other cable networks, CNN's exclusive cume in this period was only 12 million. In December 2004, 12 million people watched CNN for at least six minutes on at least one day and did not watch the Fox News Channel, MSNBC, CNN Headline News, or CNBC. The cumulative audience for Fox News in this period was 54 million, with an exclusive cume of 14 million. MSNBC's cume was 40 million, and its exclusive cume was 7 million. Many cable news viewers routinely watch more than one cable

---

14 Survey data and dairies of television viewing also indicate considerable overlap of audiences for Fox News Channel and CNN (DellaVigna and Kaplan 2005).

channel.[15] More generally, audience data point to the same conclusion as the preference distributions in the N&E Survey: There are relatively few news junkies, but they consume a lot of news.

CONCLUSION

In the first decade of commercial cable television, the new technology provided hardly any news, but plenty of entertainment content. As a consequence, growing cable penetration lowered turnout. This negative effect was limited only by the relatively low number of cable subscribers at the time. The period before the establishment of the first cable news channel was an atypical expansion of media choice. Beginning in the early 1980s, cable television and later the Internet provided both more entertainment content and more news and public affairs content. Before CNN, cable lacked this diversity of content.

The asymmetric expansion of choice in the early cable years offers another possibility to test the Conditional Political Learning model. When new technologies increase the availability of both news and entertainment content, the model does not offer a prediction for changes in average political involvement because increases in involvement among news fans offset involvement declines among entertainment fans. The model does not specify the expected relative magnitude of the gains and losses. But for the period in which cable only made more entertainment available, Conditional Political Learning predicts a decline in involvement because news fans had no additional opportunities to learn about politics and increase their turnout rates. The analysis in this chapter confirms this prediction of the model empirically with regard to turnout.

The negative effect of cable television did not last. After the mid-1980s, the impact of cable became more neutral in the aggregate as the positive involvement effects on news fans began to be felt. Over the entire period of analysis, the results are consistent with overall trends in turnout, which show only modest, if any, declines after 1972 (Freeman 2004; McDonald 2004; McDonald and Popkin 2001). Average political knowledge, too, seems to have remained fairly stable (Delli Carpini and Keeter 1996;

---

15 Although these data suggest a relatively heavy concentration of cable news viewing, they cannot provide a precise assessment of specialization in news viewing. The Nielsen data reviewed here measure audience overlap in the aggregate among viewers who watch a particular cable news network at least once during a week or month. On average, these viewers also watch a lot of cable news on other channels. But this is not necessarily true for very heavy viewers of a particular news channel. The best nonproprietary evidence cannot rule out completely that particularly heavy cable news viewers watch mostly one cable news channel.

Gilens, Vavreck, and Cohen 2005; Smith 1989). And in the second half of this chapter, I have offered some evidence that average news consumption has not changed much over the last twenty years. Television news consumption appears to have risen in recent years compared to the 1980s and 1990s. Together with online news media use, increased cable news viewing might well make up for the decline in network news viewing and newspaper circulation.

The central argument of this book is of course that the stability in average news exposure, knowledge, and turnout hides important changes in the distribution of political involvement. News junkies get more news, and entertainment fans and Switchers get less news than before. The variance in news exposure has increased, as has the variance in political knowledge and turnout. In all cases, it is much more difficult to estimate the variance. But the substantial amount of cable news viewing among today's news junkies evident in cumulative audience data offers at least an illustration of the concentration of television news exposure. This concentration of news viewing in a relatively small segment of the population contrasts markedly with the large number of Americans who watched their daily half hour of network news in the low-choice media environment.

Constant average political involvement implies that the gains in involvement among the news junkies are roughly of the same magnitude as the losses among the Switchers. The size of the two groups is not the same, however. There are relatively few news junkies, but they watch and read a lot more news than before. Switchers outnumber news junkies, but their news consumption in the broadcast era should not be exaggerated. As a result, news media use by relatively fewer news junkies can make up for the declining consumption among the larger group of Switchers.

A higher concentration of news exposure and political knowledge poses problems for a democratic system. It widens differences in turnout rates between more and less interested segments. Increasing inequality in news exposure, political knowledge, and turnout exacerbates concerns about the quality of public opinion and voting decisions. Without attention to the distribution of political involvement in the population – even when average involvement remains stable – we cannot detect the problem or assess the consequences of rising political inequality. In Chapter 7, I focus on one such consequence: the growing partisan polarization of elections. But first, Chapter 6 moves us back to a time when knowledge and turnout were more equally distributed. To understand the political consequences of cable television and the Internet, we need to begin by considering politics in the low-choice media environment.

Part 2

The Political Effects of Media Choice

6

Broadcast Television, Partisanship, and the Incumbency Advantage

Just as television grew across the country and established itself as Americans' most important source of news (at least according to their own assessment), the American political scene began to experience important changes. After a period of stability in the aggregate distribution of partisanship in the 1950s and early 1960s, which Converse (1976) called a "steady-state period," partisanship began to decline in the mid-1960s, voters became more likely to vote for different parties in presidential and congressional elections, and incumbents in Congress received more support from voters who did not identify with their party.

At least since *The American Voter* (Campbell et al. 1960), party identification had been considered a fundamental and highly stable component of people's political identity. It was also the most important determinant of their voting decisions. Knowing only a voter's party identification allowed scholars to predict his or her vote with remarkable accuracy. But in the mid-1960s, partisanship began to weaken. After dropping for another decade, it eventually rebounded (Bartels 2000). An explanation for these ups and downs in the importance of the most central predictor of voting behavior remains elusive. Such an explanation gains added significance because weaker impact of partisanship is often thought to go along with a greater role for individual candidates in deciding elections (and vice versa). And for better or worse, the strength of partisanship among voters is related to the salience of partisan divisions at the elite level.

In the second part of this book, I investigate how changes in the media environment affect individual and aggregate vote decisions and whether they can explain trends in the importance of partisanship. In this chapter, I start by examining the impact of broadcast television on people's voting decisions in the 1950s and 1960s to determine if the rise of television contributed to declining partisanship and higher vote margins for congressional incumbents. This chapter looks back at politics in an earlier era, the low-choice days of broadcast television. Even though the media environment has changed since then, it is important to understand the political impact of low choice in order to appreciate the implications of greater media choice for current politics, which are the topic of the next chapter.

The Conditional Political Learning model links the media environment to the role of partisanship in voting behavior. As I showed in Chapter 3, the broadcast era was an unusual period in recent history in that television's combination of popularity and lack of content choice led less educated Americans to watch news, learn about politics, and turn out at higher rates. Television thus increased the share of less educated voters and, ceteris paribus, improved their representation at the polls.

These effects suggest at least two ways in which television could have influenced elections. The first possibility is a purely compositional effect. By increasing the proportion of less educated voters, broadcast television may have diminished the role of partisanship in election decisions simply because it encouraged people to vote who were not as partisan as those voters who turned out even before television. I begin this chapter by examining this most parsimonious prediction of the Conditional Political Learning model.

According to a second possibility, it matters what these newly drafted voters learned from television, what kind of political messages they encountered, and who was favored by those messages. All voters who tuned to the new medium could have been affected by its content, whether or not they used to vote even before television. But the less educated should have been the most impressionable. The major part of the chapter is devoted to an examination of the second possibility in the context of congressional elections.

BROADCAST TELEVISION, EDUCATION, AND PARTISAN VOTING BEHAVIOR

The predicted compositional effect of television on voting behavior rests on the assumption that less educated Americans encouraged by the new medium to participate in elections were less partisan than their more educated counterparts. A first step in assessing the political consequences of increased (relative) voting rates among the less educated is to verify the relationship between education and strength of partisanship.

Table 6.1 presents several indicators of partisanship and perceptions of parties for people with different levels of education for the period between 1952 and 1970. The first column shows the percentage of respondents who believed that there were "any important differences in what the Republicans and Democrats stand for." Only 45 percent of the least

Table 6.1. *Partisanship and Level of Education, 1952–1970*

		Percentage Who See Party Difference	Difference in Number of Arguments in Favor of Parties	Percentage Who Know Republican Party Is More Conservative	Percentage of Partisans (Including Leaners)	Number of Arguments in Favor of Own Party
8 grades or less	(29%)	45	2.2	43	86	2.7
9–12 grades, no diploma or equivalency	(19%)	52	2.2	51	87	2.9
High school diploma or equivalency	(20%)	50	2.2	57	89	2.8
High school diploma or equivalency, plus some nonacademic training	(10%)	57	2.4	62	89	3.1
Some college, no degree (or junior / community college degree)	(12%)	60	2.6	74	92	3.4
B.A. or graduate degree	(10%)	65	2.6	89	93	3.9
N		6,585	9,253	5,352	13,244	8,267

Note: The education breakup is from the NES Cumulative File, variable 140. The table gives the share of Americans in each education category between 1952 and 1970.

educated – those with less than 9 grades of schooling, a large group in this period – saw any important differences. This percentage rises linearly to 65 percent at the highest level of education. With education clearly came the notion that the two parties were different. The second column shows that this notion is in fact rooted in people's reasons for liking or disliking the two parties. In several surveys between 1952 and 1970, respondents were given a chance to mention up to five things they liked about each party and up to five things they disliked. The measure in the second column is the difference between the number of reasons in favor of each party (e.g., the sum of reasons for the Democrats and against the Republicans, subtracted from the sum of reasons for the Republicans and against the Democrats). The things people liked and disliked were more clearly supportive of one party or the other among the more educated.

Not only did less educated people perceive fewer differences between the parties, but their subjective impressions matched their knowledge of the parties' ideological positions. For each level of education, the third column in Table 6.1 lists the percentage of respondents who knew that the Republican Party was more conservative than the Democratic Party. In perhaps the clearest testimony to the political confusion of the less educated, only about half of the respondents without a high school diploma gave the correct answer.[1] By comparison, four out of every five of the most educated quarter of the population knew that the Republican Party was more conservative.

But there is one critical similarity across levels of education. Despite their less differentiated idea of the two parties, most Americans of lower education still identified with one of the two. The fourth column in Table 6.1 shows the percentage of respondents who identified with or felt closer to one of the two major parties. Most of them did, even among the less educated.[2] (Respondents with higher levels of education were more likely to call themselves "independents," but admit in a follow-up question that they felt somewhat closer to one of the two major parties. Keith et al. (1992) have shown that these so-called independent leaners are more similar to partisans in their voting behavior than to pure independents.) If by partisanship we mean only people's party identification – their answer to the question, "Generally speaking, do you usually think of yourself as a Republican, a Democrat, an Independent or what?" – then the less educated were almost as partisan as the more educated.

Did Television Reduce the Impact of Partisanship in Elections?

Television sent less educated Americans to the polls. Although they were less informed about the choice that was awaiting them than the more educated, most of them had one important piece of the puzzle all figured out: They knew which party was theirs. Hence, a higher share of less educated voters may not have reduced the average level of partisanship among voters. Of course, some Americans with little education voted even before the advent of television. If less educated voters with strong partisan sentiments voted all along, television could have lowered partisanship by bringing to the polls predominantly Americans who were both less educated and less partisan. In this section, I evaluate these competing

---

1 The results remain the same when respondents who lived in the South, where the Democratic Party was more conservative than in the rest of the country, are excluded.
2 Between 1952 and 1970, 59 percent of all Americans without a high school diploma identified with, or felt closer to, the Democratic Party. An additional 27 percent identified with the Republican Party. The Democratic advantage is only marginally smaller when Southern respondents are excluded.

Table 6.2. *The Effect of Television on the Role of Partisanship in Voting Behavior*

	Turnout		Presidential Vote Choice
	1952–1958	1960–1968	
Number of VHF stations (log)	0.07 (.13)	0.26* (.14)	0.01 (.06)
Strong partisan[a]	1.33** (.30)	1.81** (.37)	2.89** (.23)
Strong partisan × VHF stations (log)	−0.01 (.15)	−0.23§ (.17)	0.004 (.11)
Weak partisan[a]	0.65** (.29)	1.49** (.35)	1.46** (.15)
Weak partisan × VHF stations (log)	0.02 (.15)	−0.36* (.16)	−0.01 (.08)
Independent leaner[a]	0.64* (.34)	0.91* (.40)	1.47** (.26)
Independent leaner × VHF stations (log)	−0.05 (.17)	−0.16 (.19)	0.11 (.12)
Education	0.39** (.03)	0.35** (.02)	0.11** (.03)
Female	−0.68** (.07)	−0.25** (.06)	−0.004 (.08)
African American	−1.05** (.13)	−0.41** (.10)	−1.25** (.20)
Age	0.028** (.003)	0.023** (.002)	0.007** (.003)
Suburban area	0.05 (.10)	0.16* (.08)	0.03 (.11)
Rural area	0.07 (.10)	0.08 (.08)	0.15 (.11)
South	−1.25** (.09)	−0.77** (.07)	0.72** (.11)
N	4,714	6,413	5,258
Log likelihood	−2,383.8	−3,290.0	−2,051.5
Pseudo-R^2	0.19	0.13	0.44

[a] The partisan dummies are coded 0 or 1 in the first two models and −1, 0, or 1 in the third model. See text for details.

** $p < .01$, * $p < .05$, § $p < .10$ (one-tailed).

Note: Cell entries are logit coefficients with standard errors in parentheses. Year dummies are included. Weights are used when required (NES 1958, 1960). Number of cases is unweighted.

Source: NES 1952–68, merged with Television Access Data Set.

expectations and determine if the growth of television affected average levels of partisanship among voters.

If the compositional changes predicted by the Conditional Political Learning model did indeed occur, independents and partisan leaners should have been increasingly likely to vote – relative to more partisan Americans – in areas with television. The first two models in Table 6.2 analyze if television changed the turnout rates at different levels of partisan strength. The dependent variable, turnout,[3] is regressed on a set of dummy variables indicating the respondent's strength of party identification (strong partisan, weak partisan, and leaner, with pure independent

3 As in Chapter 3, I use variable 702 from the NES 1948–2002 Cumulative Data File.

as the omitted baseline). Now and then, with or without television, strong partisans are most likely to vote; pure independents are least likely to do so.

To test if television changed the magnitude of these differences, the model also includes the (logged) number of VHF television stations in the respondent's county of residence – the measure I used in Chapter 3 to examine the effect of television on political knowledge and turnout – and its interactions with the partisan strength dummies. In the first model, which covers elections in the 1950s, these interactions are small and insignificant. In the second model, however, television makes a difference. The positive and significant main effect indicates that television increased turnout of pure independents relative to people with stronger party affiliations. As indicated by the negative and at least marginally significant interaction effects of television with strong and weak party identification, the positive effect of television on turnout did not extend to partisans.

In the 1960s, the share of less partisan voters thus increased in areas with many television stations. Figure 6.1 illustrates this result graphically by plotting the predicted values from the second model in Table 6.2. As the number of television stations increased, the probability of going to the polls rose among independents and dropped among weak partisans. Further analysis shows that this effect occurred in both midterm and presidential elections.

The model in Table 6.2 is estimated on cross-sectional data, so the analysis cannot fully establish the causal direction of the relationship between television and turnout at different levels of partisanship. Instead of television sending more independents and leaners to the polls, perhaps turnout was less stratified by partisanship to begin with in areas with many television stations. The model does control for the most likely alternative explanation, the disproportionate presence of television stations in urban counties. The effect of television emerges despite the NES controls for size of place in the model. Additional robustness checks confirm the independent contribution of television even when the effect of partisan strength on turnout is allowed to be different in rural, suburban, and urban areas.[4]

---

4 When interactions between the two urbanism indicators and the partisan strength dummies are included in the model, the effect of television in fact becomes slightly larger. When I include interactions of the partisan dummies with a linear time trend, the effects of television remain almost identical. The television measure, which increased over time, thus does not simply pick up turnout trends that are unrelated to television. Using interactions of the partisan strength dummies with dummies for individual years instead of a time trend yields the same conclusion.

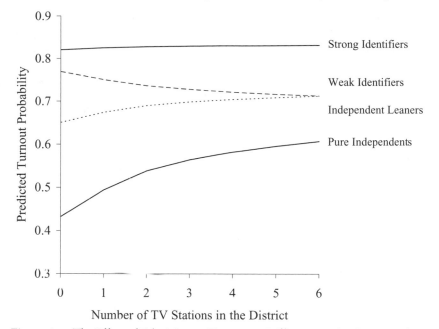

Figure 6.1. The Effect of Television on Turnout at Different Levels of Partisanship.
Note: This graph is based on predicted values from the first model in Table 6.2. Control variables are set to their sample means. Each year dummy is set to the proportion of cases for the particular year (i.e., to its sample mean).
Source: NES 1960–8, merged with Television Access Data Set.

Television lowered the impact of partisanship in elections by increasing the share of independent voters and partisan leaners. It did so even though less educated people, whose representation at the polls increased as a result of television, were on average about as likely as the more educated to identify with a party. Perhaps strongly partisan citizens with lower levels of education usually went to the polls even before television, so that television recruited predominantly less educated people whose partisan attachments were weaker.

The respective proportions of independents, leaners, weak partisans, and strong partisans among voters make up one component of the electoral impact of partisanship. A second component is the reliability with which voters at each level of partisan strength support their party (Bartels 2000; Krehbiel and Wright 1983). In addition to lowering the impact of partisanship by reducing the proportion of partisan voters, television may also have done so by affecting the second component. Even though the less educated had a good sense of which party they supported, their explanation for this support was not as detailed as among the more educated.

The last column in Table 6.1 shows the sum of things respondents liked about their own party and disliked about the other party. Even the least educated gave a few reasons explaining their partisan feelings. But explanations became richer at higher levels of education, and the most educated gave over 40 percent more reasons than the least educated. Attached to a party, but not as well prepared as the more educated to back up this attachment, less educated voters may have found it harder to resist non-partisan arguments or appeals by the other side. Television may thus have lowered the relationship between identifying with a party and voting for that party.

Another consideration, however, casts doubt on this expectation. In order to use their sense of partisan identity as a guideline for their voting decisions, less educated voters needed only one other piece of information: knowledge of which candidate represented their party. In presidential elections, that information was easy to come by. Both candidates received a lot of media attention – enough certainly to clarify their party affiliations. Poorly informed and less educated voters can apply their own partisan identities and stereotypes to the vote decision at hand, even if all they learned about the presidential contest is the party affiliation of the two major candidates (Mondak 1993a; 1993b; Rahn 1993). In contexts that make it easy for less educated voters to match their party identification with the party of the candidates, their voting behavior may appear to be just as partisan as that of more educated voters.

Television may in fact have contributed to the salience of presidential candidates and their party affiliations among the less educated. As shown in Chapter 3, television not only motivated less educated citizens to go to the polls, but it also taught them a few basic things about politics. The party affiliation of the presidential candidates may have been among those basic facts. What is more, the choice between the two parties became starker at roughly the same time that the expansion of television neared completion. Driven at least in part by the debate over civil rights, the differences between Democratic and Republican elites became more obvious. Diverging party positions should have made it easier even for the less educated to use their party identification as a voting cue because they gained greater certainty that the party with which they identified was indeed their preferred choice.[5]

---

5 The impact of divergence depends to some extent on both parties' moving away from the center by a similar amount. If divergence occurs in an asymmetric fashion – as in 1964, when Goldwater was farther from the center than Johnson – partisan voting should decline again (because partisans are increasingly likely to consider their own parties' position too extreme and select the more centrist alternative even if that means crossing party lines).

Broadcast TV, Partisanship, and Incumbency Advantage

The third model in Table 6.2 examines whether television weakened the relationship between identifying with a party and voting for it. The dependent variable is 1 if the respondent voted for the Republican presidential candidate and 0 if she voted for the Democrat. The model excludes respondents who voted for a third-party candidate or did not vote at all. Following Bartels (2000), strong partisans are coded 1 if they identify strongly with the Republican Party and −1 if they identify strongly with the Democratic Party. All other respondents are coded 0 for that level of partisanship. The two other levels of partisanship (weak identifiers and independent leaners) are coded analogously. The model is estimated by probit analysis.[6]

Not surprisingly, the results indicate strong effects of partisanship on voting behavior. Strong partisans were most reliable in voting for their party's candidate. Party identification also had a powerful impact on the votes of weak partisans and independents who feel closer to one party. But there is no sign that television changed any of this. The effect of the different levels of partisanship on vote choice is the same regardless of the number of television stations in the county.

In sum, this analysis shows that television lowered the impact of partisanship on vote choice. It did so by increasing the share of less partisan voters. Television did not affect the likelihood that those who identified with a party ended up voting for it.

Broadcast Television and the Flow of Political Information

Television not only increased turnout rates among the less educated, but it improved their political knowledge, according to the analysis in Chapter 3. The compositional hypothesis focuses on the importance of these learning effects in encouraging electoral participation, but assumes that the things people learned from watching television were politically neutral. If, in addition to motivating people to vote, television influenced people's opinions about political issues or candidates for office, looking only for compositional change misses an important element of its political impact. Television may have affected not only people's propensity to vote but also how they cast their votes.

What, then, did these political messages that educated and perhaps persuaded Americans in the 1950 and 1960s look like? Detailed data on the content of news and advertising by candidates in this period do not exist, but some basic generalizations are possible. The information flow

6 The appendix to Chapter 7 contains a more detailed description of Bartels's method, which I use more prominently in that chapter.

in presidential elections was generally balanced (Zaller 1992). Although Table 6.1 suggests that less educated citizens were less prepared to defend their party against arguments that pointed out the other side's merits, this may not have mattered a great deal in presidential elections because both candidates bombarded voters with campaign messages and the news media provided ample coverage of both sides. A good argument to defect from one's party was often neutralized by a good argument to stick with it.

In elections to the House of Representatives, on the other hand, one candidate usually enjoys a considerable advantage in both campaign resources and news coverage, at least according to research conducted when broadcast television was firmly established (e.g., Clarke and Evans 1983; Cook 1989; Goldenberg and Traugott 1984; Jacobson 2004).[7] The advantaged candidate is typically the incumbent. It seems likely that television contributed to the one-sidedness of the message flow in congressional elections. Compared to earlier media, broadcast television had less space to cover elections and therefore devoted most of its coverage to the most newsworthy candidate, the incumbent. During their term in office before challengers even emerged, congressional incumbents were in an advantaged position to affect the content of local news and public affairs programming. As one *New York Times* article put it in 1955, "with the cathode-ray tube, the key to every voter's living room is at last in the Congressman's hand" (Baker 1955b). Local television presented information from a distinctive political point of view: that of the incumbent member of Congress.

With the flow of information so heavily skewed in favor of the incumbent, television may well have affected people's voting behavior. The remainder of this chapter therefore examines the role of broadcast television in House elections. The next section describes how incumbents came to dominate the local airwaves. I then examine empirically whether television increased people's knowledge of Congress and of their representatives in particular. The last part of this chapter analyzes the effect of the new medium on voting behavior in House elections.

LEARNING ABOUT CONGRESSIONAL ELECTIONS IN THE LOW-CHOICE MEDIA ENVIRONMENT

The spread of television increased political knowledge among less educated Americans by presenting information in an attractive and more easily comprehensible fashion than previous media. In my analysis of this

---

7 The message flow is generally more balanced in U.S. Senate elections.

hypothesis in Chapter 3, I made no distinction between different kinds of political information. From network newscasts, viewers could learn about issues of national or international importance, such as presidential elections or U.S. policy toward Cuba. Local news had even larger audiences than network news (see Chapter 3) and offered information of local relevance. Could television have increased political knowledge of Congress or congressional elections among less educated Americans? Judging by the content of today's local newscasts, this seems highly unlikely because most programs offer little political information at all. Yet, early local news was different. It had a stronger focus on local politics and allowed local members of Congress greater access to the airwaves. In this section, I describe the content of early local news and the ways in which members of Congress influenced coverage. I then test empirically if the general learning effect shown in Chapter 3 also applies to Congress in particular.

Local News

Local news in the 1950s and 1960s was not the blood-and-guts spectacle that it is today (Hamilton 1998). Today's ubiquitous "Eyewitness" and "Action" news formats became commonplace only in the 1970s (Dominick, Wurtzel, and Lometti 1975). The technological limitations of early television and the high cost of film and cameras made talking-head coverage of government the easiest and cheapest way to fill the nightly local news. They were "often staffed by experienced print journalists bearing the traditional news values of their profession" (Zaller 1999, 7). In the first twenty years of local news, "nearly 100 percent of its content had consisted of just these two subjects, crime and government" (Allen 2001, 208). Based on the content of local news on stations in twenty cities in 1956, Bogart (1972, 159) concludes that "local news items most often deal with disasters or natural catastrophes, next with the activities of local legislators or officials." If local stations wanted to cover politics (instead of just buying footage of national or international events from the networks' syndication services), they had to cover local issues, simply because the technology to report distant matters quickly, such as satellite transmission and mobile satellite units, was not yet available (Mickelson 1989, 175).

According to one content analysis of the six Los Angeles television stations in 1961 (Lyle and Wilcox 1963), almost 60 percent of all local news stories covered political news, including local and state government. Less than 20 percent of the stories were on crime and disasters, and less than 10 percent were on human interest and other "soft" news. In 1973, WABC in New York, the station that had recently pioneered the *Eyewitness News* format, still broadcast more than 70 percent hard news stories in their local newscasts, about as much as the other New York network affiliates (Dominick, Wurtzel, and Lometti 1975).[8]

Even in the late 1970s, when the *Eyewitness* and *Action* news formats had become popular, local stations continued to provide local and, to a lesser extent, national and international news (Ostroff and Sandell 1984; Ryu 1982). In a systematic study of ten local television stations in Pennsylvania, Adams (1978) found that news about local and state politics filled almost two-thirds of the local newscasts. Furthermore, most stations typically started their broadcasts with local politics. Most interestingly, the heavy emphasis on local politics was evident for stations in different communities, media markets of different size, and stations with and without network affiliation.

In time, television's reputation as a good source for news extended beyond national and international politics. In a study of the 1958 gubernatorial election in New York, two-thirds of all interviewed voters said that they had seen both candidates on television. Television was as important a source as newspapers for information about this local election (Bogart 1972, 447). According to Roper surveys conducted in the 1970s and 1980s, people perceived television as a more important source of information than newspapers for all elections except mayoral elections and elections to the state legislature. Considerably more respondents reported "becoming best acquainted" with congressional candidates through television rather than newspaper (Mayer 1993, 610).

The Symbiosis of Local Television Stations and House Incumbents

Members of the House of Representatives were in an excellent position to provide local stations with cheap, professionally produced public affairs coverage with a local angle. In 1947, the government created congressional studios where members of Congress could produce radio and, starting in 1953, television reports for their districts. (In 1956, House and Senate facilities were separated.) Incumbents used the studios to record minute-long segments that could be inserted into local newscasts. "For the run-of-the-mill member of Congress aspiring to hit the screens in his home area, Mr Coar [the coordinator of the Joint Recording Facility for many years] recommends a one- or two-minute

---

8 Very few content analyses of local news exist for the time before 1970, partly because broadcasts were often live and recording facilities did not exist or were not used by stations. The study by Lyle and Wilcox (1963) is the *only* content analysis of local news published in the *Journalism Quarterly* or the *Journal of Broadcasting* between 1940 and 1970.

news clip on a subject of local interest" (Baker 1955b). In *An Introduction to Service in the U.S. House of Representatives*, co-written in 1966 by the associate director of the American Political Science Association and a member of Congress, new representatives are informed that "local outlets have been found by Congressmen to be relatively receptive to tape, film, or telephone reports from the nation's capital" (Tacheron and Udall 1966). The publication then provides advice on how to "exploit this opportunity." And so, according to a *New York Times* reporter in 1965 (Robertson 1965): "The voice may speak in the broad A of Massachusetts or sound as if each word were deep-fried in Mississippi fatback, but the opening message is always the same: 'This is your Congressman in Washington.'"

In addition to short statements for the local news, many representatives also recorded stand-alone programs. Fifteen-minute segments were the most common format (Otten 1957). These pieces were often designed as interview shows. In some of them, several representatives from the same state or area appeared in roundtable formats. Other shows featured "the legislator having a couple of newsmen from the home district peppering him with questions, in the manner of the big network panel shows" (Brown 1959). Or congressional aides posed as reporters and asked questions, the answers to which representatives read off a teleprompter (Gruenstein 1974). Interview shows often featured guest appearances by cabinet secretaries, party leaders, or other prominent politicians (Otten 1957). Among the interview guests in 1959 were vice president Richard Nixon, House Speaker Sam Rayburn, and Senate majority leader Lyndon Johnson, as well as the chairman of the Joint Chiefs of Staff and the president of the American Red Cross (Brown 1959). And "when a delegation from home comes to Washington, it is likely to be invited to take part in a TV show" (U.S. News & World Report 1955, 70).

Other long formats included generic programs produced by the studio staff or party organizations to which the representatives would add their personalized introductions, voice-over, and closings before sending the reports to their home districts (MacNeil 1968). Democrats and Republicans from the same state sometimes used the same generic material, just giving it a partisan spin with their introductions (Carter 1955). The National Republican Congressional Committee produced canned statements by President Eisenhower's cabinet members to which Republican incumbents could add their opening and closing remarks. Or the representative "may simply read the questions at the studio and his voice is dubbed in to make it sound like a face-to-face interview" (U.S. News & World Report 1955). And "thus, with a little splicing, the lawmaker produces the illusion that his power is such that the cabinet will go to the studio for him" (Baker 1955b).

In 1955, about a third of all House members used the congressional studios regularly to produce television reports (Baker 1955b; Cronheim 1957). Four years later, 160 representatives used the studios weekly or biweekly; another 110, less often (Brown 1959). The number of regulars rose to about 300 in 1964 (Broadcasting 1964), and to 353 in 1973 (Bagdikian 1974).

The recording facilities were heavily subsidized by the government. Legislators paid production fees that were considerably below market rates – by a factor of 20 or greater, according to some estimates (Baker 1955a; Otten 1957; Robertson 1965; Tracy 1975). According to MacNeil (1968, 248), "to produce one print of a five-minute film will cost about $12. It might easily cost several hundred dollars, if the Congressman had to go outside and pay union rates." Representatives used their "stationary fund" to pay for production fees and received additional help from their parties, including yearly production allowances. In 1972, for example, the Republican National Committee spent about $50,000 per month helping legislators send their video tapes back home (Anderson 1972). Production was not only cheaper for incumbents, but also of higher quality: "The congressional studio has such modern and expensive equipment that its TV footage is clearly superior in quality to the average material shot by a local television crew" (Bagdikian 1974).

There is no systematic record of how regularly these recordings found their way into the local newscasts or how frequently incumbents appeared on local talk shows. We cannot go back and check because the earliest local newscasts aired live and could not be recorded. Many stations did not archive their programming even when that became technically feasible at lower costs. The first large study of the amount of local news coverage received by members of Congress is Stephen Hess's (1991) *Live from Capitol Hill*. Hess collected his data in 1987–8 and only examined news programs, not representatives' interview programs or other candidate-supplied programming. Only a handful of House members appeared in sixty hours of local news on fifty-seven stations. Such minimal coverage might seem to invalidate any claim that local coverage of incumbents had a meaningful effect on congressional elections, especially because Hess took his snapshot at a time when the costs of reporting about Congress had decreased considerably compared to the 1960s. Satellite technology allowed local stations to report live from Washington. Members of Congress could be interviewed by the local anchor (e.g., Osterlund 1988; Tuden 1987). Broadcast chains began to employ pool reporters and sessions of Congress were televised beginning in 1979. These developments made it cheaper for local newscasts to include congressional coverage.

Yet even though cost of coverage decreased, so did local stations' inclination to use it. Local news in the 1970s showed the first signs of a trend toward softer coverage focused more on crime, disasters, and local curiosities. Coverage of Congress and the local incumbents, just as other political content, had to make room for tornadoes and car chases – which of course also became easier to cover with technological advances. Starting in 1973, the FCC required local broadcasters to identify the source of their congressional reports (Tracy 1975). Even though this policy was not strictly enforced, "news" supplied directly by a member of Congress became less attractive if stations could not implicitly claim credit for it. In the 1980s, writes Cook (1989, 59) in reference to network news, "television focused on only a handful of big stories; in the 1960s, broadcasts, which were more closely restricted to Washington and New York, covered many more aspects of congressional decisionmaking." We do not know if this was true for local news as well, but technological advances, the softening of local news in the late 1970s and 1980s, and changes in FCC requirements provide several reasons why Hess's analysis of the late 1980s may underestimate the amount of coverage incumbents received two decades earlier.[9]

In sharp contrast to Hess's results, a thorough examination of local news coverage of the House race in North Carolina's Fourth Congressional District in 1970 found 139 stories on the two major VHF stations in the district during the last six weeks of the campaign (Finney 1971). Even though these stories were only one minute long on average, the total airtime devoted to this congressional race amounted to twenty-five minutes per week. But of course it is impossible to know if this district was typical.

In the absence of systematic content analyses of early local news, we have to rely on anecdotal evidence about local stations' inclusion of incumbent-produced segments.[10] It worked for Gerald Ford, then a representative from Michigan. In a letter to Cronheim (1957, 98), he reported that "the one TV channel in my district generally uses a short film I make each week." More than half of the House members Cronheim (1957, 109, 113) interviewed said that local television stations in their district carried their telecasts regularly. In fact, "many Congressmen have been surprised

---

9 With respect to newspapers, Arnold (2004, 64) mentions a finding by Green, Fallows, and Zwick (1972) that a majority of House members managed to have their press releases or columns printed in their local newspapers (see also Saloma 1969, 175). According to Arnold's analysis, this kind of public relations is no longer common either.

10 For a detailed account of media coverage of Congress in the 1980s, see Cook (1989). Arnold (2004) and Vinson (2003) provide the picture in the 1990s. It is hard to say how much these more recent analyses can teach us about local television coverage of the House of Representatives in the 1950s and 1960s.

at the number of stations back home that stand ready to use their radio and TV shows" (U.S. News & World Report 1955, 71).

Certainly the motives for local stations are almost as clear as the motives for congressional incumbents. Broadcasting reports from Washington produced by members of Congress helped local stations fulfill the FCC's public affairs requirement without depleting their scarce news budgets. Even the cheapest locally produced program could not compete with the price of a free tape from Washington. It was the ideal environment for incumbents in Washington to get free airtime back home. "For $4.40 a Congressman can make a one-minute TV film. For a couple of dollars more he can have it shipped back home by air express where a local channel will fit it into a regular newscast as part of its public service program. Many Representatives do this as a weekly routine" (Goodman 1955, 14). Robertson (1965) describes the imaginative use of these tapes by some members of Congress in a time when satellite links were not yet available:

A Milwaukee station sends [Republican Representative Melvin R.] Laird written questions in advance. He records the answers on television in a sequence that begins with his picking up the telephone. The film is flown from Washington to Milwaukee. Then, on a Milwaukee TV news show, the commentator says "Let's talk to Congressman Mel Laird in Washington," picks up a phone and supposedly dials Mr. Laird's offices. The film has been cut and spliced so that Mr. Laird is next shown on the home screen answering the call and the questions.

The longer segments were broadcast as freestanding interview shows, often on Sunday mornings before or after national interview shows such as *Meet the Press*. Republican representative Kenneth Keating from Rochester, New York, for example, was seen on his fifteen-minute interview show *Let's Look at Congress* every other Sunday on seven television stations in northern New York (Otten 1957). In Lincoln, Nebraska, *Capitol Report* featured "Nebraska Congressmen [who] report on current Congressional affairs and activities from Washington, D.C., with particular emphasis on matters affecting their constituents." Local members of House and Senate were interviewed on *Man in Washington*, a half-hour Sunday show in Huntington, West Virginia (Television Information Office 1960, 100).

On some stations that served multiple congressional districts, the local members of Congress took turns or appeared on programs together. For example, several local representatives discussed public issues each week on *Congressional Close-Up* on WCBS in New York (Adams 1958). A San Francisco station offered *Ten Men*, a half-hour show in which "the ten men representing the area in Congress are interviewed separately by the station's news director" (Television Information Office 1960, 105).

Initially, even the networks offered interview shows. *Meet your Congress* aired on NBC in 1949 (on Fridays at 9:30 P.M.) and on the Dumont Network in 1953–4 (on Sundays at 6:30 P.M.). Four members of Congress appeared on this weekly half-hour interview show broadcast from Washington. The format was revived briefly by NBC for its *Congressional Report* in 1969 (Sundays at 6 P.M.). Other public affairs shows from Washington included *Capitol Cloakroom* on CBS in 1949–50 (on Fridays at 10:30 P.M.) (Castleman and Podrazik 1984; McNeil 1984). Networks also offered specials about Congress from time to time.[11]

By one estimate in 1959, half of all House members had regular interview shows on local stations in their home districts (Brown 1959). By 1964, 60 percent of representatives regularly used free time offered by their local stations back home, according to a survey of House members conducted by the magazine *Broadcasting* (Broadcasting 1964). In 1965, "about 360 of the 435 Representatives... [had] regular programs" on stations in their home districts (Robertson 1965). According to another survey, House members made an average of four television appearances per month when Congress was in session (Saloma 1969, 174). Incumbents even sent postcards to their constituents to let them know about their upcoming programs (U.S. News & World Report 1955).

With 96 percent of all local stations without Washington correspondents even by the early seventies (Gruenstein 1974, 39; Hess 1991), most members of Congress enjoyed a quasi-monopoly for providing news from the capital. According to one expert, "most citizens get most of their news about their Congressman from the Congressman himself" (Gruenstein 1974). In his analysis of news coverage in North Carolina's Fourth District, Finncy (1971, 112) found that one station often simply read press releases issued by the candidate. On both stations, "television reporting of the campaign was largely a relaying of messages originated by the candidates." This symbiotic relationship between local television stations and the area's representative in the U.S. House[12] occasionally bordered on

11 The Television Information Office (1965) compiled a list of programs "relating to law and the legislative process" that aired on the three networks between 1960 and 1964. Among the programs listed were an hour-long report on the House Rules Committee on CBS; *New Faces of Congress* on NBC about representatives newly elected in 1962; *Discovery '63: The Capitol*, "a visit to the Capitol where the laws of the land are made" on ABC; and *Ray Scherer's Sunday Report: Congress Summer 1963*, a "report on the accomplishments and the unfinished business of the first session of the 88th Congress" on NBC. Several other programs were devoted to legislative reapportionment and civil rights legislation. A number of the programs aired in prime time.

12 This was a symbiosis between members of Congress and local stations, not between members and individual reporters, as is perhaps more common and sometimes used

the unethical. MacNeil (1968, 248), for example, reports instances where local stations footed the bill for House members' purchase of film and other production expenses since their representative was "acting as our reporter on Washington activities."

THE EFFECT OF BROADCAST TELEVISION ON LEARNING ABOUT CONGRESSIONAL ELECTIONS

Television did not offer encyclopedic information about Congress. It did not provide more coverage than print media. But for those not regularly exposed to any political information before television, local news and public affairs programming on this new medium may have been the first periodic exposure to their representative's actions in Washington or in the home district. Here I examine if they learned anything about Congress from this exposure.

To determine if television increased political knowledge of Congress and congressional officeholders among the less educated, I use the same regression model as in Chapter 3, but change the dependent variable. Instead of combining all knowledge questions available in the National Election Studies into one index, I divide the questions into two groups. One index, knowledge of Congress, includes all items related to Congress (except for questions about challengers, which I cover later). These items include questions about majorities in Congress and about the incumbent running for reelection in the respondent's district. The second index, general political knowledge, combines all other items, among them questions about presidential candidates, the U.S. political system, and international affairs. (For a complete list, see appendix to Chapter 3.)

Studying the impact of television in congressional elections raises an issue that was of little relevance for the analyses in Chapter 3. As long as the assumed effect of television is to spread political information of national importance, it does not matter where the newscasts originate. Network newscasts generally emphasize national issues. Local news, on the other hand, focuses on topics that are of interest to the people living in the station's coverage area. This distinction matters little for the effects of television on general political knowledge and turnout that I documented in Chapter 3 because television news anywhere in the country contains general political information. If the television effect depends on watching news about their congressional districts, on the other hand, we should only find it for people whose local television stations cover the

to describe current relationships (see, for example, discussion in Cook 1989, 75–8; Vinson 2003, 2). A symbiosis involving individual reporters still leaves editors to intervene in cases of abuse.

congressional race in which they are eligible to vote. For a considerable number of citizens, this is unlikely. Residents of New Jersey receive their local news either from New York or Philadelphia. Yet the large majority of viewers who watch New York or Philadelphia stations do not live in New Jersey. This limits the incentives for news producers to cover New Jersey's congressional campaigns. Irrelevant for learning about politics in general, this consideration is consequential for learning about the candidates running in one's district.

My coding of the county-level reach of television stations (explained in Chapter 3) allows me to verify this proposition empirically. For each NES respondent, I know how many stations broadcast into his or her county of residence from within the state and from outside its boundaries. For learning about congressional elections, only the former should matter. For general political knowledge, in contrast, out-of-state stations should contribute to learning as well (though perhaps less so than in-state stations which might be closer and offer better reception).[13]

As before, I regress knowledge on the (logged) number of television stations and their interaction with education to express the expectation that television should have a larger effect among the less educated. The first column in Table 6.3 shows the impact on general political knowledge. For VHF and UHF stations that are located within the state, the coefficients reveal the familiar pattern: a positive and significant main effect of television, indicating that the number of stations is positively related to general political knowledge, and a negative and significant interaction, indicating that this effect is greater for respondents with low levels of education. At the 25th percentile of education, the difference between no and three UHF stations amounts to 8.3 points on the knowledge scale, about a third of a standard deviation. The effect of out-of-market stations is weaker, but the main effect is still significant (and the interaction approaches significance). As far as knowledge of national or international issues is concerned, stations located outside the respondent's state contributed to learning. Their effect was not as strong as that of an in-state station, presumably because they tended to be farther away and offer less reliable reception.

The Conditional Political Learning model works for congressional knowledge as well. Television increased knowledge of Congress and

13 Strictly speaking, the theoretical expectations are more complicated. Even an out-of-state station should cover the congressional election in the respondent's district if the majority of viewers in that station's coverage area reside in the same state (or, more precisely, district) as the respondent. The distinction between in-state and out-of-state is only an approximation of the market incentives – and thus the likely news content – of local stations.

Table 6.3. *The Impact of Television on General and Congressional Knowledge*

	General Political Knowledge		Congressional Knowledge	
	County TV Measure	District TV Measure	County TV Measure	District TV Measure
Number of in-state VHF stations (log)	5.2** (1.3)	–	3.2* (1.4)	–
In-state VHF stations × Education	1.2** (.4)	–	−1.5** (.4)	–
Number of In-state UHF stations (log)	3.9* (1.7)	–	4.4* (2.1)	–
In-state UHF stations × Education	−1.1* (.5)	–	−1.1* (.6)	–
Number of out-state stations (log)	2.2* (1.3)	–	0.4 (1.5)	–
Out-state stations × Education	−0.4 (.4)	–	−0.2 (.4)	–
Number of stations in district (log)	–	2.1** (.6)	–	2.7** (.7)
District stations × Education	–	−0.6** (.2)	–	−0.8** (.2)
Education	9.3** (.8)	7.4** (.3)	9.6** (.9)	8.3** (.4)
Female	−8.1** (.6)	−8.6** (.6)	−11.2** (.8)	−11.5** (.7)
African American	−9.6** (1.1)	−5.7** (1.0)	−18.1** (1.4)	−16.5** (1.2)
Age	0.14** (.02)	0.09** (.02)	0.18** (.03)	0.18** (.02)
Suburban area	1.3 (.9)	0.4 (.8)	−0.8 (1.1)	−0.8 (1.0)
Rural area	−2.0* (.9)	−3.2** (.8)	2.4* (1.1)	2.9** (1.0)
South	−0.4 (.8)	0.0002 (.69)	2.0* (1.0)	1.6* (.8)
R^2	0.40	0.37	0.22	0.23
N	5,312	6,770	6,520	7,973

* $p < .05$, ** $p < .01$ (one-tailed).

Note: The dependent variables are scored 0–100. Cell entries are OLS coefficients and standard errors in parentheses. Year dummies are included. Weights are used when required (NES 1958, 1960). Number of cases is unweighted.

Source: NES 1958–70, merged with Television Access Data Set.

congressional officeholders – if the stations were located in the same state. The effect of VHF stations in the third column in Table 6.3 is somewhat weaker than the equivalent effect on general knowledge. The effect of UHF stations is slightly stronger. These results reflect the expectation that Congress was not as widely covered as other political issues of national importance, but that the less educated still picked up a significant amount of information about their representative in Congress from the local news. The results also show that local news from another state did not affect congressional knowledge. Stations in other states tend to cover members of Congress other than the one running for reelection in the respondent's districts (e.g., Ostroff and Sandell 1984).

Later in this chapter, I examine the relationship between television and election outcomes in congressional elections. For that kind of analysis, congressional districts, not counties, are the natural unit of analysis. Election statistics provide us with the vote totals for the candidates running in each district. To relate those totals to the presence of television, we need to know how many television stations operate in the district. Because counties and districts do not always map into each other easily, a different measure of the broadcast television environment is required. In the analysis of survey data, I can use this district-level measure in the same way as the county-level measure employed so far. If this alternative measure produces similar results, the findings are unlikely to be an artifact of how the television stations operating in the respondent's vicinity are counted and grouped.

Instead of asking which stations reach a particular county, the second measure of the broadcast environment takes a particular district and assesses how many television stations reached at least part of the district. I used *The Historical Atlas of United States Congressional Districts, 1789–1983* (Martis, Lord, and Rowles 1982) to map counties onto congressional districts and to count the number of television stations operating in a congressional district during a particular election year. Each district that includes all or part of a county with a television station in operation in October of an election year was coded as having a local station. Because I had to determine television coverage for all districts, I did not use the same detailed coding as for counties with NES respondents that I used in Chapter 3. Instead, I added up all UHF and VHF stations, both independents and network affiliates.

The construction of the district-level measure assumes that local television stations in counties that do not overlap with the respondent's district do not affect his or her knowledge or voting behavior even though they might broadcast their signals into some parts of the district. That out-of-state stations had no effect on congressional learning suggests that this assumption is not unrealistic. (The county-level analysis implies, for example, that New Jersey residents learn little about their representatives from television no matter how many stations from Philadelphia or New York they receive. The district-based measure takes this into account, generating television counts of zero or one for all New Jersey districts.[14]) My estimates of the effect of local television are biased downward to

14 In 1966, WCMC-TV began operation as an independent station in Wildwood (in Cape May County, south of Atlantic City).

the extent that the assumption is wrong and that respondents learned from media coverage on out-of-district stations. Just like the county-level measure, the district-level measure can be merged with National Election Studies data.[15] As in Chapter 3, I use a log transformation to account for the marginally decreasing effects of each additional station.

The district-level measure confirms the results I obtained using the county-level television measure. As shown in columns 2 and 4 of Table 6.3, the number of television stations in the respondent's congressional district is positively related to his or her political knowledge. Again, this effect is larger among the less educated, as indicated by the negative interaction with education. There are at least two reasons why the effect is somewhat smaller when the district-level measure is used. First, some districts are a lot bigger than even the biggest counties. It is thus more likely that a television station somewhere in a district will not in fact reach the NES respondent who lives in the district. Second, the district-level measure counts all commercial television stations as long as they were located in a county that was part of the district. We already know that VHF stations had a stronger effect because their signals were more likely to actually reach a given individual in the county (or district). Including UHF stations dilutes the impact of more powerful VHF stations.[16] The main point here is that an operationally quite different measure of the television environment confirms the significant boost that

---

15 The NES 1952 and 1962 had to be excluded because they do not contain information on respondents' congressional districts necessary to merge the TV measure.

  For 1970, I collected district-level television data, but not the more detailed county-level information. I can thus conduct the survey analysis for that year using the number of stations in the district as an independent variable. The models shown in this chapter yield almost identical results when all survey analyses are restricted to the years between 1958 and 1968. (1958 was the first NES survey with congressional knowledge questions. I therefore restrict the comparison to years after 1956.)

  The NES 1970 contained the following knowledge items: Knows that Republicans are more conservative than Democrats; knowledge of House majority party before and after the election; knows defense budget; places Wallace at 6 or 7 on urban unrest and Vietnam scale; places Republicans to the right of Democrats on Vietnam, Wallace to the right of Muskie on aid to minorities, and Nixon to the right of Democrats on inflation; four questions about the constitution: "How many times can an individual be elected president of the United States?", "How long is the term of office for a U.S. senator?", "How long is the term for a member of the House of Representatives in Washington, D.C.?", "If the United States Congress passes a law, is there any way that the law can be changed without the agreement of Congress?"

16 I collected the district-level data before the county-level data without firm expectations about the possibly different impact of VHF and UHF stations.

broadcast television gave to learning about politics among less educated Americans.

BROADCAST TELEVISION AND THE INCUMBENCY ADVANTAGE IN CONGRESSIONAL ELECTIONS

When members of Congress start to produce their own interview shows and clips for the local news, and when television stations in their districts broadcast those segments eagerly, the political impact is unlikely to be neutral. The new medium of television offered more than an opportunity to educate constituents. The symbiosis between members of Congress and local stations amounted to free (or, at least, heavily subsidized) advertising for incumbents.

Television thus changed the balance of communications in the incumbent's favor. A more intense flow of information (relative to the opponent) helps on Election Day, especially among voters with less elaborate political worldviews such as the less educated. In his seminal analysis of campaign effects, Zaller (1992, 228) concludes with respect to House elections that the "incumbent's high-intensity campaign manages to reach less aware voters, whereas the challenger's less intense campaign does not. Therefore the incumbent reaps big gains among the less aware." This describes the situation after the advent of television. Before television, the less aware (or, according to Chapter 3, the less educated) did not hear much at all about congressional elections. Televisions brought them the incumbent's message, but not the challenger's.

Highly politically aware voters, in contrast, heard both sides on television. But they were also more resistant to campaign effects because they could "counterargue" campaign messages more easily. They may just have discounted what they heard from the candidate who did not share their party affiliation. Such discounting was less likely among the less educated even when they did not share the incumbent's party affiliation. The incumbent's message could still impress them because their political worldviews were not developed enough to supply them with arguments to counter the incumbent's message. In congressional elections, partisan cues were often not as readily available because officeholders, representing the entire district, tried to extend their appeal (and their constituency service and procurement of pork) to constituents who did not share their party affiliation. Party attachment among less educated voters was of little help as a cue when the incumbent appealed to his entire constituency. Instead, a second simple cue exerted a powerful influence in congressional elections: incumbency. Experiments have shown that people are more likely to consider candidates viable and support them when they are described as incumbents (Kahn 1993; McDermott 2005). In congressional elections, less educated citizens encouraged by television to go to the polls may have relied on incumbency as a cue.

In short, incumbents should have benefited handily from the availability of television because they managed to dominate the information flow and because newly drafted voters with lower levels of education were especially likely to use incumbency as a voting cue.

And in fact, vote margins for incumbents in House elections rose sharply in the 1960s (e.g., Alford and Brady 1993; Ansolabehere, Snyder, and Stewart 2000; Gelman and King 1990; Levitt and Wolfram 1997). When measured in terms of vote share, the incumbency advantage jumped from 2 or 3 percentage points in the early 1950s (and even lower levels before then) to around 8 points in the second half of the sixties. Improved reelection chances for incumbents increase the combined experience of Congress, but they may also impede the responsiveness of the institution to voter preferences (especially if the incumbency advantage reflects the persuasiveness of messages that have little issue content or are strongly biased).

Could television have something to do with rising vote margins for House incumbents? More than thirty years after the rise in vote margins in the 1960s was first noticed (Erikson 1971; Mayhew 1974), the reasons for this increase are still not fully understood. Scholars have offered several explanations, including increased constituency service (e.g., Fiorina 1977a), partisan dealignment (e.g., Cover 1977; Nelson 1978), redistricting (e.g., Cox and Katz 2002), and greater electoral impact of candidate quality (Cox and Katz 1996). But each of these explanations has encountered criticism and cannot fully account for the empirical patterns. Here, I examine whether an exogenous factor, the rise of broadcast television, did indeed improve the vote margins of congressional incumbents.[17]

---

17 It seems justified to treat local television as an exogenous variable because descriptions of the licensing process for new local stations by the FCC do not suggest that House incumbents intervened successfully on behalf of applicants in their constituencies. Wolf (1972, 74) points out that some representatives and senators owned stock in TV stations, but those cases seem to have been exceptions. Contemporary estimates put the number of legislators with major financial stakes in TV stations at thirty in 1961. Another estimate in 1967 showed even fewer (only five) cases. Some legislators also had connections to law firms that represented television stations (or had done so in the past). The most powerful efforts to influence the licensing process came from the broadcasting industry (Baughman 1985; Noll, Peck, and McGowan 1973) and occasionally incumbent senators (Baughman 1985, 18; Bendiner 1957, 29). After a station had received a license, some members of Congress tried to expedite license renewal or to help their home

Broadcast TV, Partisanship, and Incumbency Advantage

Congressional Campaigns on Television

As a result of the symbiosis between local television stations and members of Congress, incumbents with a television station back home presumably entered the campaign season with an advantage in name recognition and favorability ratings. Even safe incumbents, who are infrequently covered in modern campaigns (Clarke and Evans 1983; Kahn and Kenney 1999), should have reaped the benefits of television because a large part of the pro-incumbent effect of television accrued before the campaign started. But, as Goodman (1955, 14) describes, television continued to advantage incumbents during the campaign:

Of course, these programs [produced by incumbents in Washington] are presented as a public service only until the Congressman officially files for the upcoming elections. Then he must pay for time over his local channel, just as his opponent must pay for it. But, unlike the fellow who is trying to unseat him, he still has access to government production service at very nominal fees, and, more important, he has a long head start on the contender. The incumbent's election-day benefit from his regular appearances in his constituents' living rooms between elections is incalculable.

In addition to obtaining plenty of free news coverage during their term, incumbents were in a better position to use the new medium during their campaigns. (The equal-time restrictions that led to suspension of free-standing programs during the campaign did not apply to short film clips produced by incumbents that stations inserted into their local newscasts.) Incumbents were likely to receive more coverage than challengers during the campaign because of their greater newsworthiness (Clarke and Evans 1983; Cook 1989; Robinson 1981). And this local news coverage was usually much less critical than national news (Robinson 1981), as local stations "were more apt to cover uncritically an event that the network might consider too soft or too biased for consideration" (Mickelson 1989, 161).

Incumbents' campaign funds tended to exceed those of challengers considerably, allowing them to secure an advantage in paid media as well (Goldenberg and Traugott 1984; Jacobson 1975, 785; 2004). Paid advertising in the form of thirty-second commercials was not yet common in the 1950s (for presidential advertising, see Jamieson 1996, 97–8), but candidates – and incumbents in particular – would often buy longer

stations switch network affiliation (Baughman 1985, 74). But because licenses were hardly ever revoked for nontechnical reasons (Noll, Peck, and McGowan 1973), this preservation of the status quo does not lead to serious endogeneity concerns either.

chunks of airtime, up to fifteen or even thirty minutes, to broadcast preproduced speeches or other programs (for examples, see Goodman 1955).[18] Ads and local news coverage of congressional elections were thus more similar, both because ads were longer and less technically sophisticated and because news coverage was often produced by the candidate. Because of this similarity, it is perhaps less of a problem that we cannot know if paid or free media helped incumbents more. In any case, the similarity also emphasizes that media messages in congressional elections in the early days of television were quite different from what they are today. Regardless of whether paid or free media were more important, incumbents should have obtained greater benefits from local television stations in their districts than challengers, both before and during the campaign.

Incumbents were in fact increasingly successful in getting their messages across to their less educated constituents. Figure 6.2 plots the probability that a voter with relatively low education (8 grades of school or less, the 25th percentile of education in this time period) would know the incumbent's name, which of the two major parties contested the election in the district, and which of the two candidates was the incumbent. The probability is shown as a function of the number of television stations in the respondent's district. For all three knowledge questions, television significantly increased the probability of responding correctly. (I do not show the relationship among higher levels of education because the effect is limited to the less educated as in Chapter 3 and Table 6.3.) In sharp contrast, television did not affect people's ability to recall the challenger's name at any level of education. The results support the proposition that the learning effect of television extended to knowledge about congressional elections, but that only incumbents benefited because only they had the means to influence the content of local television or were newsworthy enough to be covered.[19] Evaluated by its effect on voters, the change

18 In the 1972 presidential campaign, 41 percent of the ads aired by the Nixon and McGovern campaigns were five minutes long. Five-minute spots accounted for over three-quarters of their total advertising time (Patterson and McClure 1976, 107).

19 The knowledge questions about the candidates were asked in several different studies between 1958 and 1970. Name recall and the question about incumbency status were asked in the surveys in 1958, 1964, 1966, and 1968. The question about which party was running a candidate appeared in 1966 and 1968. (All of these items are included in the summary measure of congressional knowledge in Table 6.1.) To estimate the relationship in Figure 6.2, I ran pooled logit models that included all valid cases in one model (per question) and dummy variables for the year of the survey. I excluded elections without incumbents. In all three models, the main effect

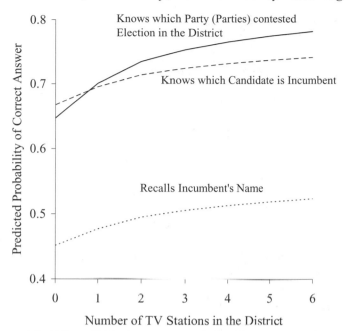

Figure 6.2. The Effect of Television on Knowledge of House Incumbents among the Less Educated.

Note: The figure plots predicted values from three pooled logit models (one for each question), each of which included all valid cases for each knowledge question in one model. The predicted values are for the 25th percentile of education (less than nine years of schooling). The independent variables are the same as those in Table 6.4. Dummy variables for the year of the survey are included. Control variables are set to their sample means. Each year dummy is set to the proportion of cases for the particular year (i.e., to its sample mean). Elections without incumbents are excluded.
Source: NES 1958, 64–8, merged with Television Access Data Set.

in the information flow brought about by television looks anything but neutral in congressional elections.

The available survey data do not allow me to examine more detailed knowledge of candidates' issue positions or past accomplishments and mistakes. But my argument is not that television taught constituents a lot about their representatives. It probably did not. Television did offer a few simple voting cues, and, as the remainder of this chapter demonstrates,

for the logged number of television stations was positive and significant at $p < .07$. The p values for the (negative) interaction of television stations and education were .02, .05, and .23. The main and interaction effects in the same model with challenger recall as the dependent variable yield small and statistically insignificant coefficients.

these cues had enough power to give political significance to the learning effects that did occur.

The Effect of Television on Voting Behavior

Familiarity with a candidate has a considerable impact on people's voting decisions (Goldenberg and Traugott 1984; Jacobson 2004; Stokes and Miller 1962). Because local television raised their familiarity with the incumbent, but not the challenger, less educated Americans should have become more likely to vote for the incumbent as the number of television stations in their district grew.[20] On top of familiarity effects, messages produced by the incumbent and favorable news coverage about the incumbent probably persuaded more than a few voters to reward their representatives with another term. To examine whether television increased people's likelihood of voting for the incumbent, I regress respondents' vote choice on education, the number of television stations, and the interaction between the two, using both the county- and the district-based measure of the television environment.

The dependent variable in the models in Table 6.4 is 1 if the respondent voted for the incumbent and 0 if she voted for the challenger. I exclude all nonvoters.[21] The models include a variety of control variables. If the presence of local television is correlated with challenger quality – either because the option or necessity of a television campaign deters strong challengers or for reasons unrelated to television – incumbents' vote shares in districts with local stations could be higher even in the absence of a television effect. Although there is little indication of such a correlation, I include challenger quality as a control variable to account

---

20 The lack of political information in the electorate helps incumbents, according to an analysis by Althaus (2001) in which he simulates how less informed citizens would vote if they were "fully informed." This does not mean, however, that television should have disadvantaged incumbents by disseminating information. First, because of the possible substitution away from newspaper reading, it is not clear that the overall effect of television was to increase knowledge. Second, information about congressional elections presented on television was often slanted toward the incumbent. Third, exposure to television news motivated less educated citizens to vote without teaching them a lot about politics. Compared to other voters, the newly drafted TV voters were relatively ill-informed and should, according to Althaus's results, have been more likely to support the incumbent because they lacked detailed information.

21 For years after 1956, the analysis excludes respondents who lived in their current district or community for fewer than six months. They could not have been affected in the same way as others by the incumbent's presence on the local airwaves. This restriction reduces the number of cases by about 3.5 percent. The variable is not available for 1956, so all valid cases are included.

Table 6.4. *The Impact of Local Television on Voting for the Incumbent*

	County TV Measure	District TV Measure
Number of in-state VHF stations (log)	0.21§ (.13)	–
In-state VHF stations × Education	−0.093** (.035)	–
Number of in-state UHF stations (log)	0.20 (.18)	–
In-state UHF stations × Education	−0.061 (.054)	–
Number of out-of-state stations (log)	0.052 (.13)	–
Out-of-state stations × Education	−0.020 (.034)	–
Number of stations in district (log)	–	0.19** (.07)
District stations × Education	–	−0.061** (.018)
Education	0.22** (.08)	0.14** (.03)
Campaign interest	−0.08 (.11)	−0.10 (.10)
Incumbent seniority	0.014 (.011)	0.014 (.011)
Challenger quality	−0.19** (.07)	−0.22** (.07)
Incumbent holds leadership position	−0.15 (.93)	−0.17 (.92)
Incumbent chairs standing committee	0.32 (.24)	0.24 (.22)
Number of candidates >2	0.089 (.087)	0.12 (.08)
Economic optimism	0.34** (.12)	0.33** (.11)
Church attendance	0.18* (.10)	0.16* (.09)
Female	0.005 (.069)	−0.02 (.07)
African American	0.28* (.17)	0.20 (.16)
Age	−0.002 (.003)	−0.001 (.002)
Suburban area	−0.41** (.10)	−0.40** (.09)
Rural area	−0.33** (.10)	−0.20* (.09)
District area (in 1,000 sq mi)	–	−0.007** (.003)
South	0.41** (.12)	0.39** (.11)
Redistricted district	0.13 (.11)	0.14 (.11)
N	3,984	4,484
Log likelihood	−2,536.2	−2,855.5
Pseudo-R^2	0.040	0.038

§ $p < .055$, * $p < .05$, ** $p < .01$ (one-tailed).

Note: Cell entries are logit coefficient estimates and standard errors in parentheses. Weights are used when required (NES 1958, 1960). Number of cases is unweighted N. The analysis excludes open and uncontested elections as well as respondents who lived in their current districts or communities for less than six months (except in 1956 where this variable is not available). All models include year dummies and dummies for Democratic and Republican respondents for each year. Dummies are included (but not shown) for respondents with missing data on incumbent seniority or economic optimism.

Source: NES 1958–60, 1964–70, merged with Television Access Data Set.

for this possibility. Quality of the challenger is defined as having previously held elective office (Cox and Katz 1996; Jacobson 2004).[22] The incumbent's seniority is included as a control because more senior members of Congress may more successfully attract news coverage. For the same reason, I collected data on other indicators of newsworthiness that have been shown to affect network news coverage (Cook 1989, 62): party leadership positions (Speaker, majority leader, minority leader, or whip) and service as chair or ranking minority member on a major standing congressional committee.[23]

Because a "considerable number of solidly entrenched Democratic representatives and senators from the one-party South...did not have to rely heavily on this medium [television] to maintain themselves in office" (Chester 1969, 163), all models include a control variable for Southern states.[24] Because urban districts are more likely than rural areas to have several television stations, I include the geographical size of the district[25] and whether the respondent lived in a city, a suburb, or rural America. With these controls in the model, it is unlikely that the television variable picks up possible changes in voting behavior of urban residents that are not related to the presence of local stations. Finally, all analyses include several demographic control variables also used in Chapter 3, including education, age, and race.

Table 6.4 contains two models, one that uses the county-level measure of the television environment employed in Chapter 3 and one that uses the district-level measure introduced earlier in this chapter. Results should be quite similar, except for out-of-state television stations, which are counted in the county measure but left out of the district measure. As Table 6.4 demonstrates, the main effect of television and its interaction with education are both of almost identical magnitude for the three counts of in-state stations (VHF stations in the county, UHF stations in the county, and all stations in the district). Stations that broadcast into the

22 Both Cox and Katz and the present analysis use Gary Jacobson's data on candidate quality.
23 I included the following committees: Appropriations, Rules, Ways and Means, Agriculture, Armed Services, Interstate and Foreign Commerce (later Energy and Commerce), Foreign Affairs, and Judiciary. Data on committee positions are from Garrison Nelson, *Committees in the U.S. Congress, 1947–1992* (available on Charles Stewart's homepage at MIT).
24 The South is defined as Alabama, Arkansas, Florida, Georgia, Louisiana, Mississippi, North Carolina, South Carolina, Tennessee, Texas, and Virginia. Alaska, Hawaii, and the District of Columbia are excluded from the analysis.
25 Data on size of the district come from Scott Adler's (2002) data set. District size is only included in the models that use the district-level television measures.

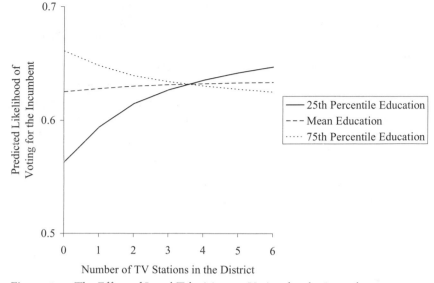

Figure 6.3. The Effect of Local Television on Voting for the Incumbent.

Note: This graph is based on predicted values from the second model in Table 6.4. Control variables are set to their sample means. Each year dummy is set to the proportion of cases for the particular year (i.e., to its sample mean).

Source: NES 1958–60, 1964–70, merged with Television Access Data Set.

respondent's county but are located in another state, in contrast, do not have any noticeable effect on voting behavior. This is consistent with the explanation that out-of-state local news was less likely to devote much airtime to in-state incumbents.

Both measurement approaches thus agree that in-state television stations increased the probability that less educated constituents would vote for the incumbent. Figure 6.3 plots the results, holding other independent variables constant at their sample means. The likelihood that a voter in the 25th percentile of education would cast her vote for the incumbent rose from .56 when her district did not have any local stations to .63 in a district with three stations. The impact of three local television stations – the median number of stations per district after 1966 – thus amounted to an 11 percent increase in the probability of voting for the incumbent. At the mean level of education, the pro-incumbent effect of television is essentially zero. Among highly educated voters, local television even decreased the likelihood of voting for the incumbent slightly.

The increased likelihood of voting for incumbents in districts with television is not simply an effect of greater success for incumbents in urban areas that happened to have more television stations. While incumbents might have become more successful in cities for other reasons – more effective constituency service, for example – the models in Table 6.4 include control variables that account for such an effect. Both models include dummies for suburban and rural counties (leaving urban counties as the omitted baseline), showing that the probability of a vote for the incumbent was indeed larger for urban residents. The model using the district-based television measure additionally includes the geographical size of the respondent's district. Incumbents did better in small (i.e., urban) districts. After accounting for these effects, however, television still had a significant effect on voting for the incumbent.[26]

The models in Table 6.4 control for partisan tides by including dummy variables for Republican and Democratic respondents. These variables are interacted with the year dummies, allowing partisan tides of different magnitude and direction in different years. The specification accounts for the possibility that Democrats or Republicans may have been more likely to reelect incumbents in some years than others – for example, when a presidential candidate carried heavy coattails or when members of one party were particularly happy or unhappy with the performance of Congress. Another way to account for the effects of partisan tides is to control for the party of the incumbent (allowing the effect to vary across elections). Doing so does not change the estimated effect of television in Table 6.4.

For additional assurance that television was indeed the causal factor in improving the fortunes of congressional incumbents, we can check to see whether self-professed news viewers were indeed more affected by television than others. Television's effect was most pronounced among less educated Americans, many of whom did not follow politics in the pre-television days when doing so required reading a paper or listening to the radio. Yet even though local and network news reached more people than any other medium before, they missed more than a few. The effect of television should have been limited to those who watched. If incumbents' ability to insert themselves into the local news generated their increased electoral success, television should have predominantly affected the votes of news viewers.[27] NES data allow a rough distinction

26 The television effects do not change either when interactions between the urbanism dummies and education (or between district area and education) are included. This further corroborates the television effect, ruling out the proposition that less educated respondents living in urban areas became more likely to vote for incumbents for some other reason in this time period.

27 To the extent that advertising was the driving force, television viewers may have been affected regardless of their exposure to news, unless most ads aired during the news, as is the case in today's campaigns.

between respondents who reported watching campaign coverage on television and those who did not.[28] The questions differentiate neither local and national news, nor presidential and congressional campaigns. Despite the noisy measure, the comparison of the television effect at high and low levels of exposure shows that the effect was strongest among respondents who watched news reports on a more or less regular basis. Using the district-based measure, the main effect of television at high exposure ($N = 2,414$) is .29 and the interaction is $-.09$. Both coefficients are significant at $p < .005$. Among respondents who reported low television exposure ($N = 2,070$), the main effect is only .11, the interaction effect is $-.03$, and neither is statistically significant (for full results, see Prior 2006). Splitting the sample in a similar way by radio or newspaper exposure does not generate any differences, suggesting that exposure to television rather than general political interest facilitated the pro-incumbent effect of local television.[29] That exposure to politics on television was a prerequisite for the pro-incumbent effect of the new medium is further evidence that rising incumbent vote margins were not a result of greater campaign activity in general, but of television in particular.[30]

28 Television news exposure is measured based on two items. The first (included in the NES cumulative file as VCF0724) asked respondents: "How about television – did you watch any programs about the campaign on television? [if yes] how many television programs about the campaign would you say you watched – a good many, several, or just one or two?" The second item asked: "Of all these ways of following the campaign, which one would you say you got the most information from – newspapers, radio, television or magazines?" The first item was included in 1960, 1964, and 1968, the second item in those three years and 1966. About half of the respondents reported watching "a good many" programs and getting most of their news from television. These respondents are included in the high exposure group, while everyone else is classified as low in television exposure. (For 1966, the second item alone distinguished high and low exposure.)

29 Main and interaction effects among frequent listeners to news on the radio were .20 and $-.08$, respectively ($N = 1,584$). The same coefficients among infrequent listeners were .18 and $-.05$ ($N = 2,892$). For newspaper use, the difference is equally small: .19 and $-.07$ for frequent readers ($N = 2,016$) compared to .19 and $-.06$ among less frequent readers ($N = 2,465$). Clearly, radio or newspaper exposure to news or campaign messages had little to do with the rising incumbency advantage.

30 The impact of television on party identification documented earlier in this chapter creates a problem for the analysis of voting behavior. If television lowered partisanship among voters by encouraging less partisan Americans to vote, then party identification becomes endogenous. When identification with the incumbent's party is included in the individual-level models, the effect of television declines. It does remain significant for the subset of voters most likely to be affected by television, those who report some television exposure to the campaign. Empirically, the likelihood of identifying with the incumbent's party was somewhat higher in areas with

The Television Effect at the District Level

The individual-level analysis suggests that television helped House incumbents get reelected. For further support of my hypothesis that the growth of television contributed to the rise in the incumbency advantage, I conduct a parallel analysis at the aggregate level to determine if incumbents did better in congressional districts with television stations. While the main reason for using both individual and aggregate data is to verify results using different methodologies, aggregate analysis also has a unique advantage. It does not have to rely on self-reported votes, but instead examines the effect of television on the vote as measured by official vote statistics. If successful, the replication with aggregate data can thus rule out that the individual-level result is an artifact of using respondents' reports of their own vote choice. The aggregate analysis also tracks the effect of television over time.

The unit of analysis in the aggregate data set is the congressional district. The data set covers House elections between 1946 and 1970. For each year, Table 6.5 shows the number of congressional districts with at least one television station and the average number of stations per district. Already before the early 1950s, up to a third of the congressional districts had at least one station in their boundaries. Television's impact on political knowledge and public opinion was muted, however, by the low number of Americans with a television set at home. The TV freeze between 1948 and 1952 is evident in the big jump in districts with television following the resolution of the issue in the early 1950s. The growth of television at the district level was marked first, until the mid 1950s, by a constant increase in the percentage of districts with at least one station (both because new television markets emerged and because an increasing proportion of districts was located in faster-growing urban areas[31]). In the second half of the period studied here, few new districts gained access to television, but the mean number of stations doubled in districts that already had at least one station.

television. Perhaps television disproportionately encouraged less educated citizens to vote who identified with the incumbent's party. Or the pro-incumbent bias on television led some people to report a closer attachment to the incumbent's party. I have found no good reason why television stations should been more likely to emerge in incumbent strongholds (see also footnote 17 in this chapter).

31 Continuing urbanization in the 1950s and 1960s together with the Supreme Court's *Wesberry v. Sanders* decision, which, in 1964, mandated roughly equal population sizes across all districts in a state, led to an increasing number of districts in cities (see, for example, Cox and Katz 2002). The percentage of districts under 100 square miles increased from 13 percent in 1950 to 19 percent in 1966.

Table 6.5. *The Growth of Television in Congressional Districts*

	All Districts				Districts with Contested Elections and No Redistricting after Previous Election					
	Number of Districts[a]	Number of Districts with at Least One TV Station	Mean Number of Stations per District	Median Number of Stations per District	Number of Districts	Percentage with at Least One TV Station	Mean Number of Stations per District	Percentage of Republican Districts[b] with TV Station	Percentage of Democratic Districts[b] with TV Station	Bivariate Regression Coefficient for Inc. Vote Share on Number of Stations[c]
1946	428	60	0.36	0	347	17	0.45	9	28	−0.61 (.62)
1948	429	113	0.90	0	330	29	1.00	28	34	−0.15 (.40)
1950	429	155	1.26	0	341	42	1.53	26	55	−0.03 (.25)
1952	427	158	1.26	0	183	(33)	(.91)	(27)	(51)	[−0.70 (.42)]
1954	428	287	1.86	1	342	70	2.10	68	71	0.25 (.23)
1956	428	305	2.07	2	353	75	2.31	71	81	0.26 (.21)
1958	431	315	2.17	2	332	74	2.38	70	82	0.63* (.27)
1960	430	322	2.25	2	350	75	2.43	70	78	0.69** (.24)
1962	417	295	2.22	2	171	(68)	(1.86)	(60)	(73)	[0.54 (.29)]
1964	427	307	2.35	2	334	71	2.48	69	73	0.74** (.24)
1966	430	325	2.67	3	208	76	3.19	76	76	1.00** (.23)
1968	432	340	3.05	3	215	74	2.57	72	77	0.73** (.26)
1970	432	346	3.17	3	322	78	3.14	74	79	0.58** (.18)

[a] At-large districts are excluded unless they are the state's only district.

[b] Republican (Democratic) districts refer to districts with a Republican (Democratic) incumbent.

[c] OLS regression coefficients with standard errors in parentheses, * $p < .05$, ** $p < .01$. Incumbent vote share is scored 0–100.

Note: Cell entries in parentheses should be interpreted with caution because they exclude a large number of redistricted districts.

The right-hand side of Table 6.5 shows the growth of television in districts that fulfilled the two conditions to be included in the analysis: They had a contested election, and they were not redistricted after the last election. (I explain in the next paragraph why these conditions are imposed.) In most years, districts with few television stations were slightly more likely to be eliminated by these conditions, but, as the table shows, this difference was small (and not always in the same direction). Table 6.5 also indicates that both parties' incumbents were in a similar position to take advantage of the new medium. Except for a few years in the early 1950s, districts represented by Republican incumbents were about as likely to have television as districts with Democratic representatives.[32]

To estimate the incumbency advantage at the district level, I use the extended Gelman and King (1990) estimator proposed by Cox and Katz (1996). The Gelman-King estimator measures the incumbency advantage by comparing incumbents' vote shares to open-seat elections. The incumbency advantage is the portion of the vote that the incumbent would not have received if he had been a candidate for an open seat (and everything else had been the same). To account for district-level differences between candidates, the estimator includes the election outcome in the previous election as a control variable. This baseline is only accurate for districts that did not change between elections, so redistricted districts have to be excluded from the aggregate analysis.[33] I also exclude uncontested elections and representatives elected by the state population at large (except in states that elect only one representative). District-level vote returns as well as information about the candidates running in the district are taken from Gary King's (1994) data set of congressional election results. The incumbent's vote share is calculated as a percentage of the two-party vote.

---

32 Between 1954 and 1960, the incumbent was a Republican in 48 (52) percent and a Democrat in 41 (38) percent of the contested elections in districts which had not been redistricted. The rest were open-seat elections. (Numbers in parentheses are for non-Southern districts only.) Republican incumbents won in 91 (91) percent of their election; Democratic incumbents, 94 (93) percent of theirs. Between 1964 and 1970, the incumbent was a Republican in 42 (46) percent and a Democrat in 49 (47) percent of the contested elections in districts that had not been redistricted. Republican incumbents won in 92 (91) percent of their election; Democratic incumbents, 94 (93) percent of theirs (numbers in parentheses are for non-Southern districts only).

33 In the individual-level analysis, I simply controlled for redistricting. It is not necessary to exclude survey respondents in redistricted districts just because they chose between a "new" incumbent and a challenger, but a control for redistricting was required to pick up the effect of potentially lower familiarity with the new incumbent.

Broadcast TV, Partisanship, and Incumbency Advantage

Cox and Katz (1996) have extended the original Gelman-King model by including direct and indirect effects of challenger quality and an indicator of incumbency status in the previous election. The primary purpose of their extension is to take into account incumbents' potential to discourage experienced opponents from challenging them (by inducing them to run in another district or wait for an open seat). This "scare-off" effect is one of the advantages of incumbency, yet the original Gelman-King estimator did not measure it.

The model expresses the Democratic share of the district vote as a function of the Democratic vote share in the previous election, the party defending the seat, and the incumbent in the current and the previous election. As proposed by Cox and Katz, the Democratic candidate's quality advantage is included as a control variable. The model also controls for the effects of the incumbent's seniority, whether or not the incumbent held a party leadership position, whether or not he or she chaired a major standing committee, as well as the size of the district, and whether or not the district is in the South. As explained earlier, these variables might be related to the effect of television, so the model should adjust for their effects. Finally, to estimate the contribution of television to the overall incumbency advantage, I add my measure of the number of television stations in the district, using the same logarithmic transformation as in the individual-level analysis.[34]

---

34 Formally, the model for each district is:

$$\begin{aligned}
DVOTE_t = {} & \beta^1\, DVOTE_{t-1} + \beta_t^2\, PARTY_t + \beta_t^3\, INCUMBENCY_t \\
& + \beta_t^4\, INCUMBENCY_{t-1} + \beta_t^5\, DQUALITY_t + \beta_t^6\, DQUALITY_{t-1} \\
& + \beta^7\, SENIORITY_t + \beta^8\, SENIORITY_t \times INCUMBENCY_t \\
& + \beta^9\, COMMITTEE_t + \beta^{10}\, COMMITTEE_t \times INCUMBENCY_t \\
& + \beta^{11}\, LEADER_t + \beta^{12}\, LEADER_t \times INCUMBENCY_t + \beta^{13}\, SOUTH_t \\
& + \beta^{14}\, SOUTH_t \times INCUMBENCY_t + \beta^{15}\, AREA_t \\
& + \beta^{16}\, AREA_t \times INCUMBENCY_t + \beta_t^{17}\, TV_t \\
& + \beta_t^{18}\, TV_t \times INCUMBENCY_t + e_t
\end{aligned}$$

$PARTY_t$ is 1 if a Democrat won the election, -1 if a Republican was the winner; $INCUMBENCY_t$ and $INCUMBENCY_{t-1}$ were 1 for Democratic incumbent, -1 for Republican incumbent, and 0 for open races. $DQUALITY_t$ and $DQUALITY_t$ are coded $+1$ (-1) if only the Democratic (Republican) candidate held elective office before; if both or neither candidate held previous office, the variable is 0. The other variables are explained in the text. Coefficients with t subscripts are estimated for each year, while the effects of the other variables are assumed to be constant across this time period.

This model decomposes the incumbency advantage into three elements: the part explained by local television (β^{18}), the part explained by the controls (β^8, β^{10}, β^{12}, β^{14}, β^{16}), and the unexplained rest (β^3). This specification distinguishes the impact of television on incumbents (β^{18}) from the impact of television on candidates of a particular party (β^{17}).

The model is estimated by OLS for each election between 1948 and 1970 (excluding the years immediately following a census, 1952 and 1962, because many districts were redistricted). Table 6.6 presents the results for contested elections with an incumbent.[35] Estimates of the impact of television on the incumbency advantage are bolded in the table. They are statistically significant starting in 1960 and increase between 1960 and 1968. The coefficient 0.0080 for 1964, for example, indicates that for each additional unit on the (logged) television measure, the incumbent in the district received an additional 0.8 percentage points of the two-party vote. The log transformation makes it difficult to interpret the magnitude of the effects. Therefore, Figure 6.4 graphs the estimated television effect, the contribution of television to the overall incumbency advantage (shown by the dotted line labeled "Direct TV Effect"). This estimate is obtained by multiplying each year's coefficient estimate by the mean number of (logged) stations for that year. Estimates rise from half a percentage point or less throughout most of the 1950s to a high of 2.8 points in 1968.

Figure 6.4 also graphs a measure of the television-based incumbency advantage that takes into account the indirect effect of television on candidate quality, following Cox and Katz's (1996) approach. An indirect advantage of incumbency is to scare off high-quality challengers. To the extent that incumbents do better against low-quality challengers, this scare-off effect is an indirect advantage of their status and should be added to the direct incumbency advantage. It turns out that television did not significantly change the scare-off effect, except in one year, 1966, which happens to be the year for which most measures of incumbency advantage find the biggest jump. In 1966, the indirect effect of television amounted to about half of the direct effect. When the two components are added (solid line in Figure 6.4), the television-based incumbency advantage traces the notorious jump in 1966 somewhat better.[36,37]

---

35 Table 6.5 details how many districts were excluded and why. A different estimation strategy would be to include fixed effects for districts (Levitt and Wolfram 1997). For the period under study here, a fixed-effects model is difficult to implement because many districts were redistricted frequently. As a robustness check, I reestimated the model with fixed effects for any district that remained unchanged for at least three elections. The estimated TV effect changed only marginally.

36 1966 is also the first year after *Wesberry v. Sanders*, which led to an unusual amount of redistricting and therefore a lower number of valid cases for analysis than in other years.

37 The direct effect of candidate quality on vote margins is not mediated by the number of stations in the district.

Table 6.6. *Effect of Local Television on District-Level Incumbency Advantage*

	1970	1968	1966	1964	1960	1958	1956	1954	1950	1948
TV_t	0.0040	0.0046	0.0047	0.0052	0.0032	0.0001	0.0056	0.0091**	−0.0005	0.0003
	(.0033)	(.0042)	(.0043)	(.0034)	(.0033)	(.0035)	(.0034)	(.0036)	(.0034)	(.0039)
$TV_t \times INCUMBENCY_t$	**0.0078***	0.0131**	0.0087**	0.0080*	0.0076*	0.00001	0.0044	0.0026	−0.0057	0.0006
	(.0035)	(.0044)	(.0044)	(.0035)	(.0035)	(.0038)	(.0036)	(.0037)	(.0036)	(.0041)
$PARTY_t$	0.005	0.012	−0.049**	−0.003	−0.023*	0.014	0.028*	0.007	0.021*	0.027**
	(.013)	(.014)	(.018)	(.012)	(.011)	(.011)	(.013)	(.012)	(.011)	(.010)
$INCUMBENCY_t$	0.068**	0.038*	0.082**	0.031**	0.039**	0.030**	0.002	0.035**	0.004	−0.003
	(.012)	(.017)	(.020)	(.012)	(.012)	(.012)	(.013)	(.012)	(.011)	(.011)
$INCUMBENCY_{t-1}$	−0.023*	−0.005	0.007	−0.010	0.012*	0.003	0.007	0.003	0.026**	0.009
	(.011)	(.008)	(.009)	(.009)	(.007)	(.008)	(.007)	(.008)	(.007)	(.007)
$DQUALITY_t$	0.037**	0.030**	0.042**	0.019**	0.021**	0.021**	0.017*	0.021**	0.027**	0.038**
	(.008)	(.010)	(.011)	(.008)	(.007)	(.007)	(.008)	(.008)	(.008)	(.008)
$DQUALITY_{t-1}$	−0.002	−0.011	0.006	0.018*	0.010	0.020**	−0.003	0.006	0.015*	0.008
	(.007)	(.010)	(.010)	(.008)	(.007)	(.008)	(.007)	(.008)	(.008)	(.008)
Year dummies	−0.039**	−0.079**	−0.121**	−0.027**	−0.080**	−0.003	−0.087**	−0.044**	−0.065**	—
	(.008)	(.009)	(.010)	(.007)	(.008)	(.008)	(.008)	(.007)	(.007)	

$DVOTE_{t-1}$	0.44** (.01)	$SENIORITY_t$	0.00068* (.00037)
$AREA_t$	−0.000001 (.0001)	$SENIORITY_t \times INCUMBENCY_t$	−0.00013 (.00044)
$AREA_t \times INCUMBENCY_t$	−0.00029** (.00010)	$COMMITTEE_t$	0.0024 (.0081)
$SOUTH_t$	−0.0086* (.0044)	$COMMITTEE_t \times INCUMBENCY_t$	0.0005 (.0082)
$SOUTH_t \times INCUMBENCY_t$	−0.0040 (.0047)	$LEADER_t$	0.0098 (.0125)
Constant	0.35** (.01)	$LEADER_t \times INCUMBENCY_t$	0.028* (.012)

* $p < .05$, ** $p < .01$ (one-tailed).

Note: Cell entries are OLS coefficients and standard errors in parentheses. The dependent variable is the Democratic share of the two-party vote in the district. For cases with missing data on seniority or open races, seniority is set to zero. A dummy variable is included for these cases, but coefficients are not reported. $N = 3{,}011$, $R^2 = .83$.

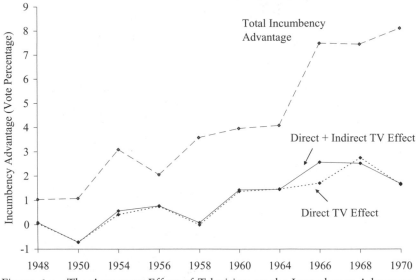

Figure 6.4. The Aggregate Effect of Television on the Incumbency Advantage, 1948–1970.

Note: This figure plots the size of the television-based incumbency advantage based on estimates in Table 6.6 and the mean number of television stations per year shown in Table 6.5. As a measure of the overall incumbency advantage, the dashed line shows the average of estimates by Gelman and King (1990), Levitt and Wolfram (1997), and Gelman and Huang (forthcoming).

Timing and trend of the estimated aggregate effect of television correspond to the rise in overall incumbency advantage, but television explains only a portion of the rise. Figure 6.4 compares the television-based incumbency advantage to the overall incumbency advantage, which is shown by the dashed line and represents the average of three different estimates, the original Gelman-King (1990) estimator and newer estimators developed by Levitt and Wolfram (1997) and Gelman and Huang (forthcoming). For the years 1966 to 1970, the combined direct and indirect (scare-off) effect of local television accounts for one-third of the overall advantage as measured by Levitt and Wolfram (1997) or Gelman and Huang (forthcoming) and one-quarter of the Gelman-King (1990) estimates. Another way of putting the size of the effect in context is to compare it to the effect of challenger quality. The difference between a high-quality and a low-quality challenger is about 3 percentage points in the 1960s, according to Table 6.6, or about twice the average effect of the first two television stations in a district. The analysis of aggregate vote returns thus confirms the individual-level analysis and demonstrates that the spread of television stations contributed noticeably to the increased incumbency advantage observed in the 1960s.

For two reasons, putting television's contribution to the overall incumbency advantage at about one-third is a conservative estimate. First, the independent variable, the number of television stations in a district, is only a rough approximation of the availability of television in a district. Some voters in uncovered areas are inaccurately coded as having access to local television (and vice versa), thereby attenuating the estimated effect of local television. Second, it is worth pointing out that I measure only the effect of the *availability* of local television stations. Undoubtedly, some incumbents made greater (or more successful) use of television than others.

The timing of the television effect reflects the gradual growth of television I discussed in Chapter 3 which continued even after most Americans had bought their first TV set. The upward trend in the television effect in Figure 6.4 arises for two reasons. The first one is the increasing number of TV stations in the country. The second factor is the strengthening effect of each station. As the coefficients in Table 6.6 indicate, a station in 1966 provided incumbents with a larger boost than a station in 1954. Even if the number of stations had remained constant, incumbents would have benefited more from them over time. What explains this strengthening effect? And why did television not affect incumbent vote shares before the 1960s? After all, the first local television stations started commercial operation in the early 1940s, long before the incumbency advantage began its more precipitous increase. And by 1956, still about ten years before the mid-sixties jump, more than two-thirds of all American households owned a television set and more than 300 congressional districts had at least one station (see Table 6.5). As described in Chapter 3, the transition to the new medium was slower and more gradual than these numbers suggest. Limited reception of UHF stations was only one reason. Television news was still in its infancy in the 1950s and continued to increase in length and quality. Television coverage of Congress grew more gradually than the number of stations around the country. For example, the number of journalists accredited by the Congressional Radio and TV Press Gallery more than doubled between 1957 and 1967, even after most Americans had access to television (Ornstein 1983, 201). While almost all Americans had access to a set by the end of the 1950s, television replaced newspapers as the most favored news source more slowly and became people's primary news source only in the mid-sixties (recall Figure 3.2). Hence, for a mix of technological and use-related reasons, it appears plausible that television's full effect only manifested itself in the 1960s.

Television benefited ordinary incumbents, not just party leaders or prominent committee chairs. When these most prominent incumbents are excluded from the analysis, the pro-incumbent effect of television remains unchanged. With or without party leaders and committee chairs (and ranking minority members) in the sample, the first three stations added, on average, 2.2 percentage points to an incumbent's vote margin in elections between 1964 and 1970. This result indicates that the effect of television was not limited to those representatives who, due to their leadership positions in the House, were most likely to appear on national television. More generally defined, newsworthiness did seem to affect how much television helped incumbents. More senior members of Congress reaped greater rewards from the new medium. Between 1964 and 1970, incumbents with at least ten years of experience in the House gained on average about 2.8 percentage points from the first three television stations, compared to only 1.5 points for incumbents with between two and four terms under their belt. Freshman representatives gained less than 1 point from the first three stations in their districts.[38]

The Effect of District Size

One of the limiting technical features of broadcast television was that the broadcast signal could travel only a certain distance before it became too weak for viewers to get a clear, or any, picture. If the effects documented so far are in fact the result of television, they should therefore depend on the reach of the broadcasting signal. The effect should rise with the percentage of people in the district who receive the signal, which in turn increases the effectiveness of television as a source for information or a channel for persuasion. The share of people reached by a station is, roughly speaking, a function of the geographical size of the district. In large districts in particular, a station is unlikely to cover the entire district. The effect of television should thus be smaller in large districts, all other things being equal.

To evaluate this conjecture, Table 6.7 presents estimates of the television effect separately for districts of different sizes (derived from the same regression model as before). Districts are divided into thirds according to their geographical area. For each of three time periods (corresponding to elections between census years), the table gives the effect of the first three television stations on incumbents' vote margins, derived from the same kind of model. The effect of television decreases as districts get larger. Between 1964 and 1970, the first three stations increased incumbents' vote margins by 2.6 percentage points on average in the smallest third of districts (districts not bigger than 60 square miles in this time period).

---

38 These estimates are calculated by running the same model as in Table 6.6 for subsets of the data based on the seniority of incumbents.

Table 6.7. *The Pro-Incumbent Effect of Television in Different
Types of Congressional Districts*

Years	1970–64 N = 1,059	1960–54 N = 1,336	1950–46 N = 948
Average TV effect	2.2*	0.7*	0.9*
Geographical size			
Smallest third	2.6*	1.2*	1.3
Medium third	1.4*	−0.6	−0.6
Largest third	0.6	−1.3	−0.2
District-market congruence			
1–3 districts (70%)	1.2*	−0.6	0.6
4–10 districts (12%)	3.3*	0.8	0.2
>10 districts (18%)	2.1*	0.8	1.6*

* Effect is significant at $p < .10$.

Note: Cell entries represent the effect of the first three TV stations on the incumbent's vote margin. To estimate effects by geographical size, districts are divided into equal thirds by district size within each time period. The congruence measure is the total number of districts served by the media market(s) that reach a congressional district.

In medium-sized districts (between 61 and 5,500 square miles), the effect was 1.4 points in 1964–70. In the largest third of districts, television had no significant effects in any of the periods. The signals simply did not reach enough constituents to make much of a difference.

Even though they are big, most of the large districts with television – about 70 percent of the largest third – received television from only one media market in the district. (Remember that my district-based measure does not count stations broadcasting from counties that do not overlap with the districts or from another state. Some of the 70 percent received signals from markets in neighboring states, but their influence on incumbents' vote margins was, according to Tables 6.2 and 6.3, relatively small.) In a large district, a second media market with additional stations should thus reach more constituents. And indeed, further analysis shows that the pro-incumbent effect of television increases with the number of media markets that are part of the district. There are too few large districts with multiple in-district markets to estimate the magnitude of this effect reliably, but it supports the notion that television was less consequential in large districts because fewer constituents could receive the signal.

The Effect of District-Market Congruence

The amount of television news devoted to any particular congressional district is modest in most circumstances. In big cities, where local stations have to keep an eye on many different districts, it is especially hard for representatives and their challengers to attract coverage. It is also more costly to reach constituents with paid messages. This makes the nature of the media market that covers the district another structural influence on the flow of television messages in congressional elections. When many districts compete for local news coverage and advertising is expensive, the total flow of information about each district is less intense. But for incumbents, this situation is often advantageous. For their electoral fortunes, it is not the overall flow of information about their district that matters, but the edge they have over their challengers. Tough competition for news coverage and inefficient and expensive advertising typically hurt challengers more than incumbents.

A small but remarkably consistent set of studies has demonstrated that incumbents benefit from poor overlap between congressional districts and media markets. The more districts and media markets overlap, the more efficiently local television reaches the district population. When the fit between market and district is poor (low congruence), "political communication in general is impeded" (Campbell, Alford, and Henry 1984, 665). Several studies (Campbell, Alford, and Henry 1984; Niemi, Powell, and Bicknell 1986; Prinz 1995; Stewart and Reynolds 1990) have shown that challengers are more disadvantaged by market incongruence than incumbents since "incumbents, because of their generally greater prominence and larger campaign warchest, can achieve some measure of attention even in incongruent districts" (Campbell, Alford, and Henry 1984, 667). As a result, the incumbency advantage is larger in districts that overlap poorly with the local media markets.

The effect is partly mitigated by the fact that stations in larger media markets, which tend to serve more congressional districts, also devoted more time to cover congressional races. Large markets had longer newscasts, offering an hour or two of news in the early evening as well as late evening newscasts (Adams 1977). On local stations in the largest markets in his sample, Hess (1991, 49–50) found an average of more than ten hours of local news per week. Stations in the smallest markets offered only about two-thirds of that amount. Local news programs in larger markets also devoted more airtime to news rather than sports or weather. Carroll's (1989) results show similar patterns in local news coverage. And yet, even several more hours of airtime per week do not allow a local newscast to cover a dozen congressional campaigns as thoroughly as a small-market station can cover the only House race in its area. According to Hess's (1991) analysis of local news coverage, the size of the market and the share of coverage devoted to members of the House are inversely related.

Incongruence subsumes two different district-media market patterns. The majority of incongruent districts are incongruent for one of the two reasons, but not both. First, incongruence arises when a district includes areas covered by different media markets. I touched on this type of incongruence in the previous section. It plays a role only in large districts, as few small or mid-sized districts are served by more than one media market located inside the district.[39] Second, incongruence exists when a district is entirely part of one media market, but this market also covers other districts. It is this type of incongruence in particular that affects news coverage of congressional candidates.

In markets with many congressional districts, incumbents must share the newshole. Rather than having their own show, several incumbents appeared together on interview programs in larger markets. In such settings, incumbents had less time to talk about their activities than their counterparts in smaller markets. But their name recognition still benefited. Empirically, television had a weaker effect on knowledge about congressional candidates among respondents in incongruent districts, but the effect continues to be marginally significant. Viewers could still pick up messages from the incumbent during their television exposure.

Challengers did not have interview shows or other regular television appearances. Tighter time constraints in incongruent districts could easily mean that challengers, lacking newsworthiness, would not receive any coverage on the local news. Higher advertising costs, too, affected poorly funded challengers before they hurt incumbents. In short, the advantage that incumbents derived from television should have been higher when districts and media markets were incongruent.

To examine how congruence conditioned the pro-incumbent effect of television, I divided the districts according to the total number of districts served by their media market(s). In small districts in large markets, such as New York or Los Angeles, this number is high (exceeding 20 in the largest cities). These are exceptions, however. Most districts share their stations with one or two other districts at the most. Table 6.7 divides the districts into those that receive their signals from television markets that cover 1–3, 4–10, and more than 10 districts. Of all districts with television, 70 percent fall in the first range, 12 percent in the second range, and 18 percent in the third.

39 There are additional districts that receive television from different media markets, not all of which are located in the district or state. On average, out-of-district markets feature less news coverage of congressional campaigns in the district. For out-of-district stations with a large share of their audience in the district, however, it makes commercial sense to focus on the district candidates. Studies of more recent elections (Campbell, Alford, and Henry 1984; Gronke 2000; Prinz 1995; Stewart and Reynolds 1990) have therefore used the proportion of a market that overlaps with a district as a finer measure of congruence.

The results in Table 6.7 confirm previous studies in showing that incumbents benefit from television more in districts whose stations also serve other districts. In 1964–70, the average effect of the first three television stations was 1.2 points in districts with relatively high congruence (1–3 districts served by media market) where challengers had their best shot at achieving news coverage. In contrast, the first three stations increase incumbent vote margins by more than three points in districts with medium congruence (4–10 districts served). This level of district–market congruence looks like the optimal environment for incumbents who receive periodic mention in the news and can still afford some advertising, while challengers rarely make it into the local news and lack the funds to buy ads. The conditioning effect of congruence is not linear, however. In districts that must share their stations with ten or more other districts, the pro-incumbent effect of television is only about two points, presumably because such a high number of congressional representatives does cut down on the amount of coverage each individual one can receive and because television advertising becomes prohibitively expensive.[40]

CONCLUSION

This chapter provides the most detailed, in-depth look at the implications of changes in the media environment. Analyses of survey data and district vote returns both confirm that television increased the incumbency advantage in congressional elections. A variety of factors contributed to the pro-incumbent effect of television, not all of which derive from the basic Conditional Political Learning model. The most vivid link between the new medium and the rising electoral fortunes of congressional incumbents is certainly the fact that members of Congress won preferential access to the local airwaves with the help of the taxpayer – something the model did not predict. This storyline appeared to make a lot of sense to contemporary observers. In several different surveys, many incumbents acknowledged that they were frequent users of the television studios in Capitol Hill and that stations in their home districts often broadcast their shows and statements. Although systematic content analyses of local television in that period do not exist, the amount of evidence clearly supports the idea that a tight symbiosis between representatives and local stations characterized the first decades of television.

40 The effect of congruence and district size are largely independent and can be distinguished. Even in the smallest third of districts, incumbents benefited more from television when the local stations covered more than three other districts.

Part of the reason why the symbiosis between local stations and members of Congress increased incumbents' vote margins was the influx of less educated voters motivated by television news. Voters with little political background knowledge to evaluate the messages they received from the candidates were most likely to pick the side that simply sent more messages. Television changed the information flow in favor of congressional incumbents and reached the kind of voters most susceptible to one-sided information flow.

The compositional changes brought about by Conditional Political Learning and the political content on television combined to help incumbents. If the influx of less educated voters had been the sole mechanism by which television affected voting behavior, local news and messages produced by congressional officeholders would not have played a role in the explanation. Instead, several findings established indirectly that television content contributed to the pro-incumbent effect. Television increased knowledge about incumbents among the less educated, but did not affect challenger name recall. That out-of-state television stations increased turnout and general political knowledge among the less educated, but failed to change their propensity to vote for congressional incumbents, also suggests that the content of local news or paid media mattered. Finally, the effects of congruence between districts and media markets indicate that newsworthiness of the candidates and efficiency of campaign communications affected the extent to which television helped incumbents.

That the content available through the new medium contributed to its effect on elections makes this chapter theoretically less parsimonious than other parts of the book. Yet after taking into account the biased information flow, the findings in this chapter still follow the notion of Conditional Political Learning. As predicted by the model, the effects of television on voting behavior occurred only among less educated voters. The popularity of television and the relative ideological innocence of those reached by the new medium were preconditions for the pro-incumbent effect of television. All factors that may have been involved in improving incumbents' fortunes – straight-up Conditional Political Learning among the less educated, local television struggling to fill airtime, candidates exploiting the new medium as an attractive channel for advertising – were made possible only by the emergence of television. It increased the share of less educated voters, offered a new venue for news about incumbents, and created structural elements of the communication environment that advantaged incumbents.

Scholars have often argued that declining partisanship, more frequent ticket-splitting, and a higher incumbency advantage were tightly related and most likely triggered by the same underlying cause. Mayhew (1974, 313), for example, speculated that "voters dissatisfied with party cues could be reaching for any other cues that are available in deciding how to vote. The incumbency cue is readily at hand." Ferejohn (1977, 174) offered a similar conjecture, arguing that incumbents may be doing better in congressional elections because incumbency cues replaced party cues: "The decreasing reliance on party as a 'shorthand' cue may not turn voters toward issue voting but may simply increase their reliance on other rules of thumb such as incumbency" (see also Nelson 1978). By this logic, some external event caused people's party identification and its impact on their vote choice to weaken, which created more room for factors related to individual candidates – and in particular incumbents – to determine vote choice in congressional elections. That in turn produced larger vote margins for incumbents and higher rates of ticket-splitting. The decreasing importance of partisan considerations reduced party-line voting and incumbents benefited disproportionately because they were more visible than the candidates challenging them. Perhaps the most tempting feature of this hypothesis is the close temporal coincidence of weakening partisanship and rising vote shares for incumbents. After twenty years of "steady state," the strength of partisanship began to decline abruptly in 1966 (Converse 1976, 70–2), exactly at the time when several measures of incumbency advantage jumped upward (Jacobson 2004, 28).

Fiorina (1977a, 180) turned the causal chain around by suggesting that the increased attractiveness of incumbents, brought about by the resources they spent in their districts, may well have preceded and caused the decline of party identification or magnified its impact. Regardless of whether weakening partisanship caused a greater incumbency advantage or a greater incumbency caused the declining role of partisanship, the explanation remains unsatisfying unless we know what triggered the change in the first place. As Cain, Ferejohn, and Fiorina (1984, 123) observed later,

once the dynamic is set in motion it is self-reinforcing; declining parties contribute to increasing personal votes which in turn detract further from the importance of party. How does the dynamic begin in the first place? Perhaps through some exogenous event(s) as with the aforementioned suggestions of bad performance or unpopular issues stands, or even as a result of more-or-less nonpolitical factors such as a changing media environment, social or technological change, or whatnot.

The spread of television was just such an exogenous event. Television lowered the share of voters who identified with the two parties, an effect that could have contributed to incumbents' greater success. But television did not reduce the electoral impact of party identification among those who felt one, neither in presidential nor in congressional elections.[41] To the extent that compositional change – increased turnout rates among less educated, less partisan citizens – led to a rise in the incumbency advantage, individuals did not replace one cue with another. Instead, television increased the share of voters who were generally more likely to rely on incumbency cues.[42]

The fact that television explains a significant portion of the increased incumbency advantage does not necessarily clash with existing accounts of what triggered the rise. According to the constituency service explanation (Cain, Ferejohn, and Fiorina 1984; Fiorina 1977a; 1981), once elected, members of Congress appropriated themselves more and more resources and used them to provide additional services to their constituents. This, in turn, made it rational to vote for the incumbent even if he or she represented a different party. Among the perks of office was the opportunity to reach constituents through the media. Incumbents "may write a short column or tape a short Washington Report for the local media" (Fiorina 1977b) to publicize their good deeds. Fiorina (1981) shows that the expectation of future casework is at least as strong a predictor of voting for the incumbent as actual past casework. This suggests that media reports of constituency service may be just as important as constituency service itself. Indeed, constituents are more likely to expect their representative to be helpful in the future if they recognize his or her name and if they recall seeing him or her in the media (Cain, Ferejohn, and Fiorina 1984). The constituency service hypothesis, then, has always been an argument for media as an important factor in explaining the increased incumbency advantage. Offered the opportunity to send their reports from Washington to their home districts and have them broadcast for free, incumbents would be foolish not to emphasize what they have done for their district and advertise their plans to bring home more goodies in the future.

41 Running the same model as in column 3 of Table 6.2 for congressional instead of presidential elections does not suggest any effect of television on the relationship between party identification and vote choice either.
42 Questioning the conjectures by Mayhew (1974), Ferejohn (1977), Nelson (1978), and others, some scholars have offered evidence indicating that party and incumbency cues are not in fact substitutes for each other (Ansolabehere et al. 2006; Ansolabehere and Snyder 2002; Born 2000). Declining partisanship, in other words, does not necessarily imply an increasing incumbency advantage, or vice versa. The effect of television does not depend on the substitution of one cue with another. Television may not have triggered a "self-reinforcing dynamic" between weaker partisanship and increased incumbency advantage, but it did both downplay partisanship and reward incumbents.

Unlike some explanations of the incumbency advantage, television as an important factor is not limited to House elections. For example, the claim that redistricting of congressional districts triggered the rise in incumbent vote margins is questioned by the observation that incumbents did increasingly well in Senate and state elections as well (Alford and Brady 1993; Ansolabehere and Snyder 2002). To the extent that a general increase in campaign intensity and an increasing proportion of less partisan voters explain the effect of television documented in this chapter, television should have helped incumbents in other types of elections as well. Senators had access to congressional production facilities and used them frequently. They also attract more network coverage than members of the House.[43] Local media do, however, cover Senate challengers more than they cover House challengers, and campaign resources are generally more balanced in Senate elections. While television may thus have helped Senate incumbents too, this boost was not necessarily of the same magnitude as for House incumbents. It is hard to imagine that incumbents in lower-level statewide elections benefited much from television because television coverage of those races (or television advertising) was probably infrequent at best. The rough correspondence between the size of the incumbency advantage for different types of incumbents shown by Ansolabehere and Snyder (2002) and the newsworthiness of their offices provides some encouragement for the conjecture that media coverage and perhaps television in particular contributed to the incumbency advantage not only for members of the House of Representatives.

The availability of media and the standards and practices that guide media output condition the way our political system works. In the 1960s, a change in the media environment linked two institutions, Congress and the media, in a symbiotic relationship that helped local television stations to comply with the FCC public affairs requirement and members of Congress to spread their message more widely – with profound implications for congressional politics. There are several reasons to expect that the symbiosis came to an end in the 1970s. Since the FCC never revoked a station's license for violating the public affairs requirement, locals became increasingly willing to cut down on news coverage. With

---

43 Unlike network news (Adams and Ferber 1977; Cook 1986; Kuklinski and Sigelman 1992), modern local news, both on television and in print, does not cover senators much more heavily than House members. Arnold (2004, 59–60) finds that Senators have a noticeable advantage in newspaper coverage only in markets with four or more districts. From the point of view of the local paper, two or three House members in the coverage area are just as important as the two senators. Vinson's (2003) data show only a modest advantage for senators on local television news, but much lower volume of coverage than in newspapers.

inexpensive entertainment programming now abundantly available in the form of syndicated shows, local stations no longer used cheap public affairs coverage to fill their programming hours. The presentation style of local newscasts changed in the 1970s. The relatively serious formats with considerable focus on political news gave way to *Eyewitness News* and *Action News*, more sensationalist formats that devoted most of their time to car chases, crime, and celebrities. As a result of these developments, local news coverage of politics decreased and incumbents were given far fewer opportunities to broadcast their own programs for free.

At least equally important, chapters 4 and 5 have demonstrated that people's news exposure, not just to local news, but to network news as well, declined as cable television began to offer more and more alternatives in slots that used to be reserved for news. In retrospect, the media environment of the 1960s that produced 75 to 80 percent market shares for news and allowed incumbents to dominate the airwaves stands out as a rather unlikely coincidence of technology, regulation, and taste. If broadcast technology and government regulation had not limited the number of channels, or if people had not liked television so much that they kept their sets on for pretty much any kind of programming, news audiences would have been smaller and incumbents not quite as successful. Once entertainment emerged as a ubiquitous competitor, only the more politically interested continued to stay with the news and go to the polls. These hardnosed news viewers are, as the next chapter shows, quite different from the average couch potato of the broadcast era.

7

Partisan Polarization in the High-Choice Media Environment

In uncommon unison, many academics, journalists, and pundits of all political leanings have recently declared that America in the early twenty-first century is more politically polarized than it used to be. Different observers stress polarization at different levels – in Congress, in the media, among activists, in the electorate, or, simply, in the "50–50 nation." Polarization at its most general describes a combination of increasing differences of opinion between opposing political camps and more consistent opinions within those camps. Allegedly, there are more consistent differences between the Republican Party and the Democratic Party and fewer differences within the two parties. Observers like to deplore this partisan "warfare" for its lack of bipartisan spirit and hostility to compromise. Perhaps more importantly, a polarized political climate threatens to drive away moderates, regardless of whether it is based on "myth" (Fiorina 2004a) or fact.

When it comes to the causes of polarization, experts point to a more ideologically divided Congress, greater influence of increasingly extreme party leadership, and the emergence of Fox News, among other things. Even in the absence of a precise definition of polarization and thorough empirical examination of its causes, the assumption has emerged that its likely roots are found at the elite level. Although changes among political elites might contribute to polarization in the public, the Conditional Political Learning model locates a major cause of polarization elsewhere.

Compositional changes caused by moving to the high-choice media environment can polarize elections all by themselves. In this chapter, I show that greater media choice explains at least part of the increasing polarization. As demonstrated in Chapter 4, greater choice leads to an increasing turnout gap between news junkies and entertainment fans. The following analysis will show that Switchers – those who become less likely to vote once they have entered the high-choice media environment – are predominantly politically moderate or indifferent. As Switchers' media choices increase, their share among the voting public declines, thereby increasing the proportion of voters with deep partisan and ideological convictions. This process is not elite-driven. Technology simply facilitates participation of the more partisan news-seekers and abstention of the less partisan entertainment-seekers.

The purpose of this chapter is to demonstrate empirically that the transition to a high-choice media environment increased partisan polarization by changing the composition of the voting public. This explanation of polarization directs more attention to the considerable differences in polarization among voters and the public as a whole. It differs from most other explanations in that it neither rests on individual-level change in political attitudes nor assumes that changes at the elite level prompted the trend toward greater polarization. Explaining polarization without individual-level attitude change is consistent with recent work that emphasizes consensus on many political issues and finds little divergence over time. An account of polarization that does not start with elite-level change is consistent with the absence of a good explanation of why Congress or presidential candidates should have polarized first.[1]

In the first part of this chapter, I review what we know about the degree and causes of partisan polarization, both in Congress and in the electorate. Existing research presents a puzzling set of findings that leaves room for another explanation. The analysis that follows then links changes in the media environment to polarization and establishes a causal chain that reaches from an exogenous change – the proliferation of media choice – to polarized elections and finally polarization in Congress. Of course, the fact that both attitude change and influences that directly polarize Congress are not necessary in this causal chain does not demonstrate that they did not occur. In fact, there is some evidence that Americans have become more partisan in recent years and that changes in party positions

---

[1] The evidence concerning the timing of polarization is ambiguous. According to Poole and Rosenthal's NOMINATE scores, the recent period of polarization in Congress began in the early 1980s. They conclude that "[c]learly, Reagan was out in front of the transformation [of Congress]" (Poole and Rosenthal 2001, 17). Roberts and Smith (2003) find a sharp increase in congressional polarization later, beginning only in the mid-1980s. Other measures of polarization reveal a different timing. Party unity voting in Congress picked up earlier – in the mid-1970s (e.g., Fiorina 2002). Differences in congressional support for the president between his party and the opposition had already begun to increase at that point (Jacobson 2003). At the mass level, Jacobson (2000b, 26) finds that "most of the trends among voters...show their largest movement in the 1990s, after the firming up of congressional party lines." Yet this conclusion is debatable in light of Bartels's (2000) analysis, which shows the beginning resurgence of partisan voting in the mid- to late-1970s for presidential elections and in the 1980s for congressional elections.

on racial and cultural issues contributed to, rather than followed, this trend. My goal in this chapter is not to argue that greater media choice is the single cause of partisan polarization but to show that it is an important one.

Polarization in Congress

The least controversial element of polarization is evident in Congress. Whereas several Republican members of Congress were ideologically more liberal than the most conservative Democrats two or three decades ago, all Republicans are to the right of all Democrats today (Poole and Rosenthal 2001). Many different measures pick up this trend. Members of Congress are rated as more ideologically split by monitoring interest groups (e.g., Fleisher and Bond 2000) and their roll-call voting reflects the growing ideological divergence (Jacobson 2000c; Poole and Rosenthal 1997; 2001). The percentage of roll-call votes in which a majority of one party opposes a majority of the other party has risen (e.g., Rohde 1991; Sinclair 2000). Evidence for polarization in both the House and the Senate has emerged (e.g., Fleisher and Bond 2004; Jacobson 2003). It is more difficult to determine if other elites have become more polarized as well. Whether President Bush and Senator Kerry offered more ideologically diverse policy proposals in 2004 than, say, Jimmy Carter and Ronald Reagan in 1980 is not immediately clear (but see Clinton, Jackman, and Rivers 2004; Erikson, MacKuen, and Stimson 2002; Poole and Rosenthal 1997).

There are many plausible explanations why Congress may have polarized. First, leaders of the two parties in Congress have created incentives and organized congressional procedures in a way that grants them more influence over individual representatives (Brady, D'Onofrio, and Fiorina 2000; Cox and McCubbins 1993). Cooperation in the drafting of legislation is said to have been discouraged, and intraparty cohesion became stronger. Newt Gingrich is the most frequently mentioned example, but Democratic leadership in the House in the years before 1994 shows signs of comparable tendencies (Roberts and Smith 2003). Second, a more prominent role of the national parties and party activists in the primary process could have led to nomination of more ideological candidates (Aldrich 1995; Fiorina 2002, 99; Fleisher and Bond 2004). Third, partisan gerrymandering has reduced the proportion of ideologically diverse districts that are most likely to produce moderate representatives. Representatives of significantly redrawn districts are more ideologically extreme than their counterparts in districts that were changed only slightly or not at all (Carson et al. 2004).

According to all these explanations, polarization could be confined to the elite level. Organizational change and stronger party leadership in

Congress, an altered nomination process, and redistricting could all lead to greater ideological divergence between Republicans and Democrats in Congress without any change in the electorate. Yet, the case for an elite-level cause of polarization is less than convincing. If redistricting did it, why do we observe polarization of the Senate and why does polarization in the House occur not in discrete jumps (in years after redistricting), but at a very steady rate (Poole and Rosenthal 2001, 19)? The same argument applies to any explanation that focuses on changes in leadership or procedures in the House of Representatives alone. If polarization occurs because the modern nominations process has made it easier for ideologues to win election, why have sitting members of House and Senate become more partisan as well (Fleisher and Bond 2004; Roberts and Smith 2003)?

Perhaps, then, we have to look for the causes of polarization elsewhere. Several scholars (e.g., Fleisher and Bond 2004; Roberts and Smith 2003) have suggested that changes in the electorate triggered polarization in Congress. According to others (e.g., Hetherington 2001; Jacobson 2000b), causality flows in the opposite direction, and ordinary citizens merely echo elite polarization—which, by that reasoning, must have other causes. Regardless of causal direction, these arguments presume that the electorate (or parts of it) in fact became more polarized. A closer look at the evidence for mass polarization reveals a picture far less clear-cut than for the elite level. To jump ahead in the story, polarization at the mass level has at least as much to do with the changing composition of the voting public as with deepening partisan divisions within the electorate as a whole. Elections have become more partisan, but the strengthening of partisan feelings appears too modest to account for this trend.[2] Before I resolve what might seem like a paradox, it is necessary to examine closely the evidence for polarization at the mass level.

Polarization among Voters

If only a fraction of the endless media coverage of "a nation deeply divided" is accurate, the mass public has become more polarized and partisan in recent years. (Fiorina (2004a) illustrates the zeal with which media outlets follow their story line of a polarized country rife with "culture war.") Increasing polarization and increasing partisanship are not the same thing. It is impossible for an individual to polarize, but an individual can become more partisan, either in her attitudes, in her political

2 For example, the percentage of (strong and weak) partisans in the electorate was 62 percent in the 1970s, 65 percent in the 1980s, and 62 percent in the 1990s. The percentage of Americans who identify themselves as "extremely" conservative or liberal has remained stable at 4 to 5 percent over those decades.

feelings, or in her voting behavior. If an individual becomes more partisan, the distance between her and those who identify with the opposite party increases, creating between-party polarization. In this sense, it is helpful to think of the electorate as an institution that – just like Congress – can polarize over time, while individual citizens – just like members of Congress – can become more partisan.

A strengthening of partisanship among voters can thus produce polarized elections in which strong partisans on both sides dominate. But such a strengthening is not a necessary precondition for polarized elections. More polarized elections can occur even when individuals have not become more partisan and the electorate has not polarized. A turnout increase among strong partisans (or a decrease among nonpartisans) can polarize elections even when partisanship in the electorate has not changed.

To understand trends in partisanship and political polarization, Bartels's (2000) analysis of party identification as a predictor of people's vote decisions, which I already described briefly in Chapters 1 and 6, is a useful starting point. Bartels estimates the joint impact of two elements of this relationship, the proportion of voters in each category of party identification (strong partisans, weak partisans, leaners), and the associations between the different categories and vote choice (that is, how likely people in these categories are to vote for their party). Since its modern low point in the 1970s, partisanship has resurged, both in terms of the number of people who consider themselves partisan and in terms of the impact that identification with a party has on vote choice. Combining these two trends, Bartels (2000, 44) concludes that party identification has become a better predictor of vote decisions since the mid-1970s in presidential and, somewhat later, in congressional elections: "The American political system has slipped with remarkably little fanfare into an era of increasingly vibrant partisanship." (Figure 1.2 graphs this trend.) The high volatility of election outcomes in the 1960s and 1970s (Bartels 1998, 295–7) also supports the claim that voting decisions were less rooted in firm partisan identities.

An increasing impact of party identification on vote choice is not the only indication of resurging partisanship in the electorate. The National Election Study has asked many of the same questions about partisanship repeatedly over the course of the last fifty years. As Figure 7.1 shows, respondents' answers leave little doubt that voters have become more partisan and that the voting public has polarized along partisan lines. The five panels in the figure show trends in partisan polarization since the middle of the twentieth century, using different indicators that tap both cognitive and affective elements of partisanship. The first panel plots the percentage of voters who identify strongly with one of the two parties. Through the mid-1960s, about 40 percent of all voters were in this

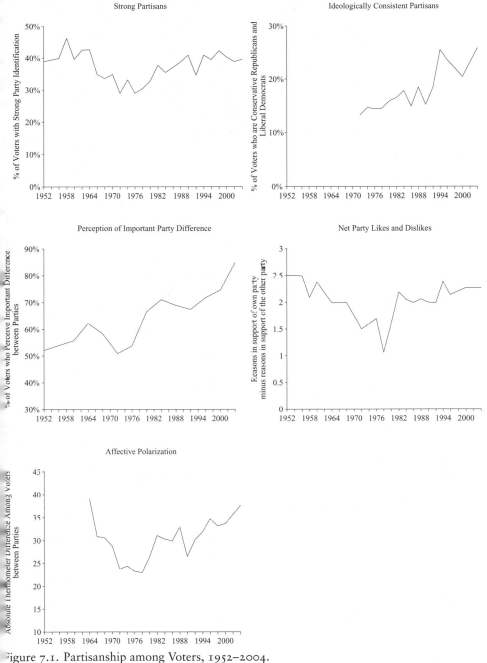

Figure 7.1. Partisanship among Voters, 1952–2004.
Source: National Election Study.

category. This number dropped to 30 percent in the 1970s before recovering to its 1950s levels in recent elections. The second panel (top row, on the right) adds an ideological dimension of self-identification by graphing the percentage of (weak or strong) partisans whose ideology corresponds to their party identification, that is, the percentage of Democrats who also identify themselves as liberals and Republicans who also call themselves conservatives. By this measure, too, which is only available after 1970, voters have become more polarized recently.

Polarization among voters appears to have a cognitive foundation. As the third panel (middle row, on the left) shows, before the 1980s between 50 and 60 percent of all voters said that there were important differences between the two parties. In the last two decades, this share passed 70 percent. In 2004, 85 percent of all voters saw important differences. Voters have not only become more likely to perceive differences between the parties, they also offer more reasons in support of their own party. In most NES interviews, a series of questions invites respondents to explain what they like and dislike about the two parties. The interviewer records up to five different likes and dislikes about each party. These questions can track how many different reasons a respondent has to support the party with which he or she identifies. The measure used in panel four (middle row, on the right) is a count of the reasons a respondent offers in support of his or her party minus the number of reasons in favor of the other party. (For example, for a Democrat, the sum of favorable mentions about the Republican Party and unfavorable mentions about the Democratic Party is subtracted from the sum of favorable mentions about the Democratic Party and unfavorable mentions about the Republican Party.) Panel four plots this net number of reasons in favor of the respondent's own party. In the 1960s, voters gave on average more than two more reasons in support of their own party. This number fell to a low point of barely more than one reason in 1978, but has since recovered almost to its 1950s levels.

Because many people do not have well-formed attitudes on more than a few political issues (e.g., Converse 1964; Delli Carpini and Keeter 1996), it may seem odd to define polarization as a function of attitudes, attitude consistency, and attitude strength. More people have affective attachments to a party or feelings about which side is right. If these feelings have become stronger, polarization may have ensued despite many voters' shaky grasp of policy details. The fifth panel in Figure 7.1 (bottom row) completes the evidence for partisan polarization by documenting its affective component. The NES uses so-called feeling thermometers to gauge respondents' affective responses to political groups, candidates, and officeholders. On these thermometers, respondents rate targets on a scale from 0 to 100 degrees, where values below 50 are described as unfavorable and cold and values over 50 as favorable and warm. The difference between thermometer ratings of the two parties can thus indicate how polarized a respondent's feelings about the two parties are. The fifth panel graphs this measure of affective partisan polarization over time.[3] It shows the familiar drop in partisanship to a low in the 1970s. Just as for the other measures of partisanship, the trend in affective polarization reverses in the 1980s. In the last years of the twentieth century, voters' feelings about the two parties were just as polarized as they were at the beginning of the time series.

Together, the five measures plotted in Figure 7.1 illustrate the resurgence of partisanship among voters in all its shades. Americans not only vote more reliably for their own party again, they also think and feel more positively about it (at least relative to the other party).

Polarization in the Electorate?

It is important to note that most of the evidence for partisan polarization at the mass level – including all evidence I have offered so far – comes from analyses of voting behavior or changes in partisan feelings among voters. For example, the correlation between party identification and vote choice has become stronger (Bartels 2000; Jacobson 2000a), and split-ticket voting, less frequent (Hetherington 2001; Mayer 1998). Whether nonvoters too would vote increasingly in line with their partisan leanings is a difficult question, both because it is hypothetical and because nonvoters are less likely to identify with a party. But we can consider those measures of partisanship that are defined regardless of turnout, such as the differences in party thermometer ratings and the reasons people give to explain why they like one party over the other. Plotting the same trends for nonvoters that showed marked increases in partisanship among voters in Figure 7.1 reveals a surprising contrast. The five panels in Figure 7.2 all indicate that nonvoters (shown by the dark lines) are not only less partisan than voters

---

3 In the late 1970s, the NES changed its thermometer rating questions from asking respondents to rate "Republicans" and "Democrats" to asking about the "Republican Party" and the "Democratic Party." In 1980 and 1982, both versions of the question were asked. Comparisons reveal that the wording change affected the difference between ratings of the two parties. Under the old wording, the average rating differences were 19.4 in 1980 and 21.3 in 1982. Using the new wording, these differences increased to 24.3 in 1980 and 27.2 in 1982. Thus, the increase due to the new wording averages 5.4 points in those two years. This is a sizable increase in apparent polarization as a result of a wording change. To remove this distortion from the time series, I add 5.4 to the difference in all years that used the old wording. (Because the effect of question wording in 1980 and 1982 is almost the same for voters and nonvoters, I do not apply separate corrections for those two groups of respondents in Figure 7.2.)

Political Effects of Media Choice

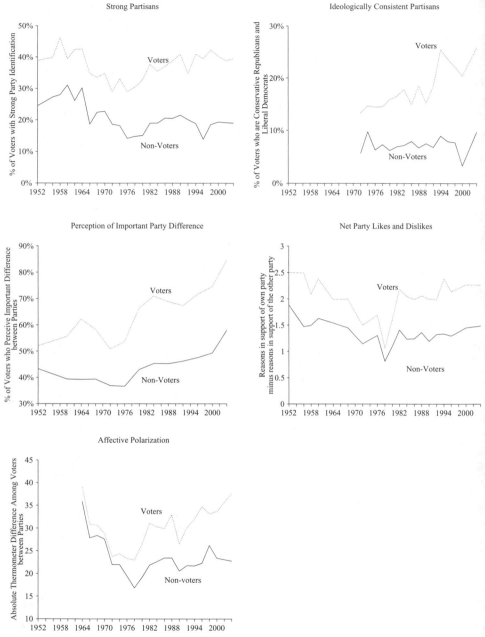

Figure 7.2. Partisanship among Voters and Nonvoters, 1952–2004.
Source: National Election Study.

(shown by the weaker lines), but that the difference between voters and nonvoters has increased noticeably since the 1970s. The first two panels – graphing the percentage of strong partisans and the percentage of ideologically consistent partisans – reveal no signs of increasing partisanship among nonvoters at all. The share of strongly partisan and ideologically consistent nonvoters remained stable over the last two decades.

The share of nonvoters who see important differences between the two parties (third panel, middle row, on the left) has increased from a low of less than 40 percent in the early 1970s to almost 50 percent by the end of the century and to 58 percent in 2004. Although significant, this increase is clearly less pronounced than the equivalent increase among voters. Furthermore, perception of differences alone does not necessarily indicate polarization. The fourth panel (middle row, on the right) plots the number of reasons that nonvoters offered in support of their own party minus the number of reasons offered in support of the other party. Among nonvoters, it shows not much of a trend at all, hovering right around 1.3 net reasons in their party's favor. (The suspiciously low values for 1978, both among voters and nonvoters, look like measurement error rather than a dramatic drop for just one year.)

Affective polarization – measured as the difference between thermometer ratings of the two parties and shown in the last panel in Figure 7.2 – increased slightly in the late 1970s even among nonvoters. Despite some ups and downs, nonvoters' affective evaluations of the parties have not diverged further since then. Voters' feelings, in contrast, have become decidedly stronger in the same time period. Until the mid-1970s, voters and nonvoters were almost equally polarized. Since then, the difference between them has increased to about 15 points.

Figure 7.3 shows this divergence more systematically by graphing the gap between voters and nonvoters for all five measures of partisanship. Each panel plots the differences between voters and nonvoters for each year and a moving average generated by a locally weighted regression of the differences on time. All gaps have substantially increased since the early seventies; in fact they have more than doubled in several instances. While the public as a whole has become somewhat more partisan in recent decades, this trend has been much stronger among voters. Perhaps this growing divergence between voters and nonvoters is often overlooked because exit polls and surveys of likely or registered voters will necessarily miss it. Surveys that do not sample the entire electorate increasingly exaggerate the level of polarization in the American public.

Two mechanisms could possibly account for the growing divergence between voters and nonvoters. Either individual voters became more partisan over time, or partisan members of the electorate became more likely to vote and less partisan Americans correspondingly more likely

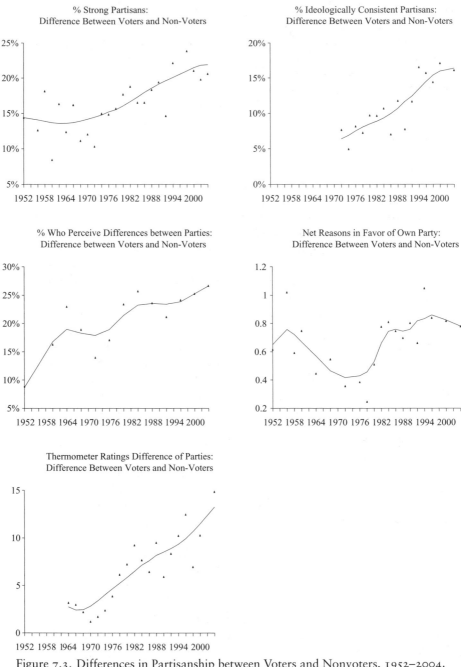

Figure 7.3. Differences in Partisanship between Voters and Nonvoters, 1952–2004.
Source: National Election Study.

to abstain.[4] The first mechanism is rooted in individual change. The second mechanism is compositional. When partisans become more likely and moderates less likely to vote, the voting public ends up more partisan even though individuals' partisanship did not change. The Conditional Political Learning model in its most parsimonious form can only explain the latter, compositional change. It predicts that, during a period in which media choice increased, the voting public should become more polarized because strong partisans become more likely to vote, while moderate or indifferent voters are more likely to abstain. It is clear from Figure 7.2 that, despite increasing divergence between voters and nonvoters, the public as a whole has become somewhat more partisan. Conditional Political Learning cannot explain that part of polarization (unless it incorporates some sort of feedback mechanism whereby greater media choice not only increases the share of partisan voters but also reinforces their partisanship, perhaps by offering more ideologically divergent media content. As I discuss in the conclusion to this chapter, such a content-driven effect, if it exists, is probably small).

The result that partisanship in the public has increased less than partisanship among voters is consistent with other studies. On most issues, Americans take moderate positions and their disagreement has not intensified noticeably in recent decades. In fact, the most thorough examination of attitudes about social issues finds convergence (that is, "depolarization") on many issues (DiMaggio, Evans, and Bryson 1996; Evans 2003). Many opinion distributions have become less dispersed and more centered on one middle position. Polarization has decreased on many social issues not only in the population as a whole but also between people with different levels of education, between people of different races, between frequent churchgoers and those who go to church less frequently or are not religious, and between Southerners and non-Southerners. Opinions of different demographic groups have in fact grown more similar to an extent that leads Di Maggio, Evans, and Bryson (1996, 738) to proclaim "dramatic depolarization in intergroup differences."[5]

---

4 Because turnout has remained fairly constant over the last thirty years (McDonald and Popkin 2001) – the period of slight polarization even in the electorate as a whole – a tendency for increasingly partisan people to turn out at higher rates cannot be the whole explanation for the diverging trends in Figure 7.2. To maintain constant turnout, a decline in electoral participation in some segments must offset any increase among the more partisan.

5 Di Maggio et al. (1996, 738) do find "striking divergence" between Democrats and Republicans on those same social issues. To reconcile the two sets of empirical observations, it must be true either that different people call themselves "Democrats" and "Republicans" now than in the past, or that roughly the same number of Republicans and Democrats switched their issue position in opposite directions. It is not

Political Effects of Media Choice

As I showed in Chapter 4, a changing media environment modified the composition of the voting public, raising the share of highly interested voters with a strong preference for following the news and reducing the share of less interested voters who prefer to be entertained rather than informed. The remainder of this chapter will demonstrate that a preference for news often comes with strong partisan views and that therefore greater media choice increased the relative representation of voters with strong partisan affiliations and contributed to increasingly polarized elections.

ENTERTAINMENT PREFERENCE AND PARTISANSHIP

The Low-Choice/High-Choice Experiment presented in Chapter 2 identified a group of people, the Switchers, who would watch the news if nothing else was on television in the early evening but would select an entertainment program instead if offered. The Switchers make up about a third of the population according to the N&E Survey. Most other respondents either said they would watch news regardless of the alternatives (Always News group) or would not watch any television unless entertainment programs were available (Entertainment Only group). Here, I return to the Low-Choice/High-Choice Experiment briefly to examine the strength of people's partisan attachments in these different groups. The Always News group is the most partisan group of the three; the Entertainment Only group is the least partisan. The Always News group contains the highest percentage of strong and weak identifiers (a combined 64.9 percent) as well as the lowest percentage of respondents who do not state a preference in the party ID question (9.3 percent). In the Entertainment Only group, the percentage of partisan identifiers is lower by about a third (46.2 percent weak or strong identifiers), while the share of respondents without a preference almost triples to 26.1 percent.

The Switchers are between these two extremes. They include 57.6 percent weak or strong identifiers and 13.8 percent respondents without a preference. In a high-choice media environment, where Switchers abandon the news for more attractive entertainment programming, the news audience thus loses some of its less partisan members. Without the educating and motivating exposure to political information, Switchers go to the polls less frequently and leave voting decisions to the more partisan Always News group.

---

clear which of the two is more common (see, e.g., Abramowitz and Saunders 1998; Layman and Carsey 2002a; 2002b; Miller and Hoffmann 1999), but the consequence in both cases is that Democrats and Republicans hold increasingly distinct issues positions. What caused this kind of sorting and the extent to which it is more common among voters remains uncertain.

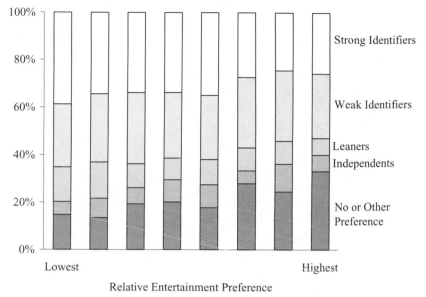

Figure 7.4. Strength of Party Identification and Relative Entertainment Preference.
Note: The sample is divided into eighths according to Relative Entertainment Preference. For each segment, the graph plots the distribution of party identification.
Source: N&E Survey.

The relationship between entertainment preference and partisanship is evident regardless of how exactly both concepts are measured. As an example, Figure 7.4 plots the association for the combined measure of Relative Entertainment Preference introduced in Chapter 4. I divided the N&E Survey sample into eighths according to their relative liking for entertainment. For each of these eight segments, Figure 7.4 shows the partisan composition. The more strongly respondents prefer news to entertainment, the more partisan they are (and vice versa). At one extreme, almost 40 percent of the people who decidedly prefer news identify strongly with a party, and an additional 26 percent, weakly. Respondents at the other extreme – those who most clearly prefer entertainment – are the least partisan of all. Only 25 percent of them identify strongly with a party. Two-fifths are either independent or completely apolitical, not reporting any party preference. As we move from low to high Relative Entertainment Preference, the share of strong partisans drops by about a third, while the share of apoliticals and independents doubles.

Judging by the strength of people's party affiliations, entertainment fans are indeed less partisan than people who like the news. Some o them are politically attuned independents, but a considerable share is indifferent to politics rather than deliberately moderate. Another measure of the strength of partisan attitudes is the absolute difference between thermometer ratings of politically opposed groups or individuals, such as liberals and conservatives or the two parties' presidential candidates. The absolute difference between ratings of liberals and conservatives in the N&E Survey is 35 among strong news fans, but barely half that among avid entertainment fans. News fans' feelings concerning the two parties and George W. Bush and Al Gore are also more than 25 percent more polarized than the respective feelings of entertainment fans. The same negative relationship between Relative Entertainment Preference and the strength of people's partisan feelings is evident in the NES data used in Chapter 4. Entertainment fans express less polarized feelings toward liberals and conservatives and toward Democratic and Republican candidates for office. Compared to strong entertainment fans, strong news fans are 10 to 50 percent more polarized in their assessments (using the same type of thermometer question format). In short, no matter which measure of entertainment preference or partisanship is used, entertainment-seekers are noticeably less partisan than the people motivated to watch the news.

As I already demonstrated, greater media choice reduces turnout among entertainment-seekers but increases it among news fans. Together, the growing turnout gap and the close correlation of entertainment preference and strength of partisanship generate the following prediction: The spread of cable and the Internet increased partisan polarization among voters by changing the composition of the voting public because less partisan entertainment-seekers drop out, while more partisan news fans vote even more reliably than before. Although measures of entertainment preference do not exist for past decades, it is at least possible to verify that the predicted change in turnout patterns occurred. Drawing on the NES time series, Figure 7.5 graphs the turnout rates (in House elections) at different levels of party identification. The upper panel shows turnout rates for presidential election years; the lower panel, for midterm elections. While turnout among strong partisans in presidential elections has remained constant over time, independents and apoliticals[6] have become much less likely to cast a vote.[7] In midterm elections, turnout rates declined most strongly among independents, although the 1994 election put a bump in this trend.[8] Figure 7.5 also makes clear that there is room for a rise in

6 These two groups are pooled here because slight changes in the administration of the party ID questions make it impossible to distinguish them for the whole time series.

7 This trend is slightly exacerbated by the lowering of the voting age to 18 in 1971, but comparing only voters older than 20 yields an almost equally steep decline among independents and apoliticals, and hardly any difference among strong partisans.

8 I do not include estimates from the NES 2002 because it was conducted entirely by phone, which exacerbates the problem of vote overreporting.

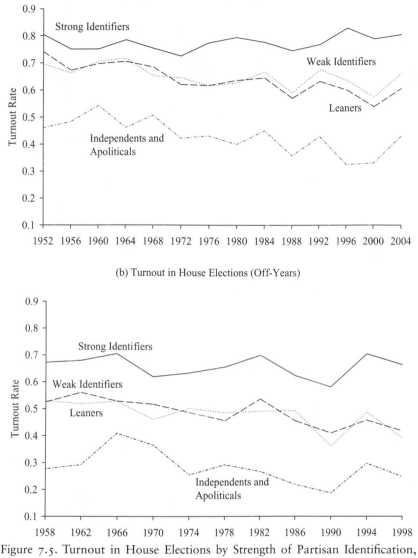

Figure 7.5. Turnout in House Elections by Strength of Partisan Identification, 1952–2004.

Note: Except in 1998 (when not enough face-to-face interviews were conducted), NES respondents interviewed by telephone (in 1984, 1992, 1994, 1996, and 2000) are excluded because overreporting is more severe in phone interviews. The NES 2002 was conducted entirely by phone and is therefore not used here.

Source: National Election Study.

turnout among strong partisans. Although they turn out at higher rates than the rest of the public, greater media choice can increase their turnout even further.

For turnout in presidential elections, the last data point – the election in 2004 – deviates from the long-term trend, especially among independents. The elections of 2004 saw the highest turnout in over thirty years (McDonald 2004). The unusual closeness of the election increased turnout rates at all levels of partisanship. Perhaps because turnout among strong partisans is very high even in uneventful election years, the effect of greater intensity in 2004 was to lower the turnout gap between partisans and people who do not identify with a party. The 2004 presidential election thus serves as a useful reminder that while the media environment sets the stage for politics – and does so in different ways than in the past – politicians, journalists, and citizens still put on the show. And in 2004, it happened to be a show of high stakes and big suspense that inspired even some of the less partisan Americans to go to the polls.

Although turnout is lower in midterm elections, the difference between more and less partisan segments is similar in on- and off-year elections. It has become considerably larger in the last twenty-five years. The growing gap is obvious in Figure 7.6, which plots the difference in turnout rates between strong partisans and independents (and apoliticals) for both

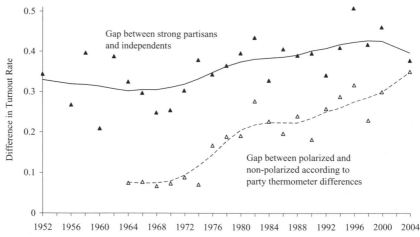

Figure 7.6. The Growing Turnout Gap between Strong Partisans and Independents.

Note: This figure graphs the difference in the turnout rates of strong partisans and independents (or apoliticals) shown in Figure 7.5 (dark triangles) and in the turnout rates of respondents who rate the parties the same on the thermometer items and respondents who rate the parties at least 40 degrees apart (light triangles). The lines are moving averages generated by a locally weighted regression on time. *Source:* National Election Study.

on- and off-year elections. (The dark triangles indicate the yearly differences. The solid line is a moving average.) After oscillating wildly around a mean of approximately 30 percent until the mid-1970s, the turnout difference has grown by about a third since then. In 1996 and 2000, the difference exceeded 45 percent. It remains to be seen if the lower gap in 2004 is more than an aberration.

The second trend in Figure 7.6 (marked by the dashed line and the light triangles) reinforces the conclusion of a growing turnout gap between more and less partisan people. It represents the difference in turnout rates of respondents who have the same affective response to both parties and respondents who rate the parties at least 40 degrees apart. About 30 percent of the respondents are in the former group. It includes not only respondents who give both parties the same thermometer rating, but also those who do not know how to rate both parties. Another 30 percent of the respondents rate one party at least 40 degrees more favorably than the other party. These more partisan citizens have always (as long as we have data) been more likely to go to the polls than those whose feelings toward both parties are the same. But this turnout difference has increased quite dramatically from less than 10 percentage points before 1974 to over 25 percentage points in 1992 and 35 points in 2004. By this measure of partisan attachment, the trend toward greater partisan polarization through compositional change continued unabated in 2004 despite the close election.

In sum, over the past three decades diverging trends in turnout of strong partisans, on the one hand, and people with no partisan attachments and similar affective reactions toward both parties, on the other, have changed the composition of the voting public. This change has increased the share of voters with a deep attachment to their own side and much less favorable feelings toward the opposition.[9] According to my Conditional Learning Model, this is a consequence of greater media choice. Entertainment-seekers are less partisan and their turnout rates have decreased relative to more partisan news-seekers. As a result, representation of partisan voters has increased, and elections are more guided by partisan sentiments than before the growth of cable and the Internet. Up to this point, the evidence that connects greater media choice and polarized elections has been indirect. In fact, there may be other explanations for the trends in Figure 7.5. Demonstrating more directly that the increase in partisan

9 The effect of these diverging turnout trends has been complemented by a slight rise in the proportion of strong partisans in the electorate (see Figure 7.2) and a decrease in the proportion of independents or apoliticals. To reiterate, those changes are not compositional and can therefore not follow directly from the mechanisms outlined by the Conditional Political Learning model.

polarization would not have been as strong in the absence of changes in the media environment requires inferences about the hypothetical votes of entertainment fans who no longer go to the polls because they have access to new media.

THE ROLE OF MEDIA CHOICE:
ALLOWING MODERATES TO ESCAPE

The analysis so far has demonstrated that entertainment-seekers are less partisan than news-seekers. They are also less likely to vote in the first place because many of them have cable or Internet access. According to the key hypothesis of this chapter, they would have been a moderating element, had they cast a vote. In order to test this hypothesis, it is necessary to get an idea of what their vote choice would have been and to examine how strongly this hypothetical vote is determined by their partisan identification. It then becomes possible to infer what the level of partisanship or polarization would have been if people with a strong entertainment preference had cast a vote despite having access to new media.

One way to learn about this counterfactual scenario is to use a question in the National Election Studies that asks nonvoters how they would have voted. This analytic strategy is uncomplicated, but it requires that nonvoters have reached a hypothetical vote decision. In practice, not every nonvoter gives an answer, so a small, but presumably very apolitical segment of the electorate still escapes the analysis. The second way to study hypothetical vote choice among nonvoters is to infer their likely vote choices from the other things we know about them. This analytic strategy is more complex, but it avoids the problems associated with asking nonvoters how they would have voted. I pursue both strategies here. Reassuringly, they lead to the same conclusion.

In the NES 1996, 164 nonvoters reported a preference for one of the two major party candidates for Congress and lived in districts with a contested election.[10] The probit coefficient for the impact of party identification on their (hypothetical) vote choice was .24. Among voters, that coefficient was almost twice as large at .45. Of course, it does not come as a big surprise that voters are more partisan in their actual voting behavior

---

10 This number excludes 188 nonvoters who did not prefer a candidate. Four non-voters were asked for their hypothetical vote choice, but are excluded because they lived in a district with an uncontested House election or named a candidate who was not on the ballot. Eighty-five respondents who reported voting in the presidential but not in the House election were not asked for their hypothetical House vote choice.

than nonvoters are in their hypothetical voting choices. Strong partisan sentiment is after all one of the things that stimulate people to vote. More interesting is the difference between news- and entertainment-seekers in the two groups. Among voters, party identification is almost as strongly related to vote choice for respondents above the median Relative Entertainment Preference as below. The probit coefficients are .48 for low REP and .42 for high REP. Among nonvoters, in contrast, those with a taste for entertainment would cast decidedly less partisan votes than those with a preference for news. At .38, the probit coefficient for news-seekers is more than twice as large as the same coefficient for entertainment-seekers (.17).[11] Compared to both voters and nonvoters with a preference for news, the vote decisions of abstaining entertainment fans would have been much less partisan. Judging by the stated vote preferences of nonvoters, elections would be less polarized in the absence of greater media choice.

If we do not want to rely on the assumption that nonvoters' hypothetical vote choices are meaningful but want to get a sense of how the respondents who did not even state a hypothetical preference would have voted, we need to turn to more complicated inferential machinery. This method uses Bartels's (2000) algorithm of calculating the estimated impact of party identification on vote choice as its starting point. Bartels estimates the associations between the different categories of party identification (strong partisan, weak partisan, leaner), weights these associations by the proportions of voters in the respective categories, and sums across categories to generate a measure of the average impact of party ID on vote choice. Bartels calculates partisan voting scores for presidential and congressional elections between 1952 and 1996 to compare the importance of partisanship over time. To get a sense of the magnitude of difference in the following analysis, it helps to consider Bartels's results. For congressional elections, the focus of my analysis, partisan voting scores drop from around 1.2 in the early 1960s to a low of 0.6 in 1978. In recent decades, partisan voting scores have rebounded to levels around 0.9. (Partisan voting scores for presidential elections are shown in Figure 1.2.) I use Bartels's method not to compare the impact of party identification over time, but rather to compare it at different levels of entertainment preference. Moreover, I must extend the estimation in order to figure out how partisan the voting decisions of nonvoters would have been.

---

11 More formally, the impact of party identification on actual vote choice is not significantly conditioned by entertainment preference. The interaction is significant only for hypothetical vote choice, which is affected by party identification only for those with a high relative preference for news.

In technical terms, the added difficulty of inferring the (potential) strength of partisan voting among nonvoters represents a missing data problem. The dependent variable is only observed for respondents who reported voting – in the 2002 House election in the case of the N&E Survey. Simply estimating the probit model and discarding all nonvoters provides an estimate of the partisan voting score *for voters*. When examining partisanship in the entire electorate, however, the estimates are inaccurate for two reasons. First, the proportions in each category of party identification are different for the electorate as a whole. As we have already seen, the proportion of partisans is lower in the public than among voters. Second, the effect of party identification on actual vote choice may not be the same as the (hypothetical) effect among nonvoters. Typically less informed nonvoters may abandon the party line quite easily, especially in House elections where incumbency cues stand out (see Chapter 6) and candidates often downplay their party affiliation.

For these two reasons, calculating partisan voting scores based on voters only would result in an overestimate of potential partisan voting, especially among people with high entertainment preference. Relative Entertainment Preference affects partisan voting scores not only directly but also indirectly by reducing the likelihood that moderates will vote in the first place. To assess the effect of entertainment preference on partisan voting – including the effect entertainment preference has on whether to vote or not – I use a Heckman selection model. This model takes into account the process that determines whether a respondent has missing data on the dependent variable in addition to the relationship between the dependent and independent variables. I present the technical details of this procedure in the appendix to this chapter. Here, I simply explain the substantive conclusions.

For both the N&E Survey (top half) and the NES 1996 (bottom half), Table 7.1 offers three estimates of partisan voting, each at two levels of Relative Entertainment Preference. The first estimate, in columns 1 and 2, is for voters. The second estimate, in columns 3 and 4, is based on the distribution of party identification in the public as a whole, but still assumes that the effect of party identification on vote choice is the same among nonvoters as among voters. It shows the extent of partisan voting if the entire electorate had turned out *and* if nonvoters had based their vote on their party identification in exactly the same way as voters. The third estimate, in columns 5 and 6, is also for the entire electorate, but it relaxes the second assumption and simulates what the impact of party identification on nonvoters' votes would have been (instead of forcing that impact to be the same as among voters). For each of six groups of partisans – from strong Republicans to strong Democrats – each pair of columns shows the regression coefficient and the proportion of voters

	No Selection, Proportions among Voters		No Selection, Proportions in the Electorate		Selection, Proportions in the Electorate	
	Coefficient	Proportion	Coefficient	Proportion	Coefficient	Proportion
N&E Survey						
Low REP						
Strong Republican	2.56**	0.20	2.56**	0.26	2.96**	0.26
Weak Republican	1.39**	0.15	1.39**	0.15	1.76**	0.15
Lean Republican	1.55**	0.09	1.55**	0.08	1.84**	0.08
Lean Democrat	0.90**	0.10	.90**	0.07	0.45	0.07
Weak Democrat	0.87**	0.16	.87**	0.16	0.49	0.16
Strong Democrat	1.54**	0.17	1.54**	0.20	1.44**	0.20
Partisan Voting Score	1.52		1.36		1.40	
High REP						
Strong Republican	1.43*	0.14	1.43*	0.20	1.00	0.20
Weak Republican	1.62**	0.13	1.62**	0.16	1.39**	0.16
Lean Republican	0.40	0.08	0.40	0.09	0.28	0.09
Lean Democrat	1.57**	0.10	1.57**	0.09	1.37**	0.09
Weak Democrat	2.22**	0.17	2.22**	0.17	2.16**	0.17
Strong Democrat	1.97**	0.16	1.97**	0.22	1.99**	0.22
Partisan Voting Score	1.55		1.29		1.17	
NES1996						
Low REP						
Strong Republican	1.31**	0.13	1.31**	0.17	1.10*	0.17
Weak Republican	0.80*	0.15	0.80*	0.16	0.83	0.16
Lean Republican	0.37	0.12	0.37	0.11	0.38	0.11
Lean Democrat	1.13**	0.13	1.13**	0.12	1.16**	0.12
Weak Democrat	1.02**	0.20	1.02**	0.17	0.96*	0.17
Strong Democrat	1.61**	0.20	1.61**	0.22	1.73**	0.22
Partisan voting score	1.07		1.00		1.00	
High REP						
Strong Republican	2.37**	0.14	2.37**	0.14	2.12**	0.14
Weak Republican	0.74**	0.16	0.74**	0.16	0.55	0.16
Lean Republican	0.70*	0.11	0.70*	0.11	0.52	0.11
Lean Democrat	0.44	0.14	0.44	0.11	0.27	0.11
Weak Democrat	0.61*	0.19	0.61*	0.17	0.53	0.17
Strong Democrat	1.07**	0.14	1.07**	0.20	1.11**	0.20
Partisan Voting Score	1.02		0.89		0.77	

$** p < .01, * p < .05$

Note: This table summarizes the results of twelve probit regressions of vote choice on party identification used to generate different estimates of partisan voting scores. The models in the third pair of columns are estimated with a selection stage (see appendix for this chapter). Proportions in each category of party ID are either for voters (first pair of columns) or for the public as a whole.

(or, in columns 3–6, the proportion of the entire public) in each category. The regression coefficient indicates the strength of the relationship between being in a particular category and voting for one's party.[12] Partisan vote scores are calculated by multiplying coefficient and proportion and then summing across all six groups.

In the N&E Survey, the partisan voting score is 1.52 for news-seekers compared to 1.55 for entertainment-seekers when estimated for voters only. In the NES 1996, the respective values are 1.07 and 1.02.[13] Entertainment fans appear to be just as partisan in their voting behavior as news-seekers, according to these estimates. But these are estimates for entertainment fans who actually voted (either because they still did not have access to cable television or the Internet, or because they were interested – and partisan – enough to vote despite the allure of entertainment). The Conditional Political Learning model predicts, and Chapter 4 showed empirically, that many citizens with a strong preference for entertainment stayed at home on Election Day 2002 as an indirect consequence of having access to new media. This leaves only the most partisan entertainment fans in the voting population and inflates their proportions used in calculating partisan voting scores. Because people with high entertainment preference are least likely to vote (if they have access to new media), this distortion is more consequential for them than it is for news-seekers.

In the second pair of columns, which use the proportions in the electorate instead of proportions among voters to calculate voting scores, we begin to see lower scores for entertainment fans. Estimates drop at both levels of Relative Entertainment Preference, but the drop is larger among respondents with a preference for entertainment. Among news-seekers, the drop is 0.16 in the N&E Survey and 0.07 in the NES 1996. Among entertainment fans, partisan voting scores drop by 0.26 in the N&E Survey and by 0.13 in the NES 1996. If everybody voted, and nonvoters

---

12 Minus signs have been omitted for the probit coefficients for Democratic partisans to make the presentation more intuitive. For full results, see Tables 7A.1 and 7A.2.

13 The partisan voting scores are universally higher in the N&E Survey than in the NES 1996 or in Bartels's analysis of NES data. This difference is probably explained by the fact that the NES is conducted in two waves, one before and one after the election. Respondents are asked about their party identification in the pre-election wave, and about their vote choice, naturally, in the post-election wave. In the N&E Survey, by contrast, party identification and vote choice were assessed in the same interview. The increased temporal proximity of the two questions probably creates a closer statistical relationship between the two variables. For the purpose of this study, such inflation is not troubling as long as its prevalence does not differ by levels of entertainment preference. It is reassuring that the magnitude of the difference between voters and the electorate as a whole is so similar in the NES 1996 and the N&E Survey at each level of entertainment preference.

voted just as voters do, partisanship would be less important in determining election outcomes. Entertainment fans would contribute more to this downplaying of partisanship than news fans.

Even this adjustment still overestimates the potential importance of partisanship *especially among entertainment-seekers*. In columns 1–4 of Table 7.1, the probit coefficients are estimated using only respondents who voted in the 2002 House election (and in the 1996 House election, for NES data in the bottom half of the table). The exclusion of nonvoters exaggerates the potential relationship between each level of party identification and the vote decision in the electorate as a whole because voters are more partisan than the electorate as a whole- and because the discrepancy between voters and nonvoters is greater among entertainment-seekers, the coefficients should be disproportionately more inflated for them.

The third set of estimates in columns 5 and 6 of Table 7.1 adjusts for this sample selection problem (see chapter appendix for details). Taking into account the hypothetical voting behavior among nonvoters, the (hypothetical) partisan voting scores drop further, but only among respondents with high levels of entertainment preference. In the N&E Survey, the partisan voting score declines by another 0.12 points. In the NES 1996, the additional drop is 0.12 as well. Among news-seekers, the Heckman model yields exactly the same partisan voting score as the probit model without selection. Nonvoting news-seekers would make their vote choices in the same partisan fashion as news-seekers who actually vote. If one's aim is to draw conclusions about the potential voting behavior among current nonvoters, using a model without selection overestimates (potential) partisan voting scores *only* among people with a high entertainment preference because voters who like entertainment are clearly more partisan than nonvoters who like entertainment.

Whereas partisan voting was similar for news-seekers and entertainment-seekers who actually voted, the difference in the *potential* importance of partisanship in the electorate as a whole is considerable. In the N&E Survey, the inferred voting score for news fans is 1.40, which is not all that different from the actual score among voters of 1.52. The inferred partisan voting score among entertainment-seekers is only 1.17, by comparison. In the NES 1996, actual partisan voting and potential partisan voting in the entire electorate are almost the same for low REP (1.07 vs. 1.00.) For high REP, on the other hand, observed partisan voting is much higher (1.02) than potential partisan voting under full turnout (0.77). According to both the N&E Survey and the NES 1996, actual partisan voting among entertainment fans is 25 percent stronger than it would be if all entertainment fans voted.

The more a current nonvoter prefers entertainment programming to news, the more *unlikely* that person would have been to cast a vote based on his partisan identification, had the person in fact voted. The potential strength of partisan voting among news-seekers exceeds that of entertainment-seekers by 20 percent in the N&E Survey and by 30 percent in the NES 1996. These are sizable differences when compared to the over-time trend presented by Bartels (2000), who finds an increase of a similar magnitude among voters between the 1970s and the 1990s.[14]

In sum, results from both the N&E Survey and the NES 1996 confirm that entertainment preference is related to partisan polarization of House elections. The coefficient estimates obtained by the original Bartels approach represent estimates of partisan voting among those who went to the polls. The coefficients in the selection model, in contrast, are estimates based on voters and nonvoters combined. In other words, the selection model addresses the hypothetical case of full turnout and does so by "simulating" the voting behavior of nonvoters in addition to modeling the behavior of actual voters. If including the hypothetical behavior of nonvoters in the estimation reduces partisan voting for high entertainment preference, it follows that these nonvoters would base their votes less on partisan identification than entertainment fans who did vote. In contrast, the corresponding differences between voters and nonvoters at lower levels of entertainment preference (i.e., for those who like news) are statistically and substantively negligible.

Combining these results with the effect of entertainment preference on turnout finally allows me to connect the impact of increased media choice with partisan polarization. In Chapter 4, I provided evidence that increased media choice leads to lower turnout among people who prefer entertainment to news. This chapter showed that a preference for entertainment is negatively related to both the strength of people's party identification and feeling thermometer differences between political opposites. Finally, the last part of the analysis indicates that among people who like entertainment, nonvoters would be less partisan in their voting decisions than voters. The people who do not vote because increased media choice allows them to follow their preference for entertainment are among the least partisan members of the electorate. The exact magnitude of polarization caused by increased media choice is difficult to gauge. Certainly, only a portion of the difference between partisan voting scores among current voters and simulated scores for the full electorate can be the result of changes in the media environment. Nevertheless, it is valid to conclude

---

14 According to Bartels's analysis, party ID had its lowest impact on congressional vote choice between 1976 and 1980, with an average voting score of .66 for those three elections. The average for 1996–2000 is .86, equivalent to a 30 percent rise. In presidential elections, partisan voting scores have increased by about 50 percent over the last two or three decades.

that increased media choice disproportionately decreases the vote likelihood of politically moderate citizens, and that voting behavior would be less partisan if the expansion of media choice had not happened. Cable television and the Internet have polarized American elections by providing their audiences with more choice.

THE EFFECT OF RISING CABLE PENETRATION ON PARTISAN POLARIZATION

For a third test of my hypothesis that greater media choice polarized elections, I turn to aggregate data. The data relate changes in cable penetration to changes in aggregate voting patterns in media markets. It is the same data set I used in Chapter 5 to examine the effect of cable television on turnout. Using aggregate data has different advantages and disadvantages than using survey data. The aggregate data set does not rely on people's reports of their voting behavior. Instead, it uses official vote returns. The analysis tracks the same media markets over time, so inferences about causality are more rigorous. Finally, aggregate data allow me to extend the analysis back in time. If greater media choice polarizes elections, its effect should have been felt as early as the 1970s, when cable penetration began to pick up. Suitable survey data with questions about cable access and voting behavior do not become available until the mid-1990s. The aggregate data set covers the years from 1972 to 1990. Over this period, large variation in cable penetration occurred both over time and across media markets. Increasing cable penetration in a media market should have made voting behavior in the market more partisan, according to the Conditional Political Learning model.

The greatest disadvantage of the aggregate data is the operationalization of the dependent variable, partisan polarization. Scholars routinely use aggregate voting data to infer the level of partisanship in a constituency. The premise is that vote shares for candidates of the same party at different electoral levels will be more similar if people's voting behavior is strongly influenced by partisan consideration. Strong partisans are less likely to split their ticket. Hence, the more partisan the voters, the greater the correlation between party vote shares for different offices (e.g., Jacobson 2000b, 21; 2000c, 22).

My data set includes information on cable access and vote returns for presidential and House elections in all media markets (DMAs) between 1972 and 1990. (Details on how I created the DMA data set are available in Chapter 5.) In the following analysis, I use the relationship between voting in House and presidential elections to infer the degree of partisan polarization. Yet, whereas previous studies used district-level data, my unit of analysis is the media market. My data set does not include information on the overlap of congressional districts and media markets (a changing and often very complicated mapping), so I cannot consider the role of congressional competition in my analysis. All voters in a media market choose between the same two major-party candidates at the presidential level. In many markets, that is not true in congressional elections. This problem is most severe when some of the House elections in a media market are not contested by two candidates. By definition, an unopposed candidate gets most or all of the votes. This reflects the strength of her party base in the district only imperfectly. She would probably still have received a large majority of the votes in a contested election, but a 100 percent vote share clearly exaggerates the partisan composition in the district. To avoid distortions from uncontested House elections, I exclude media markets with low competition in House elections from my analysis. For each DMA, I calculate the share of votes cast in counties where only one candidate received votes (i.e., where the election was not contested). If this share exceeds 5 percent, I do not exclude the DMA in my analysis. This constraint eliminates about one-third of the cases.[15]

Table 7.2 presents three models that estimate the impact of cable penetration on the correspondence of House and presidential elections in different ways. The dependent variable in the first two models is the Democratic vote share in House elections in a media market. It is regressed on the Democratic vote share in the presidential election of the same year, the percentage of cable households in the DMA, and the interaction between these two variables. The model also includes a set of control variables, both as main effects and conditional on cable penetration. The key variable is the interaction of presidential vote share and cable penetration. The positive and significant coefficient for this variable indicates that voting in House and presidential elections is more closely related in DMAs with higher cable penetration. The same result emerges in the second model, which adds fixed effects for DMAs to control for idiosyncrasies at the market level.

The first two models explore the cross-sectional relationship between cable and correspondence of voting patterns. In a different specification, which is not shown, I examined the relationship between presidential

15 A second way to adjust market-level measures is to calculate a party's vote share only for those counties in which both parties received votes. Like the 5 percent cutoff, this adjustment may not exclude all uncontested elections (because it leaves counties in the sample if at least one election in the county is contested even if the county also includes parts of uncontested districts). Empirically, different measures and cutoffs for the share of contested elections did not affect the analysis of the correlation between House and presidential vote shares (see below). The analysis of absolute differences between House and presidential vote share, on the other hand, was somewhat sensitive to the cutoff.

Table 7.2. *The Effect of Cable Television on Correspondence of Presidential and House Elections*

	Democratic House Vote Share		Change in Absolute Difference of Democratic Vote Share in House and Presidential Election
Dem. pres. vote share	0.49** (.094)	−0.023 (.091)	0.043 (.068)
Cable penetration	−0.058 (.37)	−0.36 (.38)	
Change in cable penetration			**−0.131*** (.067)
Cable penetration × Dem. pres. vote share	0.013** (.002)	0.011** (.002)	
Pres. turnout			0.008 (.092)
Population density	6.4** (2.6)	19.3* (1.2)	2.3 (2.1)
TV households (in millions)	−2.1** (.65)	−4.8 (4.2)	−0.42 (.53)
% White	−0.14 (.082)	0.29 (.25)	0.11 (.067)
% with college degree	1.1** (.28)	2.4** (.73)	0.21 (.18)
Median age	0.70* (.30)	0.29 (.44)	0.0001 (.24)
Unemployment rate	1.2** (.45)	1.0* (.55)	−0.12 (.25)
Median income (in $1,000)	−0.87** (.28)	−1.1* (.60)	0.19 (.28)
Change in pres. turnout			−0.17 (.16)
Change in Dem. pres. vote share			−0.56** (.086)
Change in TVHH			7.2 (5.9)
Change in % white			0.49 (.37)
Change in % with college degree			−0.74 (1.1)
Change in median age			0.17 (.61)
Change in unemployment rate			1.2* (.61)
Change in median income			−0.078 (.75)
Cable penetration × Pop. density	−0.094 (.083)	−0.21** (.085)	
Cable penetration × TVHH	0.009 (.022)	0.035 (.024)	
Cable penetration × % white	−0.002 (.002)	−0.003 (.002)	
Cable penetration × % college	−0.021** (.007)	−0.018** (.007)	
Cable penetration × Age	−0.007 (.01)	0.005 (.011)	
Cable penetration × Unemployment	−0.021* (.012)	−0.016 (.012)	
Cable penetration × Income	0.018** (.006)	0.02** (.007)	
1976	−2.3 (1.5)	2.1 (2.2)	2.2 (3.8)
1980	−2.4 (2.2)	−3.1 (4.0)	−4.0 (3.0)
1984	1.0 (3.1)	−3.1 (5.8)	2.0 (2.1)
1988	−2.3 (4.1)	−6.6 (7.9)	
Constant	15.6 (12.4)	−16.0 (28.1)	−16.9* (9.9)
DMA fixed effects	—	Included	—
R^2	0.45	0.82	0.22
N	620	620	445

** $p < .01$, * $p < .05$ (one-tailed)

Note: The dependent variable in the first two models is the Democratic vote share in House elections in a media market. The dependent variable in the third column is the change between consecutive elections in the absolute difference of Democratic House and presidential vote shares. All models are estimated by OLS. Numbers in parentheses are standard errors.

vote shares in consecutive elections. As cable penetration increases, variations in presidential vote shares from one election to the next decline significantly, suggesting more partisan voting behavior and explicitly linking the growth of cable to the decline in electoral volatility that Bartels (1998) has documented (see Chapter 1). This alternative specification does not rely on House election, so it removes the problem of uncontested elections.[16]

The third model in Table 7.2 takes even greater advantage of the time series nature of the data set by employing a so-called difference-in-differences approach. One measure of polarization is the (absolute) difference between a party's vote share in House and presidential elections in the DMA (e.g., Born 2000). A decrease in this difference from one election to the next indicates that voting patterns for different electoral offices have become more similar, reflecting a greater impact of partisanship. The dependent variable in the third column is just this difference: the difference in the absolute difference of House and presidential vote shares obtained by Democratic candidates in consecutive elections.

The key independent variable in the third model in Table 7.2 is the change in cable penetration in the period between the two elections. The negative and significant coefficient for this variable means that an increase in cable penetration reduces the difference between House and presidential election outcomes.[17] This result confirms the conclusions from the first two models in the table, using a different (and sometimes preferred) estimation strategy. Regardless of measurement or estimation details, cable television increased the correspondence between election outcomes both over time and for different offices. The most compelling explanation for this effect – and the explanation backed up by the Conditional Political Learning model and the individual-level results presented earlier in this chapter – is that cable television polarized elections by increasing the share of partisan voters.

To illustrate the magnitude of the cable effect, Figure 7.7 plots the strength of the relationship between House and presidential elections for

16 A more explicit time series specification confirms this result. The correlation between vote shares in consecutive presidential elections depends significantly (and positively) on the *change* in cable penetration between the two elections.
17 This model is estimated by OLS, so predicted values of interelection change may imply negative absolute values in the first election of the pair. If the actual absolute difference between House and presidential vote shares at time t is smaller than the predicted increase in this difference between $t - 1$ and t, then the absolute difference at $t - 1$, impossibly, would have to have been negative. This was the case in only 8 percent of the cases, and the implied negative absolute value exceeded 5 points in only 2 percent of the cases.

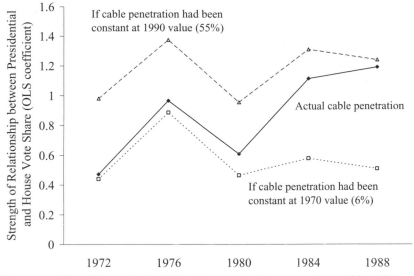

Figure 7.7. The Effect of Cable Television on the Correspondence of Presidential and House Elections, 1972–1988.

Note: This figure is based on the first model in Table 7.2. The estimations for the three different scenarios of cable penetration are explained in the text.

election years between 1972 and 1988. Based on the model in column 1 of Table 7.2, the graph shows this relationship for three different scenarios.[18] The solid line shows the actual relationship in this period during which cable penetration rose nationally from 9 to 50 percent. In this period, the strength of the relationship roughly doubled. The two other lines in the graph illustrate that the correspondence between House and presidential elections would have barely changed in the absence of rising cable penetration. The dotted line estimates what the relationship would have been if cable penetration had remained constant at its 1970 level of 6 percent. Clearly, Democratic vote shares in House and presidential elections would have remained a lot less similar. The dashed line graphs the relationship we would have observed if the 55 percent of households that had cable access in 1990 had already had cable in 1970 and if cable penetration had stayed at that level. The correspondence of House and presidential voting behavior would have been much higher to begin with, but it would not have changed much over time.

18 To estimate the relationship between Democratic vote shares in House and presidential elections for each election year, I added interactions of the year dummies with both Democratic Presidential Vote Share and the Cable Penetration × Democratic Presidential Vote Share term.

The aggregate models show effects of cable television on partisan polarization as early as the mid-1970s. (Year-by-year estimates of the models in Table 7.2 do not suggest a time trend in the size of the cable effect.) The beginnings of the cable effect thus precede polarization in Congress as measured by NOMINATE scores (Poole and Rosenthal 2001; Roberts and Smith 2003).[19] Change in the media environment polarized elections, according to my results, and it did so before Congress polarized. This timing contradicts studies that locate the reason for increased polarization at the elite level, arguing that polarization in Congress preceded polarization of voting behavior. Hetherington (2001, 619), for example, concludes that "greater partisan polarization in Congress has clarified the parties' ideological positions for ordinary Americans, which in turn has increased party importance and salience on the mass level." In contrast, the results in this chapter suggest that the causal chain began with a change in the media environment. As cable television lowered turnout of less partisan entertainment fans (and, somewhat later, increased turnout of more partisan news junkies), members of Congress had good reason to advocate more ideologically extreme positions both in Congress and during their reelection campaigns. Over the last two decades, representatives have indeed positioned themselves farther away from the center not only in Congress, but also in primary and general elections (Aldrich 1995; Ansolabehere, Snyder, and Stewart 2001; Fiorina 1999). The timing of cable effect thus strengthens the case for greater media choice as an important cause of polarization in Congress. Current levels of polarization are at least partly an unintended consequence of new media technologies.

CONCLUSION

If we still lived in a low-choice media environment, and Switchers – people who watch the news only when media choice is low – voted again, voting behavior would be less polarized than it is today. I reached this conclusion through a chain of evidence that began in Chapter 4. Greater media choice reduced turnout rates among entertainment fans. They are more moderate or politically indifferent than the rest of the electorate. Their abstention makes the voting public more partisan. This compositional change is complemented by partisan news junkies becoming even more reliable in going to the polls and casting ideologically motivated votes. Different

19 Compared to other measures of elite polarization, the timing is more ambiguous. Party unity voting in Congress, and differences in congressional support for the president by his party and the opposition, began to increase in the 1970s (Fiorina 2002; Jacobson 2003).

analyses of survey data show that party identification would be a less important determinant of voting decisions if entertainment fans returned to the polls. This conclusion is supported by the consistent finding that while American voters are more partisan today than three decades ago, evidence for more intense partisanship in the public as a whole is a good deal weaker. Cable television and the Internet set in motion a re-sorting of the electorate that polarized elections without necessarily making anyone more partisan.

Greater media choice thus amplified the impact of party identification on voting behavior in both presidential and congressional elections, which in turn increased correspondence of presidential and congressional election outcomes. Whereas idiosyncratic local factors in individual districts – including the impact of incumbency – used to play a strong role in congressional elections, national conditions that benefit one or the other party across many districts have reasserted their impact in recent decades. The correlation between the presidential vote in a district and the vote for the House candidate of the president's party first declined from its high levels in the 1950s and then resurged starting in the mid-1970s (Jacobson 2000b; 2003). Likewise, Fleisher and Bond (2004) show that presidential vote in a district or state predicts the winner of congressional elections decidedly better today than in the 1960s. As a result of these trends, the number of districts that elect a representative from one party but give a majority to the presidential candidate of the opposite party has declined (Jacobson 2003).

According to the Conditional Political Learning model, these are all consequences of the same underlying mechanism. Greater media choice triggers compositional change of the voting public that accentuates the role of partisanship in voting behavior. After the advent of television initially increased the proportion of less educated voters and helped incumbents, the spread of cable began to reverse this trend by lowering the turnout of citizens most attracted by the newly available around-the-clock entertainment. With this relatively nonpartisan segment increasingly in front of the television instead of in the voting booth, the power of party identification in congressional elections returns.

The correspondence between rising impact of partisanship and reduced impact of incumbency is often asserted. "Given that incumbency advantage is a reflection of district and personal considerations," write Brady, D'Onofrio, and Fiorina (2000, 143), "it is logical to suppose that incumbency should fade as House elections become more nationalized." Jacobson (2000c, 29) agrees that "the shrinking value of incumbency is a predictable consequence of voting patterns increasingly shaped by national partisan considerations."

Empirically, the correspondence between rising polarization and declining incumbency advantage is not as close as these statements might suggest. The incumbency advantage peaked in the late 1980s (Jacobson 2004, 28), at a time when polarization in Congress and among voters was already under way for up to a decade (see first footnote in this chapter). Since the late 1970s, voting behavior has been increasingly determined by party identification, but the rise in the incumbency advantage continued. This is even more surprising given that congressional voters are more interested and partisan than presidential voters. More important for my argument, the incumbency advantage kept increasing during the first decade of cable television. Is it possible, then, that the incumbency advantage in House elections is not an exact mirror image of rising polarization or greater partisanship? Are there reasons why the incumbency advantage did not decline sooner and more strongly?

The partisan leanings of congressional voters are certainly not the only predictor of congressional voting behavior. If incumbents become safer for other reasons – redistricting or more federal spending in the district, for example – then even a more partisan voting public, produced in part by greater media choice, may continue to support congressional incumbents. Fiorina (2004b, 149) argues that different factors contributed to the incumbency advantage at different times before it eventually began to decline:

From approximately the mid-1960s through the 1970s, I believe, it was based primarily on member resources and activities. But as increases in member resources leveled off and a high level of constituency attentiveness became a universal expectation, they declined in importance. During the 1980s elections became much more expensive, incumbents were able to raise far more money than challengers, and the nature of the incumbency advantage increasingly came to reflect those facts. Then, as alternative means of recruiting and financing challengers developed in the 1990s, elections become more national and the incumbency advantage declined.

If Fiorina is correct, greater media choice could have affected voting behavior in the 1980s, but incumbents were shielded from the consequences until the 1990s.

Several scholars have argued that the primary cause for polarization in the electorate is a change in the information about congressional officeholders and candidates that reaches the public. Jacobson (2000a) believes that party-related information about candidates (such as their issue positions relative to their party or their ideology) has become more available at the expense of party-independent information (such as individual candidates' performance or personality). Party labels have become "more informative" (Jacobson 2000c) to voters because clear issue differences between parties have emerged. Information about the correspondence of members' voting records to their parties' positions is more easily available. "Today, it is much harder for individual members to hide their votes or fudge their positions than a generation ago. Today's voters in principle have access to considerable policy information in addition to the usual local heuristics" (Brady, D'Onofrio, and Fiorina 2000, 146).

My explanation for increasingly polarized elections focuses not on the type of messages being sent but on the receivers of these messages. Independent of message content, different segments of the electorate are exposed to news about Congress and about the political process more generally. Before cable television and the Internet expanded viewing choices, news-seekers and entertainment-seekers alike received elite message, and many were sufficiently motivated by them to go to the polls. Since then, more interested, more partisan citizens have become more likely to receive political information and vote, while moderates have become less engaged. Moderates do not make it to the polls anymore, whereas partisans just keep doing what they always did: vote for their party.

Better sorting of voters and nonvoters by partisan strength alone helps explain more partisan voting behavior. Greater media choice has raised the concentration of partisans among voters. But the simple compositional effect predicted by the Conditional Political Learning model cannot account for a slight increase in partisanship even in the electorate as a whole. Furthermore, Conditional Political Learning does not rule out that news-seekers become more partisan after increased media choice allows them to watch more news. In fact, previous research suggests that more information makes people's views more partisan, simply because it leads them to see clearer differences between the alternatives (Palfrey and Poole 1987).

It is important to distinguish between factual information about objectively increasing differences between political parties and bias in reporting that increases only the perception of those differences. Hetherington, Jacobson, and Brady, D'Onofrio, and Fiorina have the former in mind when they write about clarifying ideological positions and more informative party labels. Pundits and journalists have focused largely on the impact of more ideologically diverse news options. Cable news and political Web sites, especially their more ideologically unambiguous versions, are said to persuade people to endorse more partisan opinions. The Fox News Channel in particular is often blamed (or credited) for this increasing polarization. It provides a forum for more conservative elite opinions (DiMaggio, Evans, and Bryson 1996, 740) and may reinforce the political views of its conservative audience (Lazarsfeld and Berelson 1968 [1944]). Perhaps its emergence has contributed to a changing climate of political discussion more generally by suggesting that political confrontation and opinionated reporting attracts viewers (see Mutz and Reeves 2005).

It should be quite clear, however, that Fox News, despite its more conservative appearance, cannot have caused the polarization trends discussed in this chapter. Founded in 1996, it simply emerged too late to help us understand trends that started in the late 1970s. The time series analysis of voting patterns in media markets shows strong effects of cable penetration on electoral polarization twenty years before the Fox New Channel aired its first partisan rant. Moreover, audience research reviewed in Chapter 5 suggests strongly that most Fox News viewers also spend considerable time watching other cable news channels. Tracking of people's use of multimedia content has shown that many people listen to opposing views, rather than just the political slant they agree with in the first place (Iyengar, Hahn, and Prior 2001). Fox News is only one component in the media diets of ideologically hardened news junkies. It is not likely to change many minds[20] – and even less likely to reach the minds of many entertainment fans.

Half a century ago, Angus Campbell (1960) offered the idea of "surge and decline" to explain why voting behavior in midterm elections was more partisan than in presidential elections (see Chapter 1). People without deep attachments to a party would only go to the polls when the fanfare of a presidential campaign motivated them. In midterm years, they would stay home, only to return to the polls two years later. These "in-and-out voters" (Key 1966) made presidential elections less partisan by casting their nonideological votes and midterm elections more partisan by staying at home. Today's politically moderate or indifferent entertainment fans do not come back – not even for a presidential election.[21] For Americans who take advantage of more media options to avoid the news and who also happen to be less partisan, it is all decline and no more surge. They miss even the fanfare of a presidential campaign amid the hubbub of movie channels, reality contests, and online gaming.

---

20 A recent working paper finds that Republicans increased their vote share slightly more between 1996 and 2000 in parts of the country where the Fox News Channel began airing in this period (DellaVigna and Kaplan 2005). But the effect is too small to account for a substantial portion of the polarization trends shown in this chapter.

21 I deliberately exaggerate here to emphasize usual behavior in normal times. Entertainment fans do pay attention to politics under extraordinary circumstances. They followed the news after 9/11. As noted earlier, some of them even voted in the close 2004 election. I discuss the significance of this point in the concluding chapter.

Appendix to Chapter 7: Using a Selection Model to Simulate Partisan Vote Strength in the Full Electorate

According to the key hypothesis of this chapter, entertainment-seekers who do not go to the polls anymore because they have cable or Internet access would have been a moderating element in elections, had they cast a vote. To avoid the assumption that nonvoters' hypothetical vote choices are meaningful and to get a sense of how the respondents who did not even state a hypothetical preference would have voted, I extend Bartels's (2000) algorithm of calculating the estimated impact of party identification on vote choice by adding a selection equation that models whether or not an individual voted. To estimate this two-stage model, I employ a Heckman selection model.

Bartels estimates the associations between the different categories of party identification (strong partisan, weak partisan, leaner) and vote choice, weights these associations by the proportion of voters in respective category, and sums across categories to generate a measure of the average impact of party ID on vote choice. The partisan voting score is estimated by the following probit model:

$$v_i = \alpha_0 + \alpha_1 \cdot PID_i^{strong} + \alpha_2 \cdot PID_i^{weak} + \alpha_3 \cdot PID_i^{lean} + \varepsilon_i \qquad (1)$$

The dependent variable v_i is coded 1 for a Republican vote and 0 for a Democratic vote and is missing otherwise. PID_i^{strong} is 1 if the respondent identifies strongly with the Republican Party, -1 if she identifies strongly with the Democratic Party, and 0 otherwise. PID_i^{weak} and PID_i^{lean} are coded analogously for weak identifiers and independent leaners. ε_i is the error term. After estimating this model, the coefficients α_1, α_2, and α_3 are multiplied by the actual percentages of strong identifiers, weak identifiers, and leaners to calculate the partisan voting score.

For reasons that will become obvious momentarily, I break up the three PID variables to estimate coefficients separately for Republicans and Democrats. For example, instead of PID_i^{strong} with values $(-1, 0, 1)$, I include two variables, $PID_i^{REPstrong}$ and $PID_i^{DEMstrong}$. The first is coded 1 for respondents who identify strongly with the Republican Party, and 0 otherwise. The second is coded 1 for strong Democratic identifiers, and 0 otherwise. This yields the following model:

$$v_i = \alpha_0 + \alpha_1 \cdot PID_i^{REPstrong} + \alpha_2 \cdot PID_i^{REPweak}$$
$$+ \alpha_3 \cdot PID_i^{REPlean} + \alpha_4 \cdot PID_i^{DEMstrong} + \alpha_5 \cdot PID_i^{DEMweak} \qquad (2)$$
$$+ \alpha_3 \cdot PID_i^{DEMlean} + \varepsilon_i$$

The added difficulty of inferring the strength of partisan voting among nonvoters represents a missing-data problem. The dependent variable is only observed for respondents who reported voting. Simply estimating the probit model and discarding all nonvoters provides an estimate of the partisan voting score *for voters*. When examining partisanship in the entire electorate, however, the estimates are inaccurate for two reasons. First, the proportions in each category of party identification are different for the electorate as a whole. Second, the effect of each category on the actual vote among voters differs from the effect on the hypothetical vote among nonvoters. The strength of partisan identification is not only related to vote choice v_i but also to whether or not a person decides to vote. Hence, weaker identifiers will be systematically excluded from equations 1 and 2. Because I am interested in the effect of entertainment preference on partisan voting – including the effect entertainment preference has on whether to vote or not – the simple probit model in equations 1 and 2 would result in an overestimate of potential partisan voting, especially among people with high entertainment preference.

A Heckman selection model takes into account the process that determines whether a respondent has missing data on the dependent variable (selection equation) in addition to the relationship between the dependent and independent variables (outcome equation) (Brehm 1993, Chapter 5; Greene 1997, 976–81; Winship and Mare 1992). Here, the selection equation is a model of turnout:

$$v_i^{obs}* = \varphi \cdot Z_i + \mu_i$$
$$v_i^{obs} = 1, \; if \, v_i^{obs}* \geq 0 \qquad (3)$$
$$v_i^{obs} = 0, \; if \, v_i^{obs}* < 0$$

Equation 3 is the selection equation that models which cases enter into the estimation of the outcome equation. v_i^{obs} indicates whether the dependent variable, the vote, is observed, that is, whether or not respondent i voted for one of the two major parties. As in a typical probit setup, the unobserved continuous latent variable v_i^{obs*} is determined by the variables in the matrix Z_i. If none of the variables in equation 2 are related to whether v is observed, then the error terms of equations 2 and 3 are not correlated. If, however, observing v is affected by the dependent or independent variables in equation 2, then a correlation between the error terms leads to a violation of OLS assumptions. This correlation is $\rho = \text{corr}(\varepsilon, \mu)$. Assuming that ε and μ are distributed normally with a mean of zero and variances σ and 1, respectively, a Heckman selection model provides consistent and asymptotically efficient estimates if the model is identified. In addition to the regression coefficients, a Heckman model also estimates the correlation ρ. Hence, it is possible to test whether the selection and outcome equations are in fact dependent.

The selection equation includes the same variables as the outcome equation (and others related only to the selection process). For that reason, it is advantageous to break up the three *PID* variables in Bartels's original estimator into six indicator variables. A variable scored $+1$, -1, and 0 for strong Republicans, strong Democrats, and all others, respectively, is not a good predictor of turnout (because strong partisans of both parties are more likely to vote than the rest of the sample). Using separate indicator variables for strong Republicans and Democrats avoids this problem because it allows the effects of identifying strongly with either party on turnout to be positive. Table 7A.1 lists all variables used in the selection equation. (The equation is specified to predict voter turnout as accurately as possible, even at the expense of parsimony. It therefore differs slightly from the turnout model in Chapter 4.)

Table 7A.1 presents the coefficient estimates for the N&E Survey based on a Heckman model that incorporates both outcome (equation 2) and selection stage (equation 3). The first column shows the results for respondents with low Relative Entertainment Preference; the second column shows results for those with high REP. (I divided the sample at the median of REP.) Estimates of ρ indicate whether the two stages of the Heckman model are indeed not independent. To assess whether ρ is large enough, a likelihood-ratio test is conducted comparing the joint likelihood of the independent outcome and selection models (i.e., an OLS regression and a probit model) to the likelihood of the Heckman model. This test is significant only for respondents with high REP, indicating that the estimates of the αs are not biased for news-seekers if the probit model is estimated without selection stage. For entertainment-seekers, they are biased because voters who like entertainment are clearly more partisan than nonvoters who like entertainment. For high REP, the estimates by the Heckman model differ considerably from the probit model without selection, as Table 7.1 shows. It follows that the partisan voting scores differ, too.

Table 7A.1. *Complete Estimates of Partisan Voting Scores in N&E Survey*

	Low REP	High REP
Outcome equation		
Strong Republican	2.96** (.47)	1.00 (.60)
Weak Republican	1.76** (.33)	1.39** (.50)
Lean Republican	1.84** (.37)	0.28 (.50)
Lean Democrat	−0.45 (.37)	−1.37** (.42)
Weak Democrat	−0.49 (.40)	−2.16** (.41)
Strong Democrat	−1.44** (.46)	−1.99** (.49)
Constant	−0.85 (.44)	0.64 (.45)
Selection equation		
Strong Republican	1.17** (.29)	1.11** (.30)
Weak Republican	0.59* (.27)	0.94** (.28)
Lean Republican	0.27 (.30)	0.38 (.30)
Lean Democrat	0.06 (.29)	0.43 (.30)
Weak Democrat	1.05** (.28)	0.80** (.25)
Strong Democrat	1.33** (.30)	0.98** (.25)
Internet access	0.27 (.16)	−0.07 (.15)
Cable access	−0.18 (.17)	0.06 (.23)
Political knowledge, Wave 1	0.03 (.04)	0.02 (.04)
Current political knowledge, Wave 2	0.03 (.03)	0.13** (.03)
Education	0.09 (.07)	0.16* (.08)
Gender	0.08 (.16)	0.27 (.15)
Age	0.01 (.01)	0.01* (.01)
Income	0.07** (.02)	0.01 (.02)
R's primary language is English	1.31* (.63)	−0.67 (.68)
R is white	−0.02 (.27)	−0.23 (.22)
Religious attendance	0.15 (.28)	0.17 (.25)
R is registered to vote	1.54** (.36)	1.94** (.30)
R is married	0.22 (.17)	0.45** (.17)
Political interest	0.27 (.32)	−0.17 (.30)
Sense of civic duty	0.18 (.13)	−0.16 (.13)
Efficacy	0.27* (.11)	0.05 (.12)
Constant	−6.03** (.95)	−4.02** (.88)
ρ	−0.34 (.54)	−0.68§ (.26)
N	687	596

** $p < .01$, * $p < .05$, $^\S p < .10$

Note: Cell entries are unstandardized regression coefficients with standard errors in parentheses. The dependent variable in the outcome equation is vote choice in the 2002 House election (1, Republican; 0, Democrat). The dependent variable in the selection equation is 1 if the respondent cast a vote for one of the two major parties, 0 otherwise.

Table 7A.2. *Complete Estimates of Partisan Voting Scores in NES 1996*

	Low REP	High REP
Outcome equation		
Strong Republican	1.10* (.48)	2.12** (.45)
Weak Republican	0.83 (.43)	0.55 (.29)
Lean Republican	0.38 (.44)	0.51 (.34)
Lean Democrat	−1.16** (.41)	−0.27 (.29)
Weak Democrat	−0.96* (.40)	−0.53 (.28)
Strong Democrat	−1.73** (.42)	−1.11** (.30)
Constant	0.69 (.42)	0.23 (.25)
Selection equation		
Strong Republican	2.17** (.38)	0.54* (.29)
Weak Republican	1.01** (.31)	−0.03 (.28)
Lean Republican	0.81** (.29)	−0.28 (.31)
Lean Democrat	0.62* (.29)	−0.05 (.28)
Weak Democrat	0.79** (.26)	−0.05 (.27)
Strong Democrat	1.17** (.30)	0.70* (.29)
Internet access	0.22 (.19)	−0.06 (.19)
Cable access	0.31 (.17)	0.06 (.14)
Congressional knowledge	2.05** (.33)	2.12** (.32)
General knowledge	0.34 (.34)	0.54 (.30)
Education	0.11 (.06)	0.08 (.05)
Gender	0.47** (.16)	−0.11 (.15)
Age	0.02** (.01)	0.01* (.005)
Income	0.65 (.34)	1.10** (.31)
Income is missing	0.02 (.01)	0.06** (.01)
Black	0.08 (.24)	−0.22 (.22)
Other non-white	−0.24 (.47)	0.34 (.35)
Hours worked per week	0.003 (.004)	−0.003 (.004)
Religious attendance	0.38 (.22)	0.67** (.18)
Efficacy	0.17 (.32)	0.23 (.29)
Political interest	0.23 (.13)	0.38** (.11)
Constant	−4.51** (.57)	−3.31** (.48)
ρ	−0.16 (.35)	−0.60** (.17)
N	582	653

** $p < .01$, * $p < .05$

Note: Cell entries are unstandardized regression coefficients and standard errors in parentheses. The dependent variable in the outcome equation is vote choice in the 1996 House election (1, Republican; 0, Democrat). The dependent variable in the selection equation is 1 if the respondent cast a vote for one of the two major parties, 0 otherwise.

Table 7A.2 contains the results for the Heckman selection model that estimates partisan voting scores in the 1996 National Election Study. Again, the correlation between error terms, ρ, is statistically significant only for respondents with high REP, indicating that the impact of partisanship among voters differs from the (potential) impact in the entire electorate only in this segment. I discuss the substantive conclusions from these analyses in the chapter.

8

---

*Divided by Choice: Audience Fragmentation
and Political Inequality in the Post-Broadcast
Media Environment*

Few people could deny that life would be different without television. Most Americans with cable or satellite television would agree that greater media choice has affected their evenings. Many Internet users might not remember when they last picked up a phone book or went to a book store. It may be a cliché that new media change people's lives, but with regard to many routine tasks, it is also a truism.

And yet, political scientists use the same models that were used twenty years ago to explain political behavior. Judging by their models, most political scientists believe that politics would not be so different without television, that they can safely ignore the expansion of viewer choice that came with cable, and that the Internet is little more than a newspaper without the paper. The media environment is barely on the map of political science. Studies that state explicitly whether and how political behavior would be different in a different media environment are few and far between.

This study has demonstrated that changes in the media environment affect politics. The advent of television changed news exposure, political knowledge, and turnout. Cable television and the Internet changed them again. The political relevance goes beyond political involvement. Changes in the media environment caused congressional incumbents to do better in the 1960s and elections to become polarized in recent decades.

In this chapter, I briefly summarize the key findings as well as some limitations of this study. My findings are at odds with common interpretations of declining news audiences and increasing partisan polarization. In the third section of this chapter, I juxtapose the competing accounts. A major part of this chapter is devoted to a discussion of the explanations and implications of political inequality in our current media environment. This book has documented how rising inequality in political involvement emerges as a consequence of irreversible technological progress and voluntary consumption decisions. My findings provide a cautioning counterargument to the technological optimism inherent in most discussions of the digital divide. This study also contributes to ongoing debates about the political impact of audience fragmentation and the potential of soft news to reach citizens with little interest in politics.

Accentuating the new burdens that greater media choice creates within a democratic system without considering the self-healing powers of the system would be a mistake. Greater availability of information and its abundant use by some citizens may limit the damage from mounting inequality and polarization. Toward the end of this chapter, I consider whether it might be possible to stop the undesirable consequences of high media choice in their tracks. Perhaps policy interventions can counteract rising political inequality. Perhaps political campaigns can balance the effects by mobilizing entertainment fans. Perhaps new forms of news that mix information and entertainment do just fine in reaching those that I diagnosed as beyond the reach of politics in a high-choice media environment.

KEY FINDINGS: MEDIA ENVIRONMENTS
AND POLITICAL BEHAVIOR

Before television, news was more difficult. Understanding the news required a relatively high level of ability, so learning about politics was more strongly determined by formal education and cognitive skills. Broadcast television provided less educated citizens with more basic information, which increased their political knowledge and their likelihood of going to the polls (at least relative to the more educated). Starting in the 1970s, cable television slowly offered television viewers more programming choices. Some viewers – the entertainment fans – began to abandon the nightly newscasts in favor of more entertaining programs. In the low-choice environment, they encountered politics at least occasionally because they liked watching television – even television news – more than most other leisure activities. Neuman (1996, 19) characterized this pattern as "politics by default." Cable television and the Internet have transformed "politics by default" into politics by choice. By their own choice, entertainment fans learn less about politics than they used to and vote less often.

"Politics by default" made the 1960s and 1970s a period of unusually widespread news consumption. More people watched television news in this period than at any other time. Only television, by virtue of being both easy to follow and hard to resist, drew the less educated into the news audience. That news reaches fewer people today is thus not an irregularity, but rather a return to the days before television. The anomaly that stands out is that so many Americans decided to watch the news in the 1960s and 1970s, even though nobody forced them, and they were happy to abandon the news as soon as alternatives became available.

The transition from the low-choice environment to the high-choice world of cable and Internet reversed trends generated by the advent of broadcast television. For example, broadcast television lowered inequality in political involvement before cable and the Internet increased it again. But the changes underlying the two transitions involved different sub-populations. The advent of broadcast television modified the relationship between ability and political involvement, but it did little to change the effect of motivation. Cable television and the Internet, in contrast, confer greater importance to individual motivations in seeking political information out of the mass of other content. At the same time, they leave the role of ability more or less constant. In other words, broadcast television helped the less educated learn more about politics, whether or not they were particularly motivated to follow the news. The current high-choice environment concentrates political knowledge among those who like the news – largely independent of their levels of education or cognitive skills. (Education continues to affect political learning in the high-choice media environment, but media content preferences are increasingly important predictors and only weakly related to education.)

Widespread news consumption was not the only consequence of the unusual broadcast television environment. Throughout this book, the 1960s and 1970s stand out because of their relative equality in political involvement, a direct result of the broad reach of broadcast news. Elections, too, were unusual in the 1960s and 1970s. The impact of party identification on vote decisions dropped to its modern low point (Bartels 2000). Electoral volatility was higher than either today or in the middle of the twentieth century (Bartels 1998). Politicians took atypically moderate positions, both in Congress and during their election campaigns (Ansolabehere, Snyder, and Stewart 2001; Poole and Rosenthal 1997). I have argued that the relative absence of polarization in this period reflects the properties of the low-choice media environment. Because the political views of less educated citizens who were led to the polls by broadcast television were less firmly grounded in partisanship, they were more susceptible to nonpartisan voting cues such as incumbency. Although this did not have a systematic effect in presidential elections, where partisan cues dominate, it did affect congressional elections. The symbiosis between local television stations and members of Congress allowed incumbents to dominate the airwaves and send favorable cues. As a result, incumbents increased their vote shares as television spread across the country.

Beginning in the 1970s, greater media choice widened the turnout gap between news and entertainment fans. Advances in cable technology and the emergence of the Internet continue to feed this gap today. As a result of the fact that those who do not tune out are more partisan, greater turnout inequality produces more polarized elections. Entertainment fans are less partisan than those who continue to follow politics and vote in the high-choice media environment. The stronger partisan preferences of remaining voters reduce the volatility of election outcomes. Elections become more strongly determined by partisanship even though partisanship in the public as a whole has changed to a much lesser degree.

Many Americans live in a high-choice media environment already. More than 80 percent of them have access to cable or satellite television. More than half access the Internet from their homes. With the transition from low choice to high choice so far advanced, have the bulk of the political changes happened already? In some ways, the biggest change that cable television brought about was the removal of the quasi-monopoly for news in the early evening. Once the first dozen cable channels removed this monopoly, the structural reasons for inflated news audiences had largely disappeared. Yet even though cable television removed the biggest bottleneck in the quest for around-the-clock entertainment, Internet access accelerated the effect, according to my analysis. Access to two new media appears to roughly double the impact of preferences compared to either one of them.

Analog cable systems and dial-up Internet connections – currently the modal ways of new media access – are only the first technological steps toward greater choice. The convergence of media is likely to increasingly blur the difference between cable and the Internet. Digital transmission will without a doubt multiply the number of choices and the efficiency of choosing. In the absence of preference changes, future technological advances such as video-on-demand and widespread broadband access are likely to exacerbate inequality. Media content preferences will only become more important for our understanding of American politics.

QUALIFICATIONS, FUTURE RESEARCH, AND THE LIMITS
OF THE CONDITIONAL POLITICAL LEARNING MODEL

Any study that starts with the world in 1935 and aims to explain how we arrive in the present must confront the criticism that it ignores too many significant political and societal developments. Mine is no exception. Instead of trying to somehow control for such influences, I have pursued a strategy of methodological pluralism. My empirical analysis began with an experiment in which randomization held constant all factors but media choice. The analysis of Nielsen ratings for network newscasts added realism to the same research question, but I had to surrender all control over assignment of the treatment (high choice). Between these two extremes was the analysis of survey data. A panel survey allowed me to examine learning over time. Repeated cross-sectional surveys showed that although times changed, the effects of choice did not. Finally, tracking of turnout and voting patterns in media markets over time – just as cable penetration grew across the country, but at different speeds in different locales – added the causal rigor of time series analysis, albeit with less than perfect dependent variables. Individually, none of these methods would have been very convincing. Collectively, they make a strong case for the causal impact of media choice.

No comparable plethora of methodological approaches vouched for the causal impact of broadcast television in the third quarter of the twentieth century. Although I examined both aggregate and individual-level data, weaknesses are apparent to an extent that even the collective evidence leaves some questions. In fact, the available empirical evidence failed to support directly some of the predictions by the Conditional Political Learning model regarding broadcast television's influence on voting behavior. I was unable to provide conclusive evidence that television reduced the impact of party identification in the 1960s. It did seem to grant incumbents a longer career in Congress, but a direct link between broadcast television and the impact of party identification proved elusive. The implications of data limitations are exacerbated by the variety of political changes at about the same time that broadcast television matured. The civil rights movement and the political realignment in the South are only the most obvious ones. If and how they caused, followed, or complemented the advent of television remains a big unanswered question.

The Conditional Political Learning model aims to explain broad trends in political involvement. Extraordinary circumstances can temporarily disturb these trends. With greater media choice, entertainment fans leave the news audience. But under extraordinary circumstances, many of them return. In the aftermath of the terrorist attacks on September 11, 2001, Americans watched news and visited news Web sites in record numbers (Althaus 2002; Prior 2002). In the terms of the Conditional Political Learning model, the media environment and people's motivations both contributed to these unusual spurts of political involvement. Interest in the news surrounding the attacks was obviously very high. But the media environment, too, was temporarily changed as the broadcast networks provided uninterrupted news coverage for four days and many cable channels, including MTV, TNT, and ESPN, carried news feeds instead of their usual entertainment and sports programming. The military interventions in Iraq in 1991 and 2003 also increased news interest considerably, though not nearly as much as 9/11 (Althaus 2002; Baum 2003b; Gantz and Greenberg 1993). The impact of content preferences is bound to be muted in these moments of crisis.

In normal times, content preferences affect political learning and electoral participation. I developed three different measures of Relative Entertainment Preference. All have essentially the same effect on political involvement, even though they differ in how specifically they refer to news and entertainment. The ranking measure assumes that people either have preferences over television genres or can generalize from particular program examples for each genre. The Manski measure only requires people to distinguish news from movies, music videos, and sports programming. The third measure, briefly discussed elsewhere (Prior 2003), is even more generic as it only refers to news and entertainment in general without mentioning genres or programs. These different approaches yield scales of Relative Entertainment Preference that are highly correlated.

This broad distinction between liking news and liking entertainment is obviously a big simplification. Even if people typically select media content in accordance with their content preferences, they may not do so in every instance. Over the course of a day, week, or month, people may not watch their favorite kind of programming exclusively. Even the strongest fans of news might turn to entertainment at some point (and vice versa). Future research should explore whether people achieve diversity in their media diets by going to their second or third preference for media content or by simply varying the formats of their preferred genres. After the first shoot-'em-up of the evening, does an entertainment fan become more likely to select news for balance or just more likely to switch to pro wrestling or *The Sopranos*? If people aim only for a mix of shows within their preferred genres, learning will be more concentrated among news fans than if people value a mix of genres.

The question of mixing content is related to the question of moderate preferences. How does greater media choice affect political knowledge among people who like news, but also enjoy entertainment? It may be possible to satisfy one's entertainment preference and watch, read, or hear a considerable amount of news. Hence, even people with only a moderate preference for news might learn more and vote more as their media choices increase. This study has successfully illuminated the most general effects of media content preferences, but it reaches its analytic limits when it comes to these more detailed questions. The empirical results show that people with a moderate relative preference for news learn less and turn out less than those with a strong preference for news (and this result is not driven by the fitting of a linear function to the relationship). The positive effects of media choice begin to show up for people with a Relative Entertainment Preference below the mean, but these differences become statistically reliable only at lower values of REP. To answer this question more precisely, larger data sets and more knowledge questions are necessary.

The list of interesting questions for future research does not end there. In addition to the strength of content preferences, the opportunity to act upon them should condition the effects on political involvement. In the Opportunity-Motivation-Ability framework (Delli Carpini and Keeter 1996; Luskin 1990) that laid the foundation for the Conditional Learning Model (see Chapter 2), the media environment is not the only element of learning opportunity. Even a strong news fan in a high-choice media environment may not pick up a great deal of information if other things keep her busy. Employment status, child-rearing obligations, and many other demands on time should affect the relationship between preferences, news exposure, and political involvement. Moreover, media content preferences are clearly not the only motivational determinant of content selection. With respect to the choice between news and entertainment, the most obvious other contender seems to be a sense of civic duty. Some people may not like news as much as entertainment, but they still follow it because they consider it their duty as citizens to be informed about the major political issues of the day. We might expect a greater impact of civic duty, too, in the high-choice media environment where entertainment lures whenever news is an option. Convenience, social interactions, and incomplete information about viewing choices can all dilute the relationship between content preferences and viewing decisions. One purpose of media marketing, after all, is to get people to follow programming they would not otherwise select. Yet despite these distorting influences, even the simple distinction between a taste for news and a taste for entertainment has proved to drive content selection and its political consequences to a remarkable degree.

Another possible objection to the power of media choice concerns not the demand for different programming, but its supply. Actual choice between different types of media content, not simply the number of channels or media, is the key variable behind many of the effects described in this book. Access to a medium, the measure I use in the empirical analysis, is nothing more than a convenient simplification. Some have argued that actual choice between different content has not increased much at all as a result of technological advances. Barber (1998–9, 578–9), for example, contends that "despite the fact that outlets for their product have multiplied, there has been little real substantive diversification.... The actual content available is pretty much identical with what was available on the networks ten years ago.... Media giants make nonsense of the theoretical diversification of the technology."

Although Barber overstates his case and although cable television would still make it easier to select one's preferred content, even if media content had not changed at all, he offers a useful warning against technological determinism and urges continued attention to the impact of media consolidation. The prediction that "a thousand niches will bloom" (Rich 2002) in the high-choice media environment needs an empirical assessment. Even leaving aside the issue of media ownership concentration, the choice between different news formats is clearly not limitless. News is costly, so demand needs to surpass a profitability threshold for news formats to be available (unless news production is subsidized by the government). Television news is available around the clock (although not always live even on most twenty-four-hour news channels), but some issues are covered more than others. Quality of news and the resources devoted to specific issues vary. If the potential audience for an issue is too small, the fixed costs of covering the issue can outweigh the benefits that news providers can expect, so the issue may receive little or no coverage. In principle, similar constraints apply for online news (Hamilton 2004, 190–4). Geographical boundaries and proximity to the media outlet are largely irrelevant for online news, however. Internet users can easily access news from other regions of the country or from foreign media outlets. Although economic constraints are present for online news, "the low fixed costs of website operation and potential for aggregating like-minded individuals from many different areas or countries implies great variety in news provision on the Internet" (Hamilton 2004, 192).

Although it is clearly possible to extend the Conditional Political Learning model in several directions, its general applicability and parsimony are, on balance, a virtue. These properties allowed me to examine the media environment over more than half a century within one theoretical framework. And they make Conditional Political Learning a model that will still apply in the future, even though the media environment keeps changing. A lot of today's Internet infrastructure and appearance, for example, may be obsolete in the near future. But choice and preferences will continue to condition the effects of media content.

MEDIA ENVIRONMENTS AND THE INTERPRETATION OF POLITICAL TRENDS

Changes in the media environment affect indicators that researchers and journalists frequently use to describe and evaluate the performance of American democracy. When doing so, it is important to keep in mind the influence of the media environment on those indicators. The decline of network news audiences over the last two and a half decades has been interpreted as a sign of waning political interest and a disappearing sense of civic duty. Yet this interpretation ignores the circumstances under which high news ratings emerged. Taking into account these circumstances yields a very different conclusion. News consumption can change even while people's media content preferences (and their civic duty and their political interest and their trust in the media) remain constant. In this case, cable television and later the Internet modified the relationship between content preferences and news exposure. The decline in news audiences was not caused by reduced political interest (see Chapter 1). Interest in politics was simply never as high as audience shares for evening news suggested. A combined three-quarter market share for the three network newscasts takes on a different meaning if one considers that people had hardly any viewing alternatives.

The same caution is warranted when interpreting the recent partisan polarization of elections. Many analysts believe that America has become a deeply polarized nation. This study provides a corrective to this view. Comparing survey data from the 1970s to today's polls, analysts often jump to the conclusion that the American public has become vastly more partisan. This sets off a hunt to explain how individuals were converted from ambivalent moderates to rabid partisans. I have provided a less radical explanation for the polarization of elections in recent decades. Greater media choice has made partisans more likely to vote and moderates more likely to abstain. Politics by choice is inherently more polarized than politics by default. This is not to deny that conversion may have played some role. But a far simpler change, higher turnout of partisan news-seekers and lower turnout of less partisan entertainment fans, contributes to polarization. This change polarizes elections but leaves the country as moderate and indifferent as it used to be.

This study has been different from most work on the role of mass media in American politics because it has hardly focused on trends in *average* political involvement at all. Past work in this tradition has mostly examined whether television increases or decreases political knowledge or whether it depresses or encourages turnout. Because average levels of both knowledge and turnout have not experienced dramatic changes in recent decades (e.g., Delli Carpini and Keeter 1996; Freeman 2004; McDonald and Popkin 2001), the case for media effects has been less than convincing. Putnam's (1995; 2000) work is the most influential recent example. Putnam has argued that television is one of the causes for people's decreasing participation in the political process.[1] He declares that "more

---

1 Whereas I have examined what Americans know about politics and how frequently they go to the polls, Putnam's main goal is to explain the decline of social capital. Interpersonal contact and community involvement are important components of social capital. Political learning and turnout, in contrast, "are not, strictly speaking, forms of social capital at all, because they can be done utterly alone" (Putnam 2000, 37). Putnam does examine knowledge and turnout, since "voting is almost always a socially embedded act" and since its correlation with more collective forms of civic engagement "makes it a very useful proxy measure of social engagement"

television watching means less of virtually every form of civic participation and social involvement" (2000, 228) and that "the culprit is television" (1995, 677). He attempts to figure out how television "destroy[s] social capital" (1995, 678).[2]

Unlike Putnam, I cannot conclude that television depressed political involvement. Putnam argues that television takes time away from other activities. Habitual viewing and channel surfing in particular, he maintains, are responsible for the negative effects of television on civic engagement. In contrast, the Conditional Political Learning model implies that the impact of all three factors should depend on the content. If people watch a lot of news, they learn about politics and increase their electoral participation – even when they watch alone. Likewise, habitually viewing cable news channels or surfing from one newscast to another is likely to produce greater learning effects than many other leisure activities. As Chapters 4 and 5 have indicated, these behaviors are not at all uncommon among news junkies.

The effect of television depends on the availability of content and characteristics of the viewer. Television and other media can be used for many different purposes and the degree to which this is true has changed over time. For these reasons, Conditional Political Learning supplied only a prediction for relative changes in political knowledge and turnout, but no hypothesis regarding the absolute effect on these variables. Holding other things constant, broadcast television helped less educated Americans learn more about politics. But it also seemed to replace newspaper reading among the more educated. My theory is silent on the relative magnitudes of these countervailing effects. For average turnout, too, the effect of television is undetermined in the Conditional Political Learning model.[3]

The negative impact of television on political involvement even among people who were primarily attracted by television entertainment was initially limited because the amount and availability of entertainment was limited too. Television may have offered them more vivid and convenient diversion than either movie theatres or radio, but political engagement

(2000, 447, note 2). And although I have only examined voting, conceptually the Conditional Political Learning model applies to other forms of participation as well.

2 Campbell, Yonish, and Putnam (1999) show that watching television news and watching television to acquire information are positively related to civic participation. In *Bowling Alone*, Putnam (2000) mentions the positive effects of television only briefly. They are clearly not strong enough, in Putnam's view, to compensate for the negative influence of television on civic engagement.

3 Recent empirical evidence indicates that broadcast television contributed to the decline in turnout in the 1960s and 1970s (Gentzkow 2006).

among entertainment fans took a greater hit after cable television opened the floodgates for entertainment. Again, however, increasing knowledge and turnout rates among news fans compensated at least partly for this decline. With the exception of the period before CNN began operation, my theory does not specify whether or not the increase among news fans compensated entirely for the decline among entertainment fans. It offers no ex ante reason to believe that cable television, or later the Internet, either increased or decreased average turnout levels. Empirically, turnout rates have been either stable (McDonald and Popkin 2001) or slightly down (Freeman 2004) since the beginnings of cable television. My aggregate analysis in Chapter 5 showed that cable penetration depressed turnout by a percentage point or two. As predicted by the theory, it did so primarily in the 1970s and early 1980s when cable offered little or no news. After CNN spread across the country's cable systems, the new technology produced turnout gains among some viewers. Putnam underestimates this side of television.

Characterizations of the news audience in the post-broadcast era often miss the distinction between mean and variance. Yet in the case of news consumption, arguments are further obfuscated by the difficulties in measuring the mean. While the share of Americans who watch television news has dropped over the last three decades, total television news consumption has not. Fewer Americans watch more news. This pattern extends to other media. In general, fewer Americans follow the news, but as a whole Americans do not consume less news than in the past. Like network (and local) news ratings, newspaper circulation has declined considerably, but cable news and online newspapers seem to make up for this decline, at least according to my back-of-the-envelope calculations in Chapter 5. Summing across all media, the total amount of news and political information that Americans read, watch, and hear has, if anything, increased recently (even on a per capita basis). With regard to all elements of political involvement examined in this study – news consumption, political knowledge, and turnout – the mean has been remarkably stable, while inequality has increased. The latter is the crucial effect of greater media choice.

THE VOLUNTARY ORIGINS OF POLITICAL INEQUALITY

As far as immediate gratifications are concerned, the case for greater media choice is clear-cut. Having the opportunity to view hundreds of television channels makes for more satisfying viewing than being limited to just three or four. And being able to choose from among hundreds of television channels and thousands of Web sites is even better. Despite the occasional difficulty in finding the desired content online or doubt about the added value of another dozen new cable channels, few inhabitants of the high-choice media environment would like to turn back the clock.[4]

Yet although this wide variety means greater viewing, reading, and listening pleasures, the implications of greater choice for the health of democracy are more ambiguous. Rising inequality in political involvement and increasing partisan polarization of elections make it more difficult for a democratic system to achieve equal representation of citizens' interests. Unlike most other forms of inequality, however, this one arises due to voluntary consumption decisions. Entertainment fans abandon politics not because it has become harder for them to be involved – many people would argue the contrary – but because they decide to devote their time to media that promise greater gratification than the news. The mounting inequality between news fans and entertainment fans is due to preference differences, not differences in abilities or resources. In this regard, the contrast to the pre-television media environment is stark. Print media and even radio excluded those with low cognitive abilities and little education; entertainment fans in the current high-choice environment exclude themselves. This trend creates a question for modern democracies: When media users get what they want all the time, does anyone get hurt?

The voluntary basis of rising inequality in political involvement clashes with the conventional wisdom on the implications of the "digital divide." Many casual observers emphasize the great promise new technologies hold for democracy. They deplore current socioeconomic inequalities in access to new media but predict increasing political knowledge and participation for current have-nots after these inequalities have been overcome. The notion of Conditional Political Learning leads to the decidedly less optimistic conclusion that any gap based on socioeconomic status will be eclipsed by a preference-based gap once access to new media becomes cheaper and more widely available.

DiMaggio et al. (2004) review several dimensions of the digital divide. Mere access to the Internet is only one of many aspects of the divide. Differences in hardware, software, and connection speed all introduce additional inequality. Using the Internet in a library or at school is not the same as using it in one's own home. Demographic differences in access to the Internet persist today. Unlike broadcast television and radio, the Internet is a service that is available only for a regular fee (at least in today's business model), not a product that, once purchased, provides free access to media content. It is not a foregone conclusion that almost every

---

4 The degree of media choice affects media content when content providers compete for advertising or subscription dollars. Some content may be underprovided even in a cable lineup of several hundred channels (see, e.g., Hamilton 2004; Napoli 2003; Owen and Wildman 1992).

American will eventually have easy and efficient access to the wealth of political information online (for a summary of the difficulties in predicting trends in Internet access, see DiMaggio et al. 2004).

Lack of education and functional illiteracy are no longer big obstacles to learning about politics, both because Americans are much better educated today and because news media have become easier. Before television, during a period when formal education levels were much lower, an inability to comprehend political information posed a real obstacle to political learning. These same barriers to learning do not exist today. Television made the news easier. Graphical illustrations in print media, although often ridiculed, can help readers understand complex arguments. Streaming video online offers another source of political information for those with reading difficulties or an aversion to print news. A high school education should provide most Americans with the skills necessary to read and understand a newspaper. Although print media may still discourage some people by presenting politics in complex ways, the major fault line in explaining political engagement and participation has shifted to motivation (and, perhaps, other resources, such as time).

This is not to say that ability has entirely disappeared as an obstacle to political involvement. New technologies require new skills, such as knowledge of how the Internet is organized and how desired content can be located most easily. These skills are important in making the most out of the political resources available online. They, too, are not evenly distributed across the population (Bonfadelli 2002; DiMaggio et al. 2004; Hargittai 2003). Like variation in Internet access, these dimensions of the digital divide differ from the preference divide in one crucial respect. The preference-based gaps in political involvement emerge for voluntary reasons. Differences in access and skills, on the other hand, create inequality in involvement in a similar way as education did before television. That inequality was (and continues to be) resource based. Yet, at least as far as accessing and successfully navigating major news sources online is concerned, the resource-based digital divide appears to be narrowing. Strong and growing preference-based inequality, however, is likely to persist even when (or if) resources are distributed more equally.

It is not immediately clear if the rising inequality in political involvement hurts social welfare. I have so far eschewed assessing my empirical findings in light of some normative standard. In some sense, assessing political involvement among entertainment fans does not need a normative standard: Their political knowledge and turnout rates are dropping. And they surely did not drop from such highs that their involvement in the high-choice environment represents a welcome decline to more healthy levels. Yet, it is not convincing to argue reflexively that only maximum political involvement creates the conditions under which democracy can function. Both the Downsian perspective of political ignorance as rational and Schudson's (1998; 2000) recent reconsideration of what makes a "good citizen" force us to specify more carefully how well and how equally informed we need an electorate to be.

In Schudson's view, the ideal of an informed citizen who carefully studies political issues and candidate platforms before casting a vote needs adjustment. It was, first of all, always an ideal against which most citizens looked ill-informed and ineffective. But, argues Schudson, it also ignores an arena for citizenship that has expanded dramatically in the last fifty years. Beginning with the civil rights movement, litigation became a way to instigate social change that gave citizens both the opportunity and the obligation to claim their rights: "The new model of citizenship added the courtroom to the voting booth as a locus of civic participation" (1998, 250). Together with increasing regulatory powers of the federal government, the "rights revolution" extended the reach of politics into many areas of private life. This new dimension has added considerable complexity to the role of the citizen, making citizenship "a year-around and daylong activity" (1998, 311). Although Schudson does not deny the benefits of an informed citizenry, it is neither realistic nor necessary, in his view, to expect citizens to be well informed about every aspect of their increasingly complex role in society. Instead, he proposes a modified model of citizenship, the "monitorial citizen." Rather than being widely knowledgeable about politics, citizens merely need to "be informed enough and alert enough to identify danger to their personal good and danger to the public good" (Schudson 2000, 22). In order to fulfill this "monitoring obligation," citizens "engage in environmental surveillance rather than information-gathering" (1998, 310–11).[5]

How do the news junkies, Switchers, and entertainment fans that we have encountered in this book measure up against Schudson's model of citizenship? Even by his relaxed standards, the citizenry in the high-choice media environment seems handicapped by the growing inequality of political involvement. The drop in news exposure and knowledge among entertainment fans reduces the monitoring capabilities of the electorate. According to Schudson (1998, 310), "monitorial citizens scan (rather than read) the informational environment in a way so that they may be alerted on a very wide variety of issues for a very wide variety of ends." Although available data do not allow a precise assessment, this does not sound like the entertainment fans we have encountered in this book. Many of them

---

5 Zaller (2003) has subsequently suggested modified expectations of the news media's performance that build on Schudson's model of citizenship. According to Zaller, most media should be evaluated based on how well they alert viewers to danger, not based on how well they inform them on mundane political matters.

probably do considerably less than "scan...the informational environment." It is doubtful that entertainment fans can be effective monitors.[6] To the extent that the success of Schudson's model depends on monitoring by all or most citizens, my empirical analysis indicates a growing problem for democracy.

An optimist might grant that entertainment fans would not make good monitors but point out that the high-choice media environment provides news junkies with unprecedented resources to perform as monitorial citizens. If it is not necessary for all citizens to engage in monitoring because some citizens can in fact fill in as monitors for others, the expansion of media choice could actually make it easier to spot the dangers. Can news junkies be super-monitorial citizens? News junkies certainly look like excellent monitors. They consume a lot of information – and a lot more than before the choice explosion. Collectively at least, they may be quite close to the ideal of an informed citizenry. They also take advantage of new media technologies to share and debate the results of the monitoring. (Perhaps we should think of bloggers as the quintessential monitorial citizens of our day.) Most importantly, news junkies do not mind the monitoring obligation. They enjoy following the news. According to an optimistic interpretation, the less equitable knowledge distribution benefits democracy (in the absence of a change in the mean) because those who become more knowledgeable guide policy in a more "enlightened" direction.

Empirical evidence dampens the optimism. Because politicians pay more attention to voters than nonvoters (e.g., Griffin and Newman 2005; Rosenstone and Hansen 1993), the views of politically less motivated citizens may not be reflected in political outcomes as much as before. Polls may not adequately represent the views of the electorate because respondents who lack information give responses that do not reflect their preferences or do not provide substantive responses at all (Althaus 2003).

The optimistic interpretation rises and falls with the validity of one key assumption: The happily monitoring news junkies will keep the interests of the happily news-avoiding entertainment fans in mind. For that to happen, either the super-monitorial news junkies of the high-choice media environment would have to approximate a random sample of the population, in which case their political views would correspond roughly to the views of entertainment fans. Or, if news junkies resemble an elitist sample of activists, they would have to consider the collective interest of

---

6 According to Schudson (2000, 22), "in some ways, monitorial citizenship is more demanding than informed citizenship, because it implies that one's peripheral vision should always have a political or civic dimension."

the citizenry, rather than their own self interest, while performing their monitoring tasks.[7]

Demographically, news fans and entertainment fans are remarkably similar. Although my analysis produced a few significant demographic differences, they were substantively very small. The only partial exception was a sizable age difference between news and entertainment fans, but even this difference paled in comparison to the unexplained variation in Relative Entertainment Preference. Yet despite demographic similarities, it is far from obvious that news fans can effectively and fairly represent the interests of their friends, colleagues, and relatives who prefer to avoid the news. In one respect, news fans differ substantially from entertainment fans: They are far more partisan. At the very least, this encourages candidates to take more extreme political positions, especially in primaries (Aldrich 1995; Fiorina 1999). News junkies are unlikely to advocate the moderate policy positions that entertainment fans seem to favor.

A related danger lies in the possibility that voluntary abstention becomes entrenched and harder to reverse over time. Nothing keeps entertainment fans from taking advantage of plentiful news options, becoming more knowledgeable, and going to the polls. Over time, however, the consequences of their declining participation may reinforce the very reasons for their abstention, thus creating a cycle that makes their return into the news audience and the political process increasingly unlikely. Highly partisan politics may confirm the decision of less motivated people to avoid news and devote their time to entertainment, thereby reinforcing or even intensifying the divide between the motivated and the unmotivated. In sum, entertainment fans hurt the political representation of their interests when they avoid the news and cut down on political participation. Whether or not the harm from lack of representation outweighs the added consumption value of more entertainment is a difficult question to answer. By relying on news fans to get it right for them, entertainment fans are entering in a dangerous bargain.

Greater media choice exacerbates tensions between citizens' immediate gratifications and the health of the political system in which they live. One can debate whether inequality is less worrisome when it begins with voluntary consumption decisions. Most entertainment fans are probably unaware of the possibly profound consequences of their viewing decisions. They do not consciously weigh the added gratification from

---

7 The optimistic interpretation also assumes that entertainment fans will accept the judgment of news junkies. It is not implausible that entertainment fans might instead actively jeopardize the division of labor if ignorance leads them to support policies that hurt their own interests (e.g., Bartels 2005).

media entertainment against the possible downside of encouraging elected representatives to pay less attention to their socioeconomic needs. Political scientists and economists, in fact, cannot tell entertainment fans if the bargain is worth it for them. More research is sorely needed on the link between political involvement and distributive politics. One thing is clear: The transition to the high-choice media environment has changed who does the weighing. In the past, the structure of the media environment made the decision for the viewer, at least on occasion; today, entertainment fans are on their own. Although it is comforting to know that they finally get to watch what they always wanted to watch, their newfound freedom may hurt both their own interests and the collective good.

AUDIENCE FRAGMENTATION

Recent years have seen a lively discussion of the societal and political implications of new media technologies. First and foremost, people have more choice. Increasingly, they also have the opportunity to customize their media use and to filter out content in advance. Some scholars have sounded the alarm bells over these developments, warning of dire consequences of customization, fragmentation, and segmentation. In *Breaking Up America*, Turow (1997, 2, 7) sees the emergence of "electronic equivalents of gated communities" and "lifestyle segregation." Sunstein (2001b) predicts the demise of "shared experiences" and increasing group polarization as media users select only content with which they agree in the first place. Others emphasize the benefits of choice and customization (e.g., Negroponte 1995). In this debate, some seemingly mundane conceptual details have not received enough consideration.

Audience fragmentation, the starting point for this debate, is empirically well established. As the number of television channels increases, the audience for any one channel declines and more channels gain at least some viewers. Audience fragmentation increases the diversity of media exposure in the aggregate. This much is uncontroversial. But audience fragmentation tells us nothing about the diversity of individuals' media use. Individuals may take advantage of greater media choice either by watching a mix of many newly available channels or by "bingeing on their favorites" (Webster 2005, 369). Webster (1986; 2005) uses the concept of "audience polarization" to capture the concentration of viewing of a particular channel. If a few viewers account for most of the channel's viewing, its audience is polarized. If viewing is distributed across a large number of people who individually make up only a small share of the channel's viewing, audience polarization is low. From the viewer's perspective, audience polarization is high when people watch a lot of a particular program format or genre and not much else. (In order not to confuse audience polarization and partisan polarization, I will refer to the former concept as audience specialization.[8])

Even audience fragmentation and specialization are too broad to evaluate the political implications of audience behavior. As these concepts are used in audience analysis, they refer to channels. Yet the political implications of changing audience behavior depend at least in part on fragmentation and specialization by genre. The concerns about political inequality raised by the Conditional Political Learning model are not a consequence of audience fragmentation and specialization in general, but only insofar as they affect the specialization of news viewing. Audience fragmentation in particular need not doom civic life. Certain kinds of fragmentation seem completely harmless. Imagine three individuals in the fall of 2005, John, Larry, and Claire, who all used to watch *Friends*. Now John watches *Desperate Housewives*, Larry watches *South Park*, and Claire watches *Lost*. The proliferation of choices allows people who used to watch the same entertainment programming to now watch different entertainment programming. It is hard to see how this change threatens our society (except perhaps in that John, Larry, and Claire cannot talk about the same show at work – which might itself be an incentive to coordinate on one show and limit fragmentation).

Likewise, if John, Larry, and Claire all used to watch the *CBS Evening News with Dan Rather*, but now John watches the *NBC Nightly News*, Larry watches *The Situation Room*, and Claire tunes in to *Special Report with Brit Hume*, the political implications of fragmentation are limited. Although they now watch different news programs, the three of them still learn roughly the same things about politics. To the extent that exposure to political information motivates political participation, none of the three would seem to be less likely to participate than in the past.

In one respect, this fragmentation of news audiences does seem to make democracy more vulnerable. If some former Rather viewers switch to very conservative outlets, while others turn to a news source with a decidedly liberal slant, their political views may polarize. Such a trend has raised concerns because it might limit the diversity of arguments that viewers encounter and expose them to biased information. Sunstein (2001b) conjures up a world of almost perfect selection in which media sources conform neatly and reliably with one's prior beliefs and expectations. Such constant and nearly exclusive encounters with like-minded viewpoints

8 Tewksbury (2005) distinguishes "audience specialization" and "outlet specialization." The former is defined as the extent of selective exposure to specific media content. Outlet specialization refers to the distinctiveness of different media outlets' audience profiles.

will, he argues, lead to group polarization. In Turow's (1997) view, the marketing strategies of advertisers, not technology per se, cause the fragmentation of society. Media offer specialized content and formats that allow advertisers to target desired populations more effectively: "The creation of customized media materials... will allow, even encourage, individuals to live in their own personally constructed worlds, separated from people and issues that they don't care about or don't want to be bothered with" (p. 7). Mutz and Martin (2001) find the media to be a source of more exposure to political opposition than interpersonal relationships. Their study was conducted in the 1990s, however, and they echo the fear of increasing selectivity because "as the number of potential news sources multiplies, consumers must choose among them, and that exercise of choice may lead to less diversity of political exposure" (p. 111).

As Webster (2005) points out, Sunstein and Turow assume more than just audience fragmentation. In order for their dire predictions to materialize, audiences also need to become more concentrated. The danger lies not in the growing audience for politically biased news outlets per se, but in *exclusive* exposure to outlets that are all biased in the same direction. Several important pieces of evidence suggest that fears of audience specialization may be exaggerated. Webster (2005, 380) finds little evidence of overall audience specialization by channel. Even heavy consumers of a particular television channel devote only a small fraction of their total viewing to that channel, so "if these viewers live in cloistered communities, they evidently spend a good deal of time out and about." With regard to political information, it appears that many people do not routinely tune out the other side. The evidence I reviewed in Chapter 5, although far from conclusive, indicates a considerable overlap between audiences for CNN and the Fox News Channel (as well as other cable news channels).

Another recent test of Sunstein's hypothesis provides little evidence that users tune out opposing viewpoints. During the 2000 presidential campaign, a random sample of Americans received one of two multimedia CDs, one with all candidate speeches and advertisements, the other with a wide selection of media coverage of the candidates and the campaign. The use of these CDs, which was evaluated for study participants who returned a tracking file after the election, indicated that most people accessed both materials about the candidate with whose party they identified and materials about the opposition. To the extent that participants engaged in selective exposure, they mostly did so by focusing on specific issues (Iyengar, Hahn, and Prior 2001). This evidence on how people actually search political information comports with their own assessments of what they are doing. Few Internet users say that they visit only sites that they know to be congruent with their political attitudes (DiMaggio and Sato 2003).[9]

Although they suggest limited selective exposure along partisan or ideological lines, these results need to be viewed as preliminary. Audience data used to examine ideological audience specialization, both here and elsewhere, are quite poor. All I could point to in Chapter 5 was a considerable overlap between viewing of the Fox News Channel and viewing of other cable news networks. We lack data to effectively assess selective exposure across media (the correlation between exposure to Fox News, conservative blogs, and conservative talk radio, for example). Furthermore, the data I presented did not address the amount of overlap among heavy cable news viewers.[10]

Exaggerated or not, the audience specialization along ideological lines that does exist was largely made possible by the increase in media choice. The same development, a proliferation of media choice, also causes increasing segmentation between news and entertainment fans. Yet this audience specialization has not received as much attention as ideological audience specialization. Sunstein, and the debate he prompted (e.g., DiMaggio and Sato 2003; Iyengar, Hahn, and Prior 2001; Jenkins 2001; Sunstein 2001a), is primarily concerned that people may be following customized news and come to the polls with heavily biased information. My concern is that people may not be following any news and not show up at the polls at all.[11] In the low-choice environment, John, Larry, and Claire were all pretty likely to watch both *Friends* and Rather. Today, John and Larry watch *Desperate Housewives*, *South Park*, and *Lost*. Claire, on the other hand, watches *NBC Nightly News*, Blitzer, and Hume.

Even if some media exposure is indeed selective with regard to partisan slant, ideological audience specialization poses a lesser problem than audience specialization along the fault lines of news and entertainment. The latter not only exacerbates inequalities in political involvement, it

---

9 These results are not terribly surprising. A classic early study of selective exposure found mixed evidence at best for partisan selectivity in exposure to political campaigns (Sears and Freedman 1967). More recently, Mutz and Martin (2001, 98) wrote that "findings [on selective exposure to media content] have been so inconsistent as to discourage much research."

10 It should be noted that selective exposure is not a necessary condition for polarization. Even exposure to both sides can strengthen partisan stereotypes (Vallone, Ross, and Lepper 1985).

11 Sunstein (2001b, 2, 3) does acknowledge that many people find news "incredibly boring" and that they may take advantage of customization to tune out news altogether. One of his three "fundamental concerns" is about the effect of news media technologies on "the need for exposure to substantive questions of policy and principle, combined with a range of positions on such questions" (p. 167).

also contributes to partisan polarization in a very different way. Ideological audience specialization raises the specter of partisan polarization because exposure to ideologically biased political content may persuade moderates or reinforce partisans. In other words, if audience specialization polarizes politics, it does so because of the particular content of news. This is clearly different from the path to polarized elections evident in the Conditional Political Learning model. According to that model and the empirical evidence in Chapter 7, there are fewer moderate voters today not because they have been converted by increasingly partisan media, but because they have been lost to entertainment. They are still alive and moderate, but politically less relevant because of their tendency to abstain.

NEWS AND ENTERTAINMENT: CONTRAST OR BLUR?

The increasing divide between news and entertainment devotees sits uneasily with recent political science and communication research that sees entertainment as a way to broaden audiences for news and politics. It has recently been popular to argue that politics and entertainment are being mixed more frequently, and that therefore a distinction between the two is becoming less meaningful. This blurring is indeed happening, but its significance is easily exaggerated when it is viewed in isolation. Networks and cable channels offer many programs that mix news and entertainment. But by orders of magnitude, they offer more entertainment that lacks informational or political elements. And arguably, they also offer more news that is not all that entertaining. Thanks to infotainment, some viewers may learn more about some political issues than they would in the absence of news-entertainment mixtures. But thanks to greater media choice, a much larger number of viewers know a lot less about politics than they did thirty years ago. The flight from the news by entertainment fans, in other words, is a more profound influence than the slowing of this flight through infotainment.

The mixing of news (or politics) and entertainment occurs both because news programs incorporate entertainment elements and because the plots of fictional entertainment shows revolve around political issues. Generously defined, "soft news" comprises television programs that cover politics at least occasionally but are not traditional news programs with the primary objective to inform the viewer. Patterson (2000a, 4) describes soft news as "typically more sensational, more personality-centered, less time-bound, more practical, and more incident-based than other news." This description fits a wide variety of programs. Shows like *Entertainment Tonight*, *Hardcopy*, and *Extra*, to which some scholars refer as "tabloid news shows" (e.g., Baum 2002, 93; Delli Carpini and Williams 2000), cover primarily the glamorous or scandalous aspects of the entertainment industry, but they also devote time to political scandals and crises. Prime-time programming on some cable news channels resembles this format, although with a heavier focus on crime. Late-night comedy shows such as the *Late Show with David Letterman* and *The Tonight Show with Jay Leno* cover politics when it lends itself to ridicule. On Comedy Central's *Daily Show*, news and politics, both fake and real, make up a greater portion of the airtime, but the show is shorter. The afternoon talk show is a third important format that is often included as soft news. Although programs like *The Oprah Winfrey Show* or *Life with Regis and Kelly* do not usually cover political topics, they offer politicians a forum on special occasions, and both presidential candidates made several appearances in 2000 and 2004.

The counterpart to soft news could be called political drama. Shows like *West Wing* or *Commander in Chief* mix politics and entertainment, but they are fictional. The most prominent blend, exemplified by *Law and Order*, mixes entertainment with information about the American justice system. Although not written to reflect news as it happens (see, e.g., Holbert et al. 2003, 431), political dramas offer information about the organization of government and the practice of governing.

Mixing entertainment and politics is not new. In the past, viewers mixed news and entertainment over the course of an evening. Today, some programs mix it for them. Overall, it is probably less common for a typical television viewer today to encounter a mix of politics and entertainment. Viewers with choice are less likely than in the past to watch a soap opera followed by a news program, a syndicated game show, and then a prime-time drama – the sequence typically offered on the networks, both today and thirty years ago. Even if the number of entertainment-news hybrids has increased, their impact is overshadowed by the disentangling of news and entertainment viewing.

Soft news and political drama may affect political learning, one of the main variables in my analysis. Graber (2001, 99), for example, maintains that "average Americans are far more likely to witness discussions of political issues when viewing non-news rather than news shows during the many hours of daily television viewing" (see also Summers and Summers 1966, 306–7). The most convincing case for the political importance of soft news has been made by Matt Baum. He argues that a mix of entertainment and politics provides political information to people not sufficiently interested in politics to watch hard news. By focusing on the more entertaining, shocking, or scandalous aspects of politics, soft news offers these people an alternative that maximizes their utility because it combines entertainment and information. Baum (2002; 2003b) shows that some people who would otherwise not watch any news at all pay attention to coverage of wars and foreign policy crises in soft-news programs. When presidential candidates appear on entertainment talk shows, they sway a segment of the population that would otherwise not hear much about the campaign (Baum 2005).

At the heart of my Conditional Political Learning model is the argument that Switchers only follow the news as long as they live in the low-choice media environment of the past. Once cable television reaches them, they avoid news programming. Yet if they largely migrated to news-entertainment hybrids and if they learned from this exposure, the mixing of entertainment and politics might counteract some of the trends described in this book. I have argued that media content preferences become powerful determinants of news exposure and learning about politics in the high-choice media environment. Yet in Baum's "incidental by-product model," viewers select programs based on the desire to be entertained, but still learn about politics because the programs they pick also contain information. If this kind of by-product learning were common, the relationship between content preferences and learning would be a good deal weaker than I have argued. Despite a preference for entertainment, viewers would still learn about politics, even in a high-choice environment.

Whether or not soft news and political drama can inform entertainment fans and motivate them to vote depends on three factors. Do these hybrid programs actually increase learning and turnout? If they occur, are these positive effects on involvement of significant magnitude? And do news-entertainment hybrids reach people who do not also watch more traditional news programs (or read newspapers or visit news Web sites)?

One examination of learning effects among people who prefer soft news to hard news suggests that such learning is rare (Prior 2003). Baum (2003a; 2003b, 279–81) points to one instance of learning from soft news, but emphasizes influences on engagement other than political knowledge (such as reporting attention to a political issue). Learning from soft news is likely to be sporadic because soft news programs cover politics only sporadically. Bush and Gore both appeared on *Oprah* during the 2000 campaign, but the large majority of episodes do not touch on politics. *Leno* and *Letterman* may refer to politics more frequently, but also more briefly. Other hybrids, such as the *Daily Show with Jon Stewart*, devote a higher share of their airtime to politics. But they also have decidedly smaller audiences than more entertainment-heavy soft news or political drama. Audience size is the second precondition for sizable learning effects. Traditional news sources remain considerably more popular than soft news (Prior 2003). Despite popular myth, for example, each of the three network news programs reaches more young people than the *Daily Show*.[12]

Third, the potential for soft news to counteract the widening knowledge gap is limited because many soft-news viewers also watch hard news. Many current soft-news viewers would remain as knowledgeable and involved as they are even if they could not watch soft news. In other words, the share of the population that would not encounter any political information without soft news is considerably smaller than the share of the population that watches soft news. Viewers of late-night comedy (*Leno*, *Letterman*, *Jon Stewart*) also report frequent exposure to traditional television news programs (Young and Tisinger 2006). They even report higher newspaper consumption than their counterparts who do not watch late-night comedy.[13] More politically interested individuals are more likely to report watching *Leno*, *Letterman*, and *Oprah* (Moy, Xenos, and Hess 2005).[14] It is difficult to know how much to make of these findings because they rely exclusively on notoriously unreliable self-reports of media use (Prior 2005b). In the absence of better behavioral measures, however, they provide the only characterization of the soft-news audience. Rather than reach many entertainment fans, soft news appears to attract predominantly regular news viewers.

The same argument applies to political drama. Judging by the popularity of different news-entertainment hybrids, political drama would seem to have the best shot at informing large audiences. The caveat is that too much political detail – even when it is fictional and part of the plot – drives away the news avoiders to entertainment programs with a lower risk of exposure to politics. Many of the remaining viewers of *West Wing* or *Law and Order* are thus likely to follow the news and be quite knowledgeable about politics to begin with.

Those who advocate using entertaining politics as a way to encourage exposure to information make much of the Downsian notion of obtaining information as a by-product of consuming entertainment. Yet accidental exposure to political information, the famous "inadvertent audience" (see

---

12 According to Horst Stipp, vice president of research at NBC, on most days each of the three evening network news programs has more viewers between 18 and 34 than the *Daily Show* (personal communication, March 2006).

13 Young and Tisinger report results for young viewers only. The relationship between reported soft and hard news exposure is even stronger for older viewers (Young, personal communication, March 2006).

14 Using self-reports of media use, Baum (2003b, 111–12) himself finds a positive relationship between hard and soft news consumption. According to his "gateway hypothesis," exposure to soft news can lead people to watch hard news because soft news attracts people's attention to an issue and provides them with a simple narrative for understanding more complex information.

Chapter 3), was much more likely before media choice expanded. According to the by-product model, people watch news-entertainment hybrids because those formats best satisfy their entertainment needs. The political information provided by Al Gore's surprise visit on *Oprah* or a war story on *Hardcopy* do not reduce the payoffs from the entertainment. Entertained just as much as when the guest on Oprah's couch is Tom Cruise, people keep watching and learn something about politics.

One might imagine that people who watch soft news to satisfy their entertainment needs would switch the channel when they see Al Gore. In fact, as Baum (2005, 214) reports, the opposite was true during the 2000 presidential campaign. Gore's appearance on *Oprah* attracted a larger audience than other *Oprah* shows in the same period. That people tolerate the politics in their entertainment suggests that they are not after pure entertainment at all. Who would tune in to *Oprah* just to see a politician? It certainly would not be entertainment fans to whom any information is entirely a by-product. That some people tune in specifically to see Al Gore on *Oprah* suggests that they expect political information that cannot be obtained elsewhere or that is presented in a way that provides them with greater rewards than hard news. The size of this group is unknown. Aggregate Nielsen ratings do not tell us how many viewers tuned in specifically to see Al Gore and how many *Oprah* regulars switched the channel specifically to avoid him.[15]

To those who watch soft news because it covers politics in an entertaining style, the informational or political element does not seem to be merely an unanticipated by-product. Their Relative Entertainment Preference leads them to this combination of news and entertainment. It is not particularly high (or else they would turn to hard news instead), but it is not so low either that pure entertainment maximizes their viewing pleasure. This perspective on soft news viewing is fully consistent with Baum's findings and does not take away from his pioneering research. Yet it resolves one puzzle relevant to my study. If information came as a by-product to soft-news viewers who simply value the entertainment of those programs, then entertainment fans who, according to the Conditional Political Learning model, abandon the news audience as more choices become available might end up as soft-news consumers. Hence, soft news might stop or even revert the widening of knowledge and turnout gaps. This potential contradiction with my conclusion disappears when we instead consider the soft-news audience as a segment interested in a particular mix of entertainment

---

15 Baum (2005, 228–30) does show that political involvement of self-identified viewers of daytime talk shows was very similar in weeks with and without candidate appearances in 2000. He concludes that a sufficient number of regular talk show viewers did not switch the channel when they encountered political information.

and information. Some Switchers have found a new home in soft news, but increasing the supply of soft news would not further increase the size of its audience, because pure entertainment remains more entertaining to the strong entertainment fans. In Patterson's (2000a, 15) words, "entertainment programming is more entertaining than news for those who desire to be entertained," even in the presence of soft-news formats.[16] In general, by-product learning should become *less*, not more common, as media choice increases because greater choice makes it easier to find the desired mix of news and entertainment (see Chapter 1).[17] Baum of course does not intend to explain political learning *in general*, but focuses on learning about wars and foreign policy crises instead. His incidental by-product model applies to extraordinary circumstances, whereas my Conditional Political Learning model describes learning in normal times.

None of this is to deny that news and entertainment are blurring in some places. Politicians and news producers may indeed have to make political communication more entertaining than thirty years ago, but this is a reaction to the consequences of greater media choice. The appearance of soft-news programs is a predictable consequence of the proliferation of media outlets. Cable television and Internet have multiplied the supply of media content. The result is greater diversity of content. Neither can there be much doubt that fewer people would hear about certain political issues without soft news. What remains unclear is the magnitude of the impact of soft news compared to the impact of greater media choice more generally. My examination of the changing media environment adopts a different reference point than studies of soft news. In order to value the contribution of soft news, scholars tend to compare the current news environment to the hypothetical world in which soft news does not exist. My interest, on the other hand, is in trends in political knowledge and

16 Zaller (forthcoming, 61–2) recognizes this complication, noting that "citizens who turned to political news for entertainment must do so for some special reason, since they would otherwise consume the more conveniently pure entertainment offered up by Hollywood and the professional sports business." In his view, "that special reason has to do with the charisma of power. What makes political news distinctively entertaining is that it involves powerful and important people." I am not aware of any empirical tests of this proposition.

17 Baum (2003b, 29–33) argues that exposure to political information incurs lower opportunity costs for entertainment-seeking viewers than in the past because soft news offers them both entertainment and information. Exposure to information no longer requires viewers to miss out on entertainment. But greater media choice adds to the opportunity costs. Dozens of cable channels are entirely devoted to offering attractive pure entertainment. For entertainment fans in particular, the overall opportunity costs from watching news – even if it is soft and entertaining – have risen. As a result, they should watch less news of any kind.

turnout gaps over time. Some soft-news consumers – those who do not also watch hard news – are more attentive to politics than they would be in the absence of soft news, but are they as attentive as in the past?

Millions of Americans no longer watch network news. Some of them now watch cable news, but most of them are looking for something more entertaining. For some of the entertainment-seekers, soft news offers the preferred mix of news and entertainment. The important point is that they are former hard-news consumers. Compared to the counterfactual world in which media choice is high, but soft news does not exist, these viewers encounter more political information. Compared to thirty years ago, they encounter a lot less. Soft news merely slows down a trend toward growing information inequality, which began with an increase in choice. For most entertainment fans, most of the time, the draw of pure entertainment is greater than the draw of infotainment. Hybrids attract an audience among entertainment fans, but their general battle against the windmills of pure entertainment is a defensive one. Most entertainment fans are leaving news and politics behind altogether in the high-choice media environment.

PROMOTING POLITICAL EQUALITY IN A HIGH-CHOICE MEDIA ENVIRONMENT

Any potential intervention to stop or even reverse the rising inequality in political involvement is complicated by two fundamental truths about the impact of greater media choice. First, political inequality rises as a result of voluntary consumption decisions. Second, technological progress is the ultimate cause of this rise, and we cannot simply go back to low choice. Short of turning back the technological clock or severely restraining the free market, is there a way for political information to reach entertainment fans and to reduce inequality in political involvement in a high-choice media environment? I consider three options: communications policy, campaign mobilization, and socialization.

One possibility is to use public policy to design media systems that serve the public good. If media environments affect the knowledge levels of the least informed citizens, the question arises whether a democratic society should then use the structure of the media to "force" its citizens to be informed about the political process. The American media system of the broadcast era had elements that did indeed force its citizens to learn more about politics than they wanted. But these elements had very little to do with public policy (with the partial exception of the FCC's Fairness Doctrine which encouraged networks and local stations to offer news and public affairs programming). For the most part, the degree to which the U.S. media environment forces citizens to be politically knowledgeable was and is determined by technological change and commercial interests.

Different countries have approached technological progress and the expansion of media choice in different ways. While I have focused on the political impact of changes in the media environment as they occurred in the United States, a comparative perspective offers some valuable insights here. Technological change manifests itself differently in different countries. To some extent, its implications depend on historical contingencies and political conditions. For example, the centrality of print media in different countries today is related to literacy rates in the early twentieth century (Hallin and Mancini 2004). Even though the advances in print technology that made mass circulation newspapers feasible and economically profitable (Hamilton 2004) became available in different countries at roughly the same time, literacy rates – and presumably other factors – accelerated or impeded this development, so that it occurred in different variations in different countries.

Policy interventions also created differences in the media environments of different countries. Policy approaches differed more distinctly in the past than today. With slight modifications, the expansion of choice is occurring worldwide. The multiplication of television channels – especially via satellite – and the Internet are both global phenomena that often defy national regulation. In the 1970s and 1980s, however, political and regulatory decisions delayed the commercial use of cable television in several Western European countries compared to the United States. As a result, the consequences of high media choice should have been felt later there than in the United States.

In most Western democracies, the expansion of media choice used to be addressed more as a matter of public policy than as a market mechanism. Despite its technical feasibility, cable television began operating in most Western European countries only after a lengthy debate about its merits. In Germany, for example, Chancellor Helmut Schmidt declared in 1979 that commercial television posed "a danger more acute than atomic energy" and would "change the structure of our democratic society" (Vinocur 1979). Until well into the 1980s, the Social Democratic Party advocated the continuation of the monopoly for public-service broadcasting (Humphreys 1994, 193–285). Among opponents of cable television and commercial providers, "the essential argument was that 'soft' pressure, in the sense of limiting program choices so as to enforce exposure to informational programs, was desirable for its contribution to maintaining a democratically oriented citizenry" (Kaase 2000, 389–90). The first local pilot projects to study the impact of cable television began in West Germany only in the mid 1980s, when almost 40 percent of American households already had cable.

In 1968, Israel's first television channel began operation. It remained the only one for almost twenty-five years until parliament authorized a second national channel and the introduction of cable television. The decision to have just one television channel was driven by public policy considerations, not commercial interest or technological progress (Katz 1996). As far as providing citizens with the necessary political information, it had the intended effect: "Television controlled by the Broadcasting Authority was the only show in town.... Almost everybody watched almost everything on the one monopolistic channel" (Katz 1996, 28). On average, about two-thirds of the population tuned in for the 9 o'clock newscast. After a second channel began operation, the combined audience for news on both channels dropped considerably. Predictably, the introduction of cable further increased entertainment viewing, in particular movies and music videos (Weimann 1996).

These differences to the U.S. system all reflect a different and deliberate weighting of the two competing values: free choice of content and a widely informed and participating public. The U.S. system consistently put a higher value on free choice, yet analysts have rarely linked the domination of market values to more unequal distribution of knowledge and participation or to increasing partisan polarization among voters. Today, Western European countries and Israel, who for several decades tried to avoid these problems by limiting choice, are forced to address the consequences of almost limitless media choice in much the same way as the United States. Even if a consensus emerged to reduce choice for the public good, it would be technically impossible and have an unappealing paternalistic flavor. Long before media choice reached its current level, Downs (1957, 247) suspected that "the loss of freedom involved in forcing people to acquire information would probably far outweigh the benefits to be gained from a better-informed electorate." And in a high-choice environment with all its possibilities, the loss of freedom would be felt even more acutely than in the broadcast era.

Technological advances dictate the boundaries for policy making. Although it does not determine the use of new media, the current state of technology does rule out certain solutions to the problem of greater political inequality. Policy interventions aimed at restoring the old system of low choice and forced news exposure seem utterly unfeasible. Consider, for example, the "five-minute fix" proposed by Taylor (1992, 61–3) as a way to reach people who do not normally watch news or public affairs. Presidential candidates would receive free airtime "simultaneously on every [broadcast] television and radio station in the country" in the final weeks of the campaign. But Taylor is realist enough not to assume that many cable channels could be persuaded to join in. He acknowledges that "millions would no doubt resent this forced feeding of politics. These viewers could escape to cable channels." Of course these "safety valves to coerced viewing" defeat the whole purpose of the road-blocking strategy.

In the short run, changes in news content cannot help either. Making news more attractive – either by improving (Patterson 2000a) or by lowering its quality (Zaller 1999; 2003) – will not increase its appeal among politically uninterested people with cable or Internet access because they do not make it into the news audience in the first place. Entertainment fans do not avoid the news because they dislike its presentation or selection of topics. They turn to entertainment content because it is more exciting, diversionary, imaginatively or predictably plotted, and attractively cast. No matter how its format is changed, news cannot offer this combination.

A more promising way to reach entertainment fans might be mobilization. If entertainment fans do not come to politics, could politics come to entertainment fans? New digital technologies, perhaps foremost the Internet, offer more than greater choice. They lower the costs of political participation, organization, and mobilization (Bimber 2003). This study has indicated that the direct effects of exposure on knowledge and of knowledge on turnout are not the only relevant effects. Exposure to the news also motivates people to go to the polls. In my theoretical framework, lower costs of participation and organization affect only media users with at least a moderate preference for news. The increasing ease of participation and organization is lost on those who prefer entertainment because they rarely encounter the political world at all and therefore have little idea of how and where to participate. The model does not incorporate the possibility that news fans and political entrepreneurs may actively target entertainment fans. Is this a crucial omission? Bimber (2003, 230) offers the strong claim that in the current media environment, "the information citizens choose to learn is often less important than the information directed to them by elites and organization." If email or other hard-to-screen messages can reach entertainment fans through the wall of disinterest, even people with a clear preference for entertainment may end up participating in the political process. Such instances should be rare given the obstacles and inertia any such message would have to overcome. But entertainment fans are not unreachable. And lower mobilization costs should make attempts to reach them more common.

Political advertising may already contribute to a more evenly informed electorate. The greatest chance to encounter political advertising for people who do not voluntarily seek out political information occurs in the form of commercials inserted into their regular entertainment diet. Research has demonstrated that exposure to political ads can increase viewers' political knowledge (Ansolabehere and Iyengar 1995; Freedman, Franz, and Goldstein 2004; Patterson and McClure 1976). At least for the time being, before recording services like TiVo and Replay TV, which easily skip commercials, or subscriber-financed premium cable channels without advertising become more widespread, political advertising is more likely than news coverage to reach these viewers.

Political advertising is only one type of campaign activity that can take politics closer to citizens who typically avoid the news. Unusually high turnout and debate viewing in 2004 illustrate the mobilization effects of a hard-fought campaign leading up to a close election. Unfortunately, the potential positive effects of political advertising would not benefit all parts of the country to the same extent. Presidential campaigns concentrate their advertising on battleground states (e.g., Johnston, Hagen, and Jamieson 2004), and many congressional elections are so uncompetitive that advertising expenditures are not necessary. Hence, even if political advertising can contribute to informing entertainment fans, a substantial share of them would still not be reached. Assessments of possible changes in the electoral system – with regard to both redistricting and most states' winner-take-all allocation of electoral votes in presidential elections – should consider the likely impact on the distribution of political involvement.

It would be ill-advised to exaggerate the potential effect of political advertising on the equality of political knowledge and turnout. Over time, greater targeting of political advertising and shorter ads may in fact have exacerbated inequality in political involvement. In 1972, many Nixon and McGovern ads were five minutes long and aired nationally (rather than in selected media markets) during prime-time entertainment shows (Patterson and McClure 1976). Prime-time ratings in those days were astonishingly high, so these ads amounted to another dose of accidental exposure to politics for entertainment fans. Today, most advertising airs during (local) news programming (Freedman, Franz, and Goldstein 2004, 728), so the chances for true entertainment fans to be exposed to politics via advertising may be lower despite the higher volume of advertising. Furthermore, mobilization campaigns will be of limited help if they primarily reach out to citizens who are assumed by the campaigns to be reliable partisans. Politically indifferent entertainment fans are the hardest segment to reach. They are probably also the least interesting segment to political advertisers.

The implications of my empirical research for mobilization are not encouraging. Although I did not incorporate the possibility of mobilizing entertainment fans in my theoretical framework, any such effects would be picked up by the empirical models. The fact that entertainment fans move to the low end of knowledge and turnout distributions in the high-choice environment indicates that mobilization effects on them are either limited or not effective enough to counteract the appeal of entertainment. On balance, Internet access contributes to widening gaps in political knowledge and turnout. In the future, we may find that the ease of political participation or the opportunities for custom-made information delivery via the Internet help to reach entertainment fans. So far, the opposite appears to be true. If they are to find empirical support one day, these potential benefits of the Internet must overcome the negative impact that content choice and the allure of entertainment have on the political knowledge and participation of politically uninterested citizens.

In a media environment where people can avoid news and even mobilization efforts so easily, the potentially most compelling, but also most difficult way to reduce inequality in political involvement might well be to change preferences. One of my most important departures from previous work has been the inclusion of people's content preferences in a theoretical account of political learning and the development of empirical measures of preferences for different media content. The Conditional Political Learning model suggests that a change in content preferences would be followed by a change in political involvement. It thus raises a set of very important questions: How do content preferences form and how easily can they be changed?

An assumption in my analysis has been that content preferences are stable and exogenous to media use and the media environment. I assumed, in other words, that acquiring new political information, watching a great entertainment program, or gaining access to the Internet does not lead people to update their Relative Entertainment Preference. If people engaged in such updating, it would be much more difficult to disentangle the reciprocal effects of preferred media content and political involvement. There is some empirical evidence that content preferences are indeed quite stable, at least in the short term. Whereas only the first wave of the N&E Survey included the measures of Relative Entertainment Preference that I used in this analysis, respondents were asked a set of identical questions about their general liking of news and entertainment in both panel waves (for a brief description of these measures, see Prior 2003).[18] The correlation between responses in the two waves, which were conducted fourteen months apart, was strong, suggesting considerable short-term preference stability.[19] Since 1994, the Pew Research Center has asked

---

18 In contrast to the relative measures of entertainment preference I use in this book, the alternative measure does not require respondents to choose between news and entertainment content. Instead, it assesses respondents' absolute liking of news and entertainment separately. When this absolute measure is transformed into a relative one (by creating the ratio of absolute news to absolute entertainment preference, for example), it correlates strongly with the REP measures I employ here.

19 Pearson correlations of Wave 1 and Wave 2 summary scales exceed .6 without any corrections for measurement error.

random samples of Americans how much they "enjoy keeping up with the news." In six out of seven different surveys, the percentage of respondents who said that they enjoyed it "a lot" was between 48 and 54 (the largest outlier, in April 2000, was 45 percent). In the aggregate, this indicator of news preference is quite stable, even during a time when network news ratings dropped by over a third and Internet penetration rose from barely 10 percent to more than 50 percent.

If media content preferences are indeed very stable over time, it becomes even more urgent to understand their origins since "people's preferences do not come from nature or from the sky" (Sunstein 2001b, 106). For many children, the first encounters with politics occur via television (e.g., Chaffee and Yang 1990; Delli Carpini 2000a; McLeod 2000). But the changes in the media environment that I have documented in this study affect young people just as much as old people. Today, childhood and adolescence involve much less "politics by default" than in the past. Patterson (2000a, 13) has suggested that growing up with broadcast news at the dinner hour is a reason why older generations pay more attention to news and are more interested: "The current generation of young adults was raised on cable television. Entertainment programming was readily available at all hours, and it dominated their TV exposure." As changes in the media environment have reduced the possibility that television by itself will acquaint young people with political life, other institutions may have to take its place.

Unlike high-choice media environments, school curricula can still get away with limiting choices. Thorough civics education may become more and more important in reaching those children who would otherwise not give politics a try. Large-scale studies have documented the influence of civics education on students' political engagement (Niemi and Chapman 1998; Niemi and Junn 1998; Torney-Purta et al. 2001). Evaluations of *Kids Voting USA*, a curriculum designed to emphasize the importance of political participation, have found positive effects on political knowledge and engagement (e.g., McDevitt and Chaffee 2000; Meirick and Wackman 2004). As Gimpel, Lay, and Schuknecht (2003, 15) emphasize, "adolescence is one of the few periods during the life cycle when there are nearly universal opportunities to collect and absorb political facts and information through coursework in social studies and history." A demanding test of civic engagement effects of school curricula would assess whether they form lasting media content preferences so that graduates continue to "collect and absorb" political information even after the stimulus and reinforcement of civics classes has faded.

Young people's first experiences with news are bound to be very important for the formation of their content preferences. After content preferences have formed, news content may have little additional impact on them, at least in the short run. This is true among entertainment fans in particular. If your first experiences have taught you that entertainment programming can reliably offer you greater enjoyment than news programming, you have little reason to try news programming again. Although evaluations of the news may initially shape your content preferences, you will not update your preferences based on subsequent changes in news formats and presentation because you will try to avoid news in the first place. (Preference updating based on news content may be more common among news fans who encounter the news regularly.)

The validity of the argument in the last paragraph depends a lot on the relationship between the content preferences and media exposure. Even though this relationship is growing stronger in the high-choice media environment, it is not deterministic. Extraordinary political circumstances can temporarily reduce preference-driven media exposure. Social encouragement or a sense of duty may also lead entertainment fans to watch, read, or listen to the news on occasion. In these situations, the content and presentation of news may produce changes in content preferences. If an entertainment fan – against the odds – happened to watch the news, would some news presentations be more likely than others to raise his initially low preference for news? To the extent that people update their content preferences after media exposure, appealing presentations of political information might provide another way to stop the trend toward growing inequality of political knowledge in the population (see, e.g., Entman 1989). If Sunstein (2001b, 106) is correct that preferences "are a product, at least in part, of social circumstances, including existing institutions, available options, and past choices," a better empirical understanding of the long-term reciprocal relationship between news content and content preferences should be an urgent research priority.

References

Abramowitz, Alan I., and Kyle L. Saunders. 1998. Ideological Realignment in the U.S. Electorate. *Journal of Politics* 60 (3):634–52.

Adams, Val. 1958. News of Television and Radio. *New York Times*, June 1.

Adams, William C. 1977. Television as a Source of Local Political News. Ph.D. dissertation, Baylor University, Waco, Texas.

——— 1978. Local Public Affairs Content of TV News. *Journalism Quarterly* 55 (4):690–5.

Adams, William C., and Paul H. Ferber. 1977. Television Interview Shows: The Politics of Visibility. *Journal of Broadcasting* 21 (2):141–51.

Adler, E. Scott. 2002. *Congressional District Data File, 1946–70.* Boulder: University of Colorado.

Aldrich, John. 1995. *Why Parties?* Chicago: University of Chicago Press.

Alford, John R., and David W. Brady. 1993. Personal and Partisan Advantage in U.S. Congressional Elections, 1846–1990. In *Congress Reconsidered* (5th ed.), edited by Lawrence C. Dodd and Bruce Ian Oppenheimer (pp. 141–57). Washington, D.C.: CQ Press.

Allen, Craig M. 2001. *News Is People. The Rise of Local TV News and the Fall of News from New York.* Ames: Iowa State University Press.

Althaus, Scott L. 1998. Information Effects in Collective Preferences. *American Political Science Review* 92:545–58.

——— 2001. Who's Voted in When the People Tune Out? Information Effects in Congressional Elections. In *Communication in U.S. Elections: New Agendas*, edited by Roderick P. Hart and Daron Shaw (pp. 33–53). Lanham, Maryland: Rowman and Littlefield.

——— 2002. American News Consumption During Times of National Crisis. *PS: Political Science and Politics* 35 (3):517–21.

——— 2003. *Collective Preferences in Democratic Politics.* Cambridge: Cambridge University Press.

Anderson, Jack. 1972. Nixon's Operatives Enrage Hill GOP. *Washington Post*, February 23, B15.

Ansolabehere, Stephen, and Shanto Iyengar. 1995. *Going Negative: How Attack Ads Shrink and Polarize the Electorate.* New York: Free Press.

Ansolabehere, Stephen, and Shanto Iyengar. 1998. *Message Forgotten: Misreporting in Surveys and the Bias toward Minimal Effects.* Unpublished manuscript.

References

Ansolabehere, Stephen, and James M. Snyder, Jr. 2002. The Incumbency Advantage in U.S. Elections: An Analysis of State and Federal Offices, 1942–2000. *Election Law Journal* 1 (3):315–38.

Ansolabehere, Stephen, Shigeo Hirano, James M. Snyder, and Michiko Ueda. 2006. Party and Incumbency Cues in Voting: Are They Substitutes? *Quarterly Journal of Political Science* 1 (2):119–37.

Ansolabehere, Stephen, Shanto Iyengar, and Adam Simon. 1999. Replicating Experiments Using Aggregate and Survey Data: The Case of Negative Advertising and Turnout. *American Political Science Review* 93 (4):901–10.

Ansolabehere, Stephen, James M. Snyder, Jr., and Charles Stewart, III. 2000. Old Voters, New Voters, and the Personal Vote: Using Redistricting to Measure the Incumbency Advantage. *American Journal of Political Science* 44 (1):17–34.

2001. Candidate Positioning in U.S. House Elections. *American Journal of Political Science* 45 (1):136–59.

Arnold, R. Douglas. 2004. *Congress, the Press and Political Accountability*. Princeton, New Jersey: Princeton University Press.

Bagdikian, Ben H. 1974. Congress and the Media: Partners in Propaganda. *Columbia Journalism Review* 12 (5):3–10.

Baker, Robert E. 1955a. Lawmakers 'Air' Selves at Cut Rate. *Washington Post and Times Herald*, February 13, E8.

1955b. Congress Flocks to TV Bandwagon. *New York Times*, June 27, 43.

Baldwin, Thomas F., Marianne Barrett, and Benjamin Bates. 1992. Influence of Cable on Television News Audiences. *Journalism Quarterly* 69 (3):651–8.

Barber, Benjamin R. 1998–9. Three Scenarios for the Future of Technology and Strong Democracy. *Political Science Quarterly* 113 (4):573–89.

Barber, James David. 1979. Not the New York Times: What Network News Should Be. *Washington Monthly* (September):14–21.

Bartels, Larry M. 1996. Uninformed Votes: Information Effects in Presidential Elections. *American Journal of Political Science* 40 (1):177–207.

1998. Electoral Continuity and Change, 1868–1996. *Electoral Studies* 17 (3):301–26.

2000. Partisanship and Voting Behavior, 1952–1996. *American Journal of Political Science* 44 (1):35–50.

2002. Question Order and Declining Faith in Elections. *Public Opinion Quarterly* 66 (1):67–79.

2005. Homer Gets a Tax Cut: Inequality and Public Policy in the American Mind. *Perspectives on Politics* 3 (1):15–31.

Bartels, Larry M., and Wendy M. Rahn. 2000. Political Attitudes in the Post-Network Era. Paper presented at the Annual Meeting of the American Political Science Association, Washington, D.C.

Barwise, T. P., and A. S. C. Ehrenberg. 1988. *Television and Its Audience, Sage Communications in Society Series*. London; Newbury Park, California: Sage Publications.

Barwise, T. P., A. S. C. Ehrenberg, and G. J. Goodhardt. 1982. Glued to the Box. Patterns of TV Repeat-Viewing. *Journal of Communication* 32 (4):22–9.

Baughman, James L. 1985. *Television's Guardians: The FCC and the Politics of Programming, 1958–1967*. Knoxville: University of Tennessee Press.

References

1997. The Republic of Mass Culture: Journalism, Filmmaking, and Broadcasting in America since 1941 (2nd ed.). Baltimore: Johns Hopkins University Press.

Baum, Matthew A. 2002. Sex, Lies, and War: How Soft News Brings Foreign Policy to the Inattentive Public. *American Political Science Review* 96 (1):91–110.

2003a. Soft News and Political Knowledge: Evidence of Absence or Absence of Evidence? *Political Communication* 20 (2):173–90.

2003b. *Soft News Goes to War.* Princeton, New Jersey: Princeton University Press.

2005. Talking the Vote: What Happens When Presidential Candidates Hit the Talk Show Circuit. *American Journal of Political Science* 49 (2):213–34.

Baum, Matthew A., and Samuel Kernell. 1999. Has Cable Ended the Golden Age of Presidential Television? *American Political Science Review* 93 (1):99–114.

Becker, Lee B., and Klaus Schoenbach. 1989. When Media Content Diversifies: Anticipating Audience Behaviors. In *Audience Responses to Media Diversification: Coping with Plenty*, edited by Lee B. Becker and Klaus Schoenbach (pp. 1–27). Hillsdale, New Jersey: Lawrence Erlbaum Associates.

Becker, Lee B., Pamela J. Creedon, R. Warwick Blood, and Eric S. Fredin. 1989. United States: Cable Eases Its Way into the Household. In *Audience Responses to Media Diversification: Coping with Plenty*, edited by Lee B. Becker, Klaus Schoenbach, et al. (pp. 291–331). Hillsdale, New Jersey: Lawrence Erlbaum Associates.

Bendiner, Robert. 1957. The FCC: Who Will Regulate the Regulators? *The Reporter* 17 (4):26–30.

Bimber, Bruce A. 2003. *Information and American Democracy: Technology in the Evolution of Political Power.* Cambridge: Cambridge University Press.

Bishop, George. 1987. Context Effects on Self-Perceptions of Interest in Government and Public Affairs. In *Social Information Processing and Survey Methodology*, edited by Hans- J. Hippler, Norbert Schwarz, and Seymour Sudman (pp. 179–99). New York: Springer Verlag.

2005. *The Illusion of Public Opinion.* Lanham, Massachusetts: Rowman and Littlefield.

Bogart, Leo. 1972. *The Age of Television; a Study of Viewing Habits and the Impact of Television on American Life* (3rd ed.). New York: Frederick Ungar Publishing.

Bonfadelli, Heinz. 2002. The Internet and Knowledge Gaps: A Theoretical and Empirical Investigation. *European Journal of Communication* 17 (1):65–84.

Born, Richard. 2000. Congressional Incumbency and the Rise of Split-Ticket Voting. *Legislative Studies Quarterly* 25 (3):365–87.

Bower, Robert T. 1973. *Television and the Public.* New York: Holt, Rinehart and Winston.

1985. *The Changing Television Audience in America.* New York: Columbia University Press.

Bowman, Gary. 1975. Consumer Choice and Television. *Applied Economics* 7 (3):175–84.

Brady, David W., Robert D'Onofrio, and Morris P. Fiorina. 2000. The Nationalization of Electoral Forces Revisited. In *Continuity and Change in House Elections*, edited by David W. Brady, John F. Cogan, and Morris P. Fiorina (pp. 130–48). Stanford, California: Stanford University Press.

References

Brady, Henry E., and Stephen Ansolabehere. 1989. The Nature of Utility Functions in Mass Publics. *American Political Science Review* 83 (1):143–63.

Brady, Henry E., and Paul M. Sniderman. 1985. Attitude Attribution: A Group Basis for Political Reasoning. *American Political Science Review* 79 (4):1061–78.

Brehm, John. 1993. *The Phantom Respondent. Opinion Surveys and Political Representation*. Ann Arbor: University of Michigan Press.

Broadcasting. 1964. How Congressmen Use Radio-TV. March 16, pp. 70–71.

Broadcasting Publications. 1969. *Broadcasting Yearbook 1969*. Washington, D.C.: Broadcasting Publications, Inc.

Brosius, Hans-Bernd. 1989. Influence of Presentation Features and News Content on Learning from Television News. *Journal of Broadcasting and Electronic Media* 33 (1):1–14.

Brown, Nona B. 1959. Willing Guests in Washington. *New York Times*, June 14, X13.

Burden, Barry C., and David C. Kimball. 2002. *Why Americans Split Their Tickets: Campaigns, Competition, and Divided Government*. Ann Arbor: University of Michigan Press.

Cain, Bruce E., John A. Ferejohn, and Morris P. Fiorina. 1984. The Constituency Service Basis of the Personal Vote for U.S. Representatives and British Members of Parliament. *American Political Science Review* 78 (1):110–25.

Campbell, Angus. 1960. Surge and Decline: A Study of Electoral Change. *Public Opinion Quarterly* 24 (3):397–418.

Campbell, Angus, Philip Converse, Warren E. Miller, and Donald Stokes. 1960. *The American Voter*. New York: Wiley.

Campbell, David E., Steven Yonish, and Robert D. Putnam. 1999. Tuning in, Tuning out Revisited: A Closer Look at the Causal Links between Television and Social Capital. Paper presented at the Annual Meeting of the American Political Science Association, Atlanta.

Campbell, James E., John R. Alford, and Keith Henry. 1984. Television Markets and Congressional Elections. *Legislative Studies Quarterly* 9 (4):665–78.

Cancian, Maria, Angela Bills, and Theodore Bergstrom. 1995. Hotelling Location Problems with Directional Constraints: An Application to Television News Scheduling. *Journal of Industrial Economics* 43 (1):121–4.

Cantril, Hadley. 1951. *Public Opinion 1935–1946*. Princeton, New Jersey: Princeton University Press.

Cappella, Joseph N., and Kathleen Hall Jamieson. 1997. *Spiral of Cynicism*. New York: Oxford University Press.

Carroll, Raymond L. 1989. Market Size and TV News Values. *Journalism Quarterly* 60 (Spring):49–56.

Carson, Jamie L., Michael H. Crespin, Charles J. Finocchiaro, and David W. Rohde. 2004. Linking Congressional Districts across Time: Redistricting and Party Polarization in Congress. Paper presented at the Annual Meeting of the American Political Science Association, Chicago, September 2–5.

Carter, Douglas. 1955. Every Congressman a Television Star. *Reporter* 12 (12):26–28.

Castleman, Harry, and Walter J. Podrazik. 1982. *Watching TV: Four Decades of American Television*. New York: McGraw-Hill.

1984. *The TV Schedule Book: Four Decades of Network Programming from Sign-on to Sign-Off*. New York: McGraw-Hill.

References

Chaffee, Steven H., and Joan Schleuder. 1986. Measurement and Effects of Attention to Media News. *Human Communication Research* 13 (1):76–107.

Chaffee, Steven H., and Donna G. Wilson. 1977. Media Rich, Media Poor: Two Studies of Diversity in Agenda Holding. *Journalism Quarterly* 54 (3):466–476.

Chaffee, Steven H., and Seung-Mock Yang. 1990. Communication and Political Socialization. In *Political Socialization, Citizenship Education, and Democracy*, edited by Orit Ichilov (pp. 137–57). New York: Teachers College Press.

Chaiken, Shelly. 1980. Heuristic Versus Systematic Information Processing and the Use of Source Versus Message Cues in Persuasion. *Journal of Personality & Social Psychology* 39 (5):752–66.

Chang, LinChiat, and Jon A. Krosnick. 2002. Measuring the Frequency of Regular Behaviors: Comparing the "Typical Week" to the "Past Week". *Sociological Methodology* 33:55–80.

Chester, Edward W. 1969. *Radio, Television, and American Politics*. New York: Sheed and Ward.

Clarke, Peter, and Susan Evans. 1983. *Covering Campaigns: Journalism in Congressional Elections*. Stanford, California: Stanford University Press.

Clarke, Peter, and Eric Fredin. 1978. Newspapers, Television, and Political Reasoning. *Public Opinion Quarterly* 42 (2):143–160.

Clinton, Joshua D., Simon Jackman, and Doug Rivers. 2004. "The Most Liberal Senator"? Analyzing and Interpreting Congressional Roll Calls. *PS: Political Science & Politics* 37 (4):805–11.

Comstock, George A., and Erica Scharrer. 1999. *Television: What's on, Who's Watching, and What It Means*. San Diego: Academic Press.

Converse, Philip E. 1962. Information Flow and the Stability of Partisan Attitudes. *Public Opinion Quarterly* 26 (4):578–99.

———. 1964. The Nature of Belief Systems in Mass Publics. In *Ideology and Discontent*, edited by David E. Apter (pp. 206–61). New York: Free Press.

———. 1976. *The Dynamics of Party Support: Cohort-Analyzing Party Identification*. Beverly Hills, California: Sage Publications.

Cook, Timothy E. 1986. House Members as Newsmakers: The Effects of Televising Congress. *Legislative Studies Quarterly* 11 (2):203–26.

———. 1989. *Making Laws and Making News: Media Strategies in the U.S. House of Representatives*. Washington, D.C.: Brookings Institution.

Cook, Timothy E., Paul Gronke, and John Rattliff. 2000. Disdaining the Media: The American Public's Changing Attitudes toward the News. Paper presented at the Annual Meeting of the International Society of Political Psychology, Seattle, July 1–4.

Cover, Albert D. 1977. One Good Term Deserves Another: The Advantage of Incumbency in Congressional Elections. *American Journal of Political Science* 21 (3):523–41.

Cox, Gary, and Mathew D. McCubbins. 1993. *Legislative Leviathan: Party Government in the House*. Berkeley: University of California Press.

Cox, Gary W., and Jonathan N. Katz. 1996. Why Did the Incumbency Advantage in U.S. House Elections Grow? *American Journal of Political Science* 40 (2):478–97.

———. 2002. *Elbridge Gerry's Salamander*. Cambridge: Cambridge University Press.

Craig, Douglas B. 2000. *Fireside Politics: Radio and Political Culture in the United States, 1920–1940*. Baltimore: Johns Hopkins University Press.

References

Cronheim, Dorothy H. 1957. Congressmen and Their Communication Practices. Ph.D. dissertation, Ohio State University, Columbus.

Danna, Sammy R. 1975. The Rise of Radio News. In *American Broadcasting*, edited by Lawrence W. Lichty and Malachi C. Topping (pp. 338–44). New York: Hastings House.

DellaVigna, Stefano, and Ethan Kaplan. 2005. *The Fox News Effect: Media Bias and Voting*. Unpublished manuscript, University of California, Berkeley.

Delli Carpini, Michael X. 2000a. Gen.Com: Youth, Civic Engagement, and the New Information Environment. *Political Communication* 17 (4):341–9.

    2000b. In Search of the Informed Citizen: What Americans Know About Politics and Why It Matters. *Communication Review* 4 (1):129–64.

Delli Carpini, Michael X., and Scott Keeter. 1996. *What Americans Know About Politics and Why It Matters*. New Haven, Connecticut: Yale University Press.

Delli Carpini, Michael X., and Bruce A. Williams. 2000. Let Us Infotain You: Politics in the New Media Environment. In *Mediated Politics: Communication in the Future of Democracy*, edited by W. Lance Bennett and Robert M. Entman (pp. 21–52). Cambridge: Cambridge University Press.

Delli Carpini, Michael X., Scott Keeter, and J. David Kennamer. 1994. Effects of the News Media Environment on Citizen Knowledge of State Politics and Government. *Journalism Quarterly* 71 (2):443–56.

DiMaggio, Paul, and Kyoko Sato. 2003. Does the Internet Balkanize Political Attention? A Test of the Sunstein Thesis. Paper presented at the American Sociology Association, Atlanta.

DiMaggio, Paul, John Evans, and Bethany Bryson. 1996. Have Americans' Social Attitudes Become More Polarized? *American Journal of Sociology* 102 (3):690–755.

DiMaggio, Paul, Eszter Hargittai, Coral Celeste, and Steven Shafer. 2004. Digital Inequality: From Unequal Access to Differentiated Use. In *Social Inequality*, edited by Kathryn M. Neckerman (pp. 355–400). New York: Russell Sage Foundation.

Dominick, Joseph R., Alan Wurtzel, and Guy Lometti. 1975. Television Journalism vs. Show Business: A Content Analysis of Eyewitness News. *Journalism Quarterly* 52 (2):213–18.

Downs, Anthony. 1957. *An Economic Theory of Democracy*. New York: Harper.

Entman, Robert M. 1989. *Democracy without Citizens*. New York: Oxford University Press.

Epstein, Jay Edward. 1973. *News from Nowhere*. New York: Random House.

Erikson, Robert S. 1971. The Advantage of Incumbency in Congressional Elections. *Polity* 3 (3):395–405.

Erikson, Robert S., Michael B. MacKuen, and James A. Stimson. 2002. *The Macro Polity*. New York: Cambridge University Press.

Evans, John H. 2003. Have Americans' Attitudes Become More Polarized? – An Update. *Social Science Quarterly* 84 (1):71–90.

Eveland, William P., Jr., and Dietram A. Scheufele. 2000. Connecting News Media Use with Gaps in Knowledge and Participation. *Political Communication* 17 (3):215–37.

Farhi, Paul. 2003. Everybody Wins. *American Journalism Review* (April).

Federal Communications Commission. 1946. *Public Service Responsibility of Broadcast Licenses*. Washington, D.C.

References

Ferejohn, John A. 1977. On the Decline of Competition in Congressional Elections. *American Political Science Review* 71 (1):166–76.

Fielding, Raymond. 1972. *The American Newsreel, 1911–1967*. Norman: University of Oklahoma Press.

Finney, Robert G. 1971. Television News Messages and Their Perceived Effects in a Congressional Election Campaign. Ph.D. dissertation, Ohio State University, Columbus.

Fiorina, Morris P. 1977a. The Case of the Vanishing Marginals: The Bureaucracy Did It. *American Political Science Review* 71 (1):177–81.

1977b. *Congress: Keystone of the Washington Establishment*. New Haven, Connecticut: Yale University Press.

1981. Some Problems in Studying the Effects of Resource Allocation in Congressional Elections. *American Journal of Political Science* 25 (3):543–67.

1990. Information and Rationality in Elections. In *Information and Democratic Processes*, edited by John A. Ferejohn and James H. Kuklinski (pp. 329–42). Urbana: University of Illinois Press.

1999. Whatever Happened to the Median Voter? Paper presented at the MIT Conference on Parties and Congress, Cambridge, Massachusetts, October 2.

2002. Parties and Partisanship: A 40-Year Retrospective. *Political Behavior* 24 (2):93–115.

2004a. *Culture War? The Myth of a Polarized America*. New York: Longman.

2004b. Keystone Reconsidered. In *Congress Reconsidered* (7th ed.), edited by Lawrence Dodd and Bruce Oppenheimer (pp. 141–62). Washington, D.C.: CQ Press.

Fleisher, Richard, and Jon R. Bond. 2000. Partisanship and the President's Quest for Votes on the Floor of Congress. In *Polarized Politics: Congress and the President in a Partisan Era*, edited by Jon R. Bond and Richard Fleisher (pp. 154–85). Washington D.C.: CQ Press.

2004. The Shrinking Middle in the U.S. Congress. *British Journal of Political Science* 34 (3):429–51.

Freedman, Paul, Michael Franz, and Kenneth Goldstein. 2004. Campaign Advertising and Democratic Citizenship. *American Journal of Political Science* 48 (4):723–41.

Freeman, Richard B. 2004. What, Me Vote? In *Social Inequality*, edited by Kathryn M. Neckerman (pp. 703–28). New York: Russell Sage Foundation.

Gantz, Walter. 1978. How Uses and Gratifications Affect Recall of Television News. *Journalism Quarterly* 55 (4):664–72.

Gantz, Walter, and Bradley S. Greenberg. 1993. Patterns of Diffusion and Information-Seeking. In *Desert Storm and the Mass Media*, edited by Bradley S. Greenberg and Walter Gantz (pp. 166–81). Cresskill, New Jersey: Hampton Press.

Gaziano, Cecilie. 1997. Forecast 2000: Widening Knowledge Gaps. *Journalism and Mass Communication Quarterly* 74 (2):237–64.

Gelman, Andrew, and Zaiying Huang. Forthcoming. Estimating Incumbency Advantage and Its Variation, as an Example of a Before/after Study. *Journal of the American Statistical Association*.

Gelman, Andrew, and Gary King. 1990. Estimating the Incumbency Advantage without Bias. *American Journal of Political Science* 34 (4):1142–64.

Genova, B. K. L., and Bradley S. Greenberg. 1979. Interests in News and the Knowledge Gap. *Public Opinion Quarterly* 43 (1):79–91.

References

Gentzkow, Matthew. 2006. Television and Voter Turnout. *Quarterly Journal of Economics* 121 (3): 931–972.

Gilens, Martin. 2001. Political Ignorance and Collective Policy Preferences. *American Political Science Review* 95 (2):379–96.

Gilens, Martin, Lynn Vavreck, and Martin Cohen. 2005. *Mass Media and Public Perceptions of Presidential Candidates, 1952–2000.* Unpublished manuscript.

Gimpel, James G., J. Celeste Lay, and Jason E. Schuknecht. 2003. *Cultivating Democracy.* Washington, D.C.: Brookings Institution Press.

Goldenberg, Edie N., and Michael W. Traugott. 1984. *Campaigning for Congress.* Washington, D.C.: CQ Press.

Goodman, Walter. 1955. Television and Politics: Candidates and the Camera. *New Republic,* May 9, 13–16.

Gould, Jack. 1951a. TV Makes Inroads on Big Radio Chains. *New York Times,* June 27, 1.

——— 1951b. TV Transforming Social Scene; Challenges Films. *New York Times,* June 24, 1.

Grabe, Maria Elizabeth, Annie Lang, Shuhua Zhou, and Paul David Bolls. 2000. Cognitive Access to Negative Arousing News. *Communication Research* 27 (1):3–26.

Graber, Doris A. 1980. *Mass Media and American Politics* (1st ed.). Washington, D.C.: Congressional Quarterly Press.

——— 1988. *Processing the News: How People Tame the Information Tide* (2nd ed.). New York: Longman.

——— 1990. Seeing Is Remembering: How Visuals Contribute to Learning from Television News. *Journal of Communication* 40 (3):134–55.

——— 2001. *Processing Politics: Learning from Television in the Internet Age.* Chicago: University of Chicago Press.

Green, Mark J., James M. Fallows, and David R. Zwick. 1972. *Who Runs Congress?* New York: Grossman.

Greene, William H. 1997. *Econometric Analysis* (3rd ed.). Upper Saddle River, New Jersey: Prentice Hall.

Griffin, John D., and Brian Newman. 2005. Are Voters Better Represented? *Journal of Politics* 67 (4):1206–27.

Grimes, Thomas. 1991. Mild Auditory-Visual Dissonance in Television News May Exceed Viewer Attentional Capacity. *Human Communication Research* 18 (2):268–98.

Gronke, Paul. 2000. *The Electorate, the Campaign, and the Office: A Unified Approach to Senate and House Elections.* Ann Arbor: University of Michigan Press.

Gruenstein, Peter. 1974. Press Release Politics: How Congressmen Manage the News. *The Progressive,* January, 37–40.

Hallin, Daniel C., and Paolo Mancini. 2004. *Comparing Media Systems: Three Models of Media and Politics.* New York: Cambridge University Press.

Hamilton, James T. 1998. *Channeling Violence. The Economic Market for Violent Television Programming.* Princeton, New Jersey: Princeton University Press.

——— 2004. *All the News That's Fit to Sell: How the Market Transforms Information into News.* Princeton, New Jersey: Princeton University Press.

Handel, Leo A. 1950. *Hollywood Looks at Its Audience.* Urbana: University of Illinois Press.

References

Hargittai, Eszter. 2003. How Wide a Web: Inequalities in Accessing Information Online. Ph.D. dissertation, Princeton University, Princeton, New Jersey.

Hawkins, Robert P., Suzanne Pingree, Jacqueline Hitchon, Bradley W. Gorham, Prathana Kannaovakun, Eileen Gilligan, Barry Radler, Gudbjorg H. Kolbeins, and Toni Schmitt. 2001. Predicting Selection and Activity in Television Genre Viewing. *Media Psychology* 3:237–63.

Headen, Robert S., Jay E. Klompmaker, and Roland T. Rust. 1979. The Duplication of Viewing Law and Television Media Schedule Evaluation. *Journal of Marketing Research* 16 (3):333–40.

Heeter, Carrie. 1985. Program Selection with Abundance of Choice: A Process Model. *Human Communication Research* 12 (1):126–52.

Hess, Stephen. 1991. *Live from Capitol Hill*. Washington, D.C.: Brookings Institution.

Hetherington, Marc J. 2001. Resurgent Mass Partisanship: The Role of Elite Polarization. *American Political Science Review* 95 (3):619–31.

Holbert, R. Lance, Owen Pillion, David A. Tschida, Greg G. Armfield, Kelly Kinder, Kristin L. Cherry, and Amy R. Daulton. 2003. *The West Wing* as Endorsement of the U.S. Presidency: Expanding the Bounds of Priming in Political Communication. *Journal of Communication* 53 (3):427–43.

Humphreys, Peter J. 1994. *Media and Media Policy in Germany: The Press and Broadcasting since 1945* (2nd ed.). Oxford: Berg.

Hutchings, Vincent. 2001. Political Context, Issue Salience, and Selective Attentiveness: Constituent Knowledge of the Clarence Thomas Confirmation Vote. *Journal of Politics* 63 (3):846–68.

Iyengar, Shanto. 1990. Shortcuts to Political Knowledge: Selective Attention and Accessibility Bias. In *Information and Democratic Processes*, edited by John A. Ferejohn and James H. Kuklinski (pp. 160–85). Urbana: University of Illinois Press.

Iyengar, Shanto, and Adam Simon. 2000. New Perspectives and Evidence on Political Communication and Campaign Effects. *Annual Review of Psychology* 51:149–69.

Iyengar, Shanto, Kyu S. Hahn, and Markus Prior. 2001. Has Technology Made Attention to Political Campaigns More Selective? An Experimental Study of the 2000 Presidential Campaign. Paper presented at the Annual Meeting of the American Political Science Association, San Francisco.

Iyengar, Sheena S., and Mark R. Lepper. 2000. When Choice Is Demotivating: Can One Desire Too Much of a Good Thing? *Journal of Personality and Social Psychology* 79 (6):995–1006.

Jacobson, Gary C. 1975. The Impact of Broadcast Campaigning on Electoral Outcomes. *Journal of Politics* 37 (3):769–93.

  1990. The Electoral Origins of Divided Government: Competition in U.S. House Elections, 1946–1988. Boulder: Westview Press.

  2000a. The Electoral Basis of Partisan Polarization in Congress. Paper presented at the Annual Meeting of the American Political Science Association, Washington, D.C.

  2000b. Party Polarization in National Politics: The Electoral Connection. In *Polarized Politics: Congress and the President in a Partisan Era*, edited by Jon R. Bond and Richard Fleisher (pp. 9–30). Washington, D.C.: CQ Press.

References

2000c. Reversal of Fortune: The Transformation of U.S. House Elections in the 1990s. In *Continuity and Change in House Elections*, edited by David W. Brady, John F. Cogan, and Morris P. Fiorina (pp. 10–39). Stanford, California: Stanford University Press.

2003. Partisan Polarization in Presidential Support: The Electoral Connection. *Congress & the Presidency* 30 (1):1–36.

2004. *The Politics of Congressional Elections* (6th ed.). New York: Pearson-Longman.

Jamieson, Kathleen Hall. 1996. *Packaging the Presidency* (3rd ed.). New York: Oxford University Press.

Jenkins, Henry. 2001. Challenging the Consensus. *Boston Review* 26 (3–4):16–17.

Johnston, Richard, Michael G. Hagen, and Kathleen Hall Jamieson. 2004. *The 2000 Presidential Election and the Foundations of Party Politics*. Cambridge: Cambridge University Press.

Kaase, Max. 2000. Germany: A Society and a Media System in Transition. In *Democracy and the Media*, edited by Richard Gunther and Anthony Mughan (pp. 375–401). Cambridge: Cambridge University Press.

Kahn, Kim Fridkin. 1993. Incumbency and the News Media in U. S. Senate Elections: An Experimental Investigation. *Political Research Quarterly* 46 (4):715–40.

Kahn, Kim Fridkin, and Patrick J. Kenney. 1999. *The Spectacle of U.S. Senate Campaigns*. Princeton, New Jersey: Princeton University Press.

Katz, Elihu. 1996. And Deliver Us from Segmentation. *The Annals of the American Academy of Political and Social Science* 546:22–33.

Katz, Elihu, Jay G. Blumler, and Michael Gurevitch. 1973. Uses and Gratifications Research. *Public Opinion Quarterly* 37 (4):509–23.

Katz, Elihu, Michael Gurevitch, and Hadassah Haas. 1973. On the Use of the Mass Media for Important Things. *American Sociological Review* 38 (2):164–81.

Keaggy, Diane Toroian. 2004. All Things (NPR) Considered. *St. Louis Post-Dispatch*, April 4, F4.

Keeter, Scott, and Harry Wilson. 1986. Natural Treatment and Control Settings for Research on the Effects of Television. *Communication Research* 13 (1):37–53.

Keith, Bruce E., David B. Magleby, Candice J. Nelson, Elizabeth Orr, Mark C. Westlye, and Raymond E. Wolfinger. 1992. *The Myth of the Independent Voter*. Berkeley: University of California Press.

Kelley, Jr., Stanley. 1983. *Interpreting Elections*. Princeton, New Jersey: Princeton University Press.

Key, Jr., V. O. 1966. *The Responsible Electorate*. Cambridge, Massachusetts: Belknap Press.

Kinder, Donald R. 1998. Opinion and Action in the Realm of Politics. In *The Handbook of Social Psychology*, edited by Daniel T. Gilbert, Susan T. Fiske, et al. (pp. 778–867). Boston: McGraw-Hill.

2003. Communication and Politics in the Age of Information. In *Oxford Handbook of Political Psychology*, edited by Leonie Huddy and Robert Jervis David O. Sears (pp. 357–93). New York: Oxford University Press.

King, Gary. 1994. *Elections to the United States House of Representatives, 1898–1992 [Computer File]*. Ann Arbor, Michigan: Inter-university Consortium for Political and Social Research.

Kingson, Walter. 1952. The Second New York Television Survey. *Quarterly of Film Radio and Television* 6 (4):317–26.

References

Klein, Paul. 1972. The Television Audience and Program Mediocrity. In *Mass Media and Society*, edited by Alan Wells (pp. 76–9). Palo Alto, California: National Press Books.

Krehbiel, Keith, and John R. Wright. 1983. The Incumbency Effect in Congressional Elections: A Test of Two Explanations. *American Journal of Political Science* 27 (1):140–57.

Krosnick, Jon A., and Lin Chiat Chang. 2001. *A Comparison of the Random Digit Dialing Telephone Survey Methodology with Internet Survey Methodology as Implemented by Knowledge Networks and Harris Interactive.* Unpublished manuscript, Ohio State University, Columbus.

Krotki, Karol, and J. Michael Dennis. 2001. Probability-Based Survey Research on the Internet. Paper presented at the 53rd Conference of the International Statistical Institute, Seoul, South Korea.

Krugman, Herbert E. 1965. The Impact of Television Advertising: Learning without Involvement. *Public Opinion Quarterly* 29 (3):349–56.

Krugman, Herbert E., and Eugene L. Hartley. 1970. Passive Learning from Television. *Public Opinion Quarterly* 34 (2):184–90.

Kuklinski, James H., and Paul J. Quirk. 2000. Reconsidering the Rational Public: Cognition, Heuristics, and Mass Opinion. In *Elements of Reason: Cognition, Choice, and the Bounds of Rationality*, edited by Arthur Lupia, Mathew D. McCubbins, and Samuel L. Popkin (pp. 153–82). New York: Cambridge University Press.

Kuklinski, James H., and Lee Sigelman. 1992. When Objectivity Is Not Objective: Network Television Coverage of U.S. Senators and the "Paradox of Objectivity". *Journal of Politics* 54 (3):810–33.

Kwak, Nojin. 1999. Revisiting the Knowledge Gap Hypothesis: Education, Motivation, and Media Use. *Communication Research* 26 (4):385–413.

Ladd, Jonathan. 2006. Attitudes toward the News Media and Political Competition in America. Ph.D. dissertation, Princeton University, Princeton, New Jersey.

Lang, Annie. 1995. Defining Audio/Video Redundancy from a Limited-Capacity Information Processing Perspective. *Communication Research* 22 (1):86–115.

Lau, Richard R., and David P. Redlawsk. 2001. Advantages and Disadvantages of Cognitive Heuristics in Political Decision Making. *American Journal of Political Science* 45 (4):951–71.

Layman, Geoffrey C., and Thomas M. Carsey. 2002a. Party Polarization and 'Conflict Extension' in the American Electorate. *American Journal of Political Science* 46 (4):786–802.

2002b. Party Polarization and Party Structuring of Policy Attitudes: A Comparison of Three NES Panel Studies. *Political Behavior* 24 (3):199–236.

Lazarsfeld, Paul F. 1940. *Radio and the Printed Page* (2nd ed.). New York: Duell, Sloan and Pearce.

Lazarsfeld, Paul F., and Bernard Berelson. 1968 [1944]. *The People's Choice; How the Voter Makes up His Mind in a Presidential Campaign* (3rd ed.). New York: Columbia University Press.

Lehmann, Donald R. 1971. Television Show Preference: Application of a Choice Model. *Journal of Marketing Research* 8 (1):47–55.

Leighley, Jan E., and Jonathan Nagler. 1992. Socioeconomic Class Bias in Turnout, 1964–1988: The Voters Remain the Same. *American Political Science Review* 86 (3):725–36.

References

Levitt, Steven D., and Catherine D. Wolfram. 1997. Decomposing the Sources of Incumbency Advantage in the U.S. House. *Legislative Studies Quarterly* 22 (1):45–60.

Lichty, Lawrence W., and Thomas W. Bohn. 1975. Radio's March of Time: Dramatized News. In *American Broadcasting*, edited by Lawrence W. Lichty and Malachi C. Topping (pp. 324–33). New York: Hastings House.

Lichty, Lawrence W., and Malachi C. Topping. 1975. *American Broadcasting*. New York: Hastings House.

Lichty, Lawrence W., Joseph M. Ripley, and Harrison B. Summers. 1965. Political Programs on National Television Networks: 1960 and 1964. *Journal of Broadcasting* 9 (3):217–29.

LoSciuto, Leonard A. 1972. A National Inventory of Television Viewing Behavior. In *Television and Social Behavior. Television in Day-to-Day Life: Patterns of Use*, edited by Eli A. Rubinstein, George A. Comstock, and John P. Murray (pp. 33–86). Washington, D.C.: U.S. Government Printing Office.

Lundberg, George A. 1975. The Content of Radio Programs. In *American Broadcasting*, edited by Lawrence W. Lichty and Malachi C. Topping (pp. 322–4). New York: Hastings House.

Lupia, Arthur. 1994. Shortcuts Versus Encyclopedias: Information and Voting Behavior in California Insurance Reform Elections. *American Political Science Review* 88 (1):63–76.

Luskin, Robert C. 1987. Measuring Political Sophistication. *American Journal of Political Science* 31 (4):856–99.

1990. Explaining Political Sophistication. *Political Behavior* 12 (4):331–61.

Lyle, Jack, and Walter Wilcox. 1963. Television News. An Interim Report. *Journal of Broadcasting* 7 (2):157–66.

MacNeil, Robert. 1968. *The People Machine. The Influence of Television in American Politics*. New York: Harper & Row.

Manski, Charles F. 1999. Analysis of Choice Expectations in Incomplete Scenarios. *Journal of Risk and Uncertainty* 19 (1/3):49–66.

2002. Probabilistic Polling. In *Navigating Public Opinion: Polls, Policy, and the Future of American Democracy*, edited by J. Manza, F. Cook, and B. Page (pp. 251–71). Oxford: Oxford University Press.

Martis, Kenneth C., Clifford Lee Lord, and Ruth Anderson Rowles. 1982. *The Historical Atlas of United States Congressional Districts, 1789–1983*. New York: Free Press.

Mayer, William G. 1993. Trends in Media Usage. *Public Opinion Quarterly* 57 (4):593–611.

1998. Mass Partisanship, 1946–1996. In *Partisan Approaches to Postwar American Politics*, edited by Byron E. Shafer (pp. 186–219). New York: Chatham House.

2005. *The Swing Voter in American Presidential Elections: An Initial Inquiry*. Unpublished manuscript, Northeastern University.

Mayhew, David. 1974. Congressional Elections: The Case of the Vanishing Marginals. *Polity* 6 (Spring):295–317.

McDermott, Monika L. 2005. Candidate Occupations and Voter Information Shortcuts. *Journal of Politics* 67 (1):201–19.

McDevitt, Michael, and Steven H. Chaffee. 2000. Closing Gaps in Political Communication and Knowledge: Effects of a School Intervention. *Communication Research* 27 (3):259–92.

References

McDonald, Michael P. 2004. Up, up and Away! Voter Participation in the 2004 Presidential Election. *The Forum* 2 (4).

McDonald, Michael P., and Samuel L. Popkin. 2001. The Myth of the Vanishing Voter. *American Political Science Review* 95 (4):963–74.

McLeod, Jack M. 2000. Media and Civic Socialization of Youth. *Journal of Adolescent Health* 27 (2):45–51.

McNeil, Alex. 1984. *Total Television: A Comprehensive Guide to Programming from 1948 to the Present*. New York: Viking Penguin.

Media Dynamics, Inc. 2001. *TV Dimensions 2001*. New York: Media Dynamics.

Meirick, Patrick C., and Daniel B. Wackman. 2004. Kids Voting and Political Knowledge: Narrowing Gaps, Informing Votes. *Social Science Quarterly* 85 (5):1161–77.

Mickelson, Sig. 1989. *From Whistle Stop to Sound Bite: Four Decades of Politics and Television*. New York: Praeger.

Miller, Alan S., and John P. Hoffmann. 1999. The Growing Divisiveness: Culture Wars or a War of Words. *Social Forces* 78:721–46.

Mondak, Jeffery J. 1993a. Public Opinion and Heuristic Processing of Source Cues. *Political Behavior* 15 (2):167–92.

1993b. Source Cues and Policy Approval: The Cognitive Dynamics of Public Support for the Reagan Agenda. *American Journal of Political Science* 37:186–212.

1995. *Nothing to Read: Newspapers and Elections in a Social Experiment*. Ann Arbor: University of Michigan Press.

Moy, Patricia, Michael A. Xenos, and Verena K. Hess. 2005. Communication and Citizenship: Mapping the Political Effects of Infotainment. *Mass Communication & Society* 8 (2):111–31.

Mutz, Diana C., and Byron Reeves. 2005. The New Videomalaise: Effects of Televised Incivility on Political Trust. *American Political Science Review* 99 (1):1–15.

Mutz, Diana C., and Paul S. Martin. 2001. Facilitating Communication across Lines of Political Difference: The Role of Mass Media. *American Political Science Review* 95 (1):97–114.

Napoli, Philip M. 2003. *Audience Economics: Media Institutions and the Audience Marketplace*. New York: Columbia University Press.

National Telecommunications and Information Administration. 2002. *A Nation Online: How Americans Are Expanding Their Use of the Internet*. Washington, D.C.: U.S. Department of Commerce.

Negroponte, Nicholas. 1995. *Being Digital*. New York: Knopf.

Nelson, Candice. 1978. The Effects of Incumbency on Voting in Congressional Elections. *Political Science Quarterly* 93 (4):665–78.

Nestvold, Karl J. 1973. Diversity in Local Television News. *Journal of Broadcasting* 17 (3):345–52.

Neuman, W. Russell. 1976. Patterns of Recall among Television News Viewers. *Public Opinion Quarterly* 40 (1):115–23.

1986. *The Paradox of Mass Politics: Knowledge and Opinion in the American Electorate*. Cambridge, Massachusetts: Harvard University Press.

1991. *The Future of the Mass Audience*. New York: Cambridge University Press.

1996. Political Communication Infrastructure. *The Annals of the American Academy of Political and Social Science* 546:9–21.

References

Neuman, W. Russell, Marion R. Just, and Ann N. Crigler. 1992. *Common Knowledge: News and the Construction of Political Meaning*. Chicago: University of Chicago Press.

Nie, Norman H., Jane Junn, and Kenneth Stehlik-Barry. 1996. *Education and Democratic Citizenship in America*. Chicago: University of Chicago Press.

Nielsen Media Research. 1972. *Nielsen Station Index*. Chicago: A. C. Nielsen Company.

2000. *2000 Report on Television*. New York: A. C. Nielsen Company.

2005. *Television Audience 2004*. New York: A. C. Nielsen Company.

Nielsen, Ted. 1975. A History of Network Television News. In *American Broadcasting*, edited by Lawrence W. Lichty and Malachi C. Topping (pp. 415–21). New York: Hastings House.

Niemi, Richard G., and Chris Chapman. 1998. *The Civic Development of 9th-through 12th-Grade Students in the United States: 1996*. Washington, D.C.: U.S. Department of Education, National Center for Education Statistics.

Niemi, Richard G., and Jane Junn. 1998. *Civic Education: What Makes Students Learn*. New Haven, Connecticut: Yale University Press.

Niemi, Richard G., Lynda W. Powell, and Patricia L. Bicknell. 1986. The Effects of Congruity between Community and District on Salience of U.S. House Candidates. *Legislative Studies Quarterly* 11 (2):187–201.

Noll, Roger G., Merton J. Peck, and John J. McGowan. 1973. *Economic Aspects of Television Regulation*. Washington, D.C.: Brookings Institution.

Ornstein, Norman J. 1983. The Open Congress Meets the President. In *Both Ends of the Avenue: The Presidency, the Executive Branch, and Congress in the 1980s*, edited by Anthony S. King (pp. 185–211). Washington, D.C.: American Enterprise Institute.

Osterlund, Peter. 1988. Media-Savvy Congress Turns to TV. *Christian Science Monitor*, June 3, 3.

Ostroff, David H., and Karin Sandell. 1984. Local Station Coverage of Campaigns: A Tale of Two Cities in Ohio. *Journalism Quarterly* 61 (2):346–51.

Otten, Alan L. 1957. Expansive Uncle. *Wall Street Journal*, June 27, 1.

Owen, Bruce M., and Steven S. Wildman. 1992. *Video Economics*. Cambridge, Massachusetts: Harvard University Press.

Page, Benjamin I., and Robert Y. Shapiro. 1992. *The Rational Public: Fifty Years of Trends in Americans' Policy Preferences*. Chicago: University of Chicago Press.

Palfrey, Thomas R., and Keith T. Poole. 1987. The Relationship between Information, Ideology, and Voting Behavior. *American Journal of Political Science* 31 (3):511–30.

Parker, Edwin B. 1963. The Effects of Television on Public Library Circulation. *Public Opinion Quarterly* 27 (4):578–89.

Parkman, Allen M. 1982. The Effect of Television Station Ownership on Local News Ratings. *Review of Economics and Statistics* 64 (2):289–95.

Patterson, Thomas E. 1993. *Out of Order*. New York: Random House.

2000a. *Doing Well and Doing Good: How Soft News and Critical Journalism Are Shrinking the New Audience and Weakening Democracy – and What News Outlets Can Do About It*. Cambridge, Massachusetts: Joan Shorenstein Center.

2000b. The United States: News in a Free-Market Society. In *Democracy and the Media*, edited by Richard Gunther and Anthony Mughan (pp. 241–65). Cambridge, U.K.: Cambridge University Press.

References

Patterson, Thomas E., and Robert D. McClure. 1976. *The Unseeing Eye: The Myth of Television Power in National Politics.* New York: Putnam.

Petty, Richard E., and John T. Cacioppo. 1986. *Communication and Persuasion: Central and Peripheral Routes to Attitude Change.* New York: Springer-Verlag.

Pew Internet and American Life Project. 2003. America's Online Pursuits.

Pitkin, Hanna F. 1967. *The Concept of Representation.* Berkeley: University of California Press.

Poole, Keith T., and Howard Rosenthal. 1997. *Congress: A Political-Economic History of Roll Call Voting.* New York: Oxford University Press.

——— 2001. D-Nominate after 10 Years: A Comparative Update to Congress: A Political-Economic History of Roll-Call Voting. *Legislative Studies Quarterly* 26 (1):5–29.

Popkin, Samuel L. 1991. *The Reasoning Voter: Communication and Persuasion in Presidential Campaigns.* Chicago: University of Chicago Press.

Popkin, Samuel L., and Michael A. Dimock. 1999. Political Knowledge and Civic Competence. In *Citizen Competence and Democratic Institutions*, edited by Stephen L. Elkin and Karol Edward Soltan (pp. 117–46). University Park: Pennsylvania State University Press.

PR Newswire. 1987a. Early Evening Local TV News Up in 1987. August 3.

——— 1987b. Trend toward Sandwiching Hour-Long Local Newscasts. August 24.

Price, Vincent, and John Zaller. 1993. Who Gets the News? Alternative Measures of News Reception and Their Implications for Research. *Public Opinion Quarterly* 57 (2):133–64.

Prinz, Timothy S. 1995. Media Markets and Candidate Awareness in House Elections, 1978–1990. *Political Communication* 12 (3):305–25.

Prior, Markus. 2002. Political Knowledge after September 11. *PS: Political Science and Politics* 35 (3):523–9.

——— 2003. Any Good News in Soft News? The Impact of Soft News Preference on Political Knowledge. *Political Communication* 20 (2):149–72.

——— 2005a. News v. Entertainment: How Increasing Media Choice Widens Gaps in Political Knowledge and Turnout. *American Journal of Political Science* 49 (3):577–92.

——— 2005b. The Pitfalls of Self-Reported News Exposure. Paper presented at the 60th Annual Meeting of the American Association for Public Opinion Research, Miami Beach, May 12–15.

——— 2006. The Incumbent in the Living Room: The Rise of Television and the Incumbency Advantage in U.S. House Elections. *Journal of Politics* 68 (3): 657–673.

Project for Excellence in Journalism. 2004. *The State of the News Media 2004.* Washington, D.C., http://www.stateofthenewsmedia.com/

——— 2005. *The State of the News Media 2005.* Washington, D.C., http://www.stateofthenewsmedia.com/

Project for Excellence in Journalism. 2006. *The State of the News Media 2006.* Washington, D.C., http://www.stateofthenewsmedia.com/

Putnam, Robert D. 1995. Tuning in, Tuning Out: The Strange Disappearance of Social Capital in America. *PS: Political Science and Politics* 28:664–83.

——— 2000. *Bowling Alone: The Collapse and Revival of American Community.* New York: Simon & Schuster.

Rahn, Wendy M. 1993. The Role of Partisan Stereotyping in Information Processing About Political Candidates. *American Journal of Political Science* 37 (2):472–96.

References

Ranney, Austin. 1983. *Channels of Power: The Impact of Television on American Politics*. New York: Basic Books.

Rich, Frank. 2002. The Weight of an Anchor. *New York Times Magazine*, May 19, 35.

Roberts, Jason M., and Steven S. Smith. 2003. Procedural Context, Party Strategy, and Conditional Party Voting in the U.S. House of Representatives, 1971–2000. *American Journal of Political Science* 47 (2):318–32.

Robertson, Nan. 1965. Most in Congress Broadcast Home. *New York Times*, August 1, 63.

Robinson, Michael J. 1976. Public Affairs Television and the Growth of Political Malaise: The Case of "the Selling of the Pentagon." *American Political Science Review* 70 (2):409–32.

———. 1981. Three Faces of Congressional Media. In *The New Congress*, edited by Thomas E. Mann and Norman J. Ornstein (pp. 55–96). Washington, D.C.: American Enterprise Institute.

Rohde, David W. 1991. *Parties and Leaders in the Postreform House*. Chicago: University of Chicago Press.

Roper, Burns W. 1971. *An Extended View of Public Attitudes Towards Television and Other Mass Media, 1959–1971*. New York: Television Information Office.

Rosenstein, Aviva W., and August E. Grant. 1997. Reconceptualizing the Role of Habit: A New Model of Television Audience Activity. *Journal of Broadcasting & Electronic Media* 41 (3):324–44.

Rosenstone, Steven J., and John Mark Hansen. 1993. *Mobilization, Participation, and Democracy in America*. New York: MacMillan.

Rubin, Alan M. 1984. Ritualized and Instrumental Television Viewing. *Journal of Communication* 34 (3):67–77.

Ryu, Jung S. 1982. Public Affairs and Sensationalism in Local TV News Programs. *Journalism Quarterly* 59 (1):74–8.

Saloma, John. 1969. *Congress and the New Politics*. Boston: Little, Brown and Company.

Sanders, Tony. 2005. That Was the Year That Was. *Billboard Radio Monitor*, December 9, 2005.

Scheufele, Dietram A., and Dhavan V. Shah. 2000. Personality Strength and Social Capital: The Role of Dispositional and Informational Variables in the Production of Civic Participation. *Communication Research* 27 (2):107–31.

Schudson, Michael. 1998. *The Good Citizen: A History of American Civic Life*. New York: Martin Kessler Books.

———. 2000. Good Citizens and Bad History: Today's Political Ideas in Historical Perspective. *Communication Review* 4 (1):1–20.

Schwarz, Norbert, and Howard Schuman. 1997. Political Knowledge, Attribution, and Inferred Interest in Politics: The Operation of Buffer Items. *International Journal of Public Opinion Research* 9 (2):191–5.

Sears, David O., and Jonathan L. Freedman. 1967. Selective Exposure to Information: A Critical Review. *Public Opinion Quarterly* 31 (2):194–213.

Sharbutt, Jay. 1987. The State of the Network News Business. *Los Angeles Times*, December 28, 1.

Signorielli, Nancy. 1986. Selective Television Viewing: A Limited Possibility. *Journal of Communication* 36 (3):64–76.

Simmons, Steven J. 1978. *The Fairness Doctrine and the Media*. Berkeley: University of California Press.

References

Simon, Herbert A. 1957. *Models of Man – Social and Rational*. New York: John Wiley and Sons.

Simon, Herbert A., and Frederick Stern. 1955. The Effect of Television upon Voting Behavior in Iowa in the 1952 Presidential Election. *American Political Science Review* 49 (2):470–7.

Sinclair, Barbara. 2000. Hostile Partners: The President, Congress and Lawmaking in the Partisan 1990s. In *Polarized Politics: Congress and the President in a Partisan Era*, edited by Jon R. Bond and Richard Fleisher (pp. 134–53). Washington D.C.: CQ Press.

Singer, Jerome L. 1980. The Power and Limitation of Television: A Cognitive-Affective Analysis. In *The Entertainment Functions of Television*, edited by Percy H. Tannenbaum (pp. 31–66). Hillsdale, New Jersey: L. Erlbaum Associates.

Smith, Eric R. A. N. 1989. *The Unchanging American Voter*. Berkeley: University of California Press.

Smythe, Dallas W. 1953a. *New Haven Television, May 15–21, 1952*. Urbana, Illinois: National Association of Educational Broadcasters.

——— 1953b. *Three Years of New York Television, 1951–1953*. Urbana, Illinois: National Association of Educational Broadcasters.

Smythe, Dallas W., and Angus Campbell. 1951. *Los Angeles Television, May 23–29, 1951*. Urbana, Illinois: National Association of Educational Broadcasters.

Sniderman, Paul M., Richard A. Brody, and Philip Tetlock. 1991. *Reasoning and Choice: Explorations in Political Psychology*. Cambridge, U.K.: Cambridge University Press.

Springsteen, Bruce. 1992. 57 Channels (and Nothin' on). *Human Touch* (Sony).

Stanley, Harold W., and Richard G. Niemi. 2006. *Vital Statistics on American Politics, 2005–2006*. Washington, D.C.: CQ Press.

Starr, Paul. 2004. *The Creation of the Media: Political Origins of Modern Communications*. New York: Basic Books.

Steiner, Gary A. 1963. *The People Look at Television. A Study of Audience Attitudes*. New York: Alfred A. Knopf.

Steiner, Peter O. 1952. Program Patterns and Preferences and the Workability of Competition in Radio Broadcasting. *Quarterly Journal of Economics* 66 (2):194–223.

Stepp, Carl Sessions. 1999. State of the American Newspaper Then and Now. *American Journalism Review* (September):60–75.

Sterling, Christopher H. 1984. *Electronic Media: A Guide to Trends in Broadcasting and Newer Technologies 1920–1983* (2nd ed.). New York: Praeger.

Sterling, Christopher H., and John M. Kittross. 1990. *Stay Tuned: A Concise History of American Broadcasting* (2nd ed.). Belmont, California: Wadsworth.

Stewart, Charles III, and Mark Reynolds. 1990. Television Markets and U.S. Senate Elections. *Legislative Studies Quarterly* 15 (4):495–523.

Stokes, Donald E., and Warren E. Miller. 1962. Party Government and the Saliency of Congress. *Public Opinion Quarterly* 26 (4):531–46.

Strömberg, David. 2001. *Radio's Impact on Public Spending*. Unpublished manuscript, Stockholm University.

——— 2004. Radio's Impact on Public Spending. *Quarterly Journal of Economics* 119 (1):189–221.

Summers, Robert E., and Harrison B. Summers. 1966. *Broadcasting and the Public*. Belmont, California: Wadsworth.

References

Sunstein, Cass R. 2001a. Is the Internet Bad for Democracy? Cass Sunstein Replies. *Boston Review* 26 (3–4):19.

———. 2001b. *Republic.Com*. Princeton, New Jersey: Princeton University Press.

Tacheron, Donald G., and Morris K. Udall. 1966. *The Job of the Congressman: An Introduction to Service in the U.S. House of Representatives*. Indianapolis: Bobbs-Merrill.

Taylor, Paul. 1992. Political Coverage in the 1990s: Teaching the Old News New Tricks. In *The New News V. The Old News: The Press and Politics in the 1990s*, edited by Suzanne Charle (pp. 35–69). New York: Twentieth Century Fund.

Television Digest. 1960. *Televison Factbook*. Radnor, Pennsylvania: Triangle Publications.

Television Information Office. 1960. *Interaction. Television Public Affairs Programming at the Community Level*. New York: Television Information Office.

———. 1965. *Television Programs Relating to Law and the Legislative Process, 1960–1964*. New York: Television Information Office.

Tewksbury, David. 2005. The Seeds of Audience Fragmentation: Specialization in the Use of Online News Sites. *Journal of Broadcasting and Electronic Media* 49 (3):332–48.

Tichenor, Philip J., George A. Donohue, and Calice A. Olien. 1970. Mass Flow and Differential Growth in Knowledge. *Public Opinion Quarterly* 34 (2):149–70.

Tiedge, James T., and Kenneth J. Ksobiech. 1986. The "Lead-in" Strategy for Prime-Time TV: Does It Increase the Audience? *Journal of Communication* 36 (2):51–63.

Topping, Malachi C., and Lawrence W. Lichty. 1971. Political Programs on National Television Networks: 1968. *Journal of Broadcasting* 15 (2):161–179.

Torney-Purta, Judith, Rainer Lehmann, Hans Oswald, and Wolfram Schulz. 2001. *Citizenship and Education in Twenty-Eight Countries: Civic Knowledge and Engagement at Age Fourteen*. Amsterdam: IEA.

Tracy, Phil. 1975. Canned Goods from Capitol Hill. *MORE*, 20–3.

Tuden, Dan. 1987. Hometown TV Coverage Is Booming. *National Journal*, August 29, 2174–5.

Turow, Joseph. 1997. *Breaking up America: Advertisers and the New Media World*. Chicago: University of Chicago Press.

U.S. News & World Report. 1955. Some Votes Are Made This Way. July 15, 70–1.

Vallone, Robert P., Lee Ross, and Mark R. Lepper. 1985. The Hostile Media Phenomenon: Biased Perception and Perceptions of Media Bias in Coverage of the Beirut Massacre. *Journal of Personality & Social Psychology* 49 (3):577–85.

Variety. 1969. Tv's Toprated Events of 1960s. August 27, 39.

Vavreck, Lynn. 2005. *The Dangers of Self-Reports of Political Behavior: Observational v. Experimental Evidence*. Unpublished manuscript, University of California, Los Angeles.

Verba, Sidney, Kay Lehman Schlozman, and Henry E. Brady. 1995. *Voice and Equality: Civic Voluntarism in American Politics*. Cambridge, Massachusetts: Harvard University Press.

Vinocur, John. 1979. Television in West Germany Becomes Hot Political Issue. *New York Times*, October 15, A2.

References

Vinson, Danielle. 2003. *Local Media Coverage of Congress and Its Members: Through Local Eyes*. Cresskill, New Jersey: Hampton Press.

Viswanath, Kasisomayajula, and John R. Finnegan, Jr. 1996. The Knowledge Gap Hypothesis: Twenty-Five Years Later. In *Communication Yearbook*, edited by Brant Burleson (pp. 187–227). Thousand Oaks, California: Sage Publications.

Waldfogel, Joel. 2002. Consumer Substitution among Media. Working Paper, Media Ownership Working Group, Federal Communications Commission.

Walker, James R. 1988. Inheritance Effects in the New Media Environment. *Journal of Broadcasting & Electronic Media* 32 (4):391–401.

Walker, James Robert, and Douglas A. Ferguson. 1998. *The Broadcast Television Industry*. Boston: Allyn and Bacon.

Webster, James G. 1982. *The Impact of Cable and Pay Cable Television on Local Station Audiences*. Washington, D.C.: National Association of Broadcasters.

———. 1984. Cable Television's Impact on Audience for Local News. *Journalism Quarterly* 61 (2):419–22.

———. 1986. Audience Behavior in the New Media Environment. *Journal of Communication* 36 (3):77–91.

———. 2005. Beneath the Veneer of Fragmentation: Television Audience Polarization in a Multichannel World. *Journal of Communication* 55 (2):366–82.

Webster, James G., and Gregory D. Newton. 1988. Structural Determinants of the Television News Audience. *Journal of Broadcasting & Electronic Media* 32 (4):381–9.

Webster, James G., and Patricia F. Phalen. 1997. *The Mass Audience: Rediscovering the Dominant Model, Lea's Communication Series*. Mahwah, New Jersey: Erlbaum.

Webster, James G., and Jacob J. Wakshlag. 1983. A Theory of Television Program Choice. *Communication Research* 10 (4):430–46.

Webster, James G., and Ting-Yu Wang. 1992. Structural Determinants of Exposure to Television: The Case of Repeat Viewing. *Journal of Broadcasting & Electronic Media* 36 (2):125–35.

Weimann, Gabriel. 1996. Cable Comes to the Holy Land: The Impact of Cable TV on Israeli Viewers. *Journal of Broadcasting & Electronic Media* 40 (2):243–57.

Wilbert, Caroline. 2004. Fox Fattens Lead on CNN in Peak Year for Cable News. *Atlanta Journal-Constitution*, January 6, 1D.

Winship, Christopher, and Robert D. Mare. 1992. Models for Sample Selection Bias. *Annual Review of Sociology* 18:327–50.

Wolf, Frank. 1972. *Television Programming for News and Public Affairs*. New York: Praeger.

Youn, Sug-Min. 1994. Program Type Preference and Program Choice in a Multichannel Situation. *Journal of Broadcasting & Electronic Media* 38 (4):465–75.

Young, Dannagal G., and Russ Tisinger. 2006. Dispelling Late-Night Myths: News Consumption among Late-Night Comedy Viewers and the Predictors of Exposure to Various Late-Night Shows. *Harvard International Journal of Press/Politics* 11 (3):113–34.

Zaller, John. 1986. Analysis of Information Items in the 1985 NES Pilot Study: Report to the NES Board of Overseers. Center of Political Studies, University of Michigan.

References

1992. *The Nature and Origins of Mass Opinion*. New York: Cambridge University Press.

1999. Market Competition and News Quality. Paper presented at the Annual Meeting of the American Political Science Association, Atlanta.

2003. A New Standard of News Quality: Burglar Alarms for the Monitorial Citizen. *Political Communication* 20 (2):109–30.

2004. Floating Voters in U.S. Presidential Elections, 1948–2000. In *Studies in Public Opinion*, edited by Willem E. Saris and Paul M. Sniderman (pp. 166–212). Princeton, New Jersey: Princeton University Press.

Forthcoming. *A Theory of Media Politics: How the Interests of Politicians, Journalists, and Citizens Shape the News*. Chicago: University of Chicago Press.

Zukin, Cliff, and Robin Snyder. 1984. Passive Learning: When the Media Environment Is the Message. *Public Opinion Quarterly* 48 (3):629–38.

Index

Index

Index

Index

Index

surge and decline, 7, 248
swing voter. *See* floating voter
Switchers, 41–7, 156, 214
  partisanship of, 226

Taylor, Paul, 283
technological determinism, 22–5
television. *See also* broadcast
    television, cable television
  and use of other media, 66–8
  cognitive demands, 15, 48, 73n5,
    72–4
  daily viewing time, 1–2, 69
  diffusion, 59
  local stations
    licensing of, 187n17
    number per media market, 68
    spread of, 60–2
    VHF vs. UHF, 1, 61–2, 68, 74–8,
      181, 184
  measurement of access to, 74–8,
    180–1, 183–4, 196–8
  models of program selection, 37–41
  popularity, 59–60, 90
  scheduling, 68
  TV freeze of 1948, 61, 196
Tewksbury, David, 272n8
The Daily Show with Jon Stewart,
  276
  audience, 277
The Oprah Winfrey Show, 276, 279
The Tonight Show with Jay Leno,
  276–8
Theory of Least Objectionable
  Program, 39
Tichenor, Philip J., 136
Total News Consumption, 149–55
  definition, 150
trust
  in government, and declining news
    audience, 21, 41
  in the media, and declining news
    audience, 21

turnout, 98
  aggregate-level studies of television
    effects, 86–7
  and campaign stimulus, 7–9
  and partisan polarization, 51,
    228–32
  change in, 18, 149, 159, 265
  definition of inequality in, 98n4
  effect of broadcast television on
    turnout of party identifiers,
    167–9
  effect of cable television on, 143–9
  effect of radio on, 59
  effect of Relative Entertainment
    Preference on, 120–31
  impact of broadcast television on,
    84–7
  indirect effect of television through
    political interest, 86, 123
  turnout gap, 49–50
    definition, 98n4
Turow, Joseph, 157, 271–5

UHF (ultra high frequency). *See*
  television
uses-and-gratifications, 38

VHF (very high frequency). *See*
  television
viewer inertia, 39
Vinson, Danielle, 177n10, 212n43
volatility, electoral, 18. *See also* vote
  swing,
  effect of cable television on, 242
vote swing, 19

Webster, James G., 37n7, 156–9,
  271–5
Wolfram, Catherine D., 202

Zaller, John, 7, 74, 101n7, 185,
  268n5, 280n16
Zukin, Cliff, 44

Books in the Series

Asher Arian, *Security Threatened: Surveying Israeli Opinion on Peace and War*

James DeNardo, *The Amateur Strategist: Intuitive Deterrence Theories and the Politics of the Nuclear Arms Race*

Robert S. Erikson, Michael B. Mackuen, and James A. Stimson, *The Macro Polity*

James L. Gibson and Amanda Gouws, *Overcoming Intolerance in South Africa: Experiments in Democratic Persuasion*

John R. Hibbing and Elizabeth Theiss-Morse, *Congress as Public Enemy: Public Attitudes Toward American Political Institutions*

John R. Hibbing and Elizabeth Theiss-Morse, *Stealth Democracy: Americans' Beliefs about How Government Should Work*

John R. Hibbing and Elizabeth Theiss-Morse, *What Is It about Government That Americans Dislike?*

Robert Huckfeldt, Paul E. Johnson, and John Sprague, *Political Disagreement: The Survival of Diverse Opinions within Communication Networks*

Robert Huckfeldt and John Sprague, *Citizens, Politics, and Social Communication*

James H. Kuklinski, *Thinking about Political Psychology*

Richard R. Lau and David P. Redlawsk, *How Voters Decide: Information Processing in Election Campaigns*

Arthur Lupia, Mathew McCubbins, and Samuel Popkin, *Elements of Reason: Cognition, Choice, and the Bounds of Rationality*

George E. Marcus, John L. Sullivan, Elizabeth Theiss-Morse, and Sandra L. Wood, *With Malice Toward Some: How People Make Civil Liberties Judgments*

Diana C. Mutz, *Impersonal Influence: How Perceptions of Mass Collectives Affect Political Attitudes*

Paul M. Sniderman, Richard A. Brody, and Philip E. Tetlock, *Reasoning and Choice: Explorations in Political Psychology*

Karen Stenner, *The Authoritarian Dynamic*

Susan Welch, Timothy Bledsoe, Lee Segelman, and Michael Combs,
Race and Place

John Zaller, *The Nature and Origins of Mass Opinion*